# EDUCATION
## IN A
## RESEARCH UNIVERSITY

# EDUCATION
## IN A
# RESEARCH UNIVERSITY

Edited by

Kenneth J. Arrow, Richard W. Cottle,
B. Curtis Eaves, and Ingram Olkin

STANFORD UNIVERSITY PRESS
Stanford, California

Stanford University Press
Stanford, California
© 1996 by the Board of Trustees
of the Leland Stanford Junior University
Printed in the United States of America

CIP data appear at the end of the book

Stanford University Press publications
are distributed exclusively by
Stanford University Press within
the United States, Canada, Mexico, and
Central America; they are distributed
exclusively by Cambridge University
Press throughout the rest of the world.

To Gerald J. Lieberman

for his contributions to the University

and the friendship he has bestowed

# Foreword

In the summer of 1992, a *Stanford Daily* photographer captured both the image and the essence of Gerald Lieberman. The image is of Provost Lieberman and Stanford's new president-elect sitting under a fig tree at the Center for Advanced Study in the Behavioral Sciences. Framed by this tranquil setting, Lieberman is looking intently toward his new colleague and puncturing the calm air with his index finger. It is initiation into the Lieberman circle, in which the thrust of that finger signals Jerry's sharing of the sagacious, the significant, the sensible. Thus, the photograph captures not just the Lieberman image but the Lieberman essence: that of wise teacher and shrewd guide.

Jerry Lieberman joined the Stanford faculty straight out of graduate school in the early fifties, the selection of his predecessor generation of Stanford leader. Fred Terman, then dean of the School of Engineering and soon to be provost, spotted Jerry, who had just succeeded in bridging the fields of mathematical statistics and industrial engineering. This expertise fit right in with Terman's interest in industrial renewal and with the School of Engineering's studies on standardization and quality control. Jerry also fit right in with Terman's system of faculty renewal, in which distinguished scholars and scientists brought and mentored junior colleagues, ensuring not only eminence but continuity. In biochemistry, Arthur Kornberg cultivated Paul Berg; in chemistry, Bill Johnson drew in Carl Djerassi, Paul Flory, and Henry Taube; in academic leadership, Fred Terman fostered Jerry Lieberman.

Lieberman fit the Terman approach in other ways as well. Bringing together theoretical science initiatives and the applied science industries on Stanford's periphery, Terman built a university that was resourceful and dynamic. Spurred by the challenge to innovate, faculty and students learned to cross the boundaries of traditional disciplines, creating new areas of study.

Jerry pioneered the interdisciplinary field of operations research, becoming one of its founding fathers and the first chair of the Department of Operations Research at Stanford. Jerry modestly prefers to cite as the principal patriarch of the field Al Bowker, with whom Jerry produced the *Handbook of Industrial Statistics and Engineering Statistics*. Regardless, Jerry's influence on the field has been remarkable, including coauthoring with Fred Hillier the leading basic textbook in the field, *Introduction to Operations Research* and two other volumes, *Introduction to Mathematical Programming* and *Introduction to Stochastic Models in Operations Research*.

Jerry's own work and familiarity with the cooperative ventures between the university and industry and government made him, not only a spokesman for Stanford policies governing research and technology transfer, but eventually Dean of Research. In that role, he endeavored to safeguard faculty interests in the face of external demands, ensuring fiscal viability while preserving the faculty's capacity to explore.

Inevitably, Jerry's statesmanship brought him to leadership of other university organizations, including the Faculty Senate. The Senate gatherings at which Jerry presided sparkled with lively, often brilliant, debate, as recorded by the artful academic secretary, Arthur Coladarci. Perhaps even more lasting than those words was the precedent of adjourning meetings punctually at 5:30 that Jerry, abetted by John Brauman, established. Subsequent Senate chairs have reverently invoked "the Lieberman tradition." When Jerry stepped down as chair of the Twentieth Senate of the Academic Council, Marsh McCall paid the customary tribute to the departing chair on behalf of his fellow senators. He cited the Senate's warm regard for Jerry's genial disposition, unfailing humor, abundant wisdom, and most of all, his resolute integrity.

A rabid backer of Stanford athletics, Jerry also made evident his support for the students in his role as Dean of Graduate Studies. Jerry believed that students formed a vital part of the research enterprise and encouraged programs to provide stipends and increased student access to research funding. To improve student living conditions, he laid the groundwork for what is now the Rains Housing Complex.

As dean and as provost, Jerry anticipated and encouraged the growing diversity of the student population. And just as he had bridged disciplines, he sought to help Stanford bridge cultures, nations, and generations. This was a theme of his leadership of the Centennial Committee from 1985 to 1991, thereby celebrating Stanford and projecting it as a world university that spanned both boundaries and eras to unite alumni, faculty, staff, and students in common experiences and goals.

In honor of Jerry's work, and to extend his influence into the future, the university marked his retirement as provost with the establishment of the Gerald J. Lieberman Fellowships. These are awarded to graduate students who intend to pursue a career in university teaching and research, and who exhibit promise in assuming leadership roles in the academic community.

The Lieberman Fellowships honored Jerry for his scholarship and academic statesmanship. Stanford's Cuthbertson Award in 1985 recognized his tireless efforts on behalf of students. The National Academy of Engineering paid him tribute for his foresight in developing an interdisciplinary field. To those, and to his many other honors, we modestly add this collection of articles. We offer it in thanks for his innumerable contributions to teaching, learning, and research, and to the greatness of Stanford.

Gerhard Casper
Condoleezza Rice

# Contents

## C. Research Reaching Society *371*

# Contributors

S. Christian Albright is Professor of Decision & Information Systems in the Business School at Indiana University, where he has taught since 1972. He has published over twenty articles in applied probability, has written a managerial statistics textbook, and is currently writing two textbooks that incorporate spreadsheets into management science and statistics courses.

Kenneth J. Arrow is Joan Kenney Professor of Economics Emeritus, Professor Emeritus of Operations Research, and Director of the Stanford Center on Conflict and Negotiation at Stanford University. He has been President of the Econometric Society, the Institute of Management Sciences, the American Economic Association, the Western Economic Association, the International Society for Inventory Research, the International Economic Association, and the Society for Social Choice and Welfare. He has received the John Bates Clark Medal of the American Economic Association, the Alfred Nobel Memorial Prize in Economic Science, and the von Neumann Prize. He is the author or co-author of *Social Choice and Individual Values*, *Essays in the Theory of Risk-Bearing*, *Studies in Linear and Nonlinear Programming*, *General Competitive Analysis*, *Studies in Resource Allocation Processes*, and *Collected Economic Papers*.

J. Myron Atkin, Professor of Education at Stanford University, formerly was Dean of Education at Stanford University and at the University of Illinois at Urbana-Champaign. He co-directs a twelve-country study of innovations in science, mathematics, and technology education for the Organization for Economic Cooperation and Development (OECD) in Paris.

His writings include co-authoring *Improving Science Education through Local Alliances* and *Getting Serious about Priorities in Science Education*. He currently serves as a member of the National Committee for Science Education Standards and Assessment of the National Research Council.

Donald Bentley is the Burkhead Professor Mathematics at Pomona College where he has spent the past thirty years introducing undergraduate students to the field of statistics. Approximately forty of his former students now hold doctorate degrees in statistics, biostatistics and epidemiology. He is a co-author of *Linear Algebra with Differential Equations*. He has served as a statistics consultant on biomedical problem, and has published over fifteen articles based on this work.

Frederick Biedenweg is a founding partner of the Pacific Consulting Group, Inc. He has written on a number of topics influencing policy in higher education including planning and budgeting models, studies of indirect cost policies, predictive models of physical plant renewal, faculty early retirement programs, and organizational studies.

Volker Brendel is Research Associate in the Department of Mathematics, Stanford University. His research interests include molecular sequence analysis and mathematical modeling of biological phenomena.

David A. Butler is Professor of Statistics, Oregon State University. He received his Ph.D. degee from the Department of Operations Research at Stanford University in 1975, and subsequently worked in both academia and private industry. His research interests include machine vision, computer automated manufacturing, applications of operations research to forestry, and reliability and maintenance models wherein he has published over twenty papers.

Gerhard Casper is President and Professor of Law at Stanford University. Prior to joining the Stanford faculty he served as the William B. Graham Professor of Law, Dean of the Law School, and Provost at the University of Chicago. He has written and taught primarily in the fields of constitutional law, constitutional history, comparative law, and jurisprudence. From 1977 to 1991 he was an editor of *The Supreme Court Review* and is a member of the American Law Institute and a Fellow of the American Academy of Arts and Sciences.

Richard W. Cottle is Professor and Chairman of the Operations Research Department at Stanford Univesity. His research is rooted in mathematical programming, especially in quadratic programming, linear complementarity and variational inequalities. He is editor or co-editor of eight books on mathematical programming, complementarity and variational inequalities and is a co-author of *The Linear Complementarity Problem*. In 1977, Professor Cottle received the U.S. Senior Scientist Award from the Alexander von Humboldt Stiftung in Bonn.

George B. Dantzig, Professor Emeritus of Operations Research and Computer Science at Stanford University, was awarded the National Medal of Science "for inventing linear programming that led to wide-scale scientific and technical applications to important problems in logistics, scheduling, and network optimization, and in the use of computers to implement efficiently mathematical theory." Chief among his contributions are the linear programming model and the method for its solution, the simplex method, in 1947 "which enabled for the first time, government and industrial managers to model and solve extremely complex systems in order to optimally allocate scarce resources."

B. Curtis Eaves is a Professor of Operations Research at Stanford University. His research is centered in mathematical programming; publications include over sixty papers on the subject, the book *A Course in Triangulations for Solving Equations with Deformations*, and the co-edited *Studies in Optimization* and *Homotopy Methods and Global Convergence*. He has served as associate editor of *Mathematical Programming* and of *Mathematics of Operations Research*, and has received a Guggenheim Fellowship.

Jean H. Fetter is Assistant to President Gerhard Casper at Stanford University. She is the former Dean of Undergraduate Admissions; her book, *Questions and Admissions: Reflections on 100,000 Admissions Decisions at Stanford University*, is based on this experience. Among other positions, she previously served as Associate Dean of Graduate Studies and Research at Stanford.

Stephen E. Fienberg is Maurice Falk Professor of Statistics and Social Science, at Carnegie Mellon University. He has served as Dean of the College of Humanities and Social Sciences at Carnegie Mellon and as Vice President for Academic Affairs at York University in Toronto. He has published two books and over 100 papers on statistical methods for the analysis of categorical data, and on aspects of sample surveys and randomized experiments. His research interests include the use of statistics in public policy and the law, and the role of statistical methods in censustaking.

Randall E. Fleming received his Ph.D. in Operations Research in 1980; his doctoral dissertation developed under the guidance of Gerald J. Lieberman is entitled *Coherent System Repair Models*. He has fifteen years progressive experience evaluating and resolving management and technical problems through application of the principles and practices of operations research and system engineering. He was a consultant at System Control Technology, Inc. from 1980 through 1989, and is currently a system engineer in the Space Systems Division, of the Lockheed Missiles and Space Company, where he has played key roles in the development and improvement of spacecraft products. His publications include papers on such diverse subjects as reliability modeling and design, project management, system engineering, and product development processes.

Alexander L. George is Professor Emeritus of International Relations at Stanford University. He is an author or co-author of *Woodrow Wilson and Colonel House: A Personality Study, Deterrence in American Foreign Policy, Presidential Decision Making in Foreign Policy*, and *Avoiding War: Problems of Crisis Management*. His most recent publication, for the United States Institute of Peace, is *Bridging the Gap: Theory and Practice of Foreign Policy*. He is preparing a book on the use of case studies for theory development.

Kathryn Gillam is Associate Provost for Faculty Affairs at Stanford

University. Prior to coming to Stanford, she was a member of the faculty at the University of Redlands, where she served as Chair of the Department of Biology and Director of the Johnston Center for Individualized Learning. Her work at Stanford concerns policy matters involving the professoriate, including appointments and tenure, compensation, and retirement.

Albert Hastorf is Benjamin Scott Crocker Professor of Human Biology and Psychology Emeritus at Stanford University where he served as Dean of the School of Humanities and Sciences and Provost. He has co-authored *Person Perception* and *Social Stigma: The Psychology of Marked Relations*, as well as co-editing *Cognitive Social Psychology*. He is a Fellow of the American Psychological Society and the American Academy of Arts and Science and was awarded honorary degrees by Dartmouth and Amherst. He is now Director of the Terman Study of the Gifted at Stanford University.

Frederick S. Hillier is Professor of Operations Research, Stanford University. He is co-author (with Gerald J. Lieberman) of *Introduction to Operations Research*, *Introduction to Mathematical Programming*, and *Introduction to Stochastic Models in Operations Research*. His other books are *The Evaluation of Risky Interrelated Investments* and *Queueing Tables and Graphs*.

David S. P. Hopkins is Vice President, Client Services and Corporate Development, of International Severity Information Services, Inc., a medical severity indexing software and consulting firm, and Consulting Professor in Health Research and Policy at Stanford University School of Medicine. He is co-editor of *Clinical Practice Improvement: A New Technology for Developing Cost-Effective Quality Health Care* and co-author of *Planning Models for Colleges and Universities*, which was awarded the 1981 Frederick Lanchester Prize by the Operations Research Society of America. He served as an officer on the Board of Directors of The Alan Guttmacher Institute (a special affiliate of Planned Parenthood Federation of America), and is currently a Director of Fair, Isaac and Company, Inc., which develops statistically-based decision systems and services for the banking, direct marketing, and insurance industries.

Samuel Karlin is Professor Emeritus of Mathematics at Stanford University. A recipient of the National Medal of Science, he has been productive in a variety of fields with applications in inventory processes and queueing systems, operations research, population models in genetics, and statistical analysis and development of algorithms for identifying and evaluating patterns in DNA sequences. He has authored *Total Positivity*, the two-volume work *Mathematical Methods and Theory in Games, Programming and Mathematical Economics*, and has co-authored *A First Course in Stochastic Processes* and *Tchebycheffian Systems*.

Donald Kennedy is Bing Professor of Environmental Science and President Emeritus, Stanford University. He is a member of the National Academy of Sciences, and the author of publications on neurophysiology and behavior as well as various science policy issues. He is a former Senior Consultant to the Office of Science and Technology Policy and served as Commissioner of the Food and Drug Administration from 1977 to 1979. As Stanford's eighth President (1980-92) he served as co-chair of the DoD-University Forum and wrote frequently on issues in the university-government relationship.

Richard W. Lyman is President Emeritus and Sterling Professor Emeritus in the Humanities at Stanford. A historian of modern Britain, he has written on the British Labour Party and on philanthropy and higher education in the United States. He was President of Stanford from 1970 to 1980, and of the Rockefeller Foundation in New York from 1980 to 1988. He is a former Chairman of Independent Sector and of the Association of American Universities, and vice-Chairman of the National Council on the Humanities. His publications include *The First Labour Government, 1924* and, as co-author, *The Future of the Non-Profit Sector*.

Alan S. Manne is Professor Emeritus of Operations Research, Stanford University. He is the author or co-author of seven books including the recent *Buying Greenhouse Insurance - the Economics Costs of CO2 Emission Limits*. He has published 110 papers in the area of industrial scheduling, development planning and energy policy analysis.

Gary C. McDonald is Head of the Consumer and Operations Research Department, General Motors Research & Development Center. He has chaired several National Research Council Panels: Applied Mathematics Research Alternatives for the Navy; Computing and Applied Mathematics for the Board on Assessment of the National Institute of Standards and Technology Programs. He has served on the Editorial Boards of *Technometrics, Naval Research Logisitcs Quarterly*, and other statistical journals, and has published approximately fifty articles in diverse areas of applied and mathematical statistics.

Lincoln E. Moses is Professor Emeritus of Statistics at Stanford University where he served in the Medical School and in the Statistics Department from 1952-1992. He was Dean of Graduate Studies at Stanford from 1969 to 1975. President Carter appointed him in 1978 to head the Energy Information Administration in the newly founded Department of Energy where he served for two and a half years. He is author or editor of books and papers in statistics and fields of application.

Ingram Olkin has been Professor of Statistics and Education, Stanford University since 1961. He is a Fellow of the Institute of Mathematical Statistics, and served as its President; he is a Fellow of the American Statistical Association, which awarded him the Samuel S. Wilks Memorial Medal and the Founders Award. He is a Guggenheim Fellow and was a Lady Davis Fellow in Hebrew University and an Overseas Fellow at Churchill College, Cambridge. He has served as editor of the *Annal of Statistics* and is currently Chair of the Committee of Presidents of Statistical Societies. He is the author or co-author of seven books in the areas of multivariate analysis and models in the behavioral and social sciences and education.

Evan Porteus is Sanwa Bank Professor of Management Science, Graduate School of Business, Stanford University, and Associate Editor of *Management Science* and *Operations Research*. He has published over thirty articles in inventory theory, Markov decision processes, and related areas.

Condoleezza Rice is Provost and Professor of Political Science at Stanford University. She served as Special Assistant to the President for National Security Affairs from 1989 to 1991, concurrent with her appointment as Senior Director for Soviet Affairs for the National Security Council. Prior to that, and also at the National Security Council, she was Director for Soviet and East European Affairs. An expert in international relations and comparative politics, she is the author of *The Soviet Union and the Czechoslovak Army*, co-author of *The Gorbachev Era*, and of the forthcoming book *German Unification and the Transformation of Europe: A Study in Statecraft*.

Saul A. Rosenberg is Maureen Lyles D'Ambrogio Professor of Medicine and Radiation Oncology, School of Medicine, Stanford University, where he served as an Associate Dean. His research, teaching and clinical emphasis has been on Hodgkin's disease and other malignant lymphomas. He has authored or co-authored more than 150 articles, and is co-editor of the textbook, *Medical Oncology and Malignant Lymphomas: Etiology, Immunology, Pathology, Treatment*. He has served as President of the American Society of Clinical Oncology.

Donald B. Rosenfield is a Senior Lecturer in Operations Management at the Massachusetts Institute of Technology Sloan School of Management and is Director of the Leaders for Manufacturing Fellows Program (run by the School of Management and the School of Engineering in partnership with thirteen leading U.S. Corporations). He has served on the faculties of the Harvard Business School, the State University of New York, Boston University and the staff of Arthur D. Little, Inc. His articles appear in the *Harvard Business Review, Operations Research, Management Science, Sloan Management Review, Journal of Business Logistics*, and *Journal of Economic Theory*. He is a co-author of *Modern Logistics Management*.

Sam L. Savage is a Consulting Professor of Operations Research at Stanford University. In 1986 he received *PC Magazine's* Technical Excellence Award for the development of *What's Best!*, a software package that couples linear programming to Lotus 1-2-3. Since then he has continued to pioneer the introduction of operations research methodologies into the electronic spreadsheet. He has published two packages of analytical tools for classroom use (*FAST QM* and *FAST POM*), which include Monte Carlo simulation, time series analysis, Markov chains, decision trees and optimization models.

Kenneth E. Scott is Ralph M. Parsons Professor of Law and Business, Stanford Law School, and Senior Research Fellow, Hoover Institution, Stanford University. His publications include as co-athor *Retail Banking in the Electronic Age: The Law and Economics of Electronic Funds Transfer*, as co-editor *Economics of Corporation Law and Securities Regulation*; and over forty articles on banking and corporate law topics.

John B. Shoven is Charles R. Schwab Professor in Economics and current Dean of Humanities and Sciences at Stanford University. He is a Research Associate of the National Bureau of Economic Research, as well as the director of its West Coast Office, and is also the former Director for the Center for Economic Policy Research at Stanford. His research has covered such topics as taxation and inflation, pension funding, various aspects of social security and the repurchase of shares by U.S. Corporations. Publications include as co-author, *Applying General Equilibrium*; as co-editor *National Saving and Economic Performance* and *Financial Aspects of the United States Pension System.*

Patrick Suppes received his Ph.D. in Philosophy from Columbia University in 1950. Since that date he has taught continuously at Stanford University where he is Lucie Stern Professor of Philosophy Emeritus. He has published in philosophy, the social sciences and especially psychology. His academic honors include election to the American Academy of Arts and Sciences and the National Academy of Sciences. In 1990 he received the National Medal of Science.

Kenneth T. Wallenius is Professor Emeritus of Mathematical Sciences, Clemson University. He has held visiting positions a the National Institute of Standards and Technology, the Office of Naval Research, Stanford University, the University of Copehagen, and the University of Athens. He is a Fellow of the American Statistical Association. His research interests include the application of statistical methods in cost analysis and in acquisition processes. For his work in developing algorithms and computer code to achieve statistically balanced samples, he was the recipient of the first Sigma Xi award as Outstanding Researcher at Clemson University.

Alan Wood is an Advisory Engineer at Tandem Computers, Inc. in Cupertino, California, where he serves as an internal consultant in the areas of reliability and availability modeling, software reliability, cost modeling, and client/server architectures. He has published over twenty papers on these subjects.

# Introduction

## Kenneth J. Arrow, Richard W. Cottle, B. Curtis Eaves, and Ingram Olkin

The research university is one of the most characteristic and important institutions of our time. It is also a complex entity, seeking to achieve a variety of aims and responding to a multiplicity of pressures. The principal obligation is that of educating the students in a broad sense, in particular, to prepare them to live in and contribute to society. To serve this function, knowledge must be collected, organized, and disseminated; but also and in the long run even more importantly, new knowledge must be created. The knowledge so developed and so imparted must ultimately be carried into the larger society, for the most part through the former students but also by other means.

The society in which the research university is embedded supports its activities in large measure and, as always, support means power. Many pressures are brought upon the university, both directly and through internalization of norms and values. It is asked to help solve social problems, both in its mode of operation and in the social value placed on the graduates and on the research.

The present volume is a collection of essays addressing the multifarious aspects of administration, education, and research. They are grouped into three parts: administration, teaching and learning, and the ways by which research reaches society at large. Within each category, the wide variety of topics mirrors the increasing complexity of the research university.

# A. Administering a Research University

The authority structure of the university is also a complex entity, seeking to achieve a variety of aims and responding to a multiplicity of pressures. It retains the original corporate and collegial elements of its origins in medieval universities. The faculty keeps many of the old guild characteristics. The choice of new faculty is primarily made by the existing faculty, though with some control by other powers in the university, and the faculty have (at least up to this date) tenure. This creates advantages in terms of security and autonomy and problems with the achievement of flexibility in the face of changes in intellectual direction and social pressures.

In the American university, the faculty has always shared its powers with a strong administration. Administrations in turn have had to respond to social pressures of many different kinds. The most direct outside control is through finances. Though universities do have endowments, these are not adequate for the operations of the university, so they have had to be responsive to student needs, to the values of donors, to the state and local governments which finance public institutions, and, in recent times, to research support from the federal government.

Universities have always had the role of educating the students. American universities have usually had the additional role of housing them and exercising some judicial control over their entire lives. In addition to all of these obligations, some universities have become centers of research, of creating knowledge and not merely transmitting it. As research has demanded more expensive equipment, the financing of research has become a major problem. The federal government and private foundations and corporations have become the chief source and with financial support has come control, frequently in realms far removed from the research itself.

Universities are large organizations and need systematic planning, to which operations research methods can contribute. Frederick Biedenweg has reported on planning models for the faculty, to anticipate vacancies in the near future, to predict the composition of the faculty (by age and other characteristics), and to locate the policy parameters that affect faculty turnover. For example, the effects of raising retirement age can be modeled.

During the 1970's, David Hopkins and others at Stanford took seriously the development and use of computer models to help administration decision-making. This development was in response to financial pressures following a period of strong growth. In addition to faculty tenure planning, also discussed by Biedenweg, there were models for long-range financial planning and for tradeoffs between different performance dimensions of the university. The Stanford models were reviewed by Hopkins in a paper originally published in 1979 and here reproduced with Hopkins's comments from today's perspective.

Stephen Fienberg discusses more generally the role of systematic and in particular statistical thinking as an aid to administration; systematic statistical analysis can be an offset to reliance on anecdotal evidence; sampling can economize on the need to check whether procedures are being carried out properly; quality control analogous to industry is needed. There needs to be analysis of teaching evaluations, which may be taken too easily at face value and need supplementation. Finally, statistical thinking can be useful even in non-statistical situations.

There are a whole series of new problems in the administration of a research university, when it is trying to achieve new social goals and being subject to outside controls. Jean Fetter analyzes the efforts at affirmative action in admissions to graduate school and in achieving faculty diversity at Stanford University. She shows the progress that has been made and the great inequalities that still persist and concludes with recommendations for further action.

Donald Kennedy, President Emeritus of Stanford University, traces the history of the Federal support for research, especially in science. He shows how the slowing of the rate of growth of support has led to strains and conflict. He points out how the support has been used to impose constraints on university freedoms; restrictions on foreign visitors, restraints on publication, and curriculum requirements have all been imposed. Kennedy also discusses the implications of industrial support of university research, which has grown, partly as a replacement for government funds, partly because of the speed with which fundamental research in biotechnology moves into products. Here, a consensus emerged as to such matters as publication restraints.

A very different form of social intervention in the research university was the student revolt of the 1960's and its implication for university operations and in particular for the student judicial system. These events, as they impinged on Stanford University, are thoroughly reviewed by Richard

Lyman, then Provost and later President. Though the changes did not prevent further disturbances and even violence, it is remarkable that the changes in the judicial system, forged in the heat of conflict, have endured to this day.

University administration is distinct from the faculty, but of course the two are intimately linked. Many university administrators have always been recruited from the faculty. As research became a stronger part of the university and therefore a more important criterion for faculty selection, the faculty members became more oriented towards their scholarly field and less to the university. Albert Hastorf gives the history of an institution at Stanford, the University Fellows, designed to meet this problem. Selected faculty were given released time to participate in university administration and to meet with adminstrators, with an evaluation of the program based on statistical data and interviews.

Two papers deal with the role of the university in scholarship. Saul Rosenberg examines the case for the existence of medical schools in a research university. He especially stresses the importance of the research environment in raising the sights of medical students and faculty and in inculcating the scientific attitude.

Patrick Suppes points to the importance of computer technology in raising performance and accomplishment by secondary school students. Through computer instruction, it will be possible for the best students to take several levels of college courses. The university will have to be prepared to make use of this learning and build on it for the future development of the students.

## B. Teaching and Learning

What should the graduate know? How do we prepare the student for the work place? How should a subject be taught? What should programs and courses look like? Who should be involved in making these decisions? These are some of the matters addressed by contributors in this part. As one reads the essays one finds a recurring theme, namely, how should academic subjects be integrated with practice to serve both learning and proficiency of the graduate in the work place? A valuable collection of answers to this question follows.

Our first contributor, J. Myron Atkin, argues from a broad perspective that educational objectives and standards vary over time and country, and further there will be little agreement within a country. Some countries are moving toward centralization, whereas others are moving away from it. Factions in Japan want a system that fosters more creativity and originality, whereas in the United States, there is a movement for more discipline. Economic competitiveness and other temporal forces generate pressures on the education system. The notion of "World-Class Standards" seems to be more of a phrase for inspiration than one of content.

Other contributors have a narrower focus and are concerned with a much more specific educational tasks; indeed we find considerable consensus here. How should mathematical sciences, statistics, operations research, management science, and so forth be taught so that the graduate is most effective in his or her specialty in the work place?

Alan Wood and Frederick Biedenweg interviewed several graduates of the Operations Research Ph.D. Program at Stanford who pursued careers in industry rather than academia. These graduates believe that their education has served them well, even though some of them do not practice operations research. Although characterizing the Ph.D. program as highly theoretical, the graduates felt that they had learned the ability to define and analyze the "big picture" in diverse settings. Given a second chance, they would again pursue the same degree. Nevertheless, the graduates suggested that certain skills that they had to learn after leaving school could be integrated into the curriculum. They recommended that the program include more case studies, be more interdisciplinary, and integrate more technology and business skills.

Our next contributor Randall Fleming was one of those interviewed by Biedenweg and Wood. Fleming gives a personal account of his own career development over the fifteen year period following receipt of his Ph.D. in Operations Research. Fleming describes himself as a broad-based system engineer who can contribute to decision making in both the business and technical operations of a company. He points out that usually he alone represents the operations research discipline in project teams. Being able to communicate his expertise to teammates with backgrounds different from his own was a constant challenge. As a student Fleming learned analytical thinking, innovation, self discipline, managing information, identifying essential facts, and drawing conclusions; in industry he found that these skills were strong relative to engineers. On the other hand, there were other skills and challenges that he had not learned, but that he found necessary in order to function effectively in a generic business or technical operations environment. These included oral and written communication skills, broad computer literacy, and the ability to focus on deliverables and deadlines.

David Butler describes the development of a computer-intensive course for teaching statistics and operations research. His literature citations indicate that, today, a statistician must have computer programming skills and facility with statistical software packages before he or she is ready to assume a place in the labor market. In operations research, computer-use skills were ranked as of primary importance. A number of difficulties, tasks, decisions, and rewards in developing and operating the course are discussed. What computer platform? What type of computer language? What software? What prerequisites? Demonstrations? Laboratory organization? How frequently should hardware, software, and demonstrations be updated? Clearly many obstacles have been encountered, thought about and dealt with. This piece will be very helpful and comforting for those trying to establish such a course; that is, to teach a subject as enhanced or revolutionized by the computing environment together with the attendant computer facility. Surely this type of instruction is one blueprint for future classrooms.

Frequently, the first lecture of a course is devoted to organization, covering such mundane facts as the number and weight of exams. Even though a significant fraction of students seems to be interested in these matters, Donald Bentley conceives of a first lecture in a first course in statistics as having a higher purpose. As an ideal he would like to communicate what the subject of statistics is, and how it relates to other fields, for example, philosophy. He is quick to point out that the identical challenge exists with respect to other disciplines, for example, philosophy, biology, theology or art. His answer is a lecture covering a collection of five or so brief but engaging examples illustrating various practical uses of statistics. The device could be applied equally well to other disciplines.

The current status of an extended and on-going effort for bringing students in operations research to a functional level for the work place is documented by Curtis Eaves. This effort now takes the form of two courses based on case studies and field projects. These courses are organized around student teams and project sponsors; the courses emphasize applications, results, modeling, communication, report writing, oral presentation, and questioning and answering. Course organization material and quotations from students and project sponsors are used to document the story.

Frederick Hillier recounts some lessons learned in keeping his well-known operations research text, jointly authored with Jerry Lieberman, on the best seller list. His messages are familiar, but we seem to forget them, and it is helpful to hear them clearly stated again: carefully identify the audience and help them into the material with examples, emphasis, perspective, and the computer.

Sam Savage observes that today's systems become tomorrow's subsystems and that education should reflect such. As an alternative to teaching mathematical modeling and linear programming in order to solve a transportation problem, one can teach that a "seed" transportation model and mathematical optimizer are subsystems of electronic spreadsheets and that this seed with optimizer can be easily expanded and modified to meet specific needs. What collection of seeds should be developed? What collection of seeds should be taught?

Chris Albright and Evan Porteus are both concerned with what and how to teach M.B.A.'s so that they can make effective use of operations research or, in the business school vernacular, quantitative methods. Both describe the evolution of such an effort and emphasize the importance of computer availability to this task. Both raise some questions for which there are currently no answers. By contrast, both have some recommendations. One important aspect of Albright's avenue lies in lock stepping the courses in quantitative methods in time and subject with other courses taken by the business students. One aspect of Porteus's answer lies in producing rich cases in the sense that there is more than a single correct model and solution. As there is a trend in business schools towards eliminating quantitative methods from the curriculum altogether, understanding and answers are urgently needed.

Donald Rosenfield describes a dual degree academic program, developed in conjunction with corporations, to produce graduates who can use operations research, statistics, and other areas to help promote world-class manufacturing in the U.S. The program integrates case studies, teamwork, and extensive internships with the traditional disciplinary material of operations research, statistics, and manufacturing. Results from three collaborative projects are included to document the approach of the program. The concept proposed is that OR and statistics can be more effective within the context of a broader program, such as manufacturing, rather than as stand-alone disciplines.

Kenneth Wallenius conveys a forward-looking Mathematical Sciences Program envisioned twenty-five years ago. The evolution, some problems, and successes of the program as well as the accompanying national scene are described. The core courses were from mathematics, statistics, operations research, computing and mathematical modeling in science, engineering, or economics. The program is administered by a department head with the advice of a council made up of representatives elected by each of six subfaculties: Analysis, Computational Mathematics, Discrete Mathematics, Operations Research, Statistics and Probability, and Undergraduate Education.

Alexander George is concerned with functionality of a policymaker in a political setting. The point is made that an otherwise well-trained specialist in an academic field is often ill prepared for a discourse in a political environment vis-à-vis his or her specialty. Such a persom may be unable to compromise or trade-off the lessons of his or her field with political feasibility, expenditure of political capital, and the cost of designing a good policy.

Our last contributor in this part, Kenneth Arrow, recounts a historical interplay of statistics, operations research, decision theory, and game theory as they have and have not influenced modern micro-economics. Here we see research in a field and related fields shaping and defining the field itself. Such evolution has considerable effect on course curricula and ultimately on the student's outlook and functionality.

## C. Research Reaching Society

Statistics and operations research provide a set of tools designed to aid in the analysis of data and for making decisions based on the data. Because the statistical procedures are generic, they have had an impact in many diverse fields—the social and behavioral sciences, the biological and physical sciences, engineering, and the judiciary. The essays in this part exhibit this diversity. Two of the essays relate to methods of operations research, and four relate to statistical methods.

George Dantzig, distinguished leader of the field of linear programming, provides a history of that field from its origins during World War II. The impact of linear programming in industry, finance, economics, and engineering is truly remarkable. To fix ideas, consider a simple situation in which there are three farms, each having a specified amount of arable land and each entitled to a certain allocation of water. There are three crops, for which we know the monetary return per unit and also the land and water requirements per unit. The problem is to decide how much of each crop to grow on each farm. The problem can be described as the maximization of a linear combination of the decision variables. The maximization is not totally free; there are linear constraints. Even in this context we can see the possibility of military applications. Dantzig's essay travels through the key developments that take place in a quarter century during and subsequent to World War II.

In his essay Alan Manne employs a particular model to provide an assessment of greenhouse gas abatement. The problem of emissions is central to environmental controls. Manne provides an example in which there are two regions with different size populations, different incomes, and so on. How much consumption of private versus public goods should take place in each region? Using the model, the author shows how we might analyze such a situation. The present development is a first step in how to think about the greenhouse gas abatement problems. There is still much to do. In particular, emissions need to be translated into climate-related variables such as mean global temperature changes. Although the problem is not urgent for this year, or the next, it will amost certainly become a critical problem in the future. This paper serves as a catalyst for additional research in this area.

The paper by Samuel Karlin and Volker Brendel shows how probability theory provides insights into gene locations, pattern counts and rare sequences in the human genome project. In its simplest form there are transition probabilities from each of the four DNA bases (or combinations thereof): adenine, thymine, guanine, cytosime denoted by $A$, $T$, $G$, $C$, respectively. From the transition matrix first passage times can be determined, as well as various other characteristics of the system. A marvelous analysis of rare and frequent words is also provided. In particular, probability statements can be made about occurrences of different types of word fragments. This paper serves to show molecular biologists how probabilistic arguments can shed light on DNA sequences. It also exemplifies to the mathematical scientist the richness of molecular biology as a field of study.

Statistical quality control has become a focus on improving products in a competitive economy. Gary McDonald, who has had a long career at the General Motors Research and Development Center, describes a set of techniques relating to the enhancement of product quality. The first is a description of sampling inspection. Although the ideas of sampling inspection originated early on, it was the military needs of World War II that gave it an impetus, and which led to the development of alternative procedures. A second area described is that of computer-aided experimental design. Here the problem is how many observations to take at different values of the characteristics. When items are expensive or destructive, experimental design is essential if costs are to be kept low. In a third section, McDonald discusses the use of control charts. In an industrial process items may be produced by a machine, say, in a conveyor-type system. How do we know if the system is in-control, that is, the system is producing what it should. The basis for determining in- or out-of-control is the control chart. From such a chart, together with statistical computations, the manager can determine when there is a problem.

The assessment of evidence obtained with uncertainty is at the heart of litigation and statistical analysis, so it is not surprising that statistical tools have been used in judicial decisions. Perhaps what is surprising is that this connection does not occur more often—given the kinship of the basic premises. Kenneth Scott has investigated the use of statistical ideas in litigation. The study includes a breakdown by year, 1962–1993, by federal and state courts, and by type of statistical analysis. A painful (to the statistician) outcome is the paucity of statistical tools used. This fact may serve to connect the two disciplines with the introduction of statistics courses in law school.

How should the statistician communicate to the non-statistical reader? The statistician's tendency to be accurate often requires telling a long story—much of which is often not understood, or worse, misunderstood.

Edward Tufte's dictum is "Less is more." Mark Kac has stated in a talk "I promise to tell the truth, nothing but the truth, but not the whole truth." Lincoln Moses discusses the issue of how to tell the truth without telling all. He provides several examples to illustrate understanding and misunderstanding together with insights on interpretation. These examples range from tables to regression and other graphical displays. The issue of statistical communication and understanding is exceedingly important, especially in the current climate in which medical, educational, and political data is so frequently reported in the news media.

# A. Administering a Research University

# Chapter 1

# A Robust Faculty Planning Model

Frederick Biedenweg

## 1. Introduction

Faculty planning models are used to analyze appointment, promotion, and retirement policies within colleges and universities. They answer questions such as:

- How many vacancies are likely to occur over the next five years?
- What will the age and composition of the faculty be at that time?
- What are the key policy parameters that affect faculty turnover rates?

In addition to answering these questions, a well-designed faculty-planning model can provide administrators with valuable insight into many of the other faculty-planning issues that face colleges and universities. It can be used, for instance, to calculate the budgetary costs of an aging faculty, to predict the possible impact of changes in mandatory retirement laws, or to determine the impact of increasing or decreasing faculty size. Other applications include helping to predict research volume growth into the next decade or the growing faculty demands for space.

I discuss here a robust faculty-planning model that was used at Stanford University along with a number of other colleges and universities belonging to CoFHE (Consortium on Financing Higher Education).

# 2. Data

As inputs, the model uses current faculty distribution broken down by age into five-year cohorts (i.e., 20–24 years old, 25–29 years old, 30–34 years old, 35–39 years old, etc.), as well as current hiring practices and retention rates. Additional inputs may be needed for advanced uses of the model.

When designing planning models, it is extremely important to aggregate data to an appropriate level. Too little aggregation results in a very complicated model (many states) in which one literally tries to predict individual behavior. Although there is sometimes value in attempting to predict the behavior of individual faculty, Stanford University has found the predictive value of these micro-models to be neither particularly accurate nor useful for help in setting longer-term policies.

Too much aggregation is also inappropriate. A model that only considers two states (for example, tenured and nontenured) will not have the richness and robustness required for policy considerations. The resulting model will frequently have minimal ability to predict and will not be useful in other contexts. This is not to say that both simpler and more complex models do not have their purposes. In fact, they do have many valuable uses, especially in explaining complex situations and dramatic policy changes. However, either they tend to require too much maintenance or they provide insufficient insight.

The model described in this paper uses five-year cohorts because over a five-year period (at Stanford), roughly 25% of the billets turn over. In actual head count, this is approximately 300 faculty positions. Studies of actual Stanford data show a remarkable consistency over the past fifteen years. A smaller period of time could have been used (one or two years, for example). However, less than five years would have been too short a period for many of the individual schools, and the predictive results would have been minimized.

As a final note, one should always consider some of the political issues associated with faculty models. The first is that most deans already understand much about faculty planning and already know to a great degree what will happen in their schools over the next two or three years. Thus, a model that pretends to tell the dean what to expect (say, in the way of retirements) in the next twelve months had better know exactly to whom the dean is talking and the contents of those conversations.

Nevertheless, a model that predicts five years out seems to predict just beyond a dean's ability to see the future. The dean will undoubtedly try a quick verification of the results but will find the model useful because it gives him or her the ability to see beyond his or her planning horizon.

# 3. The Model

Mathematically, this model falls under the general category of stochastic processes and is specifically known as a Markov Chain (with feedback). The mathematics are well known, and an interested reader can refer to any basic stochastic processes text or to a text in optimal control theory.

However, one has to understand neither the mathematics nor the underlying control theory principles to understand and use this model.

## 3.1. Inputs

This model uses four basic inputs: the actual faculty age distribution, by five-year cohorts (i.e., 20–24, 25–29, 30–34, 35–39, etc.); retention rates; new hire distributions; and the number of new billets (or changes in the numbers of billets).

TABLE 1.1
*Faculty Distribution
by Age Cohort*

| Age | Faculty Count | Age | Faculty Count |
|-----|-------|------|-------|
| 20–24 | 0 | 50–54 | 143 |
| 25–29 | 38 | 55–59 | 142 |
| 30–34 | 123 | 60–64 | 117 |
| 35–39 | 175 | 65–69 | 69 |
| 40–44 | 161 | 70+ | 0 |
| 45–49 | 170 | Total | 1138 |

### 3.1.1. Age Distribution

The data in Table 1.1 is actual 1987 data for Stanford University. Note that at this time, there were no faculty younger than 25 nor older than 69. This is because very few individuals receive their Ph.D.'s before age 25, and university policies, at that time, required retirement at age 70. The bulge in the 45–49 cohort is also interesting. (Later we will note how this bulge is expected to track through the future.)

### 3.1.2. Retention Rates

Table 1.2 is a set of five-year retention rates for each of the cohorts listed above. The interpretation of the data is best explained by an example. According to Table 1.2, 85% of those faculty aged 40–44 will still be at Stanford (in tenure-track faculty positions) five years from now. Similarly, 50% of those aged 25–29 will still be at Stanford five years from now.

TABLE 1.2
*Retention Rates by Age Cohorts*

| Age | Five-Year Retention Rates | Five-Year Retention Age | Rates |
|-----|----------|-----------|--------|
| 20–24 | 0% | 45–49 | 90% |
| 25–29 | 50% | 50–54 | 90% |
| 30–34 | 55% | 55–59 | 90% |
| 35–39 | 70% | 60–64 | 55% |
| 40–44 | 85% | 65+ | 0 |

Note that the zero in the 65+ cohort means that none of the faculty over age 65 will still be at Stanford in tenure-track faculty positions five years from now. This, once again, is a result of the then mandatory retirement laws. (See Example 3 for a discussion of today's nonmandatory retirement laws and how one can modify this table appropriately.) The 55% retention rate for faculty in the 60–64 cohort is probably due to many reasons, including a faculty early-retirement program, full social security at age 65, and faculty expectations about retirement. At the other end of the age spectrum, the attrition rate for younger faculty is relatively high. Much of this is due to a tough tenure policy, but some is also due to younger faculty responding to opportunities elsewhere.

### 3.1.3. New-Hire Distribution

The new-hire distribution is the actual experience in hiring patterns (by age) for the cohorts listed above. A difficulty here is that because one is looking over a five-year period, it is possible (actually likely) that some of the individuals hired during the previous five-year period will have already left the University. Thus, one is really interested in net new hires. Table 1.3 summarizes this data.

TABLE 1.3

*Faculty New-Hire Distribution by Age Cohort*

| Age | New-Hire Distribution | Age | New-Hire Distribution |
|-----|-----------------------|-----|-----------------------|
| 20–24 | 0% | 50–54 | 3% |
| 55–59 | 2% | 25–29 | 13% |
| 30–34 | 34% | 60–64 | 2% |
| 35–39 | 29% | 65–69 | 1% |
| 40–44 | 10% | 70+ | 0% |
| 45–49 | 6% | Total | 100% |

These data are particularly interesting for two reasons. First, they show, as expected, that virtually no new hires are made of individuals less than 25 years old or greater than 69 years old. Second, they show that younger positions (less than age 40) account for 76% of the new hires. This most likely indicates a general university policy that favors internal promotion over external hiring.

### 3.1.4. New Billets

"New billets" is shorthand for anticipated increases or decreases in billets, in five-year periods, into the future. For initial planning purposes, this chapter will assume no changes in faculty size.

### 3.1.5. Use of Historical Information

For the purposes of this chapter, and the model this data is assumed to be known. However, it is useful to note that knowing the faculty age distribution for 1984 and 1989, plus who was hired and at what age from 1984 to 1989, will allow the reader to derive the actual experience in retention rates over the past five years. Table 1.4 is an example of actual experience for six Stanford Schools (Graduate School of Business, Earth Sciences, Education, Engineering, Humanities and Sciences, and Law) from 1975 to 1980.

Note the "Losses of New Hires" column that was referred to in the "New-Hire Distribution" section. This represents individuals who were

TABLE 1.4

*Faculty Changes 1974–75 through 1979–80*

| Beginning Age Cohort | 1974–75 Actual | Losses of Faculty | Remaining Faculty | Total New Hires | Losses of new Hires | Net New Hires | 1979–80 Actual | Ending Age Cohort |
|---|---|---|---|---|---|---|---|---|
| 20–24 | 3 | −3 | 0 (0%) | 41 (19%) | −2 | 39 (20%) | 0 | 20–24 |
| 25–29 | 61 | −31 | 30 (50%) | 75 (34%) | −6 | 69 (35%) | 39 | 25–29 |
| 30–34 | 145 | −58 | 87 (60%) | 59 (27%) | −9 | 50 (26%) | 99 | 30–34 |
| 35–39 | 120 | −23 | 97 (81%) | 15 (7%) | −3 | 12 (6%) | 137 | 35–39 |
| 40–44 | 128 | −15 | 113 (88%) | 9 (4%) | −6 | 3 (2%) | 109 | 40–44 |
| 45–49 | 99 | −2 | 97 (98%) | 9 (4%) | 0 | 9 (5%) | 116 | 45–49 |
| 50–54 | 101 | −1 | 100 (99%) | 9 (4%) | 0 | 9 (5%) | 106 | 50–54 |
| 55–59 | 72 | −3 | 69 (97%) | 2 (1%) | 0 | 2 (1%) | 109 | 55–59 |
| 60–64 | 50 | −45 | 5 (10%) | 0 | 0 | 0 | 71 | 60–64 |
| 65–69 | 2 | −2 | 0 | 0 | | | 5 | 65–69 |
| 70–74 | 0 | | 0 | 0 | | | 0 | 70–74 |
| 75–79 | 0 | | 0 | 0 | | | 0 | 75–79 |
| 80+ | 0 | | 0 | | | | 0 | 80+ |
| Total | 781 | −183 | 598 | 219 (100%) | −26 | 193 (100%) | 791 | |

hired after 1975 and left before 1980. They account for 12% of the actual new hires and mean that the net new hires are understated by 13% to 14%. However, assuming this percentage is roughly constant, this under-statement will not impact the predictive abilities of this model.

Another point of interest is that for Stanford hiring patterns and re-tention rates have held remarkably stable since the early 1970's. Three different five-year periods have been examined, and the new-hire distribu-tion and five-year retention rate data were found to be remarkably constant. This indicates that unless the institution has recently undergone consid-erable changes in hiring or tenure strategies, one needs to examine only one five-year period (and then use judgment) to get reasonably accurate inputs.

Finally, the new-hire distribution data vary significantly among schools. The School of Engineering, for instance, has significantly more new young hires (on a percentage basis) than does the School of Medicine.

## 3.2. How the Model Works

The model actually works by taking the current age distribution of the faculty and projecting into the future how many of those faculty will still be tenure-line faculty (at the same college or university) five years from now. It does this by multiplying the appropriate retention rate times the number of individuals in the cohort (and then rounding to the nearest whole person) for each of the cohorts. Next, the number of the remaining faculty are summed to determine how many are left. This number is subtracted from the total number of faculty desired (the old total plus any changes) to determine the number of new faculty to be added over the five-year period. Exactly this number of new faculty are then added according to the new-hire distribution. By walking across Tables 1.5 and 1.6, the reader can see exactly how the model works. The second column in Table 1.5 is the starting counts of faculty for 1989.

Once one has calculated the remaining faculty, it is relatively simple to determine the number of open positions ($1138 - 821 = 317$) and to add that many positions back to the total. This is done by apportioning the 317 according to the new-hire distribution and then adding this to the new cohorts. Table 1.6 performs this calculation.

Remember the cohort has changed for the remaining faculty. That is, the 170 faculty in the 1989, 45–49 age cohort is now 153 faculty in the 1994, 50–54 cohort.

TABLE 1.5
*Five-Year Projection of Faculty Retention*

| Age | 1989 Starting Faculty | Retention Rates | 1994 Remaining Faculty |
|---|---|---|---|
| 20–24 | 0 | 0% | 0 |
| 25–29 | 38 | 50% | 19 |
| 30–34 | 123 | 55% | 68 |
| 35–39 | 175 | 70% | 123 |
| 40–44 | 161 | 85% | 137 |
| 45–49 | 170 | 90% | 153 |
| 50–54 | 143 | 90% | 129 |
| 55–59 | 142 | 90% | 128 |
| 60–64 | 117 | 55% | 64 |
| 65–69 | 69 | 0% | 0 |
| 70+ | 0 | 0% | 0 |
| Total | 1138 | | 821 |

TABLE 1.6
*Projection of Composition of Faculty, 1994*

| Age | 1994 Remaining Faculty | New Hire Percentage | New Hires | 1994 Total Faculty |
|---|---|---|---|---|
| 20–24 | 0 | 0% | 0 | 0 |
| 25–29 | 0 | 13% | 41 | 41 |
| 30–34 | 19 | 34% | 108 | 127 |
| 35–39 | 68 | 29% | 92 | 160 |
| 40–44 | 123 | 10% | 32 | 155 |
| 45–49 | 137 | 6% | 19 | 156 |
| 50–54 | 153 | 3% | 10 | 163 |
| 55–59 | 129 | 2% | 6 | 135 |
| 60–64 | 128 | 2% | 6 | 134 |
| 65–69 | 64 | 1% | 3 | 67 |
| 70+ | 0 | 0% | 0 | 0 |
| Total | 821 | 100% | 317 | 1138 |

# 4. Output from the Model

Typical outputs of interest include: (a) anticipated net new hires, (b) average age of the faculty, and (c) percentage of the faculty under age 40.

Many illustrative scenarios are possible with minimal adjustments to the input parameters. The first example listed below is important because it will be used as a benchmark for further analysis. Also, it is important to understand the current situation and the likely demographics changes, assuming there are no changes in current policies and regulations.

**4.1. Example 1:** Under current retirement practices, what are likely future trends?

This scenario takes the basic data from Tables 1.1, 1.2, and 1.3, and adds the assumption of no faculty billet growth. The results are summarized in Tables 1.7 and 1.8. In Table 1.7 actual data from 1974, 1979, 1984 and 1989 have been summarized first to provide context for the predictions.

TABLE 1.7
*Faculty Characteristics, 1974–1989*

|  | Actual | | | |
|---|---|---|---|---|
|  | 1974 | 1979 | 1984 | 1989 |
| Total faculty | 1000 | 1045 | 1117 | 1138 |
| Average age | 42.5 | 43.4 | 45.5 | 47.1 |
| % under 40 | 44% | 41% | 35% | 30% |
| Net new hires | | | | |
| (over previous 5 yrs.) | | | | |
|    Turnover | | 319 | 268 | 282 |
|    New positions | | 45 | 72 | 21 |
|    Total | | 364 | 40 | 303 |

Note that from 1974 to 1989, the average age of the faculty rose from 42.5 to 47.1 years. Also during that time period, the percentage of faculty under age 40 dropped from 44% to 30%. This drop in younger faculty was termed the most critical issue facing the university by a 1980 task force on retirement policies at Stanford. Part of this change was a result of the a new mandatory retirement age of 70 (up from 65) that occurred during this period; another part was due to a bulge of faculty in their early 40's who are still working their way through the Stanford system.

Table 1.8 is the model output starting with the actual 1989 data and projecting 1994, 1999 and 2004 data. (The model output yields as many years of future projections as one wishes, but we show only the fifteen-year period 1989–2004.)

TABLE 1.8
*Projected Faculty Characteristics, 1994–2004*

|  | Actual | Projected | | |
|---|---|---|---|---|
|  | 1989 | 1994 | 1999 | 2004 |
| Total faculty | 1138 | 1138 | 1138 | 1138 |
| Average age | 47.1 | 47.4 | 47.5 | 47.4 |
| % under 40 | 30% | 29% | 29% | 30% |
| Net new hires (over previous 5 yrs.) | | | | |
|     Turnover | 282 | 318 | 322 | 330 |
|     New positions | 21 | 0 | 0 | 0 |
|     Total | 303 | 318 | 322 | 330 |

Note that future projections (under the assumptions listed above) show that the impact of changing the mandatory retirement age from 65 to 70 has now been fully integrated into the system. The average age of the faculty is leveling off and is expected to be roughly constant after 1994. Similarly, the percentage of faculty under age 40 is expected to remain constant.

Another interesting piece of data is the "net new hires." The turnover data show that Stanford would today just be coming out of a hiring trough of the 1980's were it not for substantial faculty growth during the 1980's. Thus, rather than facing a hiring bulge, higher education is instead apparently coming out of a trough.

**4.2. Example 2:** What would happen if we changed hiring distributions toward more younger faculty? In this example, the new-hire distribution will change from 76% new hires under age 40 to 85%.

TABLE 1.9
*Changes in Hire Distribution for a Younger Faculty*

| Age | Original New Hire Distribution | New New Hire Assumptions | Age | Original New Hire Distribution | New New Hire Assumptions |
|-----|-----|-----|-----|-----|-----|
| 20–24 | 0% | 0% | 50–54 | 3% | 2% |
| 25–29 | 13% | 15% | 55–59 | 2% | 1% |
| 30–34 | 34% | 40% | 60–64 | 2% | 1% |
| 35–39 | 29% | 30% | 65–69 | 1% | 0% |
| 40–44 | 10% | 7% | 70–74 | 0% | 0% |
| 45–49 | 6% | 4% | | | |
| | | | Total | 100% | 100% |

TABLE 1.10
*Projected Faculty Hires*
*under New Assumptions, 1994–2004*

| | Actual | Projected | | |
|-----|-----|-----|-----|-----|
| | 1989 | 1994 | 1999 | 2004 |
| Total faculty | 1138 | 1138 | 1138 | 1138 |
| Average age | 47.1 | 46.9 | 46.7 | 46.4 |
| % under 40 | 30% | 31% | 34% | 35% |
| Net new hires (over previous 5 yrs.) | | | | |
| Turnover | 282 | 318 | 328 | 338 |
| New positions | 21 | 0 | 0 | 0 |
| Total | 303 | 318 | 328 | 338 |

Table 1.9 indicates both the original assumptions and the new assumptions. The results of this change are represented in Table 1.10. As expected, the average age decreases slightly and the turnover increases (as a result of fewer of the new faculty getting tenure). The percentage under age 40 increases significantly from 29-30% to 35%. Thus, for a substantial change in hiring strategy, one can significantly change the percentage of faculty

under age 40, but one cannot significantly change average age or turnover. Note that a policy change toward more junior faculty hires would be difficult for an institution planning to enhance its departments by strategic outside (tenure) hires.

### 4.3. Example 3: Changes in mandatory retirement laws

Modeling a change in mandatory retirement laws can be accomplished by modifying the five-year retention rates for older faculty. There has been significant debate over the anticipated impact of this change. Some institutions claim it will have no impact because all of their faculty retire by age 65 anyway. Other institutions claim that faculty surveys show a substantial number of faculty who would like to continue their tenure positions well into their 80's.

The example that follows assumes 20% of the faculty retire at age 65, 50% of the remainder retire at age 70, 60% of the remainder retire at age 75, and the remaining faculty retire at age 80. This says that about 16% ($0.8 \times 0.5 \times 0.4$) of the faculty remain until age 80.

The changes in retention assumptions are indicated in Table 1.11, and the model output is reflected in Table 1.12.

The change in retention rates has dramatically changed the ability of the institution to hire new faculty (from 318 to 254, a 20% decline), decreased the percentage under age 40 from 30% to 25% (from 44% in 1974!), and increased the average age.

To be fair, the magnitude of this decline is of a temporary nature, and by the year 2014 the percentage under 40 and turnover have stabilized at 29% and the low three-teens (i.e., 313 − 316), respectively. Still, however, these are significant changes!

TABLE 1.11

*Changes in Faculty Retention,*
*Assuming Later Retirement*

| Age | Initial Five-Year Retention Rates | Revised Five-Year Retention Rates |
|---|---|---|
| 20–24 | 0% | 0% |
| 25–29 | 50% | 50% |
| 30–34 | 55% | 55% |
| 35–39 | 70% | 70% |
| 40–44 | 85% | 85% |
| 45–49 | 90% | 90% |
| 50–54 | 90% | 90% |
| 55–59 | 90% | 90% |
| 60–64 | 55% | 80% |
| 65–69 | 0% | 50% |
| 70+ | 0% | 40% |

TABLE 1.12

*Projected Faculty Characteristics,*
*Assuming Later Retirement 1994–2004*

| | Actual | Projected | | |
|---|---|---|---|---|
| | 1989 | 1994 | 1999 | 2004 |
| Average age | 47.1 | 49.2 | 50.2 | 50.2 |
| % under 40 | 30% | 25% | 24% | 26% |
| Net new hires (over previous 5 yrs.) | | | | |
| Turnover | 282 | 254 | 269 | 292 |
| New positions | 21 | 0 | 0 | 0 |
| Total | 303 | 318 | 322 | 330 |

## 4.4. Example 4: Salary Levels

Another interesting feature that one can track from this model is total expected faculty salary expenditures in constant dollars. To do this, one needs to know the current salary distribution for faculty by age, and that the relative salaries, by age, will not change much over time.

The Stanford data illustrated in Table 1.13 show an interesting trend: average salaries tend to increase at about 3% in real terms per year from age 25 until age 50, at which time the average salary levels off in real terms. In gross terms, this means junior faculty get salary increases of about 3% percent above "inflation" and senior faculty members tend to get increases only at "inflation." *Note these are average 1980 salaries across Stanford* and do not reflect specific schools whose salary distributions vary considerably.

TABLE 1.13
*Faculty Salary Distribution by Age, 1980*

| Average Age | Faculty Salary (1980 dollars) | Average Age | Faculty Salary (1980 dollars) |
|---|---|---|---|
| 20–24 | 20,000 | 50–54 | 41,750 |
| 25–29 | 22,750 | 55–59 | 42,000 |
| 30–34 | 25,000 | 60–64 | 42,000 |
| 35–39 | 30,000 | 65–69 | 42,000 |
| 40–44 | 35,500 | 70–74 | 42,000 |
| 45–49 | 40,750 | 75–79 | |

TABLE 1.14
*Projected Total Faculty Salary Expenditures, 1979–2004*

| | 1979 | 1984 | 1989 | 1994 | 1999 | 2004 |
|---|---|---|---|---|---|---|
| Total salary | $36.3M | $40.0M | $41.6M | $41.7M | $41.7M | $41.5M |

This shows relatively constant salary expenditures into the future, which is a result of the relatively constant faculty demographics in this example. If the underlying retention or hiring assumptions are changed, these expenditures will also change. For example, under the assumptions of Example 3, the 1994, 1999, and 2004 expenditures become $42.5M, $42.6M and $42.4M, respectively.

### 4.5. Example 5: New Billets (Either Increases or Decreases)

For this example, assume that a decision is made to reduce the size of the faculty (by attrition) by 75 in each of the five-year periods ending 1994 and 1995. The result is indicated in Table 1.15.

TABLE 1.15

*Adjusted Projected Faculty Size and*
*Total Faculty Salary Expenditures*

|  | Actual | Projected | | |
|---|---|---|---|---|
|  | 1989 | 1994 | 1999 | 2004 |
| Total faculty | 1138 | 1063 | 988 | 988 |
| Average age | 47.1 | 48.1 | 48.9 | 48.3 |
| % under 40 | 30% | 26% | 24% | 28% |
| Net new hires (over previous 5 yrs.) | | | | |
| Turnover | 282 | 318 | 296 | 283 |
| New positions | 21 | −75 | −75 | 0 |
| Total | 303 | 243 | 221 | 283 |
| Total Salary | $41.6M | $39.5M | $37.0M | $36.4M |

Under this scenario, the average age increases temporarily and the percentage under age 40 decreases temporarily until the 150 positions are removed. Then the average age creeps down to about where it started and the percentage under age 40 increases. Turnover, however, is permanently lower because there are fewer faculty. (This is accomplished by a large decrease in total net new hires.)

### 4.6. Example 6: Tenure Ratios

By examining the percentage of faculty in the various cohorts who have tenure, one can look at the impact of aging upon the faculty tenure ratio. The data in Table 1.16 are 1987 Stanford data.

As expected, as the faculty age they are more likely to have tenure. This also implies that most of the older new hires are hired with tenure, or else we would see lower tenure ratios in some of the higher age cohorts.

TABLE 1.16
*Faculty Tenure Ratio, by Age Cohort*

| Age | Faculty Count | Tenure Ratio | Age | Faculty Count | Tenure Ratio |
|-----|-----|-----|-----|-----|-----|
| 20–24 | 0 | .00 | 50–54 | 143 | .99 |
| 25–29 | 38 | .02 | 55–59 | 142 | .99 |
| 30–34 | 123 | .14 | 65–69 | 69 | 1.00 |
| 35–39 | 175 | .43 | 70+ | 0 | 1.00 |
| 40–44 | 161 | .81 | Total | 1138 | |
| 45–49 | 170 | .95 | | | |

TABLE 1.17
*Projected Faculty Tenure Ratios, 1994–2004*

| | Actual | Projected | | |
|-----|-----|-----|-----|-----|
| | 1989 | 1994 | 1999 | 2004 |
| Total faculty | 1138 | 1138 | 1138 | 1138 |
| Average age | 47.1 | 47.4 | 47.5 | 47.4 |
| % under 40 | 30% | 29% | 29% | 30% |
| Net new hires (over prev. 5 yrs) | | | | |
|    Turnover | 282 | 318 | 322 | 330 |
|    New positions | 21 | 0 | 0 | 0 |
|    Total | 303 | 318 | 322 | 330 |
| Tenured faculty | 853 | 857 | 854 | 848 |
| Total faculty | 1138 | 1138 | 1138 | 1138 |
| Tenure ratio | 75% | 75% | 75% | 75% |

In 1979, 66% of the tenure-line faculty were tenured, and in 1984, 71% were tenured. Table 1.17 shows that the percentage of tenured faculty is now roughly stable at 75%. If, however, the retention rates change to the assumptions in Example 3, the future tenure ratios for 1994, 1999, and 2004 move to 79%, 79%, and 78%, respectively.

## 4.7. Example 7: Impact on Research Volume (MTDC)

The budgets of many institutions are highly leveraged on the volume of sponsored research. Some of these institutions have as much as one-third of their annual operating budgets supported by overhead on sponsored research. It would be interesting to note how demographic changes might impact these institutions. At Stanford we have collected data on sponsored research volume (MTDC) versus faculty age. These data (also) have been remarkably constant over time, not in term of actual dollars, but in terms of the shape of the curve. The data in Table 1.18 are the same form as Stanford data for 1979, 1982 and 1987.

TABLE 1.18

*Average Faculty Sponsored Research*
*Volume, by Age Cohort*

| Age | Average Research ($000) | Age | Average Research ($000) |
|---|---|---|---|
| 20–24 | 0 | 50–54 | 37 |
| 25–29 | 6 | 55–59 | 32 |
| 30–34 | 12 | 60–64 | 28 |
| 35–39 | 26 | 65–69 | 33 |
| 40–44 | 38 | 70+ | 33 |
| 45–49 | 44 | | |

These data indicate that average research increases until around age 50, then slowly drops until around age 65, at which point the average starts increasing again. It is believed that self-selection causes the increase for the latter age group.

TABLE 1.19

*Projected Faculty Characteristics and*
*Total Research Volume, 1989–2004*

|  | 1989 | 1994 | 1999 | 2004 |
|---|---|---|---|---|
| Total Faculty | 1138 | 1138 | 1138 | 1138 |
| Average Age | 47.1 | 46.9 | 46.6 | 46.3 |
| % under 40 | 30% | 34% | 34% | 35% |
| Total Research | $35.2M | $35.0M | $34.7M | $34.4M |

As expected, total research volume is reasonably flat. (If, however, the increase in research for faculty over age 65 does not hold and removing mandatory retirement has roughly the impact of Example 3, then Table 1.19 would show significant decreases in research volume.)

# Chapter 2

# Looking Back at Computer Models Employed in the Stanford University Administration

David S. P. Hopkins

The work on computer modeling to aid decisionmakers at Stanford University described in this chapter took place during the 1970's. This was a time when universities were beginning to experience significant financial constraints following a period of tremendous growth during the preceding two decades. The Stanford administration was early to recognize these constraints, to determine their root causes, and to formulate definite plans for their accommodation. It was also a pioneer in the application of operations research/management science techniques to university planning and decision making. The projects described here led to publication of many journal articles, a monograph produced by EDUCOM (a Princeton-based consortium established to facilitate and improve the use of computer technology in colleges and universities), and ultimately, a book entitled *Planning Models for Colleges and Universities* that was awarded the 1981 Frederick W. Lanchester Prize for best publication in operations research.

# 1. Introduction

The past several years have seen a dramatic increase in proposed uses of analytic techniques in university management. Various types of computer models have been developed for a number of purposes, yet documentation on their actual use is quite scarce. One suspects that in some cases this may reflect a lack of true implementation. The record should show, however, that some impact from model building in a university setting actually has occurred. This chapter will take as an example the recent experience with modeling at Stanford University and will indicate what role this activity has played in top-level decision making there.

There will be a brief discussion of three distinct areas of application: faculty tenure analysis, long-range financial planning, and trade-off analysis. But first a word about the philosophy behind the use of modeling at Stanford. Our efforts have been directed toward dealing with quite specific problems, such as the restricted number of openings for new faculty or the dynamic imbalance between operating-budget income and expense, rather than toward the adoption of general-purpose models developed elsewhere. We have found that through engaging in the actual process of model building we have been better able to discover what the components of a problem are, how they are interrelated, and what solutions exist. Once the range of possibilities has been identified, these models have served also to highlight trade-offs among those variables having the greatest impact on the process being studied.

We have not looked to models directly to solve any of our problems. Instead, by their use, we have been able to provide information that in the past has been lacking, and this has meant that analytical reasoning could form part of the basis for the decisions to be made. To maintain a proper perspective on the role of models, we must recognize that they exist to provide just one of many types of inputs to the decision-making process.

The mathematical details of the models themselves will not be discussed in this chapter. These are documented in the various technical papers that are referenced in the text.

# 2. Faculty Tenure Analysis

The first set of applications concerns the management of a university faculty during times of no growth. Up until around 1970, Stanford, like many other universities, had been accustomed to adding to the size of its faculty each year. While this growth occurred, there were plenty of opportunities to appoint outstanding scholars to the faculty from outside, and at the same time a reasonable proportion of the junior faculty could count on being promoted to tenure. This situation had turned around, of course, by four or five years ago, due to a largely unanticipated change in the University's financial condition. The abruptness of the transition from this growth situation to a no-growth one left the University administration uneasy about whether it would be able to maintain enough flexibility in the recruitment and retention of faculty, and it made many junior members of the faculty very nervous about their prospects for promotion.

Under these conditions there was an urgent need for more information about just how restrictive the no-growth situation was likely to be for both the University and its untenured faculty members. A model of faculty flow was developed to test the sensitivity of faculty turnover rates and tenure ratios to the major policy variables, such as the promotion fraction and the mix of new appointments between tenure and nontenure (Hopkins 1974a). Analyses conducted with this model revealed that flexibility was far more dependent on the promotion fraction than it was on the appointment mix, as one can see by comparing Figure 2.1 with Figure 2.2. (The "annual turnover rate" refers to the number of positions that become available during a year, divided by the faculty size. The "tenure promotion fraction" is the fraction of newly hired assistant professors who eventually make it to tenure.)

We also performed year-by-year analyses of the short- to medium-term impact of various policy alternatives on the faculty of Stanford's largest school (Hopkins and Bienenstock 1975). These runs of the model investigated how much the appointment and promotion fractions would need to be reduced if the faculty size had to be cut by 10 percent over the following three years. (By this time it had become clear that not only could Stanford not afford any further growth in its faculty, but it might have to cut back.) For various combinations of the tenure appointment and promotion fractions, and various assumptions about future resignation rates

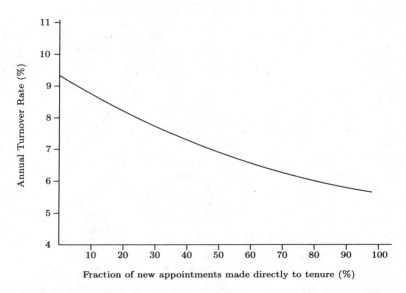

Figure 2.1. No-growth effects of appointment policy. Assumes promotion fraction
equal to 0.3 and tenure attrition rates at historical values.

from tenure, we examined changes in the annual new appointment rate,
tenure ratio, and age distribution of the faculty over a ten-year projection period. The results indicated that the faculty could continue to evolve
satisfactorily—even with the cut in size—if the appointment and promotion
fractions could be reduced from their historical values of 33 and 40 percent, respectively, to something like 20 percent each. Such changes were
generally viewed as moderate when considered against a background of the
many dire predictions that were being made at the time. These analytical
results helped to convince a Task Force on Professorial Rank and Faculty
Development, appointed by President Lyman in 1975, that the problems
for Stanford's faculty brought about by imminent retrenchment could be
managed without any radical change from past practices.

The faculty flow model also was employed in designing and evaluating
an incentive plan for early retirement (Hopkins 1974b). By encouraging
the early retirement of some older faculty members, we hoped to make
room for additional new faculty. Our initial calculations revealed, however,
that even if all tenured faculty were to retire five years early, for example,

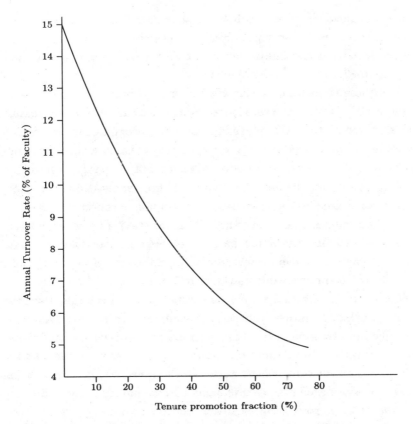

Figure 2.2. No-growth effects of promotion policy. Assumes tenure appointment fraction equal to 0.15 and tenure attrition rates at historical values.

this would have limited impact on turnover rates over the long run. In contrast, more significant gains might be obtained in the short run since, at the time these analyses were performed, the faculty included a number of individuals between the ages of 60 and 65 (the mandatory retirement age at Stanford). Another insight gained from these analyses was that it almost surely would be necessary to pay out, in early-retirement benefits, at least as much money as the University would save by replacing senior faculty members generally with junior ones; that is, an early-retirement plan could not be viewed as a device for saving money.

In spite of these findings, the Stanford administration decided that it would be desirable to provide a means whereby a faculty member nearing retirement could opt out sooner if he or she wanted to. Hence, a financial incentive scheme for early retirement, designed to appeal mainly to relatively less productive individuals out of all those who are eligible, was adopted in 1972.

Out of these applications of faculty flow models has come a better understanding of the significance of a no-growth state or even a "shrinking state," as it applies to faculty planning. A clearer recognition of the crucial variables in the system has been gained by faculty member and administrator alike, and this has raised the level of dialogue in arriving at mutually satisfactory solutions. In fact, the results of these analyses have seemed to relieve some anxiety on both parts. The administration now feels it can maintain sufficient flexibility through moderate, rather than drastic, changes in policy, and the junior faculty can see that they will probably continue to have a fair chance for promotion, although, of necessity, this will be somewhat diminished from the historical average.

*Epilogue:* From the analyses just described, one can see that the predictions have largely proved accurate. Faculty tenure ratios have crept up steadily and promotion rates have declined since constraints on faculty growth became effective. Stanford's voluntary faculty early-retirement program was implemented in 1972 and has been changed several times since. Initially, it was designed to open up a small number of faculty slots through a financial incentive structure that was meant to appeal mainly to the lowest paid (and presumably least highly valued) senior faculty, and this objective was largely achieved. In the years that followed, budgetary constraints became even more severe, and this led to a liberalization of the policy so that it would have wider appeal and a greater impact on the budget.

# 3. Long-Range Financial Planning Models

A second major area of application of computer models at Stanford has been in long-range financial planning. Although we had been in the habit for a long time of preparing five-year financial forecasts of the University's operating budget, it was not until the late 1960's that these began to reveal a tendency toward mounting operating deficits (see Figure 2.3). The factors that contributed to this rather pessimistic outlook for Stanford were the

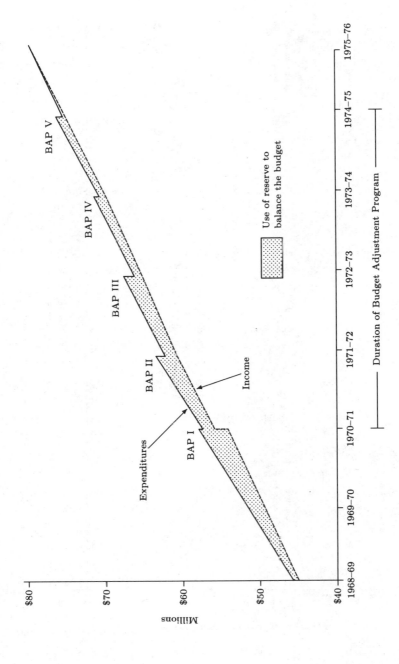

Figure 2.3. Actual and estimated operating budget expenditures and income, as modified by budget adjustment program, for 1968–69 through 1975–76.

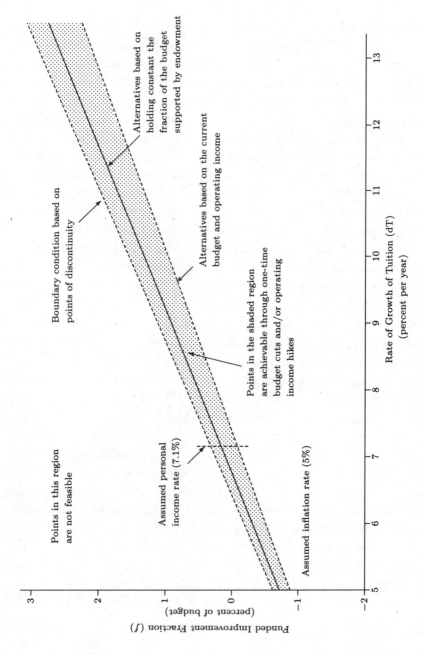

Figure 2.4. Trade-offs between tuition growth rate and funded improvement fraction.

same ones that affected most other private institutions at the time; i.e., costs were rising much faster than revenues.

The reaction of Stanford's budget planners in 1969 was to recommend a "Budget Adjustment Program" (BAP) aimed at getting the operating budget back into balance five years later. The recommendation was adopted, and the administration set about in earnest achieving that goal. By the year 1974–75, the Budget Adjustment Program had run its course and the budget was practically in balance. A fresh look at a five-year forecast, however, indicated further pressures tending to increase expenditures and reduce income that had not been anticipated five years earlier. That is, having just succeeded in closing the gap between income and expenditures, we were faced with the prospect of a new gap developing all over again.

By this time, it had become clear that achieving a balanced budget in any single year was not sufficient to assure that the budget would remain in balance. As a further condition, control over the growth rates of income and expenditure was needed to ensure that these also would be balanced. We began to develop simple models to describe the necessary control conditions for long-run financial equilibrium in terms of the critical macro-budget planning variables, that is, levels of expenditure, income, and endowment, and rates of endowment spending, cost-rise, tuition increase, and funding of new programs (Massy 1976). The models provided mathematical solutions for some of these variables in terms of the others. Their most significant use has been in identifying and quantifying important trade-offs between budget base levels and long-run growth rates.

Figure 2.4, for example, shows the feasible range of possibilities for the tuition growth rate matched against the funded improvement fraction. (The funded improvement fraction is that portion of each year's budget made available, on a net basis, for new programs in the following year; this adds to ordinary cost-rise in determining the total rate of expenditure increase.) Points inside the feasible band can be achieved through one-time base adjustments (i.e., budget cuts or operating-income hikes), but the upper boundary forms the limit on what can be accomplished in this manner. What is significant about this figure and others like it which can be prepared using the dynamic budget model is that it presents a financial trade-off in terms that are meaningful to budget planners. It thereby focuses their attention on the need to agree upon a most preferred strategy from among all those that are feasible. These models also have proved useful in analyzing the "spending-saving" trade-off with respect to return from the endowment, that is, in structuring the debate about the proper rate of endowment payout to the budget.

While it proved to be extremely instructive in delineating some major long-run financial trade-offs, the dynamic budget model did not, in and of itself, provide the solution to the chronically unbalanced budget situation that had appeared by 1974. What was missing was the means for identifying a transient solution that could describe a feasible path, starting with current budget variables and forecasted cost-rise and income growth rates, and leading to a position of long-run financial equilibrium (LRFE) within a period of, say, five years. A "transition to equilibrium" model was formulated to meet this need (Hopkins and Massy 1977).

Solutions of this model indicated the magnitude of corrective budget adjustments (i.e., expense cuts or income improvements) required during the transition period in order to bring the operating budget into dynamic equilibrium. Sensitivity analyses could easily be performed to examine the impacts of altered assumptions about endowment total return, funded improvement, and short-run tuition growth. (In the long run, this would be determined by the equilibrium conditions.) The transition model was used extensively, first as an instructive device, and then as a vehicle for communication with members of the campus community, during the fall of 1974. Ultimately, a plan for achieving LRFE by the year 1979-80 was put into effect. Stanford's publicly announced $10.2 million goal for closing the income-expenditure gap through this so-called Budget Equilibrium Program (BEP) was actually derived from these model runs.

One way of summarizing what was accomplished during the BAP and BEP eras is to look at the extent to which reserve moneys have been appropriated to balance Stanford's operating budget. According to Figure 2.5, the actual draw on reserves reached its peak in the year 1969–70, and has been diminishing ever since. In fact. the year 1976–77 ended with a small budget surplus, and the same result was projected for 1977–78. Stanford has gained a fair degree of control over its budget at a time when many other institutions still are running in the red.

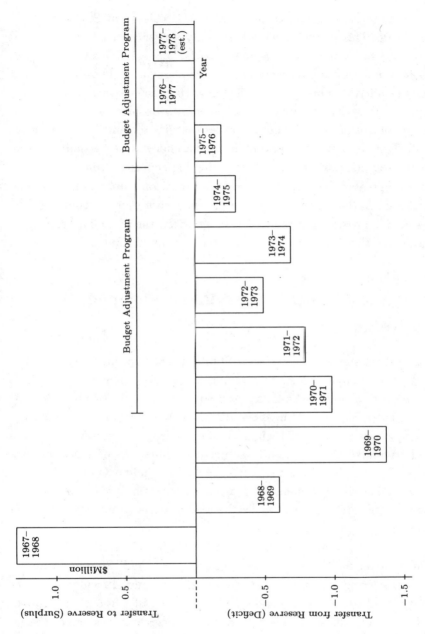

Figure 2.5. Historical budget surpluses and deficits at Stanford University (based on final, year-end accounting figures).

*Epilogue:* Budget equilibrium was indeed achieved at Stanford in the late 1970's. This period of relative stability was short-lived, however, because Stanford was hit with a major earthquake and massive reductions in federal indirect cost recovery only a few years later. Those unexpected events resulted in more severe budget cuts than anyone imagined possible during the time that the financial modeling described here was taking place. One important product of these analyses that has remained is the concept of LRFE as it applies to payout from the endowment. Administrators and trustees alike realize that authorizing expenditures from endowment at a rate greater than the LRFE rate is tantamount to deficit spending. Thus, even in the current climate of grave concern over the sustainability of academic programs at reduced funding levels, the discipline remains to continue cutting the budget until it is back in equilibrium.

# 4. Trade-off Analysis and Preference Optimization

The third area of application at Stanford is the optimization of preferences for alternative university planning configurations. A series of models have been developed to assist the top administrators in turning their attention away from purely financial details so they can focus more on the academic consequences of their decisions. Of course, there is no way to avoid having to make primarily subjective evaluations of academic outcomes. By bringing these subjective, or "value" judgments together in a single model with the financial constraints operating on the institution, however, one could hope to make the task of decision making somewhat easier.

The first step was to develop a consensus about what items should be included in a small set of "primary planning variables." Stanford's administrators selected the numbers of tenured and untenured faculty, auxiliary faculty, graduate students, undergraduate students, tuition, the growth-rate of tuition, the staff-to-faculty ratio, the degree of leverage of the institution (that is, its dependence on "soft money"), salary policy, and the funded improvement fraction.

A mathematical programming model was formulated to determine what

values of these variables were perceived by an administrator best to fulfill
the institution's objectives, subject to the conditions of LRFE. The administrator's "utility function" had to be estimated from data obtained by
filling out a lengthy questionnaire. The purpose of the questionnaire was
to get him or her to express preferences among a large number of alternative configurations of the primary planning variables. Once estimated,
the function could be used directly in a computer-optimization procedure
(Hopkins, Larreche and Massy 1977).

This technique turned out to be only partially successful. In some cases
the "optimal" solution was quite reasonable; yet, in others it was too far
from the current operating point to be of much use. The latter results
probably derived from the feelings of artificiality and detachment shared
by most of the individuals who took part in the questionnaire study.

Subsequently, several interactive versions of the model have been developed, which permit the administrator to examine the implications of his
preferences while logged on to a computer terminal (Massy 1976; Wehrung,
Hopkins and Massy 1978). The primary role being played by the computer
in these exercises is to perform "bookkeeping" calculations that will assure
the user of remaining within the set of financially feasible possibilities. The
object is to enable the user to "wander through" the feasible set in an iterative fashion, obtaining an improvement in the solution, according to his
or her own set of values, at each point along the way.

This so-called TRADES model has seen considerable use by the chief
budget planners. It has even played a role in discussions with the Board of
Trustees. Through its use, we certainly have gained a better understanding
of the significance of the financial constraints facing Stanford in terms of
its primary planning variables.

*Epilogue:* The administration's interest in the analyses described in this
section was rather transient. These trade-off analyses definitely served a
purpose at the time of focusing the key budget planners on the kinds of
decisions that had to be made in an extended period of austerity. Most
decisions have continued to be made on the margin, however, and so the
utility of these models was mainly in the insights they gave on the financial tradeoffs among primary planning variables to those who participated
directly in the exercise.

# 5. Conclusion

The foregoing discussion has given a flavor of the uses to which certain kinds of quantitative analyses have been put at Stanford. The models described have assisted us in gaining a much clearer conception of some of the more important problems facing our institution. Also, owing to their great explanatory power, these models have facilitated communication about these problems both within the administration and between it and important segments of the campus community.

As most readers will know, modeling is not always well integrated with decision making in any large organization. How, then, has this integration been accomplished at Stanford? Certainly, it is significant that the modeling activities have actually taken place in conjunction with top-level decision making. By this are meant two things: first, the models were developed in response to the need for solutions to widely recognized problems; second, the entire group of top budget officers was involved at some stage of the modeling process. Thus, there has been no risk of modelers and decision makers working in isolation from one another.

A second element that has contributed to the successful integration is the fact that the modeling efforts were restricted to a relatively small scale. Each model was built to respond to a particular need at the central administrative level and was designed to represent, in the simplest of terms, the basic structural interrelationships among a small number of planning variables. Neither the size of the models nor the complexity of their outputs has been permitted to reach a point beyond which there is a loss of intellectual control.

Finally, there was a consistent and unified effort on the parts of the model builders and the decision makers to maintain open communication at all times. This prevented the former from developing their solutions in ignorance of the real problems and led to a certain degree of intellectual ownership of the models, and hence confidence in their results, by the latter. In short, by involving the administrators at all stages of model development, we have observed a considerable willingness on their part to accept the analytical results and to factor them into the difficult decisions they must make.

# Acknowledgment

This chapter is reprinted with permission from the publishers of *Interfaces*.

# References

Hopkins, D. S. P. 1974a. "Analysis of Faculty Appointment, Promotion, and Retirement Policies." *Higher Education* 3: 397–418.

Hopkins, D. S. P. 1974b. "Faculty Early Retirement Programs." *Operations Research* 22: 455–467.

Hopkins, D. S. P. 1979. "Computer Models Employed in University Administration: The Stanford Experience." *Interfaces* 9: 13–23.

Hopkins, D. S. P., and A. Bienenstock. 1975. "Numerical Models for Faculty Planning." In Allan Cartter, ed., *Assuring Academic Progress Without Growth*, pp. 27–45. San Francisco: Jossey-Bass.

Hopkins, D. S. P., J. C. Larreche, and W. F. Massy. 1977. "Constrained Optimization of a University, Administrator's Preference Function." *Management Science* 24: 365–377.

Hopkins, D. S. P., and W. F. Massy. 1977. "A Model for Planning the Transition to Equilibrium of a University Budget." *Management Science* 23: 1161–1168.

Massy, W. F. 1976. "A Dynamic Equilibrium Model for University Budgeting." *Management Science* 23: 248–256.

Wehrung, D. A., D. S. P. Hopkins and W. F. Massy. 1978. "Interactive Preference Optimization for University Administrators." *Management Science* 24: 599–611.

# Chapter 3

# Faculty Retirement Policies: The Stanford Experience

## Kathryn M. Gillam and John B. Shoven

## 1. Introduction

On March 5, 1910, Stanford University President David Starr Jordan informed the faculty that at the Board of Trustees meeting of February 25, the resignation of Melville Best Anderson, Professor of English Literature, had been received and accepted and that he had been elected Professor Emeritus of English Literature, effective August 1, 1910. President Jordan went on to say:

> It was stated by me to the Board of Trustees, and to Professor Anderson, that by this act he is transferred to the payroll of the Carnegie Foundation, while at the same time the title of Professor Emeritus gives to him the freedom of the University, free access to all its privileges, the right to give lectures at any time or on any subject he may choose, the right to be one with his colleagues in every way that may appeal to him, the right to take part in any of the University affairs—in short, to be a

Stanford man honored of all, and beyond the reach of adverse
criticism and of all other academic dangers.[1]

Professor Anderson was the first faculty member to retire from Stanford
University. In 1985, Professor Clara Bush, Academic Secretary to the University, remarked, "the privileges seem extraordinary—even for that time,
and the promises of the last two phrases ... to be actually beyond the
power of mortal man to ensure!"[2] No doubt. However, President Jordan's
remarks are noteworthy, beyond their old-fashioned civility, because they
demonstrate the institution's early interest in both the financial and the
intellectual well-being of its retired faculty. On the financial side, the University's faculty were, in 1910, already part of the pension system of the
Carnegie Corporation, which later established the Teachers Insurance and
Annuity Association and the College Retirement Equities Fund (TIAA-
CREF). On the intellectual side, President Jordan clearly recognized that
the career of a professor did not necessarily end on the date of retirement
and that the life of the mind was not bounded by "active duty" employment.

These two themes, the financial well-being of retirees and their continued participation in the academic community, have reappeared each time
the issue of faculty retirement has been discussed and policy decisions made.
They are, of course, mutually dependent considerations, for both individuals and for the institution. In this chapter we focus on Stanford's faculty
retirement policies as they have evolved over the last twenty years. We
describe both the changes that have occurred and the legal, economic, and
institutional forces that have shaped them. We also discuss the interplay
between individual interests and the interests of the institution, as these are
defined by faculty and by university leaders, and the underlying constancy
of the values and the dynamics of the university.

# 2. The Decade of the 1970's

## 2.1. The First Early Retirement Program

At the beginning of the 1970's the mandatory age of retirement at Stanford was 65. In 1973, the administration initiated an early retirement pro-

gram for tenured faculty. The rationale for the program was later described by a committee studying retirement issues as follows:

> At the time it was adopted, it was known that several faculty members, who were in their early sixties, wanted to withdraw from active service, yet felt they could not afford to do so. This seemed particularly true for those whose salaries had not kept up with the median for their peer groups. The program was designed to provide a financial benefit that would tend to keep the effects of lower salaries from carrying over into retirement.[3]

This early retirement program was a voluntary plan that provided an eligible faculty member with an annual "interim retirement allowance" from the time of early retirement, which could be as early as age 58, to the date of mandatory retirement at age 65. The amount of the allowance was a fraction of the individual's final salary that was based on the individual's length of service and the difference between the final salary and the median full professor's salary in the individual's school. The calculation was structured so that the longer the length of service and the lower the salary relative to the median, the higher the fraction, up to a maximum of 80% of final salary. The annual amount increased each year of participation in the program by the same percentage as the median full professor salary in the individual's school. The program was open to tenured faculty with at least fifteen years of service.[4] This structure set the character for Stanford's early-retirement incentive options for faculty for fully 24 years. The principle at work, that of encouraging the retirement of relatively lower paid, relatively longer service tenured faculty, was not altered until 1994.

The Early Retirement Program operated without modification from 1973 to 1981. Table 3.1 shows the results. During this period, a total of 132 faculty retired. Ninety-six (72.7%) retired at age 65; 26 (19.7%) retired under the provisions of the Early Retirement Program; and the remaining 10 (7.6%) retired early but not under the Program (by and large these individuals were ineligible, because they were either too young or did not hold a tenured appointment). Thus, most faculty retired at the required age of 65, and the retirement-incentive program was not widely used, although those who did take advantage of it later reported that they were satisfied with their decision.[5]

TABLE 3.1

*Results of the Faculty Early Retirement Program I*
*(1973–1981)*

| Year | No. retirees under Program | No. mandatory retirees | No. other retirees | Total |
|------|------|------|------|------|
| 1972–73 | 4 | 14 | 1 | 19 |
| 1973–74 | 2 | 14 | 1 | 17 |
| 1974–75 | 0 | 13 | 1 | 14 |
| 1975–76 | 5 | 11 | 0 | 16 |
| 1976–77 | 2 | 15 | 0 | 16 |
| 1977–78 | 3 | 13 | 1 | 17 |
| 1978–79 | 6 | 4 | 1 | 11 |
| 1979–80 | 2 | 3 | 2 | 7 |
| 1980–81 | 2 | 9 | 3 | 14 |
| Total | 26 | 96 | 10 | 132 |
|  | (19.7%) | (72.7%) | (7.6%) | (100%) |

SOURCE: Office of the Provost, Stanford University

## 2.2. Legal Changes and Policy Responses

In 1977, the California legislature amended the Fair Employment Practices Act (FEPA), and in March 1978, Congress amended the Age Discrimination in Employment Act (ADEA). Effective January 1, 1978, the new state law proscribed mandatory retirement of "any individual over the age of 40 on the ground of age," although in September 1978 the legislature amended the FEPA to exclude employees between the ages of 65 and 70 who were either tenured professors or at certain executive levels. The amended federal retirement law proscribed mandatory retirement between the ages of 40 and 70. It also excluded certain executive level employees, and it did not apply to tenured faculty until July 1, 1982. The result of these changes was that Stanford could still require the retirement of tenured faculty between the ages of 65 and 70, but it was anticipated that as of July 1, 1982, mandatory retirement at or beyond age 65 would be prohibited entirely for tenured faculty. This was because after that date, federal law would prohibit mandatory retirement prior to age 70 and state law would prohibit it after age 70.[6]

Concerned about the potential significance of these changes, President Richard Lyman consulted with the University's Advisory Board, the group of seven senior faculty elected from the faculty at large that, among other duties, serves as a sounding board for the President and Provost. In typical academic fashion, the Board recommended that he establish two separate committees to study the issues arising from recent legislation affecting mandatory retirement.[7] From the University's point of view, the topics needing investigation included the prospect of many fewer appointments and promotions of faculty; as a result of fewer appointment opportunities, the possibility of a major setback in the University's efforts to achieve a better balance of women and members of minority groups through affirmative action efforts; and increasing costs for faculty salaries as well as for measures designed to encourage retirement.[8]

The first of these committees, the Administrative Panel on Retirement, chaired by Provost William Miller, submitted its report to the President in January 1979. It was published in the *Campus Report* in February 1979 and discussed in the Faculty Senate in March 1979. Among the 22 recommendations contained in the report were: (1) to retain age 65 as the mandatory retirement age for tenured faculty; (2) to encourage part-time arrangements for faculty leading up to age 65; (3) to modify the Early Retirement Program to make it more attractive to a wider range of faculty; (4) to modify the University's contributory retirement plan so as not to contribute to an individual's TIAA or CREF account after age 65; (5) to undertake a study of faculty tenure "after there has been opportunity for the legislation to stabilize and for patterns of response to the legislation to evolve."[9]

In June 1979 all of these recommendations except the first one, concerning the retention of age 65 as a mandatory retirement date, were approved.[10] This recommendation generated considerable controversy. In the February 28 issue of the *Campus Report*, Professor of Mechanical Engineering E. H. Lee published a highly critical analysis of it. He asserted that allowing tenured faculty to continue to age 70 would have a negligible effect on the University and to continue mandatory retirement for them would constitute unwarranted discrimination. In the March 15 Senate discussion

Professor Bernard Roth pointed out that none of the affected faculty had been asked about their future plans, and he charged the University administration with being deceptive in their presentation of information to the Senate. Dean of the Law School Charles Myers supported the Panel's recommendation and pointed out the prospect, in the absence of mandatory retirement, of retaining tenured faculty "regardless of competency or ability." He said, "Professor Roth has not really thought through the appalling prospect of holding a hearing for a senior member of the faculty on the question of ... competency."[11]

At Stanford and elsewhere this debate placed the greater good of the University as an institution in opposition to the rights of individual faculty members. For example, Professor Allen Calvin, of the University of San Francisco, an active faculty proponent of the uncapping of mandatory retirement, later wrote, "Because I was involved with the Civil Rights Movement in the 1960s and had the privilege of working directly with Martin Luther King Jr. and other historic figures, it seems natural for me to view the elimination of mandatory retirement as an extension of early civil rights struggles" (see Calvin, 1993). University administrators, in contrast, focused on broad institutional interests such as diminished opportunities for the future, cost, and difficult issues of addressing faculty competency in the context of strong peer relationships.

Between March and May 1979 Acting Provost Gerald Lieberman asked each school dean to inquire of the 67 faculty who would turn age 65 prior to July 1, 1982, about their plans and wishes concerning retirement, and estimates of the cost of not requiring retirement at age 65 were done. In the May 16 *Campus Report*, President Lyman announced a compromise:

> In response to federal and state legislation governing the retirement age for tenured faculty members, the University shall offer to any faculty member whose 65th birthday falls in the period between now and July 1, 1982 the opportunity to remain on duty on a half-time basis. The status of those individuals and of others who reach the "normal" retirement age after July 1, 1982 will necessarily be determined by the terms of the applicable law and University policy at the time.

In his May 16 announcement, President Lyman also said that

it is clear that we are faced with an absolute necessity of making the transition to a radically different set of circumstances surrounding the question of retirement. As the Retirement Panel clearly indicated, it will be extremely important to develop a variety of options, and to encourage faculty to think seriously about such things as gradual diminution of their time commitment—partial retirement, in effect. The deans' conversations indicate that most faculty who will reach age 65 in the next couple of years would prefer to continue on a part-time basis. Our review of the record of the last three years indicates that, in fact, most faculty do not move from full time immediately before retirement to zero time immediately after. Indeed, over two-thirds of those faculty who retired at 65 were recalled on a part-time basis.

President Lyman also criticized the legal changes resulting in prohibitions against mandatory retirement at any age as "a piece of sweeping social legislation" that was passed with a "grossly irresponsible attitude toward consequences." He believed that all institutions of higher education that faced the elimination of mandatory retirement would find it necessary to develop procedures for determining the continuing high competence of faculty members.

But one faces the prospect of putting such mechanisms in place with grave misgivings. I doubt that the sum of human happiness will have been increased when it is no longer possible for a retired scholar to say, "I was going strong but I reached that mandatory retirement age," and instead it becomes necessary for some unknown number, but surely larger than zero, to say, "They examined my competence to continue and found it wanting."

He concluded by saying that the entire University would need to think about these issues carefully, and he expressed hope that the University could "develop a system which, though no doubt complex and full of difficult day-to-day decisions, will protect a balance of interests and thereby the future of the institution."

In June, President Lyman discussed with the Senate the remaining recommendations of the Retirement Panel. In response to concern about the adequacy of pensions in a time of double-digit inflation, he said he would give further thought to the recommendations that the University end its TIAA-CREF contributions for faculty members after age 65. He had received a letter signed by 46 professors who said that prospective pensions at age 65 were "truly miserable." The President agreed that this was a serious problem, for which there were no easy solutions "so long as inflation is out of control, which it plainly is."[12] (In the end, contributions were cut off for those over age 65 for one year only; they were put in place for post–65-year-olds in October 1980.)

In September 1979 the California legislature amended its Fair Employment Practices Act to allow for compulsory retirement at age 70 for those holding a contract of unlimited tenure. This brought California law in conformity with Federal law, effective July 1, 1982. As a result, in November Stanford adjusted the policy that had been announced by President Lyman the previous May. Any faculty member whose 65th birthday fell between September 1, 1978, and August 31, 1981, would be permitted to remain on a half-time basis until August 31 of the academic year in which he or she reached age 70. Beginning September 1, 1981, age 70 would be considered the University's mandatory retirement date for tenured faculty members.[13]

# 3. The Decade of the 1980's

## 3.1. A Revised Early Retirement Program

As noted above, between 1978 and 1981, faculty who reached the age of 65 could either retire or stay on active duty at 50% time until August 31 of the year in which they turned age 70. Records in the Provost's Office show that over that three-year period, a total of 40 faculty reached age 65. Of the 1978–79 cohort of 65 year olds, 33% retired at age 65, 33% at age 70, and 33% between 65 and 70. Of the 1980–81 cohort of 65 year olds, 20% retired at age 65, 40% at age 70, and 40% in between. Beginning in 1981–82, all faculty were permitted to remain on full-time duty until August 31 of the year in which they turned age 70.

As a result of the recommendation of the Panel on Retirement, the University modified its Early Retirement Program to make it both more attractive and consistent with the new mandatory retirement age. The changes included altering the ages for participation from the previous window of 58 to 65 to a new window of 62 to 70 and instituting rights of survivorship for the interim retirement allowances. The Faculty Early Retirement Program II was announced on September 1, 1981, and was open to new participants until August 31, 1992, although those who were accepted into it by the latter date were permitted to retire as late as August 31, 1994.[14] Table 3.2 shows the results of the Program. During the period from academic year 1981–82 through 1993–94, a total of 304 faculty retired. One hundred fifty-five (51%) retired before age 70 under the provisions of the Early Retirement Program (except for 8 who retired in 1994 under the successor program), 97 (31.9%) retired at the mandatory age of 70, and 52 (17.1%) retired early but not under the program (some of these individuals were leaving Stanford to take positions elsewhere; they were old enough to retire voluntarily but did not fit the age or length of service criteria for the incentive program; others were in the non-tenure-line faculty and thus were ineligible). In contrast to the experience of the 1970's, when only about 20% of those retiring took advantage of the retirement-incentive program, fully half of those retiring during the next thirteen years took the program. Also in contrast to the earlier period, when almost three-quarters of the retiring faculty were at the mandatory age, only about one-third of the faculty who retired in this period did so at the mandatory age. Thus, the early retirement plan had a significant impact on the retirement behavior of the faculty during this period.

## 3.2. Further Policy Deliberations and Legal Changes

In April 1980, Provost Donald Kennedy appointed the second of the two committees that the Advisory Board had recommended be formed to study the impact of changes in legislation affecting retirement. Chaired by Professor Ronald N. Bracewell, the Task Force on Retirement Policies was charged with examining the desirability of continuing mandatory retirement as well as related issues of tenure, the University's early retirement program, its defined contribution pension plan, and methods for ensuring the continued influx of more junior scholars into the professoriate. The Task Force did a demographic analysis of the faculty and made projections about possible age distributions for the decade of the 1980's and beyond. They also asked participants in the Early Retirement Program about experience with it and obtained information from other universities about their policies and programs. They considered alternatives to the tenure system.[15]

TABLE 3.2

*Results of the Faculty Early Retirement Plan II*
*(1982–1994)*

| Year | No. retirees under Program | No. mandatory retirees | No. other retirees | Total |
|---|---|---|---|---|
| 1981–82 | 7 | 0 | 4 | 11 |
| 1982–83 | 11 | 1 | 3 | 15 |
| 1983–84 | 12 | 3 | 1 | 16 |
| 1984–85 | 10 | 7 | 2 | 19 |
| 1985–86 | 12 | 6 | 5 | 23 |
| 1986–87 | 9 | 9 | 3 | 21 |
| 1987–88 | 20 | 9 | 8 | 37 |
| 1988–89 | 12 | 14 | 9 | 35 |
| 1989–90 | 5 | 12 | 3 | 20 |
| 1990–91 | 5 | 7 | 2 | 14 |
| 1991–92 | 11 | 18 | 1 | 30 |
| 1992–93 | 14 | 11 | 8 | 33 |
| 1993–94 | 27* | 0 | 3 | 30 |
| Totals | 155 | 97 | 52 | 304 |
| | (51.0%) | (31.9%) | (17.1%) | (100%) |

SOURCE: Office of the Provost, Stanford University.

NOTE: Stanford's last mandatory retirement date was August 31, 1993.

* Includes eight participants in Faculty Retirement Incentive Program

The Task Force submitted its report to Provost Albert Hastorf in 1982. Its major recommendations were: (1) to retain the tenure system and a mandatory retirement age; (2) to retain the early retirement program as revised; (3) to provide investment vehicles which were alternatives to TIAA-CREF; (4) to encourage the recall of emeriti when appropriate, and seek to improve the status of all emeriti and ensure for them such participation as they may desire in the life of the University; and (5) to seek additional funds in order to maintain an adequate flux of new junior faculty during the period of adjustment to a higher mandatory retirement age .[16]

Concerning the tenure system, the Task Force report said,

> Given the full range of our charge, the current flux with regard to retirement policies, and the information presently available to us, it seems premature to focus on alternatives to tenure at this time. ... There is no reason to believe that tenure will not serve academia under the new equilibrium [of the faculty age distribution assuming mandatory retirement at age 70] as it has in the past. ... On the other hand, ... should uncapping come to pass, the tenure system itself may come into question. Alternatives to tenure involve highly sensitive issues and raise questions of their legality, implementation, and effectiveness. Moreover, one institution's abandoning tenure, still widely perceived as a benefit, might well adversely affect its ability to recruit outstanding faculty.[17]

Most of these recommendations were implemented. Mandatory retirement continued at age 70, and no changes were made in the tenure system. As noted earlier, the Faculty Early Retirement Program was maintained, with considerable success. In 1983, more investment vehicles were made available to participants in the defined-contribution pension plan, and emeriti recalls to active duty continued to be a common occurrence. Individual schools, such as the School of Humanities and Sciences received private foundation support for incremental appointments of junior faculty during the 1980's.[18]

Meanwhile, actions by the U.S. Congress during the 1980's moved the country closer to the end of mandatory retirement for tenured faculty, in spite of the ongoing concerns of university leaders and professional organizations such as the American Association of University Professors, the American Council on Education, and the Association of American Universities. In August 1982 Stanford President Donald Kennedy wrote to several members of the Senate Subcommittee on Labor and Human Resources, which was about to hold hearings on a bill eliminating mandatory retirement that had been introduced by Senator John Heinz (Republican, Pennsylvania). President Kennedy urged their support of an exemption in the bill for tenured faculty. His arguments were similar to those identified earlier by President Lyman: (1) a decrease in the number of openings for new faculty; (2) of special importance, a decrease in the number of women and minority scholars who could be offered tenured positions; and (3) the link between the tenure system and mandatory retirement. He argued that it would be very difficult to maintain a system of tenure without mandatory retirement, and he noted, "we do not have to reach as far back as the McCarthy era to realize that tenure is essential to free inquiry in colleges and universities."[19] Although this bill was not passed by the Congress, the idea of an exemption for tenured faculty persisted in later versions of the bill. However, instead of a permanent exemption, it became an exemption for a specified number of years, to allow for the mandatory retirement of as many senior faculty as possible before uncapping would take effect.

No law was passed until 1986. In the summer of that year, bills ending mandatory retirement were pending before both the House of Representatives and the Senate. In September 1986 an appeal went out to university presidents from the head of the American Council on Education, Robert Atwell, to write to their representatives advocating exemptions for tenured faculty in the bills.[20] The House bill passed on September 23, with no exemption for tenured faculty, and another urgent appeal was sent to universities to be in touch with their Senators to add the exemption to the Senate bill. In the end, the bill that passed the Senate in October 1986 and was signed by President Reagan provided a seven-year exemption for tenured faculty, during which time the National Academy of Sciences was mandated to conduct a study on the potential consequences of uncapping for institutions of higher education.[21]

In an interesting twist, Stanford retirement data were used by those who favored the uncapping of mandatory retirement to argue that the problem of faculty staying too long was not likely to be significant. In a letter to the U.S. Senate, one faculty member pointed out that "At Stanford University, for example, in June, 1986, 19 professors took emeritus status. Only 6 of these were 70 years old. More than two thirds—13 out of 19—

took early retirement."[22] However, all of these early retirees retired under the provisions of the Early Retirement Program—that is, they got paid to retire. It is not possible to say how many of them would have retired without this financial incentive. Thus, the Stanford experience did not provide a 'clean' answer to the question, how many professors would stay on in the absence of mandatory retirement? It did say, "in an environment in which there is mandatory retirement at age 70, about half of faculty will retire earlier than age 70 if financial incentives are provided to do so."

After the passage of the 1986 amendments to the Age Discrimination in Employment Act, Stanford leaders assumed that mandatory retirement for tenured faculty would end in 1994. This outcome looked increasingly inevitable as the National Academy of Science study of the impact of uncapping was delayed, and when, in 1987, the AAUP reversed its position and decided not the resist the uncapping.[23] To plan for this change and to consider related issues, such as the adequacy of Stanford's retirement pension plans, Provost James Rosse established. in March 1989, a Task Force on Faculty and Staff Retirement. This group was chaired by one of the authors (Shoven) and staffed by the other (Gillam).

# 4. The Early 1990's

The Task Force on Faculty and Staff Retirement established by Provost Rosse carried out its work under conditions of considerable uncertainty. For instance, whereas the past experience of the University with respect to faculty retirement could be studied, no one could say with certainty how faculty would respond to the lack of a mandatory retirement age. On the basis of demographic projections that used past years' data and incorporated certain assumptions about retirement behavior, the Task Force predicted that, over the first five years following uncapping, the average age of the faculty would rise from 47.4 years to between 48.1 and 48.9 years and the percentage of faculty under the age of 40 would decline from the 28.1% it would reach if uncapping did not take place to between 26.9% and 25.1%.

In addition, the Task Force carried out a survey of a sample of senior faculty who were 60 to 65 years old. Most of these faculty said that they did not think that the change in the law would have much of an effect on their behavior. Seventy percent of the respondents said they had considered when they might retire, and about 60% were able to give an age. Of that 60%, 35% said they would retire before age 70, about 50% said they would retire at ago 70, and 14% said they would retire after age 70. The factors mentioned in thinking about when to retire (apart from the changes in the law) were the adequacy of their retirement income and concern about inflation. Nonmonetary aspects of retirement, such as concern about "loss of identity" were also mentioned. The Task Force concluded that the demographic projections were cause for "concern but not alarm, and that the University should take some action to encourage retirement planning to ensure that faculty do not decide to stay on past age 70 because of financial needs." It also concluded from the survey that the University should provide mechanisms that would both inform faculty about the retirement income they could expect and provide an incentive to plan for retirement.[24]

The Task Force also discussed the issue that both President Lyman and President Kennedy had raised: the performance of senior faculty, especially those who chose to stay on active duty beyond age 70, and its relation to tenure. While fully aware of the potential pain, both institutional and individual, of stripping tenure from senior faculty whose performance was failing, this Task Force, like every committee that had preceded it, concluded that the uncertainty was too great to make a recommendation. The University's lack of experience in this area, the deep respect in which tenure is held, and the fundamental importance in the academy of peer interaction and colleagueship worked together to produce a reluctance to take on this issue, and it was simply set aside.[25]

The law continued to be another source of uncertainty. While it was assumed that mandatory retirement would go away, the fine points of the law with respect to retirement-incentive plans were not at all clear. The decision was taken to make recommendations on the basis of the best interests of the University, with the caveat that, of course, any plan that would be implemented would need to be consonant with the law. Thus, the group recommended a retirement-incentive program for faculty between the ages of 62 and 70 that would provide an incentive payment of one-half year's salary.[26]

The nature of this plan was considerably different from that of the Faculty Early Retirement Program. The incentive payment would be paid as salary prior to retirement rather than as a series of payments following retirement, and there was no weighting of the payment toward longer service and lower salaries. The principle behind this proposal was that when there would no longer be mandatory retirement, the University would be well served by having in place a voluntary program to encourage the retirement of its senior faculty. In general this would be true even for the most distinguished and still productive faculty, and it was anticipated that the long-established custom of recalling emeriti to active duty would allow those individuals who wished to continue their scholarly activities to do so. The amount of the incentive payment was intended to provide a stimulus for considering retirement rather than a mechanism for making up for lower-than-average salaries, which had been the impetus for the original plan in 1973.

The Task Force also studied the issue of the adequacy of the University's retirement pension plans for both faculty and staff. On the faculty side, the group concluded that for faculty retiring in the near future the accumulations most individuals had in their retirement accounts plus Social Security would provide for a comfortable and even generous retirement income, defined as one that would provide an income of at least 70% of preretirement net income. However, the Task Force was concerned about data that showed that many younger faculty were not participating in the University's plan (50% of those under the age of 30, for instance). This was because the plan required a 5% contribution by the individual in order to receive the University's 10% contribution. Out of concern for equity between highly paid and less highly paid employees as well as the long-term interests of the faculty, the Task Force recommended revising the contributory plan so that the University contributed 5% for everyone and then matched, on a 1:1 basis, an individual's contribution up to another 5%, so that the maximum amount would continue to be 15%.[27]

The Task Force submitted its report to Provost Rosse in April, 1990. The Senate discussed the report in June, and the Dean's Council reviewed the recommendations in August.[28] The proposal to change the contributory plan was adopted and implemented. However, the proposed new incentive plan was tabled for further study. In December, 1991, Provost

Rosse announced the end of mandatory retirement for tenured faculty effective August 31, 1993, and the end of the Faculty Early Retirement Program effective August 31, 1992 (although, as noted above, those who declared their interest in taking advantage of the program could retire as late as August 31, 1994).[29] A relatively large number of faculty retired during the years 1992 through 1994, perhaps partially as a result of Provost Rosse's announcement (see Table 3.2).

Although the administration was supportive of the retirement-incentive program proposed by the Task Force, implementation was delayed, largely because of the crisis the University faced in the area of indirect cost recovery from federally funded sponsored research. In October 1990 the University was accused of overcharging the federal government and was assaulted by unfavorable publicity, demands for huge volumes of detailed accounting information, and unilateral decreases in indirect cost recovery that led to a severe budget crisis. The University was, to a substantial degree, under siege, and coping with the crisis and its concomitant budget shortfall preoccupied the administration for the remainder of 1990 and all of 1991. In the summer of 1991, President Donald Kennedy announced that he would step down in August 1992. In April 1992 Provost Rosse left Stanford to take an executive position in Southern California. In March 1992, Gerhard Casper, Provost at the University of Chicago, was named the next President of Stanford, and also in March, Professor Gerald J. Lieberman was named Provost. Thus, by the autumn of 1992 new leadership was in place, and attention could be turned once more to policy issues that were at less than a crisis level of urgency.

One of these issues was faculty retirement, and in autumn of 1992 Provost Lieberman established a committee to follow up on the previous Task Force by focusing specifically on retirement incentive plans. The Committee was chaired by Professor of Law Alan J. Bankman, and it included faculty, recent emeriti, and senior faculty who faced retirement in the near future. Because the legal environment with respect to voluntary incentive plans was still unclear, the Committee debated the basic question of whether or not to have a plan. The Committee also considered a proposal that would provide a small annuity to faculty who retired as well as a proposal to encourage retirement by cutting off contributions to retirement accounts when an "adequate" accumulation had been reached.

In December 1993, the Committee presented the pros and cons of various alternatives to the President, Provost, and School Deans. In the end, the decision was taken to have a voluntary program that would provide a single, lump-sum payment at the time of retirement. The administration thus endorsed the principle articulated by the previous Task Force, that in the absence of mandatory retirement, the University and its faculty will be well served by a voluntary retirement-incentive program.

The terms of the proposed Faculty Retirement Incentive Program were ironed out during the autumn and winter of 1993–94 , and it was implemented May 1, 1994. In spite of the lateness of the academic year, eight faculty retired under the new plan in August 1994, and it is anticipated that at least a dozen more will do so by the end of the 1994–95 year. The program provides an incentive payment to all faculty with fifteen years of service or more of two times the final base salary for individuals aged 60 to 65. The multiple of final salary declines with increasing age (1.8 for retirement at age 66, 1.5 at age 67, etc.) to zero at age 70.[30] The full incentive payment of two times the final base salary was, however, made available to all faculty age 60 with fifteen years of service for a limited period of time at the outset of the program.

Thus, in late 1994 the long transition away from mandatory retirement has been accomplished, and the University continues to have a voluntary incentive program to encourage faculty to consider retirement.

# 5. Factors That Discourage Retirement

Stanford faces several factors that discourage faculty retirement. These include the type of pension plan it offers to faculty; other economic factors; and the nature of the professoriate at research universities.

## 5.1. The Economics of Pension Plans of Alternative Designs

As described earlier, Stanford's retirement plan for faculty is a defined-contribution plan. The University contributes 5% of an individual's gross salary, on a pretax basis, to a variety of funds designated by the individual and, on a 1:1 basis, matches individual contributions of up to another 5%, for a total of 15%. This type of plan is in contrast to a defined-benefit plan, in which a retiree receives an annuity based on years of service and a fraction (say, 2%) of final salary, or of an average of the final five years' salary.

Until 1983, the only choices for retirement accounts for Stanford faculty were those held by TIAA-CREF. TIAA had been founded in 1918 as an offshoot of the Carnegie Corporation for the Advancement of Teaching, which itself had sponsored, starting in 1908, a free pension system for professors with an endowment of $10 million from Andrew Carnegie, who had become concerned about the low level of wages of college professors. (It was this pension system that supported Stanford's first retiree, Professor Anderson.) The Carnegie free pension system was a defined-benefit plan that paid benefits to professors attaining age 65 who has at least fifteen years of service. However, by the time TIAA was founded in 1918, it was determined that a contributory plan was the only type of plan that was supportable over the long run. The Carnegie free pension system was closed to new entrants in 1932, and CREF was founded in 1952 (see Schieber 1993). In 1983, Stanford expanded its offerings of retirement funds to which it would contribute to include, in addition to TIAA-CREF, such companies as Fidelity and Vanguard.

In 1990 the Provost's Task Force briefly considered the option of shifting from a defined-contribution to a defined-benefit plan. The benefit of portability of a defined-contribution plan, as well as the difficulty of making a transition from one type of plan to a qualitatively different type and the possible perception of diminishing the quality of the benefit, discouraged the Task Force from recommending such a shift.[31] Thus, Stanford continues to have a defined-contribution plan.

Defined-contribution (DC) retirement plans and defined-benefit (DB) plans are different in several fundamental ways. First, the names are descriptive because they describe the employer's obligation. With a defined-contribution plan, all that the employer promises is to make a payment to a retirement account. The employee bears the responsibility of allocating that money to particular types of investments and faces the uncertainty about the rate of return that those assets will earn. With a defined-benefit plan the employer promises a benefit based on years of service and salary, and the employer (with regulation from the government) sets aside the funds necessary to honor its commitments. In this case the employer makes the asset allocation decisions and faces the investment risks.

The defined contribution is very simple from both the employer's and the employee's points of view. The benefits are completely portable since the retirement account belongs to the employee once full vesting is achieved (immediately for Stanford faculty). Defined-benefit plans in general do not share this simple portability feature. People who have defined-benefit plans and who change employers (even if both have equivalent DB plans) receive greatly diminished retirement benefits relative to people who stay with one employer for their entire career. Given the rigorous up-or-out tenure process faced by junior faculty, the portability of pension benefits is an extremely desirable feature in a university plan. This may be the main reason why the vast majority of private colleges and universities have opted for defined-contribution plans. Another reason may be the predictable funding requirements of these plans in contrast to defined-benefit plans. One of the determinants of how large a contribution an employer has to make to fund its DB plan is the performance of financial markets. If stock and bond markets perform poorly, universities suffer in two ways: first, their earnings on their endowment is reduced, and second, alumni and foundation contributions are likely to fall. A pension plan that requires increased contributions just when income is tight seems particularly undesirable—and that is how a defined-benefit plan would work.

So far we have mentioned important advantages of defined contribution plans for institutions of higher education. In terms of retirement incentives, defined-benefit and defined-contribution plans are once again distinctly different. In order to describe the difference, it is probably useful to consider specific plans. For this purpose, we can use the actual Stanford defined-contribution plan for faculty and assume that the total contribution is and has been 15% of salary. A generous defined benefit plan would give the employee 2 percent of final salary for each year of service commencing at retirement at age 65 or older. For retirements before age 65, the benefit formula for the DB plan would be scaled back. With these two plans in mind, consider someone who has been a very long term employee. This person joined the faculty at age 30 and now is 65 years old. The DB benefit would be a retirement annuity equal to 70 percent of current pay. For instance, if this individual currently has a $90,000 salary, the amount received in retirement would be $63,000 per year. Note that this annual benefit amount would not increase once the individual had retired. The DC benefit would be whatever annuity could be purchased from TIAA-CREF (or another insurance company) with the funds accumulated in the plan. It is difficult to say which plan would provide more money in retirement. In both cases, the retirement amount would be decreased if the employee opted for something other than a single-life annuity. For instance, most married couples opt for a joint survivor annuity where some benefits are received by the surviving spouse. The percentage reduction for choosing a joint survivor annuity would be identical for the two different types of plans.

Now, however, consider the decision of whether to retire at 65 or to continue to work and retire at age 70. In real terms, the monthly DB benefit at age 70 would be about 14 percent higher than at age 65, reflecting 40 years of service rather than 35 and assuming that the real salary of such a senior faculty member is likely to remain constant. With a DC plan, the monthly benefit could easily be 45 percent more than it would have been at age 65. The benefit goes up for three reasons rather than for one. First, the money already accumulated by age 65 has five more years to earn a return. With a relatively conservative assumption of earning a real return of 3.5 percent per year, this factor alone will increase the money available to fund an annuity by 19 percent. Second, there are the extra contributions for the additional five years of employment. These should increase the accumulated wealth by approximately 9 percent. Finally, even if the same amount of money were available, the monthly annuity amount would be about 12 percent higher owing to the shorter remaining life expectancy of someone at age 70 rather than age 65. These factors multiply out to an increase of just over 45 percent. Clearly, the defined-contribution plan rewards continued service beyond age 65 far more than a typical defined-benefit plan. The differences between the two plan types only get more pronounced if we compare retirement at age 70 versus age 75.

Figure 3.1 illustrates the example just described by showing annual pension income for alternative ages of retirement with the hypothetical defined-benefit plan, with the basic Stanford plan and with the plan augmented by the Faculty Retirement Incentive Program. The shape of the curves is more informative than the precise level since we have had to make

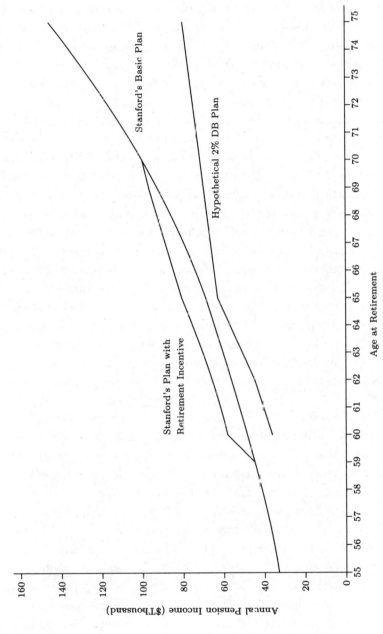

Figure 3.1. An example showing annual pension income for alternative ages of retirement with the hypothetical defined benefit plan, with the basic Stanford plan, and with the plan augmented by the Faculty Retirement Incentive Program.

up a somewhat artificial salary history and set of investment returns for this individual. The after-tax value of the bonus received for participating in the Faculty Retirement Incentive Program was converted to a life annuity so as to show its importance relative to the basic plan. All of the amounts shown in the figure are assumed to be taxable income in retirement.

We take several lessons away from this figure. First, the bonus is a nontrivial supplement to retirement resources. In the constructed example, the individual has a basic retirement account at age 60 of \$493,898, which will purchase a single-life annuity of approximately \$47,000 per year. The bonus of \$170,000 (taxable) increases the retirement resources by at least 20 percent and may make retirement at 60 affordable when it otherwise would not be. Second, we note that the hypothetical defined-benefit plan rewards service after age 60 much less than the basic Stanford plan. This is primarily because of the lack of actuarial adjustment in DB plans after the normal retirement age. Third, we see that between the ages of 65 and 70 the retirement incentive reduces somewhat the return to continuing employment. Nonetheless, the monthly income in retirement continues to climb, the later one retires. Last, the Stanford plan (with 15 percent total contributions), with or without the retirement incentive supplement, is seen to be generous for a long-term employee when compared to a benchmark defined-benefit plan, even with a conservative assumption about the earnings on assets.

One way to summarize the above analysis is to note that the defined-contribution benefits get more valuable as you delay retirement (there are more contributions, more tax-sheltered earnings on previous contributions, and an actuarial adjustment made for the shorter life expectancy that goes with retiring later), whereas the present value of defined-benefit plan payouts goes down if you postpone retirement (the monthly benefit goes up by a smaller percentage than life expectancy goes down) beyond the normal retirement age of 65. Clearly, DC plans offer a financial incentive to stay on the job whereas the DB plans offer the workers an incentive to retire at the so-called normal retirement age, usually 65. Stanford and most other private universities have retained a defined-contribution plan in the face of the lifting of mandatory retirement rules, but clearly these institutions will have to factor into their calculations the incentives of such a system to delay retirement past the previous age of mandatory retirement, namely

70. Stanford's new Faculty Retirement Incentive Program was designed with such considerations in mind.

## 5.2. Other Economic Factors

Many faculty may find themselves unprepared for the financial planning necessary to determine whether they can afford to retire. There are a large number of considerations, and this is one mathematical exercise where people get only one opportunity—one cannot rely on the old practice of learning from past mistakes. It would not be unusual for a faculty member in his or her 60's to have accumulated $750,000 in a retirement account. The problems are many. First, is that enough to finance an acceptable level of income for the rest of life? What about inflation, medical costs, taxes, long-term care, Social Security, and so on? How does one choose between single-life annuities, a whole array of joint survivor annuities, flat versus graduated payments, and so on? In 1990 the Provost's Task Force determined that most people would benefit from professional help in making these complicated decisions. As a result, in 1994, as part of the establishment of the Faculty Retirement Incentive Program, the University instituted a program whereby Stanford partially reimburses faculty when they obtain professional financial consulting services. It was the conviction of the Task Force then, and it remains our conviction today, that most long-term Stanford faculty will be able to retire when they desire to do so, given the relatively high savings rate implied by the Stanford plan.

## 5.3. The Nature of the Professoriate at a Research University

Faculty who achieve tenure at research universities are highly autonomous individuals who are devoted to scholarship and research in their disciplines. There is no predetermined end to one's scholarship—answering one question leads to more questions; finishing one book leads to ideas for the next one. Thus, there is little incentive to end one's career, so long as one's health allows one to continue. Furthermore, Rees and Smith (1991), using regression analysis to predict the age of faculty retiring at or above the age of 70, found that the quality of the student body (measured by average Scholastic Aptitude Test [SAT] scores) is the strongest predictor of delayed retirement, followed by low teaching loads and holding research grants. They suggest that faculty are more willing to continue working when they have good students, low teaching loads, and a funded research agenda. Clearly all of these characteristics apply to many, if not most, Stanford faculty.

In addition, the academic department is a far "flatter" type of organization than a typical business or corporation. It runs by peer interaction and colleagueship, and peers often are reluctant to deal with performance problems of their colleagues. Thus, even a department chair, who holds a leadership and quasi-managerial position in the department, is fundamentally a colleague and typically finds it quite difficult to approach a senior colleague about normal retirement, without even considering performance issues. This means that there is little pressure exerted on individuals at the departmental level to retire.

## 6. Conclusions

Several lessons can be drawn from the historical account of the Stanford experience provided here. The first, concerning the specific issue of faculty retirement at a research university, is that the factors that work against retirement, such as our defined-contribution pension plan, other individual economic concerns such as inflation and health care, and the nature of the professoriate, can be effectively countered by retirement-incentive programs coupled with readily available opportunities for emeriti faculty to be recalled to active duty. The second is that early recognition of a significant change in the external environment and active programmatic response to it can substantially lessen its impact on the institution. The fact that Stanford administrators recognized in 1977 that changes in mandatory retirement could have significant negative effects on the University led to policies that, in the end, not only mitigated the effect of uncapping on the demography of the faculty but, ironically, provided arguments to those who were in favor of uncapping.

The third lesson is about the dynamics of the University. Over the course of the long transition away from mandatory retirement, no fewer than four faculty/administrative committees studied the issue and its related topics. This reflects the strong commitment to consensus decision making that characterizes the University as well as the deep sense of responsibility on the part of university leaders. This sense of responsibility reflects the knowledge that decisions they take frequently have long-term consequences that must be considered prior to acting and that they are the stewards of the University's future as well as its present.

The fourth lesson is about the conservatism of the University. The committees who studied the issue of retirement were cautious in their approach and in their recommendations, and the changes that occurred were incremental and small, rather than bold and flashy. They were reported in the *Campus Report*, but they hardly made the headlines of the *New York Times*. None of the committees were willing to tackle the tenure system, for instance, and the question of performance issues of senior faculty remains open because of a fundamental reluctance to disrupt peer relationships within academic departments. At a deeper level, Stanford's attitude in 1994 toward its retiring faculty has not changed very much from David Starr Jordan's attitude in 1910. President Jordan wrote that Professor Emeritus Melville Anderson could be "one with his colleagues in every way that may appeal to him." Today, when Provost Condoleezza Rice writes to retiring faculty, she says, "Although retirement will undoubtedly give you the opportunity to pursue many other interests, and some well deserved leisure, I hope the University will be able to call upon you in a variety of ways from time to time." In other words, the emeritus faculty member remains a valued member of the academic community at Stanford.

The last lesson is that there will be, no doubt, more change in the future, which is likely to be at least as challenging as the past. Those faculty who are part of the "baby boom" generation, for instance, may well not have as favorable a return on the assets in their pension plan accounts as the generation now retiring, and issues of health care, the viability of the Social Security system, and the need for more, not less, personal saving will play a big role in retirement decisions in the decades to come. University leaders will no doubt need to continue to be vigilant in their concern about issues of faculty retirement and to act in the best interests of individual faculty and of the institution as a whole.

# Acknowledgment

The authors acknowledge with appreciation the work of Noel S. Kolak, who, during her tenure as Assistant Provost for Faculty Affairs, created and maintained the historical record on which much of this article is based.

# Notes

[1] David Starr Jordan to O. L. Elliott, Registrar of Stanford University, read to the Academic Council meeting of March 5, 1910.

[2] Clara Bush to Noel Kolak, October 23, 1985.

[3] Report to the President of Stanford University from the Administrative Panel on Retirement, January 31, 1979, p. 11.

[4] Early Retirement Program brochure, Office of the Provost, April 1, 1973.

[5] Report to the President of Stanford University from the Administrative Panel on Retirement, January 31, 1979, p. 12.

[6] Ibid., p. 18.

[7] *Campus Report*, March 21, 1979, p. 1.

[8] Private correspondence, Office of the Provost, Stanford University.

[9] Report to the President of Stanford University from the Administrative Panel on Retirement, January 31, 1979.

[10] Report to the President of Stanford University from the Administrative Panel on Retirement, January 31, 1979.

[11] *Campus Report*, March 21, 1979, p. 1.

[12] *Campus Report*, June 6, 1979, p. 1.

[13] *Faculty Handbook*, Stanford University, 1984, p. 65.

[14] The Faculty Early Retirement Program II brochure, January 1, 1992.

[15] Final Report of the Task Force on Retirement Policies to Provost Albert H. Hastorf, 1982.

[16] Ibid., p. 3.

[17] Ibid., p. 2.

[18] Private correspondence, School of Humanities and Sciences, Stanford University.

[19] Donald Kennedy to Senator Donald L. Nickles, August 13, 1982.

[20] Robert H. Atwell to university presidents, September 5, 1986.

[21] Jacyn Mitchell to Donald Kennedy and James Rosse, October 21, 1986.

[22] Lawrence Friedman to members of the U.S. Senate, cited in (Calvin, 1993), op. cit., p. 170.

[23] *The Chronicle of Higher Education,* August 5, 1987, p.9.

[24] Report of the Provost's Task Force on Faculty and Staff Retirement, April 1990, pp. 19–21.

[25] Ibid., p. 21.

[26] Ibid., p. 22.

[27] Ibid., p. 14.

[28] Minutes of the Faculty Senate, June 14, 1990.

[29] James N. Rosse to all tenure-line members of the Academic Council, December 20, 1991.

[30] Faculty Retirement Incentive Program announcement, May 1, 1994.

[31] Report of the Provost's Task Force on Faculty and Staff Retirement, April 1990, p. 2.

# References

Calvin, Allen D. 1993. "Mandatory Retirement." In Nancy B. Julius and Herbert H. Kraus, eds., *The Aging Work Force,* pp. 165–175. Washington, D. C.: College and University Personnel Association.

Rees, A., and S. P. Smith. 1991. *Faculty Retirement in the Arts and Sciences.* Princeton, N.J.: Princeton University Press.

Schieber, Sylvester J. 1993. "Retirement Programs and Issues." In Siegmund Ginsburg, ed., *Paving the Way for the 21st Century: The Human Factor in Higher Education Financial Management,* pp. 133–177. Washington, D.C.: National Association of College and University Business Officers.

# Chapter 4

# Applying Statistical Concepts and Approaches in Academic Administration

## Stephen E. Fienberg

Statistics is part of the curriculum of every institution of higher learning in the United States, and statistical methods and concepts are widely used in the sciences, management, industry, and for public policy. It is therefore surprising that these methods and concepts are rarely thought of as being applicable to the management of universities themselves, especially in the area of academic administration. In this chapter, I consider a variety of university academic management problems, drawn largely from my personal experience and that of a number of friends and colleagues in statistics, where the thoughtful application of statistics has been or has the potential to be of considerable value. Along the way, I also reflect upon some recent developments in higher education that may make it an appropriate venue for statistical pursuits.

## 1. Introduction

Imagine yourself as a dean or as a vice-president for academic affairs of a major North American university, sitting in a meeting with a group of faculty discussing student recruitment. In comes Professor Jones, from the classics department, demanding that the university change its admissions requirements for foreign students with English as a second language. "Why should we do this?" you ask. "Well, I was talking to the students in my freshman seminar," he says, "and they told me that." Soon the entire committee gets caught up in the discussion and votes to recommend the change in policy. But the only evidence invoked in support of the change was the story told by Professor Jones, which is at best an anecdote and at worst what Saks (1992) calls a *factoid*, that is, a statement that seems as though it conveys information but that on examination turns out to be either false or meaningless.

This example may sound a bit far-fetched, but I can assure you that it is far too close to the truth for comfort. How then should academic policy be changed? Clearly, a little bit of empirical knowledge goes a long way. In our example, perhaps a study of those foreign students recently admitted under the current policy would help. What do we know about those who failed to meet one or more of the current requirements? How should we get the requisite information? Well, if you think we are beginning to design a statistical investigation, you are correct. One of the themes of this chapter is that the ability to ask such questions and to direct their follow-through is clearly enhanced by statistical training and thinking.

Over the course of much of the past decade, when I was heavily engaged in academic administration, I was repeatedly asked by colleagues in statistics about the skills and background required for the job, especially those that were different from the ones associated with my other job of educator and researcher in statistics. Often, during the day-to-day press of administrative business and seemingly endless meetings, I would lament how little my background in statistics was being put to use. But on other occasions, as I was able to reflect on how I went about my job and on the ideas and approaches I brought to the table, I realized that frequently I was influenced quite strongly by my training in statistics. Further, I observed that others with exposure to statistical ideas about measurement, sampling, and inference left those ideas behind when they assumed the mantle of academic administrator. Clearly, the hallmark of the good academic administrator includes those elusive qualities of integrity, academic and social values, vision, and leadership, which are often talked about; but

I began to wonder as to whether the academic administrator with these qualities might be far more effective through the use of statistical ideas and methods.

When I first contemplated writing this chapter, I thought having some data would help, and so I wrote to a number of friends and colleagues, some statisticians and some not, but all of whom had spent some time in academic administration. I asked for their reactions to this notion that an academic administrator might be aided by the ability to use statistical ideas and methods, and I requested examples where they had occasion to use statistical approaches. One of the earliest responses directed me to a 1976 paper that begins with the following words:

> For about a quarter century, from the early 1930s to the late 1950s, I indulged heavily, though intermittently in the reading, writing and arithmetic of statistics. I have been reformed, with only rare and inconsequential episodes of backsliding.
>
> My activities since reforming have been predominantly in academic administration. There may be some interest in considering the extent to which my new activities continue to reflect the influence of statistics.

The author of these words was W. Allen Wallis, a distinguished statistician who served as dean of the University of Chicago School of Business and later as president and chancellor of the University of Rochester. The paper was based on a speech delivered at the 1970 American Statistical Association (ASA) meetings, and I had actually been there in the audience! So much for my having an original idea.

After describing some clearly nonstatistical administrative activities, Wallis made what I now appreciate as a profound observation:

> This is not to say that my statistical past does not play a substantial part in my current activities. Quite to the contrary. But that part is played not so much by tables, charts and averages, or even the nonparametric tests which used to intrigue me, as by statistical patterns of thought in contexts which normally would be considered nonstatistical. George Snedecor used to say that in teaching statistics the object should be to develop

not merely the *ability* to reason statistically but the *habit* of doing so. [T]his address has afforded me an occasion to review my past as reflected in speeches, papers and memoranda, notes, and recollections to see what evidence they reveal of persistent habits of statistical thinking, even in nonstatistical contexts.

In fact another article, by John Kemeny (1973), entitled, "What Every College President Should Know About Mathematics," also contains related observations. Kemeny, a philosopher, all-around mathematician and probabilist, and at the time president of Dartmouth College, offers mainly examples of probabilistic and statistical modeling.

In the next section, I reflect upon the distinction between formal and informal uses of statistics in the context of academic administration, and then I take up the issue of how thinking systematically about problems often leads to data requirements and both the formal and informal uses of statistical thinking. Following this, I turn quite specifically to some examples where sampling, experiments, careful measurement, and estimation can play a role in academic administration. Among the external pressures on university administrators today are demands for greater accountability, and I reflect upon how universities can and do respond. My most compelling example is something that all of us in universities regularly discuss: the quality of university teaching and its relationship to educational attainment and learning. I end by returning to Allen Wallis' theme: statistical thinking in nonstatistical contexts.

# 2. Formal Versus Informal Statistical Thinking

In responses I have received to my request for input from friends and colleagues in statistics, there seems to be two different types of reliance on statistical thinking, formal and informal. In my experience, statisticians recognize problems involving statistical ideas more easily than nonstatisticians. In the formal examples, a problem presents itself and cries out for a statistical solution. An example of this formal use relates to the current efforts underway in many universities to put the principles of Total Quality Management (TQM) to work in the management of universities. In the informal examples, it is the Snedecor-Wallis notion of thinking statistically that turns the problem into one where that use of statistical ideas yields deeper insights than would otherwise be available. I received no illustration of something as seemingly technical as the Box-Cox family of power transformations, kernel density estimates, or the bootstrap, but at least one example involved the recognition of length-biased sampling methods, and several others described a formal model for projecting faculty turnover that could be used for looking at the effects of policy changes on tenure (see also the regression model for faculty size in Kemeny 1973).

Not surprisingly, regression analysis showed up repeatedly in the responses, occasionally in surprising places. We often decry the use of possibly poorly specified regression models, but they turn out to be useful for a variety of purposes, nonetheless. Administrators at different universities use them in different ways. Several colleagues reported on their development of a regression model for faculty salaries. Using a variety of different possible predictors, they made a special point of examining the regression residuals in order to see if there were outliers. The predictors used turn out radically different from one university to the next.

At one university where they emphasize merit, the provost used variables as predictors that he believed to characterize research and creative contributions, and the question he asked was whether those with large negative residuals are in fact poor performers and those with high residuals high performers. Anomalies required careful review. At another university, a similar approach was used in the dean's office to foil an attempt by the economists to press for higher salaries to "meet market demands." (They were already outliers on the high side.) At yet another university, the faculty union wanted to use the residuals from regressions based on nonevaluative predictors such as "years from Ph.D." in order to argue for salary adjustments for the nonperformers! The union's arguments about merit were met with a negative response.

In my own administrative work, I encountered a "hidden" regression model in a staff union proposal for a "comparable worth" job ratings plan, again for use in determining salaries. I pointed out that the proposal was simply a disguised regression model where the union had made up the coefficients without any data and without explicitly discussing the principles that might lead to their relevance. My administrative colleagues, even those with some statistical training, were at first surprised and then perplexed at the notion of using principles as input to formulate a statistical model. What was clear was that the administration and the union operated under two different sets of principles and values.

Whereas these examples of regression analysis and others of faculty turnover models are reasonably complex, some examples I received were simple and pertinent to the point of thinking statistically. For example, Richard Cyert, former president of Carnegie Mellon, recalled teaching his secretary how to use a table of random numbers to select groups of students to invite to a series of breakfasts in order to learn about student experiences on campus.

One needs to be careful, however, in order not to turn every problem into a statistical one. I am reminded of an apocryphal story I have heard about a distinguished mathematical statistician. One day a colleague found him pacing the halls at the university and he asked, "Herb, what's the matter?" Herb replied, "I have an offer from another university, and I don't know what to do." His colleague then said, "But Herb, you are one of the inventors of statistical decision theory. Why don't you apply it to this problem?" Herb looked at him incredulously. "You think I should apply decision theory to my personal career decision? You must be joking. This is serious."

There are many activities that an academic administrator engages in that make no use of statistical thinking, and rightly so, but all too often statistical thinking may be disguised. John Kingman, Vice Chancellor at the University of Bristol, argued that, while ripe anecdotes are hard to recall, mathematical and statistical thinking pervaded all that he did in rather subtle ways that are much easier to remember in some specific instances. And David Cox, who served as Warden of Nuffield College at Oxford University, noted that his mathematical (and I suspect his editorial) background led him to value conciseness and precision of statement, verbal as well as quantitative. This led him to be good at adhering to "the second golden rule of administration": No administrative document or memorandum should ever exceed one side of one page in length.

In a much different context from the one being discussed here, Saks (1992) notes that the absence of systematic thinking and the reliance on anecdotes pervades much of the American legal system:

Perhaps the use of anecdotes is not entirely inappropriate or unfair, given the central role cases play in law as the device for sampling social facts, the unit of accretion of judicial authority, and the principal tool for educating new lawyers. For these reasons cases have a special power over lawyers, more so than over any other field.

Saks comments that most fields that use case studies recognize their considerable limitations as a means for gaining knowledge about phenomena of interest in their field, and the case accordingly occupies a modest position in their respective epistemologies.

We can make the same observation, I believe, about academic administrative activities. Pick up a book on the topic (there are several), and you will find a string of anecdotes about academic decision making or advice on how to deal with faculty and students that consists of some examples. Now anecdotes and case studies are not bad, in and of themselves. But to gain an appreciation of the larger context, in order to generalize, we as statisticians know that cases must be assembled with care. Anecdotes about academic administration are akin to what Saks describes as *factlets*: bits and pieces of real information about the problem, pieces one may hope can be sewn together into a serviceable quilt, but which by themselves leave much more unknown than known. Whereas factoids seem to be facts but are not, factlets present a different problem. They are true in a literal sense, but they lead directly to conclusions that are not justified by the data.

As yet, there is no theory that advises us about how to go about performing administrative and management activities, especially in academia. Nevertheless, the university is a functioning system, and we do know that to manage a system well we need information on how the system functions. Those familiar with statistical problems know that in complex systems, tinkering in one place will affect other parts of the system as well. Thus, we need to think systematically about the university as a system (and even higher education as a system) if we are to learn how to effect change in a university and to gauge what the effects of change will be. Some of this thinking will inevitably be informal, but often we need to develop formal models and gather and assess data.

As a vice-president for academic affairs at York University, I had to preside over the development of plans to reallocate faculty slots among faculties and departments. To begin this process, my predecessor, a biologist, had developed a crude "faculty complements" model based on student enrollments and a variety of other factors, both those that were common to all faculties and those that were unique. We worked quite hard to explore variations on the model using updated data and projections, and we tried to understand the implications of the model in light of our knowledge of the workings of individual parts of the university and their interconnections. Throughout the process we recognized the crudeness of the model we were working with, and we looked for robust results to target our first major round of faculty reallocations. In a related context, the vice-president for business and financial affairs and I modeled the "aging" of the faculty to determine its impact on budgets and pensions. Here our model was much more precise and the conclusions from it far more compelling.

Martin Wilk, whose administrative experience was initially corporate and then as head of a government agency, Statistics Canada, noted that his own training and knowledge in statistics, and in science and engineering more broadly, gave him self-confidence and aided his capacity to acquire new understanding and to inquire about fundamentals. But the most important influence of statistics was indirect, helping him to develop a broad perspective of the operation of the system as a whole. "Statistical concepts, philosophy, data analysis, appreciation of the frailties of data, the importance of information—all such were important, but not in terms of direct applications of sampling methods, or experimental design or analyses of variance, etc." So again we are back to the informal role that statistical thinking plays in management.

In contrast, Harry Arthurs, former president of York University and a lawyer by training, had little trouble recalling the critical role data played in shaping his judgments about the university and in what directions it should move. He found information about the demographics of the student body an important policy tool. Even more important, he commissioned a study of the academic profile of current and former students, and then used the information to refocus recruitment, admissions, and financial aid so that the university could shape its student intake. He also noted the use of statistical arguments that helped to shape the process of development of university-owned lands, both within and outside the university.

# 3.  Some Roles for Sampling, Experiments, Careful Measurement, and Estimation

I now turn to a more focused look at a few ways in which formal statistical approaches play a role in academic administration. I begin with an anecdote, with apologies to those who by now might be expecting a systematic analysis.

Almost immediately upon my arrival at York University I faced the prospect of cutting academic budgets by a substantial amount. I began a review of budgets with those in charge of each of the faculties or units that reported to me. When we went over the budget of the Faculty of Graduate Studies, the dean noted the crucial role of each staff member who worked in her office. I recall asking why there were several individuals designated to review admissions files when the actual decisions were made by those running the individual graduate programs. She replied, "We still have to check each application to be sure the Graduate Faculty rules are being properly applied." When I asked if they had ever thought of examining only a sample of admissions files, she seemed not to understand. It was as if the statistical methods she applied back in her academic home, the Department of Psychology, had no relevance to anything else.

One of the important lessons we learn as statisticians is the applicability of statistical ideas across domains. The sample principles of sampling or experimentation that are applicable in sociology are also useful in public health and medicine, albeit with modifications. Thus, bringing ideas from statistical practice around the university into administration is rather natural for a statistician, even though it may not be for a psychologist. I have been tempted to describe this ability to transfer knowledge and thinking as something unique to statistics, but it turns out to be one of the things cognitive psychologists believe distinguishes *novices* from *experts*. A psychologist steeped in statistical methods applied in a psychological context is akin to the novice, whereas the statistician who has been trained to see commonalities among methods used in disparate fields has attained statistical expertise that is much more easily transferred to a new area.

In addition to the use of sampling for auditing or quality control purposes, as a dean and vice-president I often found myself providing both formal and informal advice on the use of sampling to understand student attitudes, expectations, and retrospective evaluation of their educational experiences. On my arrival at York University I already found a commitment among my administrative colleagues to the collection and use of such "institutional research." But I did need to remind others of the need to assess the impact of nonresponse and response errors on the implications of survey results for policy purposes. In the end we worked toward a permanent budget to support an ongoing capacity for such internal survey research within the university's Institute for Social Research.

Academic administrators often must answer questions from parents, trustees, and the public about how faculty spend their time. Few outsiders can fully appreciate how a three- to six-hour-per-week teaching load can represent full-time work. Those of us who have worked in a university research environment know the foolishness of such views, but we also know a number of our faculty colleagues who put in minimal work hours in university activities. One of the responses to this outside demand is the faculty activity survey. I have examined the result of several of these surveys over the years and there are two features that seem to be constant across institutions and time: faculty members report spending far in excess of a standard 40 hours per week on direct university work, on average about 50 hours per week and often as much as 60 to 80 hours per week, especially in the sciences; and no one reports putting in less than 40 hours per week, and there seems to be less variety across individuals than personal experience suggests. To me, these surveys always raise the issue of bias in self-reports, and thus, as an administrator I balked somewhat when asked to defend them outside of the university.

The usual way we go about changing things in universities is to gather a group together, think very hard about a problem, develop a plan, and then implement it in a nonreversible and unmeasurable fashion. When a university professor talks of an experimental program, there is rarely a control group or an elaborate evaluation mechanism at hand. If someone tries to revamp the biology curriculum, the department usually plans how to phase the new curriculum in as rapidly as possible rather than to ask comparative questions about the relative merits of the old and new curricula in terms of outcomes. As a result of this type of absolutism, real opportunities for experimentation are lost. It is true that some changes are hard to implement for only some of the students or only some of the sections of a large course; but, as statisticians talking with those in other disciplines, we regularly counter such objections with the rationale underlying careful experimentation.

Here is one such example. James Hickman, who served as dean of the business school at the University of Wisconsin, described to me an experiment for which he was responsible that was intended to assist in the formulation of a policy on the use of computers in examinations. The response variable was the result on the test, the key explanatory variable was whether the students had a hand calculator. The students were assigned to the calculator and noncalculator group at random, and GPA was used as a covariate in the analysis. The experimental results led directly to a policy permitting hand calculators in all examinations.

I must confess that in my administrative experience as a department head, dean, and vice-president, I found it difficult to implement a credible randomized comparative experiment of the sort I advocate in my professional capacity, but this was not for lack of trying. Perhaps the closest I came was in the preliminary assessment of a new faculty course evaluation form at Carnegie Mellon for which we actually used matched pairs of classes and sections for a comparison of the old and new forms. I could not convince my colleagues to move to the more complete experiment, and we continue to use the old evaluation form even though everyone admits that they do not trust the data it produces.

# 4. Demands for Accountability and the TQM Movement in Universities

Over the past decade, public concerns over the quality and direction of higher education have become manifest. There are to my mind two causes. We regularly read about such matters as the decline in student performance on standardized examinations and on professional licensing examinations. This has been yoked by many to what they claim to be the dilution of the liberal arts and the rise of "political correctness," viz., Bloom (1987) and D'Souza (1991). But the current crisis in higher education, if there is one, is the result of financial matters. The claims on the public purse have multiplied, and the privileged position that universities and colleges once held when it came to government budgets has diminished, especially during the recessionary times we have been experiencing. Meanwhile, the costs of operating universities have increased at rates far outstripping the Consumer Price Index, thus leading to the steady climb of tuition. The public reaction has been to call into question the value of a university undergraduate degree and to demand greater accountability from those who manage institutions of higher education.

The result of this public attention has been a set of activities and mandates. Many states in the United States and provinces in Canada have convened special blue-ribbon panels on university educational and fiscal accountability. Questions about the balance between teaching and research abound. In Ontario, as I returned to Carnegie Mellon two years ago, a task force was considering these and other issues in order to make recommendations for budget reductions and fiscal restructuring of universities and colleges. A background paper prepared for the task force's use (Task Force on Resource Allocation 1994) revisited the issues of the structure and extent of academic work, in part by reanalyzing a decade-old survey of Canadian faculty members that had barely achieved a 50% response rate. It probably takes a statistician in a senior academic administrative position to blow the whistle on the kind of shoddy inferences drawn from running naive regression analyses on the results of such surveys; others are all too often unable to see through the masses of tables and analytical conclusions to ask the important questions of the relevance of the data and the analyses.

Two "quality-assurance"-like responses to this demand for accountability have been the "assessment movement," both within and especially across universities and colleges, and the efforts to import Total Quality Management (TQM) into university management. The two activities are intertwined and are, as we know, inherently statistical. Seymour (1992:6)notes that most states have undertaken comprehensive programs of assessment based upon the belief stated in the 1986 National Governors' Association report that assessment would be the central strategy for improving the quality of undergraduate education. The call to arms has been effective. The American Association for Higher Education's annual assessment forum draws standing-room-only crowds, and regional and disciplinary accrediting associations continue to press for the inclusion of student outcomes measures and "value-added" criteria in their evaluation procedures. Although I do not dispute that these efforts have succeeded in gaining the attention of those in charge of universities and colleges, my concerns lie with the attempts at actual implementation. In this sense there are clear parallels with the TQM movement in American industry. There is a lot of rhetoric, but there are only a few shining examples of careful measurement and sensible evaluation leading to substantial quality improvement. In universities we do not seem to do much better than in industry, and perhaps we are doing worse (for a critique of current industrial statistics, see Banks 1993).

At Carnegie Mellon we have had a major TQM effort over the past three to four years, involving faculty and staff from across the university. It involved a weeklong, off-site training session for a substantial number of people at Xerox, in Rochester, and then a series of follow-ups. The hard part, we have learned, is getting people to think about their jobs in different ways. This will be familiar to those of you who have had any experience with such training. In the end, the vice-president for business affairs proceeded to "implement" a TQM plan for his domain and has achieved some success, but the deans and faculty continue to resist the idea of even thinking about TQM in provision of learning and research.

TQM in research activities seems to be a bit of a contradiction when the most important developments are often the result of serendipitous discovery, but at least in educational (teaching) activities we know where to begin—that is, by asking: "Who are our customers?" Clearly our customers include our students; in statistics departments they also include the faculty in other departments that require our courses; in terms of students-as-products we have clients in industry and government; on the research side there are our professional peers but also the users of our research in industry and government as well as in other academic areas, and so on. Those in the English department and those in the business school would clearly answer this question in a somewhat different fashion.

The next step in implementing TQM is understanding the educational process and its goals (outputs), as well as how the customers view these outputs. This requires measurement. We need to: take stock of what we do and how we do it; measure aspects of the process in order to improve it; specify alternative outputs for different customers. These are all statistical tasks, and there are commonalities across university disciplines. Here is where careful experimentation can have major impact.

Light, Singer, and Willett (1990) is an outstanding manual on the use of comparative experiments for such evaluative research on educational teaching, with lots of examples. It is a wonderful place to begin to focus on the process of measurement, but these authors do not answer the outcomes question for us and only have hints on how to cope with the measurement of outcomes. Those in universities across the country have explored such tools as course evaluations, exit interviews on graduation, surveys of graduates and their employers five years after graduation, and even surveys of representatives of employers who come to campus to interview students. All of these provide useful information, but questions abound about the quality of the data that they generate, how to summarize it and, *most important*, how to use the information to improve our processes.

In the end, about the only thing that all universities attempt to do is measure student opinions about faculty and the courses they teach via some type of standardized questionnaire. I know of few faculty members or administrators who are enamored by the reliance by universities on student evaluation of faculty as a way to gauge the quality of their teaching. The quirky nature of the responses to questionnaires asking for opinions about the instructor is well illustrated by an incident involving my older son. As part of his job he deals with clients in Israel, and he decided to take an evening university course in Hebrew so that he could converse with them in their own language. He worked quite hard at his lessons for several months, and one day when he passed a newsstand in New York City he decided to test his newfound linguistic skills by buying a Hebrew newspaper he spotted. To his great dismay, he was unable to read more than a few words. When we spoke with him that evening he told us about what had happened and said that the teaching evaluations were the next week and that he was going to take the occasion to let the university know how incompetent the teacher was. A few days later, he called to report on his meeting with the teacher. When he demanded an explanation from the teacher about why he was unable to read anything in the newspaper, the teacher said: "It's simple. That isn't Hebrew, it's Yiddish."

The moral of this story is borne out repeatedly by empirical evidence: the timing of a teaching evaluation may affect the rating of the instructor.

Administering a questionnaire hard on the heels of a tough examination inevitably lowers the teacher's rating. Then there are also the issues of low response rates and informative nonresponse, and the relevance of such evaluations to the educational outcomes we are trying to achieve.

My experience suggests that administrators pay too much rather than too little attention to such student evaluations, especially when it comes time for promotion and tenure reviews. The consequence is that we usually have detailed and well-structured evidence on research accomplishments in a tenure file, but much poorer and impressionistic evidence on teaching accomplishments. One of the most interesting ideas being promoted in a number of institutions is the preparation of teaching portfolios that include a variety of information on teaching materials, outcomes, classroom visits by colleagues, and so on that can be evaluated as a package. What I have not seen is any careful study (e.g., an experiment) that demonstrates either the importance (and relevance) of particular kinds of teaching-portfolio information or that such teaching portfolios improve the process of faculty evaluation.

# 5. Statistical Thinking in Nonstatistical Contexts

One of my roles as Vice-President for Academic Affairs at York was to help decide if and how to respond to grievances filed against the university and the administration by faculty and staff, as part of our collective-bargaining agreements. I recall a meeting one morning where we were discussing a particularly vexing case, and the person in charge of our academic-staff relations office advised me to concede the matter so that the grievance would be withdrawn. When I pressed her for her rationale, she replied that by following her advice the university had not lost such a grievance in several years. My response was that it must be the case that the university pursued far too few grievances. She thought that I was mocking her, but in fact as I tried to explain, there was an issue of the optimal choice of a threshold. Thus, a perfectly logical explanation of why we never lost a case was that we set the threshold for cases to pursue in the wrong place. Unless we pursued cases to learn what the threshold was

we would inevitably pursue far too few, and the university would be hurt
as a consequence. (I must confess to being somewhat less original than
this story may suggest, as I actually adapted this lesson from an anecdote
attributed by a fellow statistician to Jerry Cornfield.)

My thesis in this chapter has been that when statisticians engage in academic administration, they bring a special perspective to their work that is
not necessarily shared by their colleagues from other disciplines. Sometimes
this perspective manifests itself in the use of formal statistical tools or in
a critical perspective on statistical work brought forward by others. More
important, perhaps, are the informal ways in which statisticians in academic administration often make use of statistical ideas and results. This
is what Allen Wallis called statistical thinking in nonstatistical contexts.

As I and others have reflected upon our academic administrative activities, we have identified a few qualities and aspects of our training in
statistics that are closely linked to Wallis's notion. We all recognize that
personal qualities can and often do outweigh any considerations of background for an academic administrator. But there are features of our statistical training that when taken together may distinguish the statistician
from others:

1. In consulting work statisticians are accustomed to communicating
   with those in different disciplines and thus have at least some understanding for issues that concern them. Statisticians may, in fact, be
   the only people in an administration with firsthand experience of the
   actual research and teaching activities in a wide range of university
   departments and faculties.

2. Statisticians are professional comparers of things, and comparisons
   loom large in the life of an administrator. Among the comparisons
   that deans and provosts are regularly called upon to make involve
   candidates for positions, letters of recommendation, and so on.

3. Statisticians are often better able to assess tenure and promotion files
   from departments and faculties other than their own, in part because
   of the statistical features of the research and in part because of their
   understanding of other research in the field in question.

4. Statistical decision problems are posed in such a way as to make

statisticians familiar with the costs (or lack thereof) associated with delaying a decision, and statisticians are accustomed to thinking explicitly about the range of options open, their advantages and disadvantages.

5. Statisticians are accustomed to explaining conclusions in relatively simple, nontechnical, yet precise language.

Finally, I mention a point raised by David Cox on an aspect of administrative life about which I often despaired: meetings. Cox observes that statisticians may better appreciate that meetings of highly paid people are implicitly very costly and that therefore the time should be used with great care. I wish I had been able to convince others of this point over the years.

In addressing faculty and trustees, Allen Wallis (1976) lectured:

> The appropriate objective for the University of Rochester is not just to see that our students can pass some set of examinations on some distribution of courses, but to see that each student makes the greatest advance he is capable of making in four years. The implication of such a view is that after the variability of capacity to advance is compounded with variability of attainment on admission, we will have far greater variability in our graduating seniors than in our arriving freshmen."

The translation of this quotation is: the variance of a sum is the sum of the variances (assuming zero correlation). Moreover, if we allow for a positive (rather than zero) correlation, which Wallis opined was obviously the case, the resulting variance is even larger. It is no wonder that Wallis ended his article by observing: "I conclude that statistical reasoning really is habit forming, as Snedecor said it should be. Or to put it differently: Once a statistician, always a statistician."

# Acknowledgments

I am indebted to a large number of friends and colleagues for sharing with me their own recollections of the role statistics played in their activities as administrators at universities or other research/statistical organizations. Many of their experiences and observations are reflected in this chapter, but clearly in a form for which they bear no responsibility. In particular I wish to thank Harry Arthurs, Dan Berg, Albert Bowker, Norman Bradburn, David Cox, Paul Christiano, Richard Cyert, Bradley Efron, Yves Escouffler, Ram Gnanadesikan, James Hickman, Pat Keating, John Kingman, William Kruskal, Sheldon Levy, Dorothy Rice, Donald Wallace, and Martin Wilk.

# References

Banks, D. 1993. "Is Industrial Statistics Out of Control (with discussion)." *Statistical Science* 8: 356-409.

Bloom, A. 1987. *The Closing of the American Mind.* New York: Simon and Schuster.

D'Souza, D. 1991. *Illiberal Education.* New York: Free Press.

Kemeny, J. 1973. What Every College President Should Know About Mathematics. *American Mathematical Monthly* 80: 889-901.

Light, R. J., J. D. Singer and J. B. Willett. 1990. *By Design: Planning Research on Higher Education.* Cambridge, Mass.: Harvard University Press.

Saks, M. J. 1992. "Do We Really Know Anything About the Behavior of the Tort Litigation System—and Why Not?" *University of Pennsylvania Law Review* 140: 1147–1292.

Seymour, D. T. 1992. *On Q: Causing Quality in Higher Education.* New York: Macmillan.

Task Force on Resource Allocation. 1994. *The Structure of Academic Work.* Background paper, Ontario Council on University Affairs, Toronto.

Wallis, W. A. 1976. "Statistical Thinking in Nonstatistical Contexts." *The American Statistician* 30: 159–164.

# Chapter 5

# Affirmative Action in Graduate Admissions: Stanford University in the 1980's

Jean H. Fetter

## 1. Introduction

Many universities in the United States, such as Stanford, have entered their second century in educating students. It is only just over two decades, however, since these same institutions have paid any attention to affirmative action. In the 1990's, every college and university espouses the worthy goal of appointing an ethnically diverse faculty; very few institutions have come close to achieving a faculty that could be considered representative of the population of the United States. According to the 1987 census the population of this country was 75% White, 13.5% Afro-American, 5.3% Hispanic, 0.7% Native American Indian, 2.5% Asian American, and 3% other. The comparison of this ethnic distribution with that of the faculty of leading research universities is striking and confirms the continued dominance of white faculty (Table 5.1).

TABLE 5.1

*Tenured Faculty at Selected Research Universities 1994*

| University | White | Black | Hisp. | Amer. Indian | Asian Amer. | Fem. |
|---|---|---|---|---|---|---|
| Chicago | 568 | 9 | 10 | 0 | 33 | 95 |
| Duke | 1502 | 38 | 25 | 0 | 71 | 345 |
| Harvard | 919 | 23 | 12 | 0 | 41 | 96 |
| Princeton | 421 | 11 | 7 | 0 | 30 | 60 |
| Stanford | 807 | 23 | 18 | 1 | 42 | 100 |
| Yale | 701 | 14 | 9 | 0 | 28 | 81 |
| U. Cal. (Berkeley) | 1199 | 31 | 32 | 6 | 80 | 209 |
| U. Mich. | 1501 | 47 | 17 | 2 | 102 | 229 |
| U. Tex. | 1151 | 18 | 34 | 6 | 22 | 213 |

SOURCE: Institutional Provosts' Offices

The Civil Rights movement of the 1960's and the assassination of Martin Luther King Jr. prompted the attention to affirmative action in post-secondary education. By 1980, Stanford had made significant progress in the enrollment of minority undergraduates. At that time, the undergraduate population at Stanford was 78.3% White, 6.1% Afro-American, 6.5% Hispanic, 0.6% Native American Indian, 6.3% Asian American, and 2.2% international students; 42.9% of Stanford's undergraduates were women in 1980. The enrollment of United States minorities that Stanford had achieved at the graduate level in 1980 was not as diverse as that at the undergraduate level: 67.1% White, 3.0% Afro-American, 3.6% Hispanic, 0.3% Native American Indian, 3.8% Asian American, 22.2% international students, and 25.5% female. It is quite clear that the pipeline to the faculty ranks had (and still has) a serious bottleneck at the graduate level, and there can be no progress in faculty appointments of minorities and women until at least more minorities and women earn Ph.D.'s. This reasoning formed the basis for Stanford's affirmative action efforts at the graduate level; while other research universities simultaneously acknowledged and accepted similar responsibilities, Stanford's efforts were distinctive on a number of counts. The following sections focus on these efforts during the early 1980's, when I was the Associate Dean (with the help of three minority Assistant Deans) responsible to Vice Provost Gerald Lieberman for graduate affirmative action. This chapter concludes with a brief comparison of the situation at Stanford in 1994, ten years later.

Throughout this chapter there is some apparent inconsistency in the description of ethnic groups. Part of this inconsistency may be attributed to changing times and preferred descriptions. Some is a consequence of the increased complexity of affirmative action in designating groups. At Stanford, in 1994, Black faculty includes native-born Americans, naturalized citizens, and permanent residents.

## 2. Graduate Statistics for Women and Minorities at Stanford, 1984

In May of 1973 the Senate of the Academic Council at Stanford passed legislation calling on the then Dean of Graduate Studies to make an annual report to the Senate on the enrollment of minorities and women in the University's graduate programs. By the early 1980's four minority groups had been targeted for special attention: Blacks (a descriptor subsequently changed to Afro-Americans); Mexican Americans; American Indians; and Puerto Ricans. With the exception of Puerto Ricans, these groups were also targeted for admission at the undergraduate level; the addition of Puerto Ricans as a targeted group at the graduate level was somewhat of an historical accident and the consequence of efforts made by a small group of graduate students enrolled at Stanford in the late 1970's. Figure 5.1 shows the percentages of targeted minority graduate enrollments, by School, from 1970 and 1984; Figure 5.2 shows the percentages of the enrolled graduate women, by School, for the same period.

A comparison of the two figures is striking on a number of counts. With the exception of the M.D. enrollment, the targeted minority enrollment peaked in 1973 and declined precipitously until 1978; Law was the only School to return to the enrollment reached in the banner year of 1973. The enrollment of graduate women not only showed a steady increase in every School, but in the Schools of Education and of Humanities and Sciences,

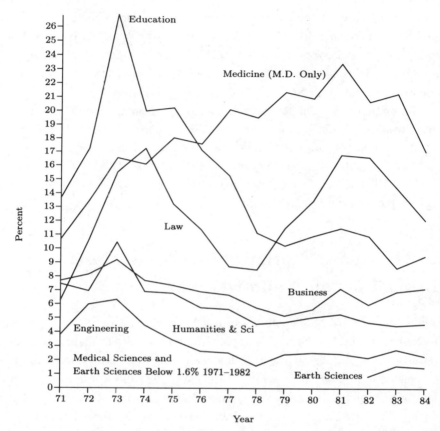

Figure 5.1. Percentage patterns of targeted minority graduate enrollment to total graduate enrollment by school 1971–1984.

N.B. In comparing these data with those in Tables 5.2 and 5.3, it is important to recall that Figure 5.1 includes international students in the total graduate enrollment; Tables 5.2 and 5.3 do not.

SOURCE: Registrar's Office (December 1984).

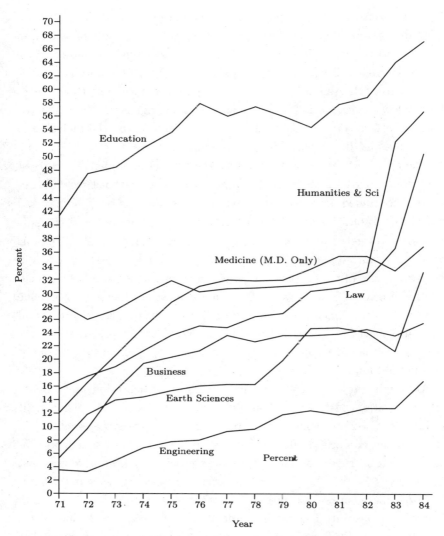

Figure 5.2. Percentage patterns of graduate women enrollment to total graduate enrollment by school 1971–1984.

N.B. In comparing these data with those in Tables 5.2 and 5.3, it is important to recall that Figure 5.1 includes international students in the total graduate enrollment; Tables 5.2 and 5.3 do not.

SOURCE: Registrar's Office (December 1984).

the percentage of enrolled women exceeded that of men. (This distinction in Humanities and Sciences was a consequence of enrollments of women in the Humanities, not in the Sciences, where even in 1994 women continue to be underrepresented, as we shall see in Table 5.6.) One notable feature common to both graduate women and targeted minorities is their exceptionally low representation in Earth Sciences and Engineering (and also the Sciences, a fact that is masked in Figures 5.1 and 5.2 by the inclusion of the Sciences in the School of Humanities and Sciences).

The year 1984 concluded my term as Associate Dean under Vice Provost Lieberman; a closer look at the graduate enrollments at that time will confirm the continued need for affirmative action focused on both women and minorities. Tables 5.2 and 5.3 show both the total numbers and the percentages of targeted minorities and women enrolled in graduate programs in each of Stanford's seven Schools in 1984. Although modest increases in the percentages of minority enrollments were seen in the Schools of Education and Business from 1983 to 1984, only Education, Law, and Medicine surpassed an enrollment of 10% whereas Earth Sciences, Engineering, and Medical Sciences remained below a dismal 5%. These representations occurred at a time when the targeted groups were represented by 20% of the total population of the United States.

Although Table 5.2 will confirm that the representation of graduate women at Stanford University in 1984 was more cause for optimism, it is clear that women continued to be significantly underrepresented. In 1984, women comprised slightly more than 50% of the national population; their total representation in graduate programs at Stanford was just above 30%. As with the graduate minority representations, some Schools presented more cause for concern than others: the graduate enrollment in Engineering was only 16% women, and Earth Sciences and Business each enrolled close to 30% women. The signs of optimism, however, were that each School continued to show gains in the total graduate enrollment of women from 1983 to 1984, with the exception of the M.D. program, which (while increasing in absolute numbers) showed a small decrease in the percentage. The School of Education actually showed an overrepresentation of graduate women in 1984; this notable feature has yet to be reflected by the representation of women in the faculty ranks even ten years down the pipeline.

## TABLE 5.2
*Total Graduate Enrollment of Targeted Minorities and Women by School with Percentages of Graduate Total[1] Fall Quarter (1983-1984)*

| School/Prog. | No. of Total Minority | | % Targeted Minority | | No. of Total Women | | % Women | |
|---|---|---|---|---|---|---|---|---|
| | 1984 | 1983 | 1984 | 1983 | 1984 | 1983 | 1984 | 1983 |
| Earth Sci. | 4 | 4 | 2.2 | 2.0 | 55 | 59 | 30.9 | 29.9 |
| Educ. | 45 | 41 | 12.5 | 11.6 | 243 | 220 | 67.3 | 62.3 |
| Engr. | 51 | 56 | 3.7 | 4.3 | 215 | 202 | 15.7 | 15.4 |
| Hum. & Sci. | 93 | 84 | 6.4 | 5.9 | 565 | 514 | 39 | 36.3 |
| Bus. | 52 | 48 | 8.8 | 8.4 | 170 | 161 | 28.9 | 28.0 |
| Law | 63 | 76 | 12 | 14.7 | 205 | 175 | 39.2 | 33.8 |
| Med. (M.D.) | 72 | 84 | 19.8 | 20.6 | 131 | 124 | 33.7 | 34.0 |
| Med. Sci. | 4 | 4 | 2.7 | 3.9 | 64 | 95 | 53.8 | 59.4 |
| Totals | 385 | 397 | 7.9 | 8.3 | 1648 | 1550 | 33.7 | 32.3 |

SOURCE: Registrar's Office

[1] Total Graduate Enrollment: 4881

## TABLE 5.3
*Graduate Enrollment of Targeted Minorities by School Fall Quarter (1984-1985)*

| School/Prog. | African American | | Chicano | | Native American | | Puerto Rican | |
|---|---|---|---|---|---|---|---|---|
| | 1984 | 1983 | 1984 | 1983 | 1984 | 1983 | 1984 | 1983 |
| Earth Sci. | 2 | 1 | 2 | 3 | 0 | 0 | 0 | 0 |
| Educ. | 13 | 15 | 27 | 23 | 5 | 3 | 0 | 0 |
| Engr. | 24 | 23 | 19 | 22 | 4 | 3 | 4 | 8 |
| Hum. & Sci. | 44 | 40 | 37 | 28 | 8 | 8 | 4 | 8 |
| Bus. | 34 | 33 | 15 | 14 | 1 | 1 | 2 | 0 |
| Law | 26 | 35 | 2 | 33 | 2 | 2 | 9 | 6 |
| Med. (M.D.) | 27 | 34 | 35 | 42 | 9 | 7 | 1 | 1 |
| Med. Sci. | 1 | 1 | 2 | 2 | 1 | 1 | 0 | 0 |
| Totals | 171 | 182 | 164 | 167 | 30 | 25 | 20 | 23 |

SOURCE: Registrar's Office

## TABLE 5.4

### Selected Degrees[1] Awarded to Targeted Minorities with Percentages of Total by Degree for Targeted Minorities and Women (1984)

| Degree[2] | 1984 Total[3] | African Amer. 1984 | African Amer. 1983 | Chicano 1984 | Chicano 1983 | Native Amer. 1984 | Native Amer. 1983 | Puerto Rican 1984 | Puerto Rican 1983 | Total % Targ. Min.[2] 1984 | Total % Targ. Min.[2] 1983 | Total % Women[2] 1984 | Total % Women[2] 1983 |
|---|---|---|---|---|---|---|---|---|---|---|---|---|---|
| M.A./M.S. | 1073 | 16 | 18 | 22 | 17 | 2 | 1 | 1 | 3 | 3.8 | 3.9 | 29 | 31 |
| Ph.D. | 347 | 9 | 6 | 3 | 5 | 3 | 1 | 1 | 0 | 4.6 | 3.7 | 29 | 27 |
| J.D. | 182 | 18 | 13 | 14 | 15 | 0 | 0 | 1 | 3 | 18.0 | 20.0 | 33 | 32 |
| M.B.A. | 260 | 12 | 16 | 2 | 11 | 1 | 0 | 0 | 1 | 5.8 | 11.0 | 27 | 28 |
| M.D. | 61 | 7 | 8 | 10 | 7 | 0 | 1 | 0 | 0 | 28.0 | 19.0 | 39 | 41 |
| Totals | 1923 | 62 | 61 | 51 | 55 | 6 | 3 | 3 | 7 | 6.3 | 6.9 | 29 | 31 |

SOURCE: Registrar's Office.

[1] Not including Doctor of Musical Arts, Master of Fine Arts, Educational Specialist, Engineer, Master of the Science of Law.

[2] The degrees are Master of Arts, Master of Science, Doctor of Philosophy, Doctor of Jurisprudence, Master of Business Administration, Doctor of Medicine.

[3] Excludes international enrollment.

Perhaps the more critical characteristic in the pipeline of faculty appointments, however, is not the numbers of women and minorities enrolled but the number of graduate degrees awarded. Table 5.4 provides the data on graduate degrees awarded for 1984. Here, the absolute numbers are a stark reminder of the challenge of appointing more minority and women faculty members: at Stanford University in 1984, only 9 African American, 3 Mexican American, 3 Native American, and 1 Puerto Rican graduate students earned the degree of Ph.D., representing a mere 5% of the total. (Stanford was close to the national percentage of doctorates awarded to minorities in 1984, which was approximately 5%.) Again, the numbers are comparatively better for women: of the 347 Ph.D.'s awarded at Stanford in 1984, women earned 29% of the total—yet still a good way from a reasonable representation when compared with the national population.

# 3. Graduate Affirmative Action Programs at Stanford in the Early 1980's

What efforts at Stanford produced these results? In the early 1980's one of the distinctive features of the Office of the Dean of Graduate Studies and Research was that four members of the staff were engaged in affirmative action programs designed to increase the enrollment of Blacks, Mexican Americans, American Indians, Puerto Ricans, and women in science and engineering. Three minority Assistant Deans were engaged full-time in efforts to recruit, enroll, and retain the four targeted groups of U.S. citizens; the author of this chapter spent approximately one-quarter time in similar efforts aimed at graduate women in the sciences and engineering. All of these efforts involved working with designated affirmative action coordinators in each of the Schools; this team constituted the Graduate Student Minority Recruitment Committee. Issues discussed by this committee included: definition of ethnicity; use of national ethnic newspaper advertisements; comparison of recruitment strategies; joint publicity efforts; revision of printed materials; and student participation in recruitment.

## 3.1. Travel

A significant part of the minority graduate student recruitment plan involved nationwide travel to colleges, universities, and reservations. During these visits, the Assistant Deans organized information meetings with

students, faculty, administrators, and tribal councils to discuss graduate
study at Stanford University. These visits often coincided with graduate
information days when many other schools participated. During 1983–84,
for example, visits were made to more than 50 schools in fifteen states and
Puerto Rico; 10 American Indian Culture Centers and reservation areas
were included. In addition, some visits were made by Stanford faculty and
minority graduate students, although travel by graduate students was not
common because of the interference with graduate study. The personal
contacts established during such visits proved effective and produced an
increase in inquiries about graduate opportunities. The travel included
participation in national conferences: the National Name Exchange; the
GRE Forum; American Indians in Science and Engineering; and the Graduate and Professional Study Fellowship Meeting of Program Directors were
among the meetings attended during 1984.

## 3.2. Name Exchange and Locator Service

Stanford staff played a primary role in organizing both the National
Name Exchange and the Western Name Exchange. These programs provided the names of minority students who, as college juniors, expressed
an interest in graduate study. In addition Stanford made good use of the
Minority Locator Service, sponsored by the Educational Testing Service,
which provided the names, addresses, majors, and grade point averages
of minority undergraduates who were interested in pursuing graduate degrees. The Assistant Deans invited promising minority students to apply
to Stanford, and the names of interested students were subsequently routed
to departments. Refinements in these programs produced improvements in
recruitment; for example, in 1984–85 close to 40% of the targeted minority students who completed an application for admission to the Schools of
Earth Sciences, Education, Engineering, and Humanities and Sciences were
on ten searches of the GRE Locator Service. Furthermore, the Name Exchange programs allowed direct participation by departments, a role that
was welcomed and encouraged by the staff of the Dean of Graduate Studies
and Research.

## 3.3. Publications

Printed materials also proved effective in graduate recruitment. In 1984,
2,000 brochures, 600 flyers and 2,000 posters with tear-off response cards

were distributed during travel visits and targeted mailings. Most of the seven Schools, in coordination with the Dean's office, produced their own publications for graduate minority recruitment. During 1983–84, full-page advertisements were purchased in three minority publications to promote inquiries about graduate studies at Stanford. We also published, with financial assistance from Hewlett Packard and Xerox corporations, a special 50-page booklet focused on Stanford, entitled "Women in Science and Engineering"; a copy of this booklet was distributed to every woman graduate applicant in the sciences and engineering.

## 3.4. An Environment of Support

In addition to affirmative action recruitment efforts, the three minority Assistant Deans helped to develop University-wide programs to maintain an environment of support for minority graduate students. These programs included special orientation sessions for new graduate students, meetings and workshops, luncheon seminars and informal counseling.

In March 1984, the Dorothy Danforth Compton Fellows Regional Conference was held at Stanford. (These Fellowships had been established by the Danforth Foundation, in a six-year grant to selected universities, including Stanford, to support Black, Chicano, American Indian, and Puerto Rican graduate students who were committed to careers in college and university teaching). The Compton Fellows from Stanford were joined by Compton Fellows from the University of California at Los Angeles, the University of Texas at Austin, and Washington University. This two-day conference, attended by the Vice-President of the Danforth Foundation and graduate student advisors, provided an opportunity for Fellows to describe their research.

Since 1971 the School of Humanities and Sciences and the Office of Graduate Studies and Research (as it was known in 1984) had collaborated in the development of the Chicano Fellows Program. This program provides opportunities for Stanford undergraduates to learn about Mexican American culture and for Stanford graduate students to teach in an interdisciplinary setting; furthermore, the program fosters faculty ties with the Chicano intellectual community. Typically, two Mexican American graduate students teach courses on Mexican American history, society, culture, language, and literature.

In 1984, the Dean's Office also contributed financially to a range of activities to support the community of minority graduate students. These included: the American Indian Festival; Black Liberation Month; Cinco de Mayo; a conference on "Affirmative Action in the 1980's" for 125 affirmative action officers from 40 colleges and universities; the Stanford chapter of American Indians in Science and Engineering; an Indian education program on the Zuni reservation in New Mexico; an information day for minority undergraduates on graduate and professional opportunities. The Dean's staff also helped organize the Minority Access to Research Careers (MARC) program at Stanford, funded by the National Institute of Health, which allows talented minority undergraduates to participate in summer research programs. The Assistant Deans spoke about graduate study to minority and low-income students who participated in the Stanford Linear Accelerator Center Summer Science Program.

## 3.5. Financial Support

In 1984 the Dean of Graduate Studies and Research administered three programs providing financial support for targeted minority students. One program used University monies, the Graduate Dean's Minority Matching Fund, and was designed to encourage the admission and enrollment of targeted minorities through a financial incentive to individual departments. This program matched up to one-half of the graduate division's entering year fellowships in departments in the Schools of Humanities and Sciences, Earth Sciences, Education, Engineering, and Ph.D. programs in the School of Medicine.

In 1983–84, the third set of Dorothy Danforth Compton Fellows enrolled at Stanford with support from a Danforth Foundation grant, and this program was also administered by the Dean of Graduate Studies. As mentioned earlier, the Compton Fellows were targeted for Black, Chicano, American Indian, and Puerto Rican students who were committed to careers in college and university teaching. Stanford was among the ten universities nationwide to receive such grants from the Danforth Foundation. In addition to the fellowship support, the Danforth Foundation provided an annual grant of $3,000 to provide an environment of support for the Compton Fellows.

The third program providing financial support was awarded through the U.S. Department of Education. After a national competition in 1983–84, Stanford was awarded eight new and fourteen continuing fellowships from the Graduate and Professional Opportunities Program. These awards, renewable for up to two years, amounted to $176,400 in 1983–84. The following year, Stanford ranked in the upper 10% of the fellowship competition.

# 4. Progress at Stanford: A Comparison of Affirmative Action 1984 to 1994

Affirmative action programs have now been in place at universities for over twenty years. What differences have such programs made at Stanford to faculty appointments and to graduate student enrollments? Some answers are revealed in Tables 5.5–5.8.

The numbers of targeted minority graduate students at Stanford (Table 5.5) are generally moving upward, although some fields have shown more significant progress than others. Over the past decade, the absolute numbers and percentages (excluding the School of Medicine) of targeted minority students have increased in every field, with Engineering, the Humanities, and Law more than doubling in absolute numbers. The Earth Sciences and Math/Sciences have shown the smallest changes in what were already very small enrollments. In 1984, the School of Medicine showed the largest percentage of targeted minority graduate students (16%); in 1993 the School of Law led the schools with a 28% enrollment, followed by Education at 22%.

The numbers of enrolled female graduate students are significantly higher than the targeted minorities in all fields, a fact that is not surprising considering that women comprise slightly more than one-half of the national population. Unlike the case with minority students, however, the absolute numbers of women enrolled in Earth Sciences, Education, Math/Science, and Social Sciences have decreased between 1984 and 1993, although the percentages of the graduate enrollment actually increased in Education and Math/Science during the same period (Table 5.6). The School of Education was the leader in the enrollment of women in both 1984 and 1993, surpassing 60% in both years. (As Table 5.8 will confirm, however, women continue to be significantly underrepresented among both tenured and untenured faculty.) In spite of the increase in enrollment from 254 to 452 between 1984 and 1993, the School of Engineering continues to enroll the lowest percentage of graduate women (16% in 1993). In addition to Edu-

TABLE 5.5

*Number and Percentages of Enrolled Targeted[1]*
*Minority Graduate Students by School*
*1984 and 1993*

| School / Program | 1984 | | 1993 | |
|---|---|---|---|---|
| | No. | $\%^2$ | No. | $\%^2$ |
| Earth Sciences | 4 | 2 | 5 | 3 |
| Education | 47 | 13 | 70 | 22 |
| Engineering | 51 | 4 | 121 | 7 |
| Humanities | 23 | 5 | 54 | 12 |
| Math / Sciences | 25 | 5 | 29 | 6 |
| Social Sciences | 39 | 8 | 43 | 12 |
| Business | 54 | 11 | 76 | 13 |
| Law | 62 | 12 | 135 | 28 |
| Medicine (M.D. & non M.D.) | 76 | 16 | 88 | 14 |

SOURCE: Registrar's Office
[1] African American, Chicano, Puerto Rican, and American Indian
[2] Excludes international enrollment

TABLE 5.6

*Number and Percentages of Enrolled*
*Female Graduate Students by School*
*1984 and 1993*

| School / Program | 1984 | | 1993 | |
|---|---|---|---|---|
| | No. | % | No. | % |
| Earth Sciences | 64 | 25 | 48 | 24 |
| Education | 291 | 61 | 237 | 64 |
| Engineering | 254 | 12 | 452 | 16 |
| Humanities | 171 | 50 | 261 | 46 |
| Math / Sciences | 205 | 22 | 188 | 27 |
| Social Sciences | 282 | 43 | 229 | 43 |
| Business | 182 | 25 | 225 | 26 |
| Law | 211 | 40 | 257 | 47 |
| Medicine (M.D. & non-M.D. | 213 | 39 | 323 | 44 |

SOURCE: Registrar's Office

cation, the fields of Humanities, Social Sciences, Law, and Medicine each currently enroll more than 40% women.

Table 5.7, which indicates tenure track appointments of minority faculty, is a dramatic confirmation of the continued need for affirmative action programs at the graduate level. Both in 1983 and in 1993, some fields can claim at most one Native American, African American, and Hispanic faculty member: Earth Sciences, Math/Sciences, and Business. The Humanities continue to lead the way in the minority faculty ranks, but even here the numbers of tenured minority faculty are extremely small: eight Blacks and four Hispanics.

The tenure-track female faculty, indicated in Table 5.8, show slightly better progress than minorities between 1983 and 1993. Again, the Humanities lead the field with 32 tenured women, but their numbers considerably lag behind the 117 tenured men. The majority of the fields (six of the nine in Table 5.8) have less than 10 tenured women. In Earth Sciences, Engineering, Math/Sciences, and Business, tenured women are less than 10% of the total number of tenured faculty.

In short, in spite of significant progress in the past decade, there is continued need for affirmative action efforts in graduate programs at every university in the United States.

## TABLE 5.7
### Tenure-Track Minority Faculty at Stanford
### by School and Tenure Status

#### 1983

| School | Asian | | Black[1] | | Hispanic | | Native American | |
|---|---|---|---|---|---|---|---|---|
| | Ten. | Unten. | Ten. | Unten. | Ten. | Unten. | Ten. | Unten. |
| Earth Sciences | 2 | 0 | 0 | 0 | 0 | 0 | 0 | 0 |
| Education | 0 | 0 | 0 | 0 | 0 | 2 | 0 | 0 |
| Engineering | 6 | 2 | 2 | 0 | 1 | 1 | 0 | 0 |
| Humanities | 4 | 1 | 6 | 5 | 5 | 3 | 0 | 0 |
| Math / Sciences | 2 | 0 | 1 | 0 | 0 | 1 | 0 | 0 |
| Social Sciences | 5 | 4 | 3 | 2 | 2 | 1 | 0 | 0 |
| Business | 2 | 2 | 0 | 1 | 1 | 0 | 0 | 0 |
| Law | 0 | 0 | 1 | 0 | 0 | 1 | 0 | 0 |
| Medicine | 5 | 5 | 0 | 0 | 1 | 1 | 0 | 0 |

#### 1993

| School | Asian | | Black[1] | | Hispanic | | Native American | |
|---|---|---|---|---|---|---|---|---|
| | Ten. | Unten. | Ten. | Unten. | Ten. | Unten. | Ten. | Unten. |
| Earth Sciences | 2 | 0 | 1 | 0 | 0 | 0 | 0 | 0 |
| Education | 1 | 0 | 1 | 0 | 4 | 0 | 1 | 0 |
| Engineering | 11 | 8 | 3 | 1 | 3 | 0 | 0 | 0 |
| Humanities | 2 | 5 | 8 | 2 | 4 | 4 | 0 | 1 |
| Math / Sciences | 3 | 6 | 1 | 0 | 1 | 0 | 0 | 0 |
| Social Sciences | 6 | 4 | 7 | 0 | 2 | 0 | 0 | 0 |
| Business | 3 | 2 | 0 | 1 | 1 | 1 | 0 | 0 |
| Law | 0 | 1 | 1 | 2 | 2 | 0 | 0 | 0 |
| Medicine | 14 | 12 | 1 | 6 | 1 | 3 | 0 | 0 |

KEY: Ten. = Tenured,    Unten. = Untenured

[1] Includes native-born Americans, naturalized citizens, permanent residents

SOURCE: Office of Institutional Planning

TABLE 5.8
*Tenure-Track Faculty at Stanford*
*by Gender, School, and Tenure Status*

### 1983

| School | Female | | Male | |
|---|---|---|---|---|
| | Tenured | Untenured | Tenured | Untenured |
| Earth Sciences | 0 | 2 | 23 | 7 |
| Education | 4 | 4 | 22 | 8 |
| Engineering | 1 | 6 | 126 | 26 |
| Humanities | 23 | 18 | 128 | 28 |
| Math/Sciences | 4 | 1 | 113 | 28 |
| Social Sciences | 7 | 8 | 93 | 25 |
| Business | 0 | 3 | 44 | 20 |
| Law | 1 | 2 | 32 | 5 |
| Medicine | 12 | 21 | 195 | 92 |

### 1993

| School | Female | | Male | |
|---|---|---|---|---|
| | Tenured | Untenured | Tenured | Untenured |
| Earth Sciences | 2 | 0 | 27 | 3 |
| Education | 6 | 4 | 29 | 0 |
| Engineering | 6 | 5 | 136 | 22 |
| Humanities | 32 | 16 | 117 | 27 |
| Math/Sciences | 6 | 7 | 90 | 26 |
| Social Science | 14 | 12 | 91 | 18 |
| Business | 3 | 3 | 54 | 18 |
| Law | 5 | 5 | 31 | 3 |
| Medicine | 26 | 29 | 206 | 74 |

SOURCE: Office of Institutional Planning

# Chapter 6

# University and Government, University and Industry: Examining a Changed Environment

## Donald Kennedy

## 1. Introduction

During the 1980's two new challenges confronted academic science in the United States. Each, in its way, was a product of the remarkable success of that venture. In the years following World War II the decision to place federal support of basic research in the universities brought rich dividends—not only in fundamental knowledge, but also in new domains of prospective application.

Advances in condensed-matter physics and electrical engineering became applicable to the national defense effort as well as to various consumer goods development. As a result, policymakers were forced to make decisions about the distribution to other nations of "dual use" technologies. A little later, the revolution in molecular biology and genetics made it possible to introduce novel, precisely selected genetic material into host organisms—either to change their properties in desired ways or to make them "factories" for making a certain product. A wave of medical and agricultural applications followed, and the new industry of biotechnology was born. But these developments, too, brought new policy challenges regarding regulation and the involvement of faculty members with for-profit ventures.

These two consequences of our postwar national research policy were plainly boons, in the first instance to our national security and in the second, to our economic health. But by the time 1980 had arrived the policy issues had also moved into the foreground—making it plain that they were going to change the character of university research, place new stresses on institutional policies, and even threaten a set of old and comfortable relationships between higher education, business, and government.

## 2. University and Government

In the first two postwar decades, federal support for academic science grew at extraordinary rates—at an average of nearly 15% per year. Few conditions were attached to this bounty: scientists applied for support for work that interested them, the university received the funds and managed the supporting infrastructure. The government's policy was to pay the full cost of the work, including not only the costs that could be directly attributed to the program but those that supported the research enterprise generally even though they could not be allocated to specific projects—the so-called indirect costs. No one thought to question several basic assumptions in this relationship: that the government's interest in a strong academic research establishment meant that it was prepared to support some training along with the project work; that the relationship was based on mutual trust; that the freedom of investigators to pursue their own work without limit and publish the results would not be interfered with; and that the university's academic rules (openness of access, responsibility for curriculum, and so on) would be respected.

As the growth rate of federal support slowed during the late 1960's and stabilized in the next decade, the kinds of tensions that often accompany resource constraints began to surface. By 1980 the National Institutes of Health (NIH) and other federal agencies were demanding increased amounts of cost sharing on research grants. Exclusions from the "base" used to determine indirect costs began to limit such reimbursements; thus, even though indirect cost recoveries for the universities during the 1980's remained a constant fraction (about one-third) of total research costs, the rates, which are calculated against the base less the exclusions, began to rise. This produced increased political pressure, in the agencies and the Congress, to view indirect costs as institutional supplements rather then real costs subject to reimbursement.

Accelerated production of new Ph.D.'s during the 1960's and early 1970's began to create upward pressure against a suddenly limited supply of research funds. The scientific community, especially in biomedical research, urged the agencies to increase the number of grants available so as to meet the demands of able young investigators. In response the National Institutes of Health adopted "targets," often funding the additional projects by making administrative reductions in all projects. The average level of hardship and dissatisfaction increased, and the added numbers made it even harder, in the 1980's, for new investigators to get funded. The situation in biomedical research by the late 1980's was described by Robert Rosenzweig, President of the Association of American Universities, in these terms: "The number of applicants for grants grows faster than the available resources, the success ratio declines, unrealistic demands for university matching accompany reduced grant support, good research goes unfunded, good researchers become frustrated, young researchers leave the field, infrastructure problems are deferred, and the price for it all will be paid in the future by people who are not around now to assert their interests" (Rosenzweig 1992). And Leon Lederman, President of the American Association for the Advancement of Science, reported at the beginning of the next decade that the scientific community in the United States was afflicted by "... a depth of despair and discouragement that I have not experienced in my forty years in science" (Lederman 1991). Nor did their dissatisfaction fall entirely on the government as the source of this diminishing support. It extended to the administrations of their universities, who were blamed for the rise in indirect cost rates and for deficiencies in the supporting infrastructure they provided for research.

Thus, a climate of growing disaffection within the academy, including faculty and administrators alike but often pitting them against one another, provides a background for the changes in the relationship between the universities and the government.

The first serious challenge came early in the decade, when the Departments of Defense (DOD) and Commerce began to worry about exports of U.S. technology overseas. The stated concern was over devices and specifications that might provide military advantages to another nation—including the possible military application of the "dual use" technologies. But a number of us who were troubled by the development wondered whether national security concerns were not often a makeweight for worries that were primarily economic. In any event, DOD began to apply regulations designed to restrict the overseas distribution of actual devices and their specifications to research and research date. The mechanism was the International Traffic in Arms regulations, which came to be used to limit publication of certain "sensitive" university research results and to bar the visits of foreigners to U.S. laboratories sponsored by the Department of Defense.

I was President of Stanford University at the time; Gerald Lieberman, Vice-Provost and Dean of Graduate Studies and Research, and I had to contend with an increasing number of problems arising from that effort. In 1981 we formed a coalition with the presidents of Caltech, the University of California, Cornell, and MIT to protest these policies to the Secretaries of State, Commerce, and Defense. The situation worsened in the next year in connection with a proposed visit by a Russian robotics expert named Nikolay Umnov. A member of our faculty had received a letter from the National Academy of Sciences, the sponsor of an exchange program under which the visit was to take place. The letter included certain restrictions that would apply to his visit: he was not to discuss unpublished research or to visit campus laboratories or programs supported by Defense Department funds, nor was he to be permitted to visit local industries. These provisions were plainly government boilerplate, and it surprised us that the National Academy of Sciences had accepted them.

Umnov's prospective faculty sponsor read these restrictions to me in the Faculty Senate and asked whether under Stanford's existing policies they would be acceptable. Without much background, I opined that they would not; and after that Lieberman and I began an effort to unwind them. We wrote to the President of the National Academy of Sciences, who made it plain that he neither knew about them nor found them acceptable. Our own point was simple: the university can not be expected to police every aspect of a foreign scientist's visit to the institution because everything here is open; most especially we are not about to stake out our visitors' hotel rooms to make sure they do not surreptitiously manage a visit to Hewlett-Packard. Eventually this argument took hold, and the result was a compromise satisfactory to us. When news reports of this outcome leaked out, the State Department cancelled the visit, in what was plainly a face-saving effort. But the Academy deleted the restrictions from future exchange letters.

An internal struggle within the Department of Defense played an important part in the development of the entire controversy and eventually in its resolution. The Assistant Secretary for Policy, Richard Perle, favored stringent limitations on the transfer of information as well as technology. In a panel discussion we had at the National Press Club in Washington, he challenged universities for their unwillingness to sponsor secret military research—and was plainly unimpressed by my argument that a university that was half-open and half-secret could not function as a university. On the other side of the issue was Richard DeLauer, Undersecretary for Research and Engineering. DeLauer formed a DOD–Universities Council, in which Lieberman and I both played roles, that attempted to work through the differences.

In an editorial in *Science,* I argued: "If a Soviet scientist is viewed with such alarm that universities must be asked to police his visit, then the Department of State can apply visa controls. And if a technology has such military value that exposure in an open environment presents clear risks to national security, the government can classify the technology —thus permitting the universities to decide in advance whether they can accept the restrictions that come along with the work" (Kennedy 1982).

With the encouragement of the DOD–Universities Council, the National Academy of Sciences formed a committee under the chairmanship of the physicist Dale Corson, former president of Cornell University. That committee essentially agreed with our position that administrative classification of security-sensitive information and visa control over scientific visitors were adequate devices, and that the provisions of the International Trade and Arms Regulations (ITAR) and the Export Administration Regulation

(EAR) were not properly applied to university research or to scientific visitors. Thus, the struggle in the Department of Defense was won by DeLauer, and although there were a few subsequent rumblings, the issue never resurfaced in a serious way.

But a quite different form of constraint on publication arose later in the decade. The National Heart, Lung, and Blood Institute sponsored a multicenter clinical trial of a ventricular assist device invented by a Stanford faculty member, Philip Oyer. Stanford was one of the centers involved, with Dr. Oyer as principal investigator. But the agency attempted to attach a condition to the grant that would have prohibited researchers from publishing until the government had given approval; the reason given was that premature disclosure from one center might compromise the entire study. We objected, and launched a long effort to negotiate the provision—an effort that failed completely. Once it became clear that there was no room for compromise, Stanford sued in federal court to have the restriction lifted. The suit was decided in the university's favor, and although the government attempted to moot the legal outcome by discontinuing the project, the decision stands as discouragement to all such prior restraints on research publication.

An entirely new form of government intervention was introduced late in the 1980's and is still unresolved. The cause was a growing public outcry over the falsification of scientific research results—the most notorious form of academic misconduct, though surely less common than the misappropriation of the intellectual property of others. Several celebrated cases in the early 1980's caught the interest of Congressional committees, and the result was heavy pressure on the National Institutes of Health and other agencies to develop regulations and conduct inquiries.

The result has been a series of intrusions into the conduct of university research and even into the curriculum. A series of investigations has been undertaken at NIH by a unit originally called the Office of Research Integrity, later moved to the Secretary's office in the Department of Health and Human Services as the Office of Scientific Integrity (OSI). Several of these were also the subjects of hearings held by the Subcommittee on Oversight and Investigations of the House Commerce Committee, chaired by Representative John Dingell (D-MI). In connection with the hearings, laboratory notebooks belonging to collaborators of scientists charged with misconduct were subpoenaed. Preliminary reports of the agency's inquiry were leaked to the press by Subcommittee staff, seriously damaging the reputations of those charged before any findings had been reached. Several of those completed in 1993 were sent to the Board of Appeals of the Department, and reversed in language that can only be described as scathing. "One might anticipate that from all this evidence, after all the sound and fury, there would be at least a residue of palpable wrongdoing. That is not the case" the Board of Appeals wrote in one of them.[1] The OSI dropped another case, but a number of others linger unfinished, still doing their damage to scientific reputations.

In response to the perceived frequency of scientific misconduct, the National Institutes of Health has taken the extraordinary (but almost unprotested) step of requiring universities receiving their funds for trainees or fellows to offer courses dealing with the problem. The result may be salutary—dozens or even hundreds of new courses dealing with a set of serious and often fascinating ethical challenges. Salutary or not, however, it represents the first case of government intervention in the course catalog. (Earlier in the decade, an effort to mandate admissions standards was beaten back narrowly. Congress very nearly passed a bill that would have required medical schools to accept candidates trained abroad in order to receive new training funds.)

The reach of federal regulation into these areas has been gradual, but its extent would astonish even those who were cautious, in the 1950's, about whether universities should become so dependent upon government funding. Required courses, accounting systems modeled after the military-procurement sector, restrictions on publication and on the access of foreign nationals to laboratories and classrooms—these would have seemed inconceivable to those who set the nation's academic science venture on its present course.

# 3. University and Industry

At the height of federal support for academic research, the zone of interaction between universities and industry was limited to a few applied disciplines. It is much expanded now, and I think the expansion can be attributed to two changes. The first, naturally enough, is the increased need for other sources of funding: as federal support reached a plateau, universities showed more interest in obtaining industrial funding for some of the work.

The second reason is the more important. Vast new areas of application were exposed by new advances in computer science and—most especially— in biomedicine. Along with those opportunities came an entirely new way of financing the development of a new idea. The traditional mode was that basic research—usually in a university—produced a thing or process that might be developed into a product. When that prospect had become sufficiently clear, risk capital was invested by some industry and the product development phase began.

Beginning in the late 1970's, this trajectory was compressed. In the new field of biotechnology especially, small start-up companies were formed on the basis of early findings. These were financed by venture-capital partnerships, and as research on the new idea went forward two or more rounds of private financing often preceded a public offering. At each of these steps, the primary investors could realize significant increases in value—long before a product had emerged for marketing. This new way of doing business made it desirable to own an idea or a technology early in its history, at a stage that in earlier times would have been characterized as basic research.[2]

Federal law changed in ways that encouraged this interdigitation of university and industry research. The Bayh-Dole patent amendments of 1980, specifically introduced to encourage the transfer of university technology to the commercial sector, effectively turned over to the universities the disposition of rights to intellectual property arising from federally-sponsored institutional research. And changes in the capital-gains provision of the tax laws and in tax credits for research and development made more private funding available for new, high-technology ventures.

The results of these changes brought new challenges to the research universities, and they arrived in force at the beginning of the 1980's. By then venture capitalists and faculty entrepreneurs had become a common sight at Faculty Club lunch tables, discussing deals or consultantships. Technology licensing, at Stanford and other universities, made its appearance as an important matter for administrations. For me a landmark was reached early in 1980 when Lieberman and I reached agreement on a policy for internal distribution of the royalties on the Cohen-Boyer patent for recombinant DNA technology—a patent that was to gather over 200 licensees and earn Stanford and the University of California over $100 million in royalty income.

In many of the start-up companies involving faculty members, the problems were more complex—if less lucrative. In some cases faculty members held significant equity and occupied positions that entailed some management responsibility. Would there be serious conflicts of commitment? There was also the possibility of crossover between research done in the faculty member's campus laboratory and the company. Would the activities of faculty and students be siphoned off into the more commercial end of a venture that used to be strictly academic? And what if the university were invited to be a coinvestor? or to license patents exclusively to the faculty company?

There were problems in the other direction as well, raised by the increasingly frequent support agreements made between established research-intensive firms, especially pharmaceutical firms, and the universities. These had come into prominence in the late 1970's; among the first were agreements between Monsanto and Washington University, and between Monsanto and Harvard Medical School. Would such agreements constrain, to an undesirable extent, the choices of the university researchers they supported? Would the quid pro quo offered by the universities (exclusive rights to intellectual property, or preferential access to information and/or students) offer an unfair advantage to the sponsoring company?

These questions and others like them began to crowd in on university administrators in the early 1980's. Stanford was very much at the cutting edge; partly that was because a long history in applied physics and engineering had prepared it, partly it was because its own strength in biomedicine and the proximity of Silicon Valley and its entrepreneurial energy made it inevitable.

At about this time, Harvard's President, Derek Bok, appeared on the front page of The New York Times in a story about exactly the kind of problem we were all beginning to face. Harvard's management company was planning to coinvest with a faculty member in a biotechnology company—but there were objections. Some faculty members felt that it might show too much institutional favoritism to commercially promising work. Another, in a burst of frankness, pointed out that he had a company too, and why should Harvard invest in his colleague's and not in his?

Harvard eventually decided against coinvestment, as we also had. But the controversy persuaded us that it might be wise to gather university and industry people together in a conference to see if we could agree on some general guidelines for these new relationships. Accordingly, we got the presidents of Harvard, MIT, Caltech, and the University of California to join us in such an exercise. Each invited senior faculty members, trustees and industry CEOs; we managed to gather a significant number of the players in the New Biotechnology.

Lieberman and I had hoped for only the broadest kind of agreement; but after two days at Pajaro Dunes on the California coast, the participants were prepared to co-sign a statement that included a number of guidelines. Among other things the Pajaro principles discouraged co-investment, called for careful examination of exclusive licensing, and advised against the migration of basic research from university laboratories into commercial ones. Although thought by some at the time to be too bland, the Pajaro principles were in fact embodied into policy at most research universities in the decade that followed their development.

Perhaps the most important recommendation of the Pajaro conference dealt with the agreements between industrial sponsors and universities. The conferees concluded that they should be made public. The Pajaro statement also included a strong guideline to the effect that the university should not accept or enforce restrictions on publication by faculty members.

Universities would surely be in a difficult position were they to countenance such restrictions—especially in view of the position they took regarding government effort to enforce secrecy. What is sauce for the goose is sauce for the gander—or, as it was put by Admiral Bobby Inman in one of the mid-1980's discussions of the issue, the universities should not be willing to do for profit what they declined to do for patriotism.

# 4. Conclusion

One would have to agree, I think, that the 1980's brought the universities a decade of extraordinary challenge. Our way of doing academic science has survived, at least in its basic outline; but we have been taught some hard lessons. Two seem particularly important to me.

First, we have learned that the acceptance of government funds, on terms that at first seemed both generous and informal, brought with it some significant requirements. Some of these—accelerated rates of cost-sharing and various forms of process regulation—fall on the university. Others, perhaps more onerous, fall on the researcher. Few of us would have thought, in the 1960's, that our government would be prepared to lay claim to our data books, or attempt to limit by regulation our ability to publish our research results. On such matters continued vigilance will be required, because Congress and the public now view the awarding of public funds as carrying with it a much intensified kind of accountability.

Second, a form of entrepreneurship has now become firmly rooted in academic science—not in just a few disciplines, but across the board. Computer software, microelectronics, fast-reaction chemistry, materials science, and many other fields are of nearly as much commercial interest as engineering and molecular biology. Today's way of commercializing good ideas reaches much farther back in the innovation cycle, invading academic laboratories in a much more pervasive way than formerly. The ethical ramifications present complex tests—for university decisionmakers no less than for individual faculty members. Defending the university's balanced interest in work without commercial application; protecting students and junior colleagues from inherently coercive situations; securing freedom of access and of publication; these are just a few of the challenges that now regularly present themselves.

Should the universities view with such alarm that they withdraw? Surely not. The relationship between the academy and society has always been changeable, and in fact the current episode has on the whole been managed well. But it has put a strongly utilitarian cast on the role of the universities, one that may have had an unanticipated effect on public attitudes about universities. In all the fuss about government funding, research accounting, scientific misconduct, ownership of intellectual property, university-industry agreements, and the like, some of our oldest and strongest supporters are beginning to ask a new and disturbing question: have we forgotten about our students? If, in our analysis of what is right and wrong about our relationship with the government and with industry, we can put them at the center, it will both help the analysis and remind our public where our priorities lie. Indeed, perhaps the best practical test of any proposed arrangement is to examine carefully how it will affect the welfare of graduate students. For it was a wise decision, at the end of World War II, to locate public support of science in the same places where the next generation of scientists is taking place. If we permit that happy synergism to be broken, the entire venture will have lost its defining character.

# Notes

[1] Department of Health and Human Services, Departmental Appeals Board, Research Integrity Adjudications Panel. Decision in the case of Mikulas Popovic, M.D. Nov. 3, 1993. Docket A-93-100, Decision No. 1446.

[2] This idea is discussed in more detail in Kennedy 1983, and consequences of such agreements are thoroughly explored in Blumenthal 1992.

# References

Blumenthal, D. 1992. "Academic-Industry Relationships in the Life Sciences." *Journal of the American Medical Association* 268: 3344–3349.

Kennedy, D. 1982. "The Government, Secrecy, and University Research." *Science* 216: 365.

Kennedy, D. 1983. "The Social Sponsorship of Innovation." *Technology and Society* 4: 253–265.

Lederman, L. 1991. "Science: The End to the Frontier?" *Science,* p. 17, supplement, January 1991.

Rosenzweig, R. M. Testimony before President's Council of Advisers on Science and Technology, July 24, 1992.

# Chapter 7

# Student Revolt and Campus Reform in the 1960's: The Case of Stanford's Judicial Charter

Richard W. Lyman

In his now classic Godkin Lectures delivered at Harvard in 1963, Clark Kerr detected signs of restiveness among the undergraduate students at the leading research universities:

> Recent changes in the American university have done them lit-
> tle good—lower teaching loads for the faculty, larger classes,
> the use of substitute teachers for the regular faculty, the choice
> of faculty members based on research accomplishments rather
> than instructional capacity, the fragmentation of knowledge into
> endless subdivisions. There is an incipient revolt of undergrad-
> uate students against the faculty; the revolt that used to be
> against the faculty in loco parentis is now against the faculty
> in absentia (Kerr 1972).

A year earlier, the drafters of the Port Huron Statement, the publication that served to introduce SDS (Students for a Democratic Society) to the world, had seen the universities as the logical starting point for a revolution that would eventually extend far beyond the campus. Kerr noted these possibilities, too.

A few of the 'nonconformists' have another kind of revolt in mind. They seek, instead, to turn the university, on the Latin American or Japanese models, into a fortress from which they can sally forth with impunity to make their attacks on society (Kerr 1972).

The campus rebellions that followed in the later 1960's focused most conspicuously on the issues of Vietnam and racial equality, but questions stemming from the discontents listed by Kerr, and relating to the purposes and functioning of universities, never entirely disappeared. Radicals who wanted the universities to cut their ties with the Pentagon and become the launching platforms for revolutionary change in the society at large also looked forward to a new era of participatory democracy on campus. Hierarchical structures would give way to communal ones; the Physics Department, and the Economics Department would become the Physics Community and the Economics Community, with custodial and clerical staff, undergraduate and graduate students empowered equally with faculty on a basis of one person–one vote on all matters, academic as well as purely administrative.[1] Such "communities" would surely have made short work of those features of the multiversity that undergraduates particularly disliked.

The moment for such utopian imaginings quickly passed. Looking at American higher educational institutions before and after the storm, one is likely to conclude that remarkably little lasting change took place. The essential conservatism of academia, at least with regard to its own customs, practices, and structural arrangements, was once again demonstrated.

Yet it would be a mistake to conclude that the radical movement left no mark on the institutions that, for a brief while, appeared to be shaken to their foundations by the havoc it caused. At Stanford, for example, governance was not revolutionized, but it was substantially altered in these years. Among the new elements were an expansion of the Board of Trustees by one-third, to make room for eight Trustees directly elected by the alumni,[2] and the addition of faculty and student representatives to most Board committees; an elected legislature for the faculty (the Senate of the Academic Council); a revised and much more formal system, with heavy student involvement, for both legislating and enforcing rules of student conduct; the elimination of ROTC and of classified research; a sweeping reformulation of academic requirements for the baccalaureate degree; changes in the dormitory and other arrangements for student living that would have been regarded as totally inadmissible just a few years earlier; the opening of Stanford Memorial Church to all faiths; and a divestiture on the part of the University of its wholly owned applied research enterprise, the Stanford Research Institute. In addition to these structural changes, the demographics of the campus population began to evolve from the overwhelming WASP domination of the past toward the multicultural panorama of the future. The quota limiting the number of women undergraduates that dated back to Mrs. Stanford's day disappeared.

All of this was duly recorded in a new periodical, *Campus Report*. The University administration, dismayed at what it saw as omissions and distortions in the student paper, the *Stanford Daily*, decided in 1968 to launch its own weekly paper. For the first time, the University had a newspaper of record.

Each of these innovations had its own particular history, of course, and connections betweeen them are not always readily discerned. Most can easily be seen in retrospect as overdue, in the sense that, even absent the radical upheavals on campus, something like them would have emerged, perhaps somewhat more gradually. And many were begun before any substantial disruptions had occurred on campus. Nevertheless, it seems clear that the breakdown of long-standing stability at Stanford played a part in making change possible on a scale and at a rate that would not otherwise have occurred.

The clearest instance of causal connection between structural changes and student protest is provided by the reform of the system for regulating student conduct. The controversy over the student judicial system provided a bridge between the protest over the war in Viet Nam and the movement for reform of University structures and procedures.

The first serious incident of the student rebellion at Stanford, a two-day sit-in by about three dozen students in the lobby of the President's Office in May 1966 was provoked by the University's participation in the selective service system through the administration of examinations to help local boards in determining which students would be eligible for continued deferment from the draft. This protest was notably unsuccessful, either in altering the University's policy or in attracting significant support from the student body as a whole. Many who opposed the war nevertheless valued their deferments and did not want the University to close any door that might lead to continuing immunity from service. And at that point, sentiment on the Stanford campus was still wary of militant confrontational tactics. Counterdemonstrators appeared outside the President's Office, and questions to the crowd by *Daily* reporters suggested that most disapproved of demonstration and counterdemonstration alike as departures from calmer discourse.[3] Far the biggest headline of the 1965–66 year announced a Board of Trustees decision in April: "Campus Drinking Approved; New Rules Effective May 10."[4]

But the episode did put in motion the system for disciplining students charged with misconduct and thereby brought to the fore the dissatisfactions on all sides with then-existing procedures. Under these procedures, cases were initiated by the Dean of Students and heard by an all-student Judicial Council, a part of the student government (the Associated Students of Stanford University, or ASSU). But if either party was dissatisfied with the outcome, appeal could be taken to the Interim Judicial Body, a panel of five faculty members, chaired by a Law Professor and appointed by the President of the University.[5]

Despite rather obvious anomalies, such as giving the plaintiff the right of appeal, the system might have worked tolerably when the gulf in attitudes between students and administrators was not too great. But as mutual trust between groups, especially between students and administrators, deteriorated in the middle and late 1960's, the inherent contradictions of the system became sharply apparent. The student Judicial Council began looking for ingenious ways to block the Dean's path to appeal, while the administration began to expect no good result (from its standpoint) from the court of first instance and to rely on appeals to get satisfactory outcomes.

As early as spring of 1965 there was general agreement that a reform of the system was needed. The Committee of Fifteen (C-15), comprising equal numbers of students, faculty, and administrators, aimed at improving communication among these groups, began meeting in March and had high on its agenda the creation of more acceptable structures both for enacting rules governing student conduct and for adjudicating cases under those rules. For various reasons, principally conflicts within student government over the appointment and accountability of the student members, progress was slow and in any event invisible to the public, since, to encourage frank exchange of views the, C-15's discussions were confidential.

Meanwhile, opposition to the war was becoming more and more vocal. Protesters attempted to prevent recruiters for the CIA from conducting interviews on campus on November 1, 1967. The administration brought charges of misconduct against ten of them. In February 1968 the Judicial Council acquitted all ten on the ground that the University's policy on disruptions was "overbroad and vague"; further, the Council rejected the administration's assumption that a violation of University rules was ipso facto a violation of the Fundamental Standard, which was supposed to govern student conduct.[6]

When the administration appealed the ruling to the Interim Judicial Body, there was a great outcry against the alleged illegitimacy of that institution, wholly the creature of the University President and lacking any student representation. The outcry increased when, predictably, the Interim Judicial Body found seven protesters guilty, suspended five for the Summer Quarter and two who were repeat offenders for Summer and Fall Quarters. Negotiations between student leaders and the administration failed to resolve the issues, and the Old Union, home of a variety of administrative offices of the University, was forcibly occupied by several hundred demonstrators on May 6, 1968.[7]

In an atmosphere of crisis one of the most heavily attended faculty meetings in the history of the University took place on May 8. The Executive Committee of the Academic Council, supported by the University Administration, presented resolutions designed both to end the sit-in and to speed the negotiation of a legislative and judicial mechanism for student conduct that would include student representation. But in a tumultuous session ending in an unprecedented roll-call vote, the full faculty tabled these measures, which of course cut off all discussion of them, in favor of urging amnesty for those sitting in and creating a new temporary judicial board of students and faculty pending the adoption of the C-15's permanent recommendations, a draft of which had been published that morning. The final vote was 284 to 245.[8]

This resolved the immediate crisis; the occupiers of the Old Union acknowledged their victory by voting to end the sit-in. But far from resolving the issues, the faculty's action created a new one: what, if any, limits would the faculty be prepared to support on the use of disruption of University operations and forcible occupation of University facilities to achieve changes in University policy? An answer to that question would not be forthcoming until many more confrontations had taken place, some of them accompanied by violence against both persons and property.

Meanwhile, the C-15's new mechanisms, accepted immediately by the administration and soon overwhelmingly approved by both students and faculty, ended the anomalies of the old arrangements.[9] The Student Conduct Legislative Council and the Stanford Judicial Council were created, each involving faculty members chosen through newly established faculty Senate channels and students chosen by the mechanisms of ASSU. Each body was chaired by a faculty member and had a narrow faculty majority. Although the new judicial council had its difficulties as long as the era of campus confrontation lasted, these arrangements have endured with little change to this day.[10]

At a rally in White Plaza attended by an estimated 900 people, Professor Hubert Marshall, Chairman of the C-15, called this reform "a major step toward community government."[11] This invocation of contemporary buzzwords was a trifle misleading, though understandable under the circumstances. Certainly student engagement in "decisions that shaped their lives," to use another catchphrase of the time, was notably advanced by these changes. To return to earlier and more paternalistic arrangements was thenceforth unthinkable. Yet it is worth noting that students have in fact availed themselves, in an overwhelming majority of cases, of an escape clause allowing a defendant to ask that the Dean of Student Affairs hear the case rather than the Student Judicial Council.[12]

Despite these dramatic events, the protest movement was scarcely dominant in the Stanford of 1968. In an unusually large turnout the student body approved by a vote of 3,924 to 1,695 a resolution calling the forcible occupation of University buildings "unacceptable behavior."[13] At least equally significant was the 3,920 to 676 vote in favor of allowing all employers equal access to recruiting facilities at the University.[14]

The Academic Council vote caused bitter divisions in the faculty for a time. That evening, both the Provost and the Vice Provost wrote letters of resignation on the ground that the faculty had shown itself to be ungovernable; we each tore up these notes in the sober light of morning, given the fact that President Sterling was a few weeks from retirement.[15]

Stanford was to be afflicted with inumerable further building occupations, sometimes accompanied by violence, in the next few years. During the months of April and May 1970, police were called to campus thirteen times; 45 police and "at least 20 students" were injured.[16] The new judicial system could not cope with such conditions; by the spring of 1970 it was far from clear that police power would be sufficient either.[17]

Amidst all the turmoil, the changes listed at the start of this chapter were proceeding, if not smoothly, at least rapidly. Where protest succeeded, it was in circumstances in which the interests of the radical movement and of academic reformers of a far more moderate stamp coincided. Both ROTC and classified research ended at Stanford. A case could be (and was) made against both on academic grounds, quite aside from the question of Viet Nam. An innovation such as the Academic Senate fell far short of radical aspirations; indeed it was attacked at the time by ASSU President Peter Lyman as a setback to the development of true community government.[18]

The reform of the student judicial system had broad support. No doubt the more militant members of the incipient Movement saw the agitation for these changes primarily as a useful way of recruiting students to their wider purposes. Radical speakers in White Plaza disowned the draft Charter as soon as it was published,[19] and when it came to a vote to present the revised document to the three constituencies for adoption, three of the five student members of the C-15 abstained.[20] But there was plenty of moderate support for reform. It was an important step away from informal—for which read "paternalistic"—campus management and toward legalism and the codification of rules.

No such radical/moderate alliance was possible concerning such questions as DOD sponsored research, and it never came close to being terminated. In the case of the Stanford Research Institute (SRI), the change that took place represented a clear rejection of radical demands: instead of the University's asserting its authority over SRI for purposes of ending its links with DOD, a commission of inquiry recommended, and the Trustees accepted, divestiture.[21]

The Stanford that emerged from the time of troubles was characterized by more formal structures for decisionmaking, with more explicit recognition of particular interest groups than existed previously and a greatly increased involvement of lawyers. Ironically, the operations of the University have come to resemble far more closely the way things are done downtown than they did before the protests of the 1960's. This should come as no surprise, for few things are more familiar in history than the triumph of unintended consequences. The "Years of Hope, Days of Rage" of 1968–70 were replete with them.[22]

# Notes

[1] *Stanford Daily*, May 5, 1970.
[2] Significantly, it was specified that four of the eight were to be under 35 years old.
[3] *Stanford Daily*, May 19, 20, and 23, 1966.
[4] *Stanford Daily*, April 25, 1966.
[5] For a convenient review of the controversy to that date, see *Stanford Daily*, May 7, 1968.
[6] See ibid. This statement, dating back to David Starr Jordan's day, says: "Students are expected to show both within and without the University such respect for order, morality, personal honor, and the rights of others as is demanded of good citizens. Failure to observe this will be sufficient cause for removal from the University." *Stanford Daily*, April 16, 1965.
[7] *Stanford Daily*, May 7 and 8, 1968.
[8] *Stanford Daily*, May 9, 1968.
[9] *Campus Report*, October 23, 1968.
[10] For the full text of the Stanford Judicial Charter recommended by C-15, see *Stanford Daily*, May 31, 1968.
[11] *Stanford Daily*, May 10, 1968.
[12] The campus Judicial Affairs Office issues statistics annually on the disposition of cases.
[13] *Stanford Daily*. May 16, 1968.
[14] See letter to the editor by Professor Gerald J. Lieberman, *Stanford Daily*, May 17, 1968. The *Daily*'s report of the voting had omitted mention of this resolution.
[15] Personal recollection. I never saw Herbert L. Packer's note, since we wrote independently and without coordination, but he told me what he had written.
[16] *Campus Report*, May 20, 1970.

17 During the strike against the invasion of Cambodia the administration announced in *Campus Report* (May 6, 1970): "The University is not presently in a position to obtain outside help in the event that access to buildings is blocked. If you are unable to enter a building, you should not fight to get in; attempt to identify persons blocking entrance, and notify Chief Tom Bell, Stanford Police, ext. 3444." The police departments of San Jose, Sunnyvale and Mountain View were all reported to be finding it impossible to continue providing manpower for Stanford while still doing their job in their own communities.

18 *Stanford Daily*, October 4, 1967. For a comprehensive rebuttal, see letter by Professor Kenneth Arrow, *Stanford Daily*, October 11, 1967.

19 *Stanford Daily*. May 10, 1968.

20 *Stanford Daily*, May 31, 1968.

21 For the committee's recommendations, see *Campus Report*, April 15, 1969.

22 Subtitle of Todd Gitlin, *The Sixties* (Toronto: Bantam Books; 1987).

# Reference

Kerr, Clark. 1972. *The Uses of the University*. 3rd ed. New York: Harper & Row.

# Chapter 8

# The University Fellows Program at Stanford: On Turning Scientists and Scholars into University Statesmen and Stateswomen

## Albert H. Hastorf

In 1967 Stanford University was still riding the crest of the boom in higher education and its own dramatic rise in status generated by the entrepreneurial activities of President J. E. Wallace Sterling and Provost Frederick Terman. After Terman's retirement one of Sterling's final significant administrative decisions was to appoint Richard W. Lyman as the new university Provost and law professor Herbert Packer to the newly created position of Vice Provost for Academic Planning. Packer proposed that he take on two major tasks. The first was to develop a major study of undergraduate education which was eventually reported to the community in a series of ten volumes in the years 1968–69. Packer also proposed that Stanford develop a program to identify relatively young, able scholars and scientists on the Stanford faculty (probably newly tenured or very strong candidates to be granted tenure in the near future) and to develop a program that would provide these young academicians with experiences that would open up the possibility of their becoming academic leaders.

This chapter will concern itself with the history of the Fellows Program. In fact, the program still exists in modified form. The chapter will also address the questions of what happened to the participants, what did they think of their experience, and would we judge the program a successful innovation? Before addressing these questions, we should note that, not surprisingly, another set of issues intruded on Lyman's and Packer's lives in that they had to engage in a series of crisis-management activities stemming from student and faculty resistance to the Vietnam War. Packer's full attention could not go to the original major tasks. Stanford had its share of upheaval (sit-ins, etc.) and discovered that its faculty decision-making processes were in no way adapted to the sorts of crisis management that the times demanded. Packer took on another task and that was to revise the self-governance system of the Stanford faculty so as to create a Faculty Senate. This required substantial effort on Lyman and Packer's part but it did not deter them from the generation of the University Fellow's Program.

# 1. Genesis of the University Fellows Program

It is my assumption that Packer and Lyman, who had both been recruited at Stanford during the dramatic growth of the Stanford faculty in the 1950's (the word *growth* should be taken in both its quantitative sense and its qualitative sense), realized that a new breed of faculty was being developed at Stanford and in other American research universities. These were able scholars and scientists who focused their attention on their research and the achievement of the forms of national status that accompany successful research performance. Department Chairs (called Executive Heads at that time) were focused on the development of strong research-based departments and saw the recruitment of research stars as a significant part of their task. A number of these people were very skilled at this which resulted in substantial increases in the national ranking of many of Stanford's departments. Stars were willing to move to Stanford, and this increased Stanford's attractiveness to able junior faculty recruits. The feeling was that individuals came to join a strong Physics Department, a strong Biochemistry Department in the Medical School or a strong History Department. Professional schools were growing markedly in the quantity and quality of their research. This "New Breed" of faculty seemed so committed to their own scholarly development, or at most to the development of their department or school, that the notion of being a citizen of the University as a whole was not at the forefront of their minds. This issue concerned Lyman and Packer; they had no notion of diminishing the scholarly aspirations of the faculty, but they were eager to try and add some "citizenship" to the mix of talents.

Packer took on the tasks of formulating a program that would meet this need and soliciting outside funds that would support it. His original proposal to the Ford Foundation was entitled "Academic Statesmen."[1] This proposal to the Ford Foundation discussed the need for the development of Academic Statesmen. He began that discussion as follows:

> The "academic statesman" is, as F. Champion Ward has defined him, "the man of good academic caliber who somehow also contributes curricular, pedagogical, and organizational ideas of general value to his institution and is willing and able to give his time to their realization." His is a rare breed, for reasons that are too clear to need much elaboration. Today's American university is more centrifugal than it is centripetal. The discipline rather than the institution commands the attention and allegiance of the individual faculty member. Rewards, including the reward of self-esteem, come from the recognition of one's work accorded by one's peers. One's peers are fellow specialists in molecular biology, or French drama of the classical period, or social stratification. In the nature of things, there are apt to be far more of them outside than inside one's home institution. And, increasingly, the professor is likely to have a number of homes away from home. Mobility combines with disciplinary loyalty to undermine the development of interest in the institution and its problems. Not surprisingly, the institution itself tends to become incoherent: a collection of more or less independent satrapies uneasily presided over by a small group of harassed bookkeepers.

The objective conditions that produce this malaise can only be altered over a long period of time. There is some reason for optimism that the increasingly fragmented nature of knowledge contains the seeds of reversal and that the need for integration will assert itself, with a corresponding integrative effect on the centers of knowledge that we call universities. But those who are concerned about the malaise can hardly afford to wait for the university to reflect subtle and long-run changes in the sociology of knowledge.

There is an immediate need for the development of counterforces. By "counterforces", we mean strategies that will induce more "men of good academic caliber" to see themselves as university men, either formally, as potential university administrators, or at least as faculty members who see a significant part of their task as relating to the welfare of the university as a whole. This proposal elaborates one such counterforce that we believe holds high promise as a model for generalized development.

The proposal rests on the proposition that a sense of educational power is the key factor in cultivating loyalty to the institution as a whole. It seeks to test the thesis that academic statesmen can be created by giving talented young faculty members, at an early stage in their academic careers, an opportunity to play a meaningful role in the development and evaluation of educational programs. As a necessary concomitant of that proposition it seeks to make possible the development and evaluation of educational programs having a supra-departmental or disciplinary orientation.

Packer went on to propose two elements of the program: Fellows of the University and Innovation Fund. This chapter will focus on the Fellows Program but the Innovation Fund was a significant part of that program for the first five years. He proposed that innovation funds would be available that were outside of the usual university budgeting procedures. These funds would be used to support high-risk academic ventures. Packer's assumptions were that University Fellows might be involved in these ventures and that after a couple years of operation a successful innovation could be included in the course of normal budgetary deliberations of the University.

Packer's application was successful, and the program was begun in 1969. The Ford Foundation made a grant of one million dollars to be used over five years. This grant was to be matched by $200,000 of university funds also to be used over five years. These funds were to support both the Fellows Program and the Innovation Fund. During the first five years the faculty fellows received handsome support. They received significant relief from teaching and full summer salary. Later periods of the program have provided substantially less support for the fellows as individuals. The first fellows were appointed for the academic year 1969–70. Four faculty were appointed; they were J. Merrill Carlsmith, Psychology; Bradley Efron, Statistics; Robert Madix, Chemical Engineering; and Mark Mancall, History. Four administrative fellows were also appointed. Administrative fellows received no relief from duty or any special stipend. The administrative fellows appointed for that first year were Raymond Bacchetti, Associate Provost; Albert Hastorf, Dean of Humanities and Sciences; Lincoln Moses, Dean of Graduate Studies; and Herbert Packer, Vice Provost for Academic Planning. The first year of the program entailed regular meetings with the faculty and administrative fellows together. These meetings were usually held over dinner. The dinner discussions were far ranging. On occasion the dinner was preceded by a talk by an invited speaker.

Another feature of the program stemmed from a university fellow opting to attach himself or herself to the office of an academic administrator to observe the process and to develop or explore alternative problem-solving methods. This activity was encouraged by the released time during the early days of the Fellows Program. The clearest example of this process occurred when Merrill Carlsmith attached himself to the Office of the Dean of Graduate Studies. Carlsmith focused his attention on redesigning Stanford's system of graduate student support. A number of departments were very eager to guarantee support to all students admitted to the Ph.D. program.

The notion was that a student would know exactly where he or she stood, contingent upon satisfactory performance; there would be no ambiguity about the level of support they would receive. Carlsmith focused his attention on his own department, psychology, which already had a system that combined university fellowships, outside fellowships (National Institutes of Health [NIH] and National Science Foundation [NSF]), and teaching assistantship funds. This had worked very effectively in psychology, partly because of psychology's access to outside federal support. Carlsmith then focused his attention on the English Department and designed a program for them that combined university fellowships, teaching assistantships, and special fellowships into a guaranteed four-year support program. Stanford was able to develop this system because Carlsmith had the released time to work on the development of the program and to educate and convince the involved faculty members. He also had the significant support of the Dean of Graduate Studies, Lincoln Moses. This program did not make any special demand on the Innovation Fund.

The most noticeable and permanent project that began with the support of the Innovation Fund was the program in "Structured Liberal Education," which in time was abbreviated to "SLE." Along with the fund the vigorous and dedicated commitment of University Faculty Fellow Mark Mancall of the History Department, was crucial. Mancall was concerned about two things; one was the neglect, as he saw it, of the educational opportunities that could be available in student living groups on campus. The term *residential education* was not heard around the Stanford campus at that time. Mancall was also concerned about the excessive specialization of introductory courses and wanted to reinstitute the notion of a group of students studying various facets of our culture in a style that came to be termed Structured Liberal Education. He began this in a living unit (Grove House). Professor Mancall's personal commitment and intellectual liveliness were crucial to the success of this program. The Innovation Fund support was a necessary condition. SLE is still an active program at Stanford.

A final comment should be made about the original Fellows Program, that is, the dinner meetings and evening discussions that were held by the fellows. The fact that the fellows had a reduction in teaching load made these evening discussions more common (biweekly) and more relaxed. These meetings and discussions were held in someone's home, or sometimes in a restaurant or at the Faculty Club. The administrative fellows were expected to attend and, in general, did so. These social activities included the enjoyment of wine in an informal setting, and they were very important to the "acquaintance processes" amongst the fellows. During the first year this meant that an historian, a social psychologist, a statistician, and a chemist had the chance to discuss and debate events of the day, significant intellectual problems, or perhaps the impact of intercollegiate athletics on academia. These are processes that occur quite naturally in small liberal arts colleges where faculty of different disciplines become acquainted and establish lasting friendships. The University Fellows Program made this possible at Stanford.

No formal evaluation was made in the first year of the Fellows Program but there was a general feeling that the program was going well. During the second year two new fellows were added to the faculty roster. They were David Abernathy of Political Science and Edwin Good of Religious Studies. The administrative fellows remained the same. Attendance at the regular meetings was very high, and the discussion very vigorous.

# 2. Evaluations of the Program

There have been two relatively structured evaluations of the program. In January of 1974 Stanford submitted to the Ford Foundation a proposal to make the University Fellows Program permanent by reducing the level of support to the fellows, dropping the Innovation Fund, and slowly increasing University-based support. Fellows would be appointed for two years; they would not have the substantial released time that the first fellows received, but they could combine one quarter of relief time with two months of summer support providing a block of time for special projects. The University's proposal to the Ford Foundation requested that it provide a transitional grant of $100,000 that would be used to buttress the University's input of budget-based support, which would provide, in the end, $40,000 a year to support six fellows. The evaluation provided to the Ford Foundation was based upon brief essays submitted by the fellows themselves. "A central tendency of the fellows' reflections suggested that the program reduced the we/they syndrome in faculty/administrative affairs. Fellows increased their understanding of the University: how multiple its goals are, how broadly power and authority are distributed, and how complex are its internal and external relations. Overall, one is struck by the ways in which the fellows speak of how they have changed in their views of the University."[2] A few selected quotes from the Fellows Memoranda illustrate the point:

Participation in the Fellows Program will make it more difficult
for me to assume a parochial departmental outlook when I return (to my department) in 1974.

(The Fellows Program) gave me time to think about a general
university problem.

I feel that the fellows offered one of the few opportunities in
which people from quite different backgrounds can discuss important University affairs in an atmosphere of mutual respect.

As for my own future (i.e., post fellow) life at Stanford, I'll always see it from ... an enlarged perspective.

My paranoid feeling that there were unseen forces controlling
my life at Stanford have been markedly relieved now that (I see
that) the institution is so diverse and diffuse that the central
administration can only guide, not dictate.

Being a university fellow does facilitate and expand the opportunities of becoming a university citizen.

It is pertinent to quote a prescient paragraph from the 1974 proposal.
"The stresses of the past few years and those projected for the future are
resulting in more centralized control, more management, and, by implication, less informality, collegiality, and faculty self-determination. Moves
in this direction will surely tend to open the very same divisions that the
Fellows Program seems so effective in narrowing."[3]
    The program continued through 1984, when another evaluation was
done by a committee of three fellows: Robert Rabin, Law School; Ewart
Thomas, Department of Psychology; and Nancy Tuma, Department of Sociology. They received comments from 14 administrative fellows out of 23
requests, and from 9 faculty fellows out of 22 requests.[4] The judgments
were very positive and it was recommended that the program be continued,
but with reduced budgetary support so that the major support was for one

three-month leave of each fellow (to accomplish a project) and for the regular dinner meetings which were preceded by presentations and discussions. The discussions were usually stimulated by an invited speaker.

In 1990, and then again in 1993, Professor Herant Katchadourian, who was at both these times serving as the coordinator of the program, recommended to the President and the Provost that the program be continued but that it be organized primarily around the dinner meetings, usually begun by a guest speaker. Katchadourian proposed eliminating any stipend for released time to the faculty fellows thus making them equivalent in support to the administrative fellows. The program was continued within the guidelines of Katchadourian's proposals; specifically, there would no longer be any sort of stipend, but there would be continuing support of the dinner meetings and other such get-togethers.[5]

Before turning to a brief summary of our interviews with past and present fellows, I should like to summarize some statistical descriptions of the fellows. These descriptions will be of the faculty fellows. On average, there were six to seven faculty fellows serving in an academic year, and fellows' terms, originally three years, were eventually reduced to two years. Added to faculty fellows would be an approximately equal number of administrative fellows. The administrative fellows usually came from the following groups: academic deans, senior members of the Provost's staff, senior members of non-academic administrative units and, as often as possible, a member of the Board of Trustees who lived near enough to the campus to make attendance possible. Various individuals have served as coordinator of the program; two should be mentioned explicitly. Ray Bacchetti, of the Provost's staff, played a crucial coordinating role early in the life of the program. Herant Katchadourian, who was one of the early faculty fellows (1971–72) has played a significant role as coordinator of the program in its latter years. His role has been especially important because the program operated on such a restricted budget.

How many people have served as faculty fellows? The program began in 1969–70 and is still going. Table 8.1 describes the demographics of the faculty fellows. Table 8.2 presents the numerical representation among the fellows by the various schools.

TABLE 8.1
*Fellow Demographics*

|        | Non-minority | Minority |
|--------|--------------|----------|
| Male   | 51           | 9        |
| Female | 17           | 2        |

TABLE 8.2
*Distribution by Schools*

| | |
|---|---|
| Business | 1 |
| Earth Sciences | 3 |
| Education | 6 |
| Engineering | 8 |
| Law | 5 |
| Medicine | 10 |
| Humanities and Sciences | 46 |
|     Humanities | 17 |
|     Sciences | 9 |
|     Social Science | 20 |

Not surprisingly, the majority of fellows came from the School of Humanities and Sciences. What is somewhat surprising is the extraordinarily small representation from the Graduate School of Business, with only one fellow. It would be very interesting to see some count of University Fellowships offered and refused. It could be said that during the period of the University Fellowship Program the zeitgeist of the Business School was dominated by a push in the direction of specialization and a peer culture dominated by research productivity. These were the norms that Herbert Packer saw as promoting centrifugal forces. It is likely that a number of the younger faculty in the Business School that showed academic-statesmen-like tendencies were rather quickly recruited into administrative services in that school as associate deans and/or the directors of programs. The same explanation would apply to the relatively low representation from the School of Engineering, where the centrifugal forces were very strong. The low representation of the Sciences is probably to be explained by the abovementioned centrifugal forces.

The contribution of the "graduates" of the University Fellows Program has been truly outstanding, although it is important to remind ourselves that one of the major selection criteria were signs of talent in research and teaching coupled with eagerness to contribute to the University as a whole.

On average fellows were 41 years of age during their first year of the fellowship; 31 years is the youngest age and 57, the oldest. Fifty-three out of the 79 have served in the Faculty Senate. On average they served five years, which means they have been reelected at least once. Five served as the elected Chair of the Senate, three have been elected to the Advisory Board, 68 of the 79 fellows have served on at least one University-wide committee. The 79 fellows have been appointed to 390 committees. Six former fellows have become deans of schools, 13 have been associate deans in schools, 19 have become chairs of their departments, one has become provost, three have become vice provosts, two have become director of the overseas study program. Very few former fellows left Stanford. Two former fellows have left the University for nonacademic jobs. One is a senior executive of a consulting firm, the other an officer in a professional association. A small number are deceased. A small number have retired. A total of five left for other universities: two for professorships in the Ivys, two to the University of California (one Berkeley, one UCLA); and one has become the president of a distinguished liberal arts college in New England. This is an impressive list of contributions to the faculty governance of the University. It would be too strong to conclude that participation in the fellows program "caused" this substantial contribution. Without, question, however, participation in the program maintained and encouraged whatever nascent talents and interests existed.

## 3. Interviews with Former Fellows

During the spring of 1994 we were able to interview fifteen former and present fellows; nine of them men and six of them women. Six of the fifteen are current fellows, and nine are former fellows. The majority of the group were faculty fellows, with a small number of administrative fellows.

All of the interviewees were asked to say something about themselves and their backgrounds. They were then asked a series of questions that entailed their explaining the program as they saw it and what they saw as its strengths and weaknesses. They were also encouraged to discuss any ways it had changed them. During the interview they were encouraged to make suggestions about how this Program could be improved. The interviewees represented both the School of Humanities and Sciences and the professional schools.

Because the interviews with the former fellows were made in confidence we shall develop only a summary of what the former fellows had to say. First of all, we should say something about "credit." A number of the fellows volunteered that participation in the Fellows Program had made a very real difference to them in their understanding of both the University and themselves. One of them said, "it made Stanford a more interesting place." Another said that both he and other fellows experienced a broader loyalty to the University as a whole. A number of them mentioned that the Fellows Program gave them a greater understanding of the University as a whole. A number of the older fellows reported their awareness of the importance of Herbert Packer to both the birth and the ethos of the program. Older fellows also mentioned Ray Bacchetti as an early coordinator. More recent fellows have mentioned Herant Katchadourian in the same role.

An interesting set of statements was made by a large number of fellows about the development of close relationships. Interviewees said such things as "The other fellows became my close friends" and "I never felt as close to members of my own department as I did to the other fellows"; "It was fun to be with smart people and talk about things—that is why I came to a university to begin with"; "There were no petty squabbles." Although just about all the interviewees talked of the advantages of learning about various administrative issues in the University, especially the nonacademic ones, and their having gained a lot from presentations by University administrators, they kept coming back to the importance of developing close relationships with people from other departments and schools.

The former fellows all seemed to be perfectly aware of their tendency to be overrepresented on University committees and in administrative posts. Many of them were not sure that being a fellow had caused that. They all granted that what they had learned as fellows about the University had helped them in their tasks and that the friendships they developed had helped them. It is interesting to note that a number of them who had been fellows at an earlier time volunteered how much they missed the fellows' reunion dinners with a guest speaker that used to occur annually. We can infer that these dinners were dropped for budgetary reasons.

When asked about changes they would suggest, some of the younger faculty fellows expressed some concern about the dinners invading the small amount of time that they had to spend with their spouses and most especially young children. These individuals granted the value of these informal get-togethers but wondered if some rearrangement of the time for such activities could be worked out.

The most common suggestion for change was decidedly task oriented; it was that the Program might develop more "structure" or more "focus." What they seemed to be getting at was the possibility of the fellows' take on some task to "get something done." One of the older fellows put it this way: "I don't know whether the fellows themselves could take on collective kinds of issues; I'm sort of toying with that idea, about whether the fellows as a group could say. 'there's something real important going on, and so as a group we're all going to pay attention to it." Another said, "There's an awful lot of brain power here, and it seems as though we ought to work on a common problem."

Our summary evaluation certainly smacks of repeating earlier evaluations. The vast majority of faculty fellows very much enjoyed the Program. The addition of some administrative fellows who had previously had very little contact with the faculty, perhaps from the Business Office or the Development Office, seems to have been a positive step both for the faculty and for those administrative fellows. the addition of one trustee fellow also appeared to be a very good idea, although their attendance was somewhat uneven.

What strikes one upon reading the various evaluation essays is that the centrifugal forces that Packer was first concerned about remain with us. Beyond that, the central administrations of research universities have been forced to engage in "more centralized control, more management and, by implication, less informality, collegiality and faculty self-determination."[6] The development of processes that promote collegiality, informal acquaintance, and cooperation across disciplinary lines are more important than ever. The University Fellows Program may not have been a panacea, but it has certainly been a counterforce to the centrifugal forces that first bothered Herbert Packer. One can wish it continued health.

## Acknowledgments

Warm thanks are due to members of the Provost's staff who provided historical information, to Jennifer Randall, who interviewed former fellows and assembled information, and to my secretary, Eleanor Walker, who provided a multitude of services.

## Notes

[1] "Academic Statesmen", a second proposal from Professor Packer to Ford Foundation, May 15, 1968, Provost's Office.

[2] "A Proposal to the Ford Foundation in Respect to the University Fellows Program of Stanford University, January 1974," Provost's Office.

[3] Ibid.

[4] Robert Rabin, Ewart Thomas, Nancy Tuma, "An Evaluation of the University Fellows Program, March 1984," Provost's Office.

[5] H. Katchadourian to Donald Kennedy and James Rosse, June 13, 1990, Provost's Office; and H. Katchadourian to Gerhard Casper and Gerald Lieberman, January 13, 1993, Provost's Office.

[6] "A Proposal to the Ford Foundation in Respect to the University Fellows Program of Stanford University, January 1974," Provost's Office.

# Chapter 9

# Why a Medical School in a Research University

## Saul A. Rosenberg

In the modern era, physicians in the United States receive their undergraduate education (pre-M.D.) in medical schools associated with universities. There are sufficient differences in the culture and processes of
the medical school with its teaching hospital(s) and its parent university
to question why they should be part of the same academic enterprise. Indeed, some university faculty suggest that medical education and faculty
are not academic at all. Some of these issues and related questions are
greatly magnified when costs, budgets, faculty-student ratios, tenure and
postgraduate (post-M.D.) training programs are examined more closely.

The education and training of physicians differs from that in other professional schools of the university in that the "laboratory" for their education is the clinic and the hospital. Medical schools, therefore, require
affiliations with and dependence on clinical facilities. Often those facilities
and enterprises are totally controlled, even owned, by the universities in
the form of university hospitals and clinics. The teaching of medicine is
done in the context of patient care. Medical schools and their teachers
strive to provide the highest possible quality of patient care while teaching
and training students. It is also the mission of medical schools and their
faculty to perform research and create new knowledge. This is done in two

general settings, though they may overlap, in so-called basic science (in the laboratory) and in clinical science (with patients). The medical school also has the responsibility to train researchers, to prepare the investigators and teachers of the future.

Only the basic science preparation of the medical student, usually confined to the first two years of medical school, resembles the undergraduate university experience. Lectures and laboratory experiences are comparable to those found in biology, chemistry, and physics courses of the university. For the next period of medical student education, usually two years, and for their postgraduate education, another three to ten years, the teaching methods are very different. The education of the advanced medical student, postgraduate, and researcher early in his or her career is much more as an apprentice. Large lectures are rare, replaced by small group discussions, seminars, and role playing under gradually decreasing supervision. There is nothing quite like this in the humanities departments of the university or even in the other professional schools.

It is possible that basic-science departments and courses such as Biochemistry and Genetics could remain within the appropriate science departments of the university rather than within the medical school. This was the arrangement at Stanford prior to 1959. Such a separation fails to recognize the continuum of basic to clinical science not only for the translation of new knowledge to clinical practice, but also for the teaching of medical students.

The economics of the total medical education of the physician is vastly different from that of both the undergraduate and graduate programs of most of the university. The faculty-student ratio, salaries paid to clinical faculty, costly modern laboratory and hospital equipment, and the dependence on soft money sources are some of the factors involved in this expense. Only a small fraction of this cost could be recovered by increasing medical students' tuition, which would also increase their financial debt at graduation beyond the approximately $50,000 per student that they currently bear. The costs must be borne by the medical school and teaching hospital, and at Stanford, by a "formula" arrangement that protects the University from medical school costs and potential debt.

I could continue developing in great detail the significant differences between medical education (and resources) and those of its parent university.

Rather, I would like to emphasize how necessary it is for medical education to remain an integral component of the university. The medical school faculty must have all the attributes of the university professoriate, and it is essential for great research universities to foster and cherish great research medical schools and hospitals. There is need in the medical school for scholars and scholarship. There is need for rigor in appointments, promotion, and conferral of tenure. And there is the need and the opportunity for new knowledge. Those attributes, so characteristic of our great universities, should not be compromised because of the unique and very real differences between a medical school and a university.

The faculty of the medical schools often have difficulty in defining and demanding of their clinical faculty university standards of scholarship. These faculty are usually physicians who must have the appropriate background and credentials of excellent clinicians, that is, patient-care providers. This requires a prolonged full-time concentration in clinical training which may require three to six years or more after receiving the M.D. degree. It is challenging for those physicians also to obtain the experience and credentials to become first-class researchers, comparable to other university faculty. Although some physician-researchers have gone through the rigor of a Ph.D. education, receiving that degree, most have not. They have obtained their scientific research training before, or after, and sometimes intermingled with their clinical education.

Yet, the attributes of the scholar, who understands and uses the scientific method and seeks new knowledge through creative research are essential for the medical school faculty. The standards and processes of the leading research university must be adhered to, imposed if necessary, on the research medical school to assure that its quality and excellence are comparable to the rest of the university. The pressures are great in a medical school to appoint and retain faculty who have strong clinical qualifications, to provide the important service needs of the clinic and hospital. As important as that need may be, only mediocrity will result if the importance of scholarship and research are too often and too greatly compromised. This importance can be maintained only by the university's insistence on the application of the same definitions of excellence, search, process, and peer review to appointments and promotions for the medical school faculty as those required for the general university faculty.

This is difficult to establish and ascertain. The culture of the medical schools, especially of the clinical fields, is very different from those of most of the fields and disciplines of the parent university. Medical school faculty rarely write books, rarely write single-authored papers, and may be known nationally to only a narrow group of subspecialists. These differences must be acknowledged and dealt with, without compromising the need for excellence, creativity, and peer review.

Research must be a major mission of a medical school, especially a school within a research university. The discoveries and understanding in the biomedical fields are as exciting and profound in their implications as any within the university. The impact of discovering the truths in biology and medicine have a very great potential to influence the human condition. This is the appropriate endeavor of the research university, requiring all the scholarship and freedom of inquiry that the university imposes upon itself and its faculty.

Research excellence and commitment is also necessary to maintain and assure the quality of the educational mission of the medical school. Without the curiosity, objectivity, and excitement that are the nature of the researcher, teachers become outdated and biased and lack the stimulation required of the educational process.

A significant factor leading to a poor appreciation of the commonality of goals of the university and medical school faculty is unfamiliarity. The medical school faculty are so preoccupied by their multiple missions and responsibilities that they do not adequately participate in general university affairs. This may be aggravated by a sense of inferiority that many medical school faculty feel. They come to believe they are not as intellectual, not as educated, not as scholarly as their university colleagues.

This is simply not true. The cultures may be different. The educational experiences and pathways may be different. But the quantity and breadth of their education and experience are no less than those of their university colleagues. The attraction of medicine as a career for some of this country's brightest young people is well known to university faculty. Those that choose medicine over the humanities or pure science do so, as a rule, for the highest of motives. They want to combine intellectual challenge with a desire to be humanitarian. They want the interpersonal relationship and rewards of helping other people. As well, they want to be respected in their communities and have a secure livelihood. These goals are not inherently less valuable than those of their nonprofessional academic colleagues.

The medical school faculty must be encouraged to participate, early in their academic career, in university affairs. By sharing administrative and committee assignments with their university counterparts, mutual respect and trust will develop. Medical school faculty have much to contribute to undergraduate advising, curricular affairs, and university governance. And they have much to learn in all of these areas from the experience.

The field of medicine cannot and should not be isolated from academia. The body of knowledge we call medicine is too significant and too far-reaching in our society to be separated from the highest standards of scholarship, education, and research.

# Chapter 10

# Education and Technology at Stanford in the Twenty-first Century

## Patrick Suppes

## 1. Historical Perspective

To put into historical perspective the great educational innovations of the past, there are at least five major technological innovations comparable to the current computer revolution: written records, libraries, printing, mass schooling, and testing.

### 1.1. Written Records

The first major educational innovation was the use of written records in ancient times for teaching. We do not know exactly when such use began, but we do have, as early as Plato's Dialogues, written in the fifth century B.C., sophisticated objections to their use.

Today no one would doubt the value of written material in education, but there were strong and cogent objections to this earliest innovation in education. The objections were these: a written record is impersonal; it is very uniform; it does not adapt to the individual student; it does not establish rapport with the student. Socrates and the Sophists, the tutors of students in ancient Athens, objected to introducing written records and destroying the essential personal relation between student and tutor. (For a detailed statement of this position, see Plato's *Phaedrus*, 273–76.)

It has become a familiar story in our own time that a technological innovation has side effects that are not always uniformly beneficial. It is important to recognize that this is not a new aspect of innovation but has been with us from the beginning.

## 1.2. Libraries

The second innovation was the founding of libraries in the ancient world, the most important example being the famous Alexandrian Library established around 300 B.C. (For a detailed presentation of the society and culture of Ptolemaic Alexandria, see Fraser 1972.) Because of certain democratic traditions and the preeminence of the creative work in philosophy and poetry, it is easy to think of Athens as the intellectual center of the Hellenic world. In fact, that center was Alexandria. From about 250 B.C. to 400 A.D. not only was Alexandria the most important center of mathematics and astronomy in the ancient world, it was also a major center of literature, especially because of the collection in the Alexandrian Library. The first critical literary scholarship in the Western world—the editing of texts, the analysis of style, and the compiling of bibliographies—took place there. This revolution in education consisted not simply of having in one place a large number of papyrus manuscripts but in the organization of large bodies of learning. Scholars from all over the Western world came to Alexandria to study and to talk to others. Substantial libraries existed also in other major cities of the ancient Mediterranean cultures and in China, India, and Korea.

## 1.3. Printing

The third innovation of great historical importance in education was the move from written records to printed books. In the West the printing of the Gutenberg Bible in 1452 marks the beginning date of this innovation. It is important to recognize, however, that block printing was used extensively in Korea and China three or four hundred years earlier (Carter 1955). The earliest printed book comes from China and is dated 868, but there is much evidence of block printing at least for the preceding hundred years. Nearly half a millennium later, it is difficult to have a vivid sense of how important the innovation of printing turned out to be. No more than five major libraries existed in the ancient world of the Mediterranean. In 100 B.C., the Alexandrian Library had few competitors; it was impossible for many copies of manuscripts to be reproduced when all copying had to be done tediously by hand. The introduction of printing in the fifteenth century produced a radical innovation—indeed, a revolution—in the distribution of intellectual and educational materials. By the middle of the sixteenth century, not only European institutions but wealthy families as well had large libraries.

Once again, however, there were definite technological side effects that were not uniformly beneficial. Those who know the beauty of the medieval manuscripts that preceded the introduction of printing can appreciate that mass printing was regarded by some as a degradation of the art of reproduction.

It is also important to have a sense of how slow the effect of a technological innovation can sometimes be. Not until the end of the eighteenth century were books used extensively for teaching in schools. In arithmetic, for example, most teachers continued to use oral methods throughout the nineteenth century; appropriate elementary textbooks in mathematics were not available until the beginning of the present century. Fortunately, the time scale of dissemination in the modern world is of an entirely different order from what it was in the past. Perhaps my favorite example is the estimate that it took more than five years for the news of Julius Caesar's assassination to reach the farthest corners of the Roman Empire. Today such an event would be known throughout the world in a matter of minutes.

It was not unusual for methods of recitation to be used in the elementary school until the nineteenth century; the same was true at some universities. According to at least one account the last professor at Cambridge University in England who insisted on following the recitative tradition, which dates back to the Middle Ages, was C. D. Broad. As late as the 1940's, he dictated, and then repeated, each sentence so that students would have adequate time to write it down exactly as dictated.

## 1.4. Mass Schooling

The fourth innovation, and again one that we now accept as a complete and natural part of our society, is mass schooling. We have a tendency in talking about our society to put schools and families into the same category of major institutions, but there is a great psychological difference between the status of the family and the status of schools. The family is an integral part of our culture. The evidence that families in one form or another have been our most important cultural unit goes back thousands of years. Schools are, by contrast, a recent innovation in our culture. In 1870, for example, only 2% of young people graduated from high school in the United States. One hundred years before that, only a very small percentage finished even third or fourth grade.

In most of the world, less than 1% of the population completed secondary school as recently as 50 years ago. In many developing countries today the best that can be hoped is that the majority of young people will receive four years of elementary-school education. Until population growth slows down, it will take all available resources to achieve that much.

The position of the United States as a world leader in education is sometimes not adequately recognized, though U.S. leadership in creating a society with mass education is one of the most important aspects of American influence in the world. The worldwide revolution in mass schooling is one of the most striking phenomena of the twentieth century.

## 1.5. Testing

The fifth educational innovation is testing, which is in many ways older than mass schooling. The great tradition of testing was first established in China; testing there began in the fifth century A.D. and became firmly entrenched by the twelfth century A.D. Tests were used continuously from the twelfth century through the nineteenth century in the selection of mandarins, the civil servants who ran the imperial government of China. The civil service positions held by mandarins were regarded as the elite social positions in the society. A variety of documents attests to the importance of these tests in Chinese society (for a recent overview, see Chaffee 1985). In examining the literature of the fifteenth or sixteenth century, for example, one is impressed by the concern expressed over performance on tests.

Literary tales often focused on the question whether sons would successfully complete the tests and what this would mean for the family. (In those days women had no place in the formal management of the society and no place as applicants for civil service positions.) The procedures of selection were as rigorous as those found in a contemporary medical school or a graduate school of business in the United States or Canada. In many periods, fewer than 2% of those who began the tests, which were arranged in a complicated hierarchy, successfully completed the sequence and were put on the list of eligible mandarins.

Although the history of testing goes back hundreds of years, in many ways it is proper to regard it as a twentieth-century innovation. Scientific and technical study of tests began only in this century, with a serious effort to understand and to define what constitutes a good test for a given aptitude, a given achievement, or a given skill.

The five innovations I have discussed—written records, libraries, printing, mass schooling, and tests—are the very fabric of our educational system today. It is almost impossible to contemplate education without each of these innovations playing an important part. Of these five technologies, the effect of none was adequately forecast at the time of introduction. Of course, a few individuals foresaw some of the consequences and had something to say about them, but the details were not accurately foreseen. No doubt the same will prove true of technologies now developing.

# 2. What Computers and Telecommunication Offer

What I have to say about the use of computers and telecommunication in education in the 21st century will also probably fall in the category of inaccurate prognostication. (For a summary of early efforts at Stanford when interactive computers had been around for less than a decade, see the two books, Suppes, Jerman and Brian 1968 and Suppes and Morningstar 1972.)   The technology and its applications are changing too quickly for one to make accurate predictions for the next century. All the same, there are several salient points about the future I want to emphasize.

## 2.1. Speech

In a variety of publications on computer applications ranging from automobiles to factories, the usefulness of speech has been emphasized. Yet I think it is fair to say that the most extended and most sophisticated use of computer-generated speech will be in education. The computers that are used for instruction twenty years from now will, almost without question, no longer be silent but fully talking and listening and doing so with a great deal of instructional sophistication. The silent computers that dominate the present scene will definitely be a thing of the past by the end of the 21st century.

## 2.2. Diversity

The second point of saliency will be the great diversity of courses that will be available. Because of budgetary constraints there has been a tendency over the past few years to reduce the variety of course offerings in colleges and universities, and also to some extent at the secondary-school level as well. This tendency I see being reversed and being reversed in a dramatic way by computers and telecommunications. Courses of a highly specialized and technical nature or, if not technical, of an esoteric nature, can be offered to a very small number of students. Moreover, they can be offered in a manner that will be economical, just as it is now economical to publish a book that has a worldwide circulation of perhaps a thousand. I see technology-based instruction as being a major force for increasing the diversity and richness of what is offered in education at all levels.

## 2.3. Individualization

What are the arguments for the individualized instruction computers can offer? First, and above all, computers offer immediate attention to individual responses. Second, computers can correct these responses and convey information about their character, especially when the student's answers are incorrect. Third, computers can adapt the pace of instruction in delicate and subtle ways to the individual student's pace of learning. Relatively simple computer systems can give us these three features, together with the virtue of the student's actively participating as opposed to passively listening.

## 2.4. Cognitive Models

Our ambitions for good computer instruction will not stop with the phenomenological features of a good tutor; we want more. We want good instructional programs also to have a good cognitive model of the student and his learning problems. (For a current survey of models in psychology, see Suppes, Pavel, and Falmagne 1994.) A good tutor intuitively has a sense of what is going on in the head of the student, but ordinarily a good tutor does not have an explicit cognitive theory of how the student is solving problems and why he is getting stuck in his problem-solving efforts. Some aspects of the process seem extraordinarily mysterious, but we should be able to make significant progress on such cognitive models even if some questions are still unanswered a century from now.

## 2.5. Accessibility of Information

The transformation of learning that will take place because of the increased accessibility of information will be greater than that which occurred with the creation of the Alexandrian Library more than two thousand years ago. Scholars of the ancient world properly stood in awe of the resources at Alexandria. The kinds of resources that were brought together there in one place will be available through computers and telecommunications in every nook and cranny of every country. The greatest potential effect of this availability of information by electronic means is the decentralization of our schools, universities, and other parts of our society, a topic that I shall examine at greater length later in this essay.

## 2.6. Augmented Technical Skills

We are all familiar with the kinds of problems that can be tackled with current computers that were simply out of reach even thirty or forty years ago. These problems range from massive computations about the weather to linear models applied to every sort of problem from medicine to economics. Students in undergraduate classes now routinely perform numerical calculations that were unheard of thirty or forty years ago and that were impossible fifty or sixty years ago. Such numerical power will continue to increase, and the number-crunching computers of today are rapidly being joined by symbol-crunching computers of comparable power. We expect symbolic analysis at our fingertips, whether it be applied to the structure of DNA, to a complicated mathematical equation that has to be transformed, or to a mathematical proof that needs completion of its combinatorial parts. We have become, both in instruction and research, as dependent on symbol crunchers as on number crunchers. The effect of these two in combination with access by telecommunication to highly specialized resources will be to augment our technical skills, and the sophisticated instruction we expect in technical skills, far beyond anything we have seen up to the present.

There is some reason to think that scientific development in many disciplines will become increasingly complex. A thesis that science will keep unifying and keep simplifying is, in my judgment, much more a romantic hope than a conclusion supported by the actual development of science over the past fifty years. If my skeptical view of unity is at all close to the truth, the problems of instruction will become ever more difficult. We will need every possible resource to augment our technical skills. Computers and telecommunications will be by far and away the most important means for doing so.

## 3. Institutional Change

The continuing developments in computers and telecommunication sketched but in no sense described in detail in the last section will have a profound effect on higher education in the 21st century. (For a detailed review of the first such experiments at Stanford, see Suppes 1981.) That effect will, in my judgment, be as profound as the most important revolution in education in the 20th century, namely, the introduction of mass schooling in most parts of the world. Although this century has seen also far and away the most massive increase in higher education in the history of the world, in many respects the way in which colleges and universities conduct their business is not too dissimilar from the way it was conducted as long ago as the 18th century or at least the 19th century. Students going to college in 1890 did not have in fundamental ways a different psychological experience from those going to school in the 1990's. It will be very surprising if this is still true in the 2090's.

I have organized my remarks about predicted changes at Stanford, but what I have to say will undoubtedly apply as well to comparable institutions. Whether the predictions are made for Stanford or for other institutions they are bound to be badly inaccurate as the 21st century progresses. The details as I sketch them are surely wrong. The general ideas should be grossly right. I have organized my remarks into three sections before, at, and after Stanford. What I mean by these headings will become clear in what follows.

## 3.1. Before Stanford

An appreciable number of entering Stanford undergraduates have essentially a year's college credit of work completed in the form of Advanced Placement exams. It is easy enough for a bright Stanford student to complete in high school the Advanced Placement exams in English, mathematics, history, one or two of the sciences, and some foreign language, in order to have full credit for a first year of college. Such students, if they so desired, could easily graduate in three years. I am not saying that they want to or even that it is the desirable thing to do. It is just that the opportunity is already there by completion of Advanced Placement courses in high school to have finished the first year before arrival. But this is only the tip of the iceberg. It is quite clear that the top 10 or 15% of the students entering Stanford could easily have completed a second year if technology had been used appropriately to offer courses to them.

Let me speak from some personal examples. For the past several years I and my colleagues have been running through the Continuing Studies Program at Stanford, the Educational Program for Gifted Youth (EPGY). We have been offering by computer and telecommunication university-level courses for very bright students in secondary schools, especially schools close to Stanford, but increasingly to students not in schools immediately adjacent to Stanford. The very best of these students are capable of finishing the Advanced Placement courses, not as graduating seniors, but in or tenth grades. (For a detailed report on the test results for the past several years, see Ravaglia, Suppes, Stillinger, and Alper, 1995.) By the time the top students are juniors in high school they will have completed the equivalent of a full year of college work and can now complete in their junior and senior years at least one more year. How should that be done?

In general terms, Stanford should admit such students early and encourage their continued rapid progress. A concrete proposal, but only one of many possible, is for Stanford to admit students who have completed the kind of Advanced Placement program I mentioned by the end of the tenth grade. But, unlike the old Hutchins program at the University of Chicago, this program does not mean that they should come to Stanford at the time when they would ordinarily be juniors in high school. They stay in place in their high schools, but in agreement with the high schools, by computer and telecommunication, Stanford offers them courses beyond advanced placement in mathematics, science, English, and foreign languages. It might even be that Stanford would not grant university credit for the learning of elementary foreign languages, something that should be really a responsibility of the high schools. However, in case the students want to learn such languages as Chinese, Japanese, or Russian, it might well be their high school does not offer them. Stanford, as part of its preparation of these students, would give them intensive work in these languages in their last two years of high school.

More important, beyond the Advanced Placement courses in mathematics and physics, the next level of Stanford undergraduate courses in mathematics and physics could be offered to the students in their last two years of high school with Stanford credit. Remember, I am talking about the top 10 or 15% of students admitted at Stanford. These students could certainly carry such a work load in these last two years. The minimum would permit them to finish the equivalent of a Stanford year and also complete some of the other standard high school requirements. More important than these standard academic high school requirements would be the fact that they were remaining in the social setting of their high school, living and learning with their social peers and remaining through their early adolescent years at home. I am skeptical that even in the 21st century we shall want to have a deluge of fifteen and sixteen year olds on the campuses of residential universities such as Stanford. What we want to do is educate them when young, but not be responsible for prematurely transferring them from home to college residence.

High school graduation should ordinarily be easy enough to orchestrate by arranging with the appropriate credentialing authorities for dual credit to be received for standard university courses taken during high school years. In some states the authority to grant such credit is decentralized to local school boards, in others it remains the responsibility of the state educational agency. In any case, such arrangements should not be difficult, particularly in view of the fact that in most cases the high schools will be supported in their usual way with a Stanford student counting as part of the average daily attendance for that high school, the basis for funding from state or local authorities.

To give you a sense that these possibilities are real and not ones that I am simply imagining, I will quote to you a few statistics from our recent EPGY results at Stanford. The youngest student in our program to complete the course for the second Advanced Placement exam in mathematics, that is, the BC Advanced Placement exam in calculus, was at the time a seventh grader. The youngest student to complete the course for the mechanics exam with a calculus prerequisite was an eighth grader, and the same student completed the course and took the electricity and magnetism exam with a calculus prerequisite as a ninth grader. But what we are offering, although still special, does not involve just single students. In 1993 in the whole of the United States there were only eight students in the ninth grade or earlier who took the mechanics Advanced Placement exam with a calculus prerequisite (1993 AP National Summary Report Tables). Of those eight students, five were students in EPGY at Stanford. Their grades were: three 5's, the top grade, one 4 and one 3. These striking results do not mean that we simply had an unusual distribution of gifted students available to us, it means that most very able students were simply not given the opportunity to take such courses at an early age, even though they were quite competent to do so.

Finally, to finish out this discussion of before Stanford, there would be nothing that would do more to promote a larger number of these students than a general decision at Stanford to run the kind of program I have described. It would encourage in many ways bright students to go ahead and complete the Advanced Placement courses at an early age, so they could move on to early admission at Stanford while still remaining at home.

## 3.2. At Stanford

Stanford students, under the setup envisaged, would arrive in a large number of cases with at least a year's work done and in some cases at least two years. For those students who did not get a fast start—and after all some of the best and brightest are late bloomers—there would be other makeup procedures Stanford could offer. Perhaps one of the best examples would be in the area of foreign languages. Consider a student who starts late but discovers he or she really wants to specialize in the economics or politics of the Pacific Rim. For this purpose he or she wants to learn both Chinese and Japanese and as yet he or she has not really started either one of these languages. That student could already begin in the summer prior to arriving on campus by taking, while still at home, an intensive course in Chinese or Japanese. This work could continue during the first year, and then a similar intensive course could be offered in the summer after the student's freshman year. These courses might not receive college credit, as we gradually eliminate such credit for elementary language learning, but the skills could be acquired and the language would be under command. This is just one example of the way in which technology could be used to facilitate a late-blooming student's needs.

While on campus a student's room would, as the 21st century progresses, increasingly be converted into a sophisticated learning center. I do not mean to suggest that students will spend most of their time in their rooms listening, looking, and responding to electronic instruction; I just mean that rich resources will be available to them, and if they do not want to attend lectures, they can look at and listen to those lectures remotely. In some cases in fact, the lectures may only be offered this way. What is more important, really, is the way in which instruction will change. The 50-minute lecture, at least in the sciences, will probably disappear and be replaced by something much more interactive and much more individualized.

In this connection I must mention one experiment I did a good many years ago with Stanford students (Crothers and Suppes 1967, p. 168). This was a study of students learning an initial segment of Russian under different regimes of instruction. The model we had for distributed learning worked rather well, but what was really surprising about the experiment were the large differences in the individual learning rates of relatively homogeneous Stanford students. The difference between the rate of learning of the slowest and the fastest of this relatively homogeneous group was astounding. (With a mean on the final test of 129 correct responses out

of 300, the range was 78 to 189 for the twenty students who were the subjects in the experiment.)  No doubt the same is true of the learning of
mathematics and physics. This suggests that lectures are a poor way of
adapting to the individual differences of students. The technology will be
used effectively in the next century to make such accommodation.

It might sound as if I were recommending the elimination of all group
learning activities, such as lectures, quiz sections, and seminars. Nothing
could be further from the truth. It is just that lectures have the wrong
natural lockstep. The brightest student in physics can look out the window
most of the time during lectures, while the slowest one is struggling to
follow an introductory course in quantum mechanics. Working together in
the laboratory on projects, doing complicated problem sets together, and
engaging in similar activities should certainly continue and be extended.

But what, above all, should be extended in a very definite way beyond
what is now the case is the teaching of seminars by faculty at all levels. It is
in the seminar room, with interaction, conversation, dialogue, and mutual
challenges, that much of the education at Stanford in the 21st century
should take place. This kind of education is expensive and extraordinarily
labor intensive. It is just for this reason that we should use technology to
do all of the preparation whenever possible. In subjects with an enormous
systematic development, such as mathematics or physics, or in subjects
in which students can be led into dialogue and discussion relatively easily,
such as philosophy, students should be brought to the frontiers by whatever
means possible and as rapidly as possible.

For example, in terms of this rapid approach to the frontiers, students
who enter Stanford with two years already completed should be ready by
what would be their third year on campus to begin intensive graduate
work and to be ready for intensive seminars in physics by what would be
their fourth year on campus. Maybe these seminars, in the case of physics,
would consist of participating in some experimental work, but whatever the
various approaches, what should be foremost in the instructional effort is
to get the student to the seminar level as rapidly as possible. It is this kind
of instruction that will return us to the glories of the Sophists in ancient
Athens but at a different level and with very much of a different subject
matter in mind. It is not the subject matter but the human interaction
that was valuable and remains valuable now. It may well be that a good

part of the role of the Sophists will be replaced by extraordinarily smart computer programs that talk, listen, and engage the student in challenging dialogue. But I am not sure that anything as bright and wonderful as this will be available even at the end of the next century. Without it we can still make wondrous progress.

### 3.3. After Stanford

Stanford has an active alumni association and the participation of many alumni in various activities, but what should be the level of their participation in the next century? We already have legislation on the books in many states requiring professionals from accountants to pharmacists to take regular continuing education courses of a certified nature in order to retain their own professional certification. In the increasingly technical world in which we live this tendency will undoubtedly continue. Lawyers, doctors, and all kinds of other professionals will be regularly taking continuing education courses, and Stanford would be remiss not to offer a wide range of such instruction to its alumni and other professional persons. It could be an activity that in terms of numbers of persons and even numbers of instructional hours, far exceeds the current teaching on campus. Technology will make it possible to run these courses from Stanford but not to require local attendance. A doctor in Alaska will be able to keep up-to-date on his specialty and receive credit for doing so without ever leaving his home or office. The same is true for all kinds of other professionals. But it is not just the professionals. Stanford will be encouraged to offer and undoubtedly will offer by technological means a great variety of courses to the adult population. There will, of course, be some occasions when it will be desirable to bring these learning professionals on to campus, but it will not be often and can only really be for purposes of a psychological boost and the satisfaction of their natural desire occasionally to return. What is important is that Stanford can play a kind of central role in the lives of its alumni that does not exist at present but that will be critical to their role in the increasingly technological society of the 21st century.

### 3.4. Psychology of the Virtual Classroom

Why be on campus at all? The new technology will permit us to conduct even a seminar with students actually located in all parts of the world. No doubt such seminars will be given and will be very effective. Take some relatively esoteric but still important topic. An example I like is Kant's *Third Critique, The Critique of Judgment,* especially the second half on teleology. I can see a seminar being offered on this text in the middle of the 21st century with the members assembled from six different countries and consisting of not more than twelve persons. I picked a topic in philosophy, but it could just as easily be a specialized topic in physics or in economics. Just how the credits will be assigned and who will pay what, I shall not venture to say.

No doubt the psychology of the virtual classroom will become increasingly intimate but will still be no match for the physical presence, so the place for Stanford as a physical institution will remain. As Stanford undergraduates have told the faculty for many years, it is not really what goes on in the classroom that is important, it is the life shared together living on campus. The joys and sorrows of those undergraduate years spent together will continue to have appeal and will continue to play a significant role.

It may be a different story at the graduate level, just because of the great desirability of specialization. Seminars will be held with the members assembled from everywhere, and that may be forecast as the great contrast between undergraduate and graduate education in the next century. But I think that also can be too sharp a contrast. There is too much, in science above all, that is like apprenticeship. You do not learn how to do experiments by just watching and listening. Hands-on work is essential, and for that continuing physical presence may be needed. But there is still a forecast that runs against even this prudent reservation. It is that the nature of experimentation will change as the role of technology rapidly increases. It may even be that in the most advanced experimentation in any one scientific domain there will be only a few places in the world with the equipment necessary to perform it, and those who want to participate will often do so remotely but still actively and essentially. If this prediction turns out to be true, graduate education will indeed be the model of the virtual university.

So the psychological needs of the undergraduates and the graduates may well diverge. The desirable socializing camaraderie of the undergraduate may well evolve into something quite different for the graduate student. The psychology of camaraderie for graduate students will be transformed, as it already is already being transformed for working scientists and scholars, into rapid, continual, and informal network communication. I, like many others, am already finding at the close of this century that most of my informal intellectual communications take place with my professional peers scattered around the world rather than with my local colleagues. It is already that way for large numbers of graduate students. There is a real likelihood that this will be the dominant trend. What will this trend mean? Will graduate students be admitted as virtual graduate students? Can a student remain in Beijing and be an integral part of graduate training, take courses, and receive a degree? Up to now such students have traveled to the universities of their choice. But there is no reason why that system cannot be reversed to have the technology bring the university to the students. Stanford, I am sure, will be able to find a way to change itself and prosper from such radical new developments in its organization as an institution of learning.

# References

Carter, T. F. 1955. *The Invention of Printing in China and Its Spread Westward.* 2nd ed. New York: The Ronald Press Co.

Chaffee, J. W. 1985. *The Thorny Gates of Learning in Sung China.* New York: Cambridge University Press.

Crothers, E., and P. Suppes. 1967. *Experiments in Second-Language Learning.* New York: Academic Press.

Fraser, P. M. 1972. *Ptolemaic Alexandria.* London: Oxford University Press.

Ravaglia, R., P. Suppes, C. Stillinger, and T. Alper. 1995. "Computer-based Mathematics and Physics for Gifted Students." *Gifted Child Quarterly* 39: 7–13.

Suppes, P., ed. 1981. *University-level Computer-assisted Instruction at Stanford: 1968–1980.* Stanford, Calif.: Institute for Mathematical Studies in the Social Sciences.

Suppes, P., M. Jerman, and D. Brian. 1968. *Computer-assisted Instruction: Stanford's 1965–66 arithmetic program.* New York: Academic Press.

Suppes, P., and M. Morningstar. 1972. *Computer-assisted Instruction at Stanford, 1966–68: Data, Models, and Evaluation of the Arithmetic Programs.* New York: Academic Press.

Suppes, P., M. Pavel, and J. Cl. Falmagne. 1994. "Representations and Models in Psychology." *Annual Review of Psychology* 45: 517–544.

# B.    Teaching and Learning

# Chapter 11

# Searching for World-Class Educational Standards

## J. Myron Atkin

## 1. Introduction

Politicians from both political parties agree that the country must develop "world-class standards" for the schools. They even agree on first steps: formulation of explicit goals for students in the major subject-matter fields of science, mathematics, English and literature, history, and geography. The stated goals, they believe, will set a needed and overdue direction for American education and provide a framework within which subsequent, concrete steps can be taken for improvement of the nation's schools.

Bipartisan determination to articulate a common vision was signaled by a manifesto issued in 1989 in Charlottesville, Virginia, at the first-ever educational summit of the president and the 50 governors. It was followed, in 1991, by an administration document prepared by the secretary of education and submitted to the president that declared

New World Standards: Standards will be developed ... for each of the five core subjects [that] represent what young Americans need to know and be able to do if they are to live and work successfully in today's world. These standards will incorporate both knowledge and skills, to ensure that, when they leave school, young Americans are prepared for further study and the work force.

In a few other countries, too, a decision has been reached to define educational standards (though other labels are usually used), and, as in the United States, the sentiment supporting such a policy encompasses the full political spectrum. On the left, the press for standards usually stems from the fact that schools vary widely in their apparent success. In particular, schools in poor neighborhoods—and especially those that serve children from minority groups—are not considered to be as successful as the others. In the name of fairness, all children should be expected to reach the same levels of attainment; a primary task is to identify those levels. On the right, talk of subject-specific expectations seems to stimulate nostalgia about the way schools once may have been: serious students, unambiguous and broadly accepted objectives, demanding teachers, high levels of performance.

There is no mistaking the seriousness with which standards are being discussed and designed. The federal government (mostly through the Department of Education but typically with other agencies joining in the effort) has begun investing millions of dollars in the effort. Federal funds have gone to about a dozen groups so far to formulate standards. Draft materials are being circulated. Legislation has been crafted to create a twenty-member National Education Standards and Improvement Council to monitor and coordinate the effort. The priority is all the more impressive at a time when money is unusually tight and there is no shortage of children's causes with plausible claims for public dollars.

There are two major conceptual obstacles, however, to this firm resolve to set a direction for American education by identifying standards. First, there is uncertainty about what the range of standards might actually look like and about the functions they will serve. Second, no one knows what is meant by "world-class." Compounding these difficulties, political issues and conflicts have arisen, some of them stemming in the United States from traditional debates about federal as against state prerogatives, and some of them associated with determining who has the credibility and the authority to determine the standards in the various subject-matter fields.

Underlying these problems is the serious possibility that professional perspectives—those of subject-matter experts, teachers, and school administrators—may, in the end, conflict with political expectations and enthusiasm. Such an outcome was indeed the result in one nation, England, where a massive attempt was made to institute a national curriculum where none had existed before.

This chapter attempts to identify and illustrate some of the key issues and challenges besetting the standards movement. The point of view proffered here is that the unprecedented national-standards-setting exercise now under way in the United States has the potential for making significant contributions to the improvement of American education, but not in the fashion that many advocates of more precise educational standards seem to think, and not without certain risks. And the term "world-class" has little operational meaning because virtually every country in the world, especially those to which the United States likes to compare itself, is trying to change its educational system in significant ways. In some places envied by the United States, significant features of educational reform are moving in directions diametrically opposite to those reflected in the American standards movement.

## 2. What Kinds of Standards?

Once the drive toward establishment of standards began in earnest and various groups started to assign resources to the task, it became apparent that the very concept of a standard was somewhat problematic to those given the responsibility of defining them. Is a standard a guideline? A minimum expectation? An aspiration? A measuring stick? A vision of a desirable state? And are there not standards associated with the quality of all the different elements of the education system, not solely the formal curriculum?

Politicians meant initially to launch an activity that identified what children were expected "to know and be able to do" as a result of their formal schooling. The wording of the Charlottesville statement makes clear that their concern was about subject matter. School programs were seen as unchallenging, student achievement as unimpressive, teachers as displaying marginal competence. Demand higher levels of performance geared to straightforward statements of content-related goals and educational quality will rise.

Standards-makers, however, quickly enlarged their charge as they began to wrestle with details of the task. They saw the job as considerably more complex than solely identifying curriculum content, though that assignment retains priority and is amply challenging in its own right. One now hears not only about curriculum (or "content") standards, but also about performance standards, assessment standards, teaching standards, program standards, and—a particularly controversial matter—support (sometimes called "delivery," or "program," or "opportunity-to-learn") standards. Many of them overlap.

Many educators who became involved in articulating national standards took the position early in the process that fairness demands that schools not be held to account unless teachers and school administrators were provided with the resources necessary to achieve the new goals. They asked, for example, "Can a school with 35 students in a class can be held to the same standards as a school with 25? Can a school without a licensed science teacher be expected to demonstrate the same achievement levels as a school with qualified teachers? Can a school with a language laboratory or state-of-the-art computer equipment be compared fairly to a school without these resources?"

At the first meeting of the National Committee on Science Education Standards and Assessment of the National Research Council (NRC) in 1992, several members of the new Committee indicated that they had professional and moral reasons for insisting that standards for support of children and teachers be a part of the NRC effort. The suggestion was not unanticipated. As a direct result of previously initiated education activities at the NRC, the organization had established a Committee on a Nationwide Education Support System for Teachers and Schools "to examine the merit and feasibility of a national delivery system for science and mathematics education." The resulting report identified requirements associated with "a standards-based support system," including "assistance to schools in adapting their programs to the diverse needs of students and teachers, ... [the support system ] must address the needs of teachers for substantial noninstructional time devoted to planning, assessing progress, and consulting other teachers within the school and beyond."

The NRC science group (next to mathematics, probably the most comprehensive of the standards initiatives) then went on to draft "program standards" to reflect the levels of support for teachers and students expected of standards-driven science programs. Supplementing the statement about professional development cited very briefly in the preceding section, program standards reflect concern about the context in which high-quality science education is to take place. In an informal working document of this group, issues were raised that elevate the importance of the "full range of science experiences for students K–12." What about the nature of the curriculum as a whole? Is it consistent across grade levels? Does it match what is known about children? Does the science relate appropriately to other subjects, especially mathematics? Does the learning environment reflect "scientific attitudes and habits of mind as well as the social values conducive to scientific learning?"

A strong emphasis on the support and resources that are necessary to reach newly articulated curriculum standards has engendered two kinds of reservations. One centers on the matter of who pays. Several governors and legislators—looking toward a probable future—see the acceptance of some sort of national content standards and, possibly, a national (voluntary) examination system. Content and achievement standards are one thing. But if the standards directly address the matter of necessary resources, where does the money come from? Is the standards movement one more example of federally initiated expectations without accompanying federal funds? States and localities are strapped financially. Formal agreement about the conditions that are necessary to achieve the new educational standards legitimates and fortifies one more demand on strained local treasuries.

The other reservation about developing standards for support of schools and teachers is based on the fear that an emphasis on resources might provide too facile an excuse for not measuring up in the case of districts that are poorly funded.

# 3. World-Class?

The standards movement in the United States is powered partly by a sense of competitiveness with other countries. The nation is concerned about becoming second-rate economically, and a strong relationship is seen among industrial productivity, a favorable balance of international trade, and the quality of education. However, anguish about education quality is universal; educational reform is a global phenomenon, regardless of balance-of-trade and productivity issues.

The initiatives that are developed for making things better in any country depend primarily on local perception of where the problems lie, circumstance, tradition, and opportunity. Each country tries to reach its own evolving ideals by modifying its education system, using the policy tools at hand. But each one also tries to exorcise its own demons. If a country does not have fears about the quality of the work force, and several do not, it has deep concerns about something else—and it tries to use the education system to fix things.

Many Americans look enviously at Japanese education, for example. Japan, however, has recently revamped its curriculum because of its own worries. Two prominent concerns among the Japanese are, first, the country's perception of a lack of creativity and originality in its students and, second, increasing alarm about problems of environmental degradation. Consequently, Japan's latest science curriculum is undergirded by several principles that may sound surprising and anachronistic to American ears. Among them are "that importance be attached to the fostering of capability of coping positively with social changes and to the cultivation of foundations of creativity, and that the willingness to learn by oneself be encouraged" and the "need to lay greater stress on closeness to nature, observation, and experiment ... and to develop a more positive attitude toward nature as a whole."

A new, required subject has been introduced: Life Environmental Studies. It stands now as the sole science subject in grades 1 and 2. One hundred fifty 45-minute hours are devoted to science at each elementary-school grade. In grades 3 through 6, the science curriculum consists of "living organisms and their environment," "matter and energy," and "the earth and space." Problem solving and student creativity are emphasized throughout.

Science education is in flux everywhere. Furthermore, priorities shift. Standards setting in such a situation is difficult. Even if agreements are negotiated, it is not clear how long they will last. The point is that there is no international standard about matters of selecting curriculum content.

Because each country sees somewhat different problems in its educational system and in its society, each one copes in a different manner.

In short no one knows what "world-class" means. It is true that many countries are trying to change their educational systems in important ways. However, in every case policymakers are responding primarily to internal pressures. In England and Wales there is a major effort to nationalize the curriculum, but not in Scotland, and not in Spain, Norway, Austria, Germany, Italy, or most other countries. Most policymakers are interested in what goes on elsewhere in the world; parallel developments sometimes profit from exchange of ideas. But few countries pattern their reforms in any precise sense on what goes on elsewhere. "World-class standards" is a slogan, probably intended to be inspirational. It carries little operational meaning.

## 4. The Heart of the Matter: Assessment

Standards and examinations are closely related: tests are the vehicle for determining how well the standards are met. In the United States, the talk so far is about "voluntary" national examinations, in deference to constitutional prerogatives that leave responsibility for education to the individual states. But it is not difficult to imagine tying federal financial support to participation in a national strategy for educational improvement, even after the 1994 election of a devolutionary-prone Congress.

As the United States moves toward nationalization of the curriculum and a possible new examination system, and in view of American interest in being "world-class," it may be instructive briefly to recognize the nature of testing practices and developments in other countries. A recent report by the Congressional Office of Technology Assessment (OTA) highlights several relevant points in this regard. First, national standardized examinations are an increasing rarity in Europe and Asia—and they are seldom given before age sixteen. Second, these examinations are almost always used for purposes of selection for university admission and hardly ever for feedback to teachers or for system monitoring. (Some variation of an inspection system is the primary method of assuring overall accountability in most countries.) Third, teachers in other countries play a major role in developing, administering, and scoring tests.

Furthermore, the OTA report states, "the trend in several countries has been to allow schools a greater say in the definition of curricula during the compulsory period of schooling." Germany leaves matters entirely to the individual states, but, in practice, to the schools. So does Austria. So do Switzerland and Denmark. Trends may change, of course. But at a time when the United States looks to identification of standards, and probably more standardized testing, to define and gauge the quality of the educational system, it should be remembered that the practice elsewhere is quite different, and, in fact, has moved in the opposite direction during the last fifteen years.

## 5. Some Challenges Ahead

Right now, most American standards are in the development stage. Professional groups are busily engaged in generating defensible goals. Well-regarded and diligent people have been enlisted in the effort. Good intentions abound. Perhaps the American standards effort will continue for several years with the same steady purposefulness. Deliberate attempts are being made to assure consensus about the results, and there is not a rush toward an examination system, voluntary or otherwise, at least not yet.

But there is also the possibility that conflicts will erupt publicly, as well as internally, among any of several areas for dispute. Underlying several of them is the confusion about the meaning of the term "standard" itself. On the current education scene, the word can be taken in at least two senses. In one, a standard is a banner, a broad statement of purpose around which people can rally. In the other, a standard is a point of reference for purposes of comparison, a measuring stick. There is considerable potential for controversy as the two meanings are confused. People find it easier to agree on general goals than on the specific operational consequences.

At a completely different level the issue of what subjects are worth teaching has not been resolved and issure to become contentious. Within a subject field there is the matter of how much of each subspecialty is to be included. The science standards are to encompass all science disciplines, but there is extended discussion and little consensus about how much physics, earth science, technology, and meteorology (to name just a few disciplines) to include. Then there is the special case of social studies. Seemingly, it has been a well-established subject. However, it is now under threat because it is seen as less rigorous (and perhaps potentially more controversial) than history, civics, and geography.

And what about cross-disciplinary activity? Much research and intellectual excitement, as well as public concern, are focused on areas where the disciplines intersect. Often, cross-disciplinary fields are created to respond to human need: in health and environmental improvement, for example, or in enhancing economic productivity. One clear curriculum trend everywhere is a move toward the study of such matters in school, partly to demonstrate to students that there are important connections between intellectual effort and practical results. At the moment, however, there is no national standards-setting committee in fields like environmental or technology education. The United States may be constraining the curriculum in undesirable ways with its stress on a subject-by-subject approach to educational standards.

Most crucially, identification of even the most educationally justifiable standards will be a force for improving the quality of American education only if teachers understand and support them. That means, in part, that the standards must reflect what the teacher sees as desirable for the students. It means also that the teacher considers the standards as sanction to teach in a fashion considered attractive and satisfying. Such perceptions are unlikely to come solely from reading the written products from the standards committees. It will be necessary for teachers to have extended opportunities to discuss the standards among themselves so that they can meaningfully incorporate them into their own vision of high-quality education and how it might be provided.

Yet some of the impetus for "world-class standards" is the belief that such standards have become necessary precisely because the United States has a teaching force that is unreliable and perhaps inept. A dilemma arises. Will a distrusting public accept standards that accord teachers greater latitude, if the whole standards exercise was intended, in significant measure, to hold teachers to account?

All this further underscores the need for teachers and other important stakeholders to have the opportunity to examine the proposed standards in considerable detail and over a relatively long period of time. They must be discussed, debated, operationalized, and understood. Consensus gained by such an approach is worth as much as the standards themselves. Without such deliberation and at least a minimum level of agreement, the standards will fall far short of whatever potential they might have to improve the quality of American schools.

# Chapter 12

# A Practitioner's View of Operations Research Ph.D. Education

## Alan Wood and Frederick Biedenweg

## 1. Study Objective

A concern frequently raised at joint meetings of The Institute of Management Sciences (TIMS) and the Operations Research Society of America (ORSA) and in the news magazine *OR/MS Today* is that operations research (OR) Ph.D. programs are slanted toward theoretical issues without practical application. The viewpoint often presented is that this theoretical OR training provides the appropriate background for those students who wish to pursue an academic career but does not provide the foundation required by OR practitioners. We decided to test that belief by surveying a group of OR practitioners about their OR education, in particular the impact that their OR education has had on their career. This group of OR practitioners consisted of those former students of Jerry Lieberman who graduated from the Stanford OR Ph.D. program and are now OR practitioners. The purpose of this is to provide feedback from these OR practitioners about an OR Ph.D. program and how it could be improved.

## 2. Summary of Findings

Without exception, the respondents to our survey valued their OR education very highly. Even those former students whose current occupations have nothing to do with OR would repeat the Stanford OR Ph.D. program if they were given a chance to do it all again. Those who ended up in business would still rather have an OR Ph.D. than an M.B.A.; those who ended up in engineering would still rather have an OR Ph.D. than an engineering or computer science degree. This reinforces the notion that OR thought processes and techniques provide a solid foundation for OR practitioners as well as for OR educators.

Notwithstanding the value that the OR practitioners place on their OR education, they had a number of recommendations for improving an OR Ph.D. program. The recommendations are summarized here and described in more detail later in this paper. The recommendations are:

- Incorporate more interdisciplinary study, either as part of standard OR coursework or in conjunction with the standard OR curriculum. Most respondents mentioned that they would have liked more breadth in their OR education. This included the suggestion for an interdisciplinary degree program—OR combined with an engineering field, computer science, or business.

- Include more case studies or OR applications, either within the standard curriculum or as separate course work. Most of the respondents expressed a desire for more exposure to "real-world" problems, "warts and all."

- Integrate technology into the OR Ph.D. program, that is, use computers to help teach fundamental concepts and expose the students to the wide variety of commercially available OR tools.

- Place more emphasis on the nontechnical skills necessary to prosper in the business world—written and oral communication and team building. It was suggested that oral reports of a case study by a team of OR Ph.D. students, similar to those produced in a current Masters course, would be useful.

# 3. The Stanford OR Ph.D. Program

All of the survey respondents are alumni of the Stanford OR Ph.D. program. This section provides background information for those readers unfamiliar with the program.

Although individual courses have been updated to take into account new discoveries and technologies, the basic philosophy and construct of the OR Ph.D. program at Stanford has remained unchanged for twenty years. The emphasis of the program is on:

1. The study of the abstract mathematical structure of models derived from real-life situations such as allocation models of an enterprise or an economy, energy modeling, network-flow models of transportation and communication systems, reliability models of complex engineering systems, queueing models of congestion, modeling and control of dynamic systems, discrete selection models for routing and pattern cutting, policy decisions for production and inventory control, and models for conflict resolution.

2. The development of the mathematical theory necessary for the study of those models.

The required courses focus on the theoretical underpinnings of the mainstays of OR: Linear Programming, Convex Analysis, Equilibrium Programming, Nonlinear Programming, Econometric Modeling, and Linear Complementarity for the deterministic side; and Dynamic Programming, Stochastic Control, Simulation Theory, Inventory Theory, Queueing Theory, and Applied Probability for the stochastic side. In addition, students can select from enhanced studies in areas such as Integer Programming, Computational Techniques, Information Theory, Applications of Game Theory, and Optimization Under Uncertainty.

# 4. Methodology

The authors are both former students of Jerry Lieberman and are now OR practitioners. We have our own views on OR education, but we wanted to include a broader perspective. Therefore, we surveyed the former Ph.D. students of Jerry Lieberman who obtained their doctorates in OR and are now practitioners. We began with a list provided by Stanford that included eighteen of Jerry's former Ph.D. students of whom twelve were thought to be practitioners. We sent a letter and questionnaire to those twelve people and received nine responses (including one phone interview). It turned out that one of the people we thought was a practitioner was a statistics professor, so we actually had eight responses from eleven questionnaires. The responses provided the basis for this paper. The survey questionnaire is appended to this chapter.

# 5. Practitioner Demography

There is a wide variety in the current use of OR by the eight respondents. Two of the respondents no longer use OR at all (one is a medical doctor, and one runs an insurance underwriting consulting company). Two do not use OR techniques (one is a senior manager; one does project scheduling) but sometimes review the use of OR or other mathematical modeling techniques. Two make moderate use of OR (both are engineers in the computer industry) as needed to solve engineering problems. Two do a significant amount of mathematical modeling (both are technical contributors; one in the defense industry, one in a consulting company), although they do not necessarily use the sophisticated OR techniques taught in the OR Ph.D. program. The last four respondents continue to create and solve mathematical models. From the wide variety of practitioner occupations, it is clear that an OR degree does not lead toward any specific career.

The types of OR tools and techniques that the practitioners have used since graduating are essentially a list of all OR tools. The tools and techniques mentioned in response to the survey were: linear programming, nonlinear programming, integer programming, dynamic programming, game theory, queueing theory, simulation, reliability, stochastic processes (renewal theory, Markov processes), networks, and statistics. From this list it is clear that practitioners should obtain a background in a wide variety of OR tools during their graduate education.

An interesting observation is that only one of the eight respondents has ever worked in an OR group. Others have worked in groups that were mathematically sophisticated but not specifically trained in OR techniques. This implies the necessity of interacting with a variety of people who do not understand the techniques, language, or benefits of OR. One comment was:

> I have found that I need to be a linguist—learn to speak the language that the specialists in a given field speak because they are not going to speak OR. Context switches, input buffers, and RAM caches can all be translated into portions of a queueing model but not by asking engineers what the parameters of a queue should be (they don't know—if they did, they wouldn't need you). Once you understand their language, it is relatively easy to cast their problem in an OR setting and make a contribution.

## 6. OR Influence on Career

The initial influence of an OR education on all the practitioners' careers was that their initial jobs were related to OR. Half of the respondents obtained their initial positions through contacts provided by Jerry Lieberman. In general, the use of OR by all respondents has declined over time. For example, the two respondents that do not currently use OR began their careers in positions that required some use of OR. A respondent who now makes minimal use of OR began his career by writing a software tool to implement his thesis. Some typical comments were:

> My OR education has affected my career by giving me skills and techniques that are frequently applicable in many different situations.

> My OR training has allowed me to pursue my interest in probability and optimization in ways which would not have been possible with a less thorough education.

Whether or not specific OR tools and techniques had affected their careers, the respondents uniformly agreed that the OR training received at Stanford had very positively affected their careers. Some general comments about OR training were:

> My training in OR has enabled me to establish myself as a
> highly technical employee, able to attack a variety of problems
> requiring detailed and objective analysis.

> My study of OR gave me the mathematical breadth and so-
> phistication to know when and how to apply a variety of math-
> ematical techniques to client problems .... Generally, I need
> not apply the sophisticated techniques I studied at Stanford.

> The mathematical maturity which I gained in my OR training
> has served me very well.

The primary reason that the respondents valued their OR training was
because of the kind of thinking required to solve OR problems. Solving
OR problems requires thinking about the entire problem and its optimal
solution instead of trying to force-fit the problem into something that can
be solved by a certain technique. It was clear from the respondents that
the OR thought process was far more important than specific OR tools
or techniques. One respondent commented that the Stanford OR program
was where he learned to think. A sampling of other comments includes:

> The OR training has taught me how to break apart and analyze
> problems.

> The analytical thinking and decision-making processes of OR
> have had a continual impact on my career, but the specific mod-
> els, tools, or techniques have had decreasing impact with time
> passage since Stanford.

> The most important part of my OR education was not the tools
> and techniques, It was the big-picture thought process — learn-
> ing to think about global optimization instead of local optimiza-
> tion.

Regardless of the suggestions for improvement described in the next section, our respondents uniformly said that they felt that their OR education
has had a positive effect on their careers. For example:

The additional information and depth that I needed as time
went on I could read by myself. But I would never have been
able by myself to develop the mental discipline or confidence
one obtains by learning mathematical proof and rigor.

# 7. Recommendations for OR Education

One of the most interesting things about our study is that no matter
how the respondents said the OR program could have been improved, they
all said they would have chosen the Stanford OR Ph.D. program if they
had it all to do over. That the respondents feel this way even though half of
them currently make little or no use of OR is a real credit to the Stanford
OR Department. A sampling of comments:

I would not change a thing about my education. My subsequent
turnings and twistings perhaps, but not my education.

I would definitely still go through the Stanford OR program.

I would not change my education if I had it to do over again.

Even though all respondents valued their OR education, they had a
number of suggestions and recommendations. Those suggestions and recommendations comprise the remainder of this section and provide valuable
feedback to OR departments about how they could make an OR Ph.D. program more suitable for practitioners. These recommendations were summarized earlier and are described in more detail in the remainder of the
paper. The suggestions relate to making the program broader, that is,
more interdisciplinary; including more case studies or OR applications; integrating more technology into the OR Ph.D. program; and emphasizing
more nontechnical business skills.

A continuing theme in the responses was that the practitioners would
have liked more breadth in their education. A variety of suggestions were
advanced about how that could be accomplished. These suggestions included modifying current courses to include OR applications from other
disciplines, new course(s) emphasizing multidisciplinary problems, and encouraging students to take courses in other departments or even to get a

degree in OR combined with another engineering or business/economics department. Some comments regarding interdisciplinary studies were:

> I would have tried to take a few more courses in engineering and computer science to broaden knowledge of common products that are necessary to understand to be an effective modeler, analyst, or system engineer.

> There is a need for cooperative ventures between the OR department and other departments. I tried, in some sense, to create my own interdisciplinary program by sitting in on business courses.

> It is interesting that OR was founded as an interdisciplinary science, but it is taught as a mathematical specialty. I would like to see its teaching reflect more of its roots.

A similar theme was the suggestion to include more practical problems and applications into the Ph.D. program. The suggestions for accomplishing that objective included:

- Making the examples and homework in the Ph.D. courses more "real-world", for example, performance modeling of computer architectures and forecasting insurance-loss projections using stochastic processes
- Having a separate course on case studies and OR applications, perhaps similar to some of the Master's courses but with more detail or mathematical rigor
- Giving problems in which the students have to determine the appropriate set(s) of assumptions to allow the problem to be solved by various modeling techniques
- Providing more real-world problems that do not necessarily have a right answer (a logical approach is the important thing) with an oral presentation
- Encouraging students to take summer or part-time jobs with OR content rather than concentrating solely on the OR coursework and thesis.

By contrast, no one advocated a radical restructuring of the OR program to make it more suitable for practitioners. One person expressed a contrary preference. "I do not long for more case studies / group projects or 'real life problem solving'. A theoretical curriculum is what is advertised at Stanford and that is what I came for—anything less and I would have been disappointed."

All the respondents thought that technology needs to be integrated into the OR Ph.D. program. Students do not need to be experts in any specific tools since they can learn that expertise on the job, and today's tools may be obsolete in a few years anyway. However, they do need exposure to the breadth of available software. OR students should be using computers to supplement OR problem solving but not at the expense of learning fundamental concepts. One interesting idea is computer lab courses, for example a one-credit course taken in conjunction with linear programming that teaches the use of linear programming packages in a spreadsheet. There were several comments stating that technology could help in the presentation and solution of case studies. It was also mentioned that technology could help in the understanding of fundamental concepts, for example, using visualization techniques to show how minor parameter changes cause major changes to a problem's solution. One comment was that "I do believe that the ability to actually experiment with systems and algorithms in real time can lead to a better understanding of the underlying mechanisms, when combined with a more traditional classroom analysis of the corresponding mathematics."

In addition to technical expertise, sound communications / presentation skills are necessary to succeed in a corporate environment. Although an OR program should not specifically teach these skills, they can be reinforced without loss of technical content. Operations Research Ph.D. students are required to do a lot of writing, a thesis for example, but the thesis defense may be the only oral presentation that a student gives. Several respondents felt that increased oral presentations would be useful, especially in conjunction with more emphasis on case studies. Team building was also mentioned, so it might be possible to have a team presentation of a case study, similar to the practice in some of the Master's courses. An alternative method for improving presentation skills is to require Ph.D. students to teach at least part of an undergraduate or Master's level OR course.

The respondents had a number of useful comments for prospective OR Ph.D. students:

> OR is by its nature an interdisciplinary activity. The student should have a strength in one or more related disciplines and be aware that many employers will consider the related discipline as the primary function of their employee. In other words, make every attempt to become facile with OR's various application areas and remember that the value of OR is in its successful application.

> Don't get so specialized that all you know how to do or are interested in doing is your thesis.

> OR tools and techniques are becoming available to the masses. However, rather than make a formal OR degree irrelevant, I think it opens up opportunities since there is a great need for experts who know how to properly set up the models to which the tools apply. I still think OR is a great field for anyone who wants to do applied mathematics.

> Try to get a breadth of experience, take a wide variety of courses, work for a year or two. OR is supposed to be an applied science, so try to apply it.

In providing advice to prospective OR Ph.D. students, our respondents indicated their appreciation for Jerry Lieberman's advice and tutelage:

> I believe that one should follow his passion, whatever it be. Jerry Lieberman said, 'Pick an area and be the best person in the world in that area.' That's still good career advice.

> My advice to a student considering a Ph.D. in OR is to get an advisor like Jerry.

# 8. Survey Questionnaire

The following questionnaire was sent to all Gerald Lieberman's former students who are currently OR practitioners.

## 8.1. Demographic Data

1. Are you a manager, individual (technical) contributor, consultant, or other?

2. Do you consider yourself an OR practitioner, OR theorist, both, or neither?

3. List the types of OR tools and techniques you have used since graduating, e.g., linear programming, non-linear programming, simulation, queueing, inventory theory, reliability, etc.

4. Do you currently do any mathematical modeling (of any type)?

## 8.2. OR and Your Career

1. How has your OR education affected your career? Do you or have you ever worked for an OR group?

2. Do you frequently use and/or apply

   (a) OR concepts,

   (b) OR tools and techniques,

   (c) OR thought process

   and how?

3. How did your advisors or professors, Jerry Lieberman in particular, influence your career?

## 8.3. Recommendations

1. Based on your career, how could an OR curriculum have better prepared you, especially for those in the commercial world?, e.g., more training in communications skills, more practical problems, case studies, labs.

2. If you had it all to do over again, what would you change about your education?

3. What trends do you think will be most important in changing the practice of OR?—e.g., global economy, math programming in spreadsheets.

4. Can current technology be used to improve OR training?

5. What advice would you have for students considering a career in OR?

# Acknowledgments

The authors would like to thank the following former students of Jerry Lieberman for responding to our requests for information: Eugene Durbin, Randy Fleming, Lola Goheen, Frederic Miercort, Mark Perkins, Marion Reynolds, and John Wagner.

# Chapter 13

# Practicing Operations Research (OR) and System Engineering in Workplaces Having Decentralized OR

Randall E. Fleming

## 1. Introduction

More and more companies today are farming out their functions involving the application of operations research (OR) techniques to the line organizations rather than keeping them in one centralized OR group. Therefore, today's OR graduate who desires an industrial career must be prepared to operate in a workplace without traditional OR functions, coworkers, or mentors. This chapter is written with the intent to provide guidance and support to those in such positions by sharing one OR Ph.D.'s career development over a fifteen-year period from a specialized mathematical modeler and analyst to a broad-based OR practitioner / system engineer contributing to mainstream decisions made on both the business and the technical operations sides of a company.

I discuss skills needed to become a good system engineer, relate these to operations research skills (Section 2), and show how I acquired them (Section 3). Lessons learned, recommendations, and pitfalls are pointed out (Sections 4 and 5). The sequence is generally chronological. This chapter is intended to provide inspiration as to the wide variety of things an OR person can learn to do (and be effective at), as well as give insight into the types of skills that make an OR practitioner or system engineer successful in a corporate environment.

# 2. System Engineering (SE) and Operations Research

The words "systems" and "system engineer" are overused and mean different things to different people. In this section, I define system engineering, the skills required to do it well, and their relationship to operations research skills.

## 2.1. What System Engineering Is

Table 13.1 presents seven definitions of system engineering. When reading the classifieds for a system engineer, one must read carefully to understand which type is desired because the skills required can be quite different. Part of the reason there is such a wide variety in interpretation of SE is that it is a relatively new technical discipline. Its technical society, the National Council of System Engineers (NCOSE) is only about three to four years old. The diversity of SE means that it overlaps with many other disciplines, especially in the areas of design integration and program planning and controls. A typical response of a team to the presence of a good system engineer on a program is: "I don't quite know what they did, but I'm sure glad he / she was around." Typically, once you get through the terminology differences and disagreements about responsibility, most SEs find that they are trying to solve the same problems. I (and my company) feel that system engineering includes all of the definitions. This is the position that will be taken in this chapter.

TABLE 13.1

*Definitions of System Engineering (SE)*

| Definition | Description |
|---|---|
| Systematic engineering | A systematic iterating process for developing any product: functions → requirements → answers → test |
| Engineering the system | A project function that focuses on managing (nurturing, balancing, and controlling) progress in the product's technical development |
| System acquisition management | Disciplined management of the system acquisition process (including preparation of program decisions) |
| System analysis | Analytical modeling and optimization of parameters and overall system performance |
| System-level engineering | Defines requirements and integrates verification at the upper levels of the system hierarchy only |
| System definition | Conceives and defines new product concepts to the point where traditional engineering development can begin |
| System marketing | A project function that provides internal advocates for customer and user needs and the primary external advocates for how the system meets the needs |

System engineering, like operations research, focuses on the big picture. Clearly system engineering is applied more often during the development phases of a system and focuses on the technical side of the problem. Operations research, because of its mathematical nature, has been most often applied in situations involving improvement of the operations of more mature businesses, longer-term strategic planning and forecasting. Many operations research tools have applicability in system analysis and decision making, and many system engineering tools for developing requirements are extremely useful in operations research applications.

## 2.2. What It Takes to Become a System Engineer

It is extremely difficult to learn system engineering without doing it in a "real" project environment. Academic or process-focused instruction is helpful but more to those with some experience seeking to improve ways of doing business than to those lacking experience. SE skills learned in a classroom are tools that can be seen as artificial "make-work" or simply not useful in the absence of a mission need, customer requirements, and cost and schedule constraints. SE tools, like OR tools, are a means to an end, not an end in themselves.

System engineers develop from any number of disciplinary backgrounds, but OR is not commonly one of them. The most common university fields of study for system engineers at the company where I currently work are mechanical engineering, aerospace engineering, electrical engineering, and physics. Most system engineers work at and become good at something else before becoming a system engineer. Most typical previous jobs address problems in: physics (most aerospace subsystems heavily involve physics principles); structures (integration of the physical configuration of a spacecraft); guidance, navigation, and control (integration of many of the functions of a spacecraft); communications (involved in many of the functions that integrate a spacecraft with its external elements); software (has a whole development process that parallels system engineering), and command and data handling (implements most spacecraft functions in hardware and / or software). As I will show in the next section, my entry was through "everything else," that is, specialty engineering, planning, process skills, and an ability to learn quickly from interactions with a large diverse cross-functional team.

Table 13.2 shows skills required to be a good system engineer. Notice the overlap of system engineering skills with the abilities to practice good OR and management science in the systems thinking and professional effectiveness skill groups.

## 2.3. When Are System Engineers Needed on a Project?

System engineers are not always needed on a project. Small-group engineering is more efficient when the project is simple enough. Some characteristics of a project needing system engineers are: many diverse parts with complex interrelationships, heavy involvement with the environment, operations concepts or existing external systems, important human interactions, many tradeoffs in design, or a variety in users or customers. System engineering applied to a system that is too simple can become unnecessary paperwork, like applying state-of-the-art algorithms and a complex mathematical model to an OR problem when a simple spreadsheet would have provided the needed result.

TABLE 13.2

*Skills Needed to Become an Effective System Engineer*

| System Engineering Engineering Group | Specific Skills Required |
|---|---|
| System engineering functions and products (refer to Wertz and Larson 1992 for a good top-level treatment of these areas) | • Requirements analysis definition and control[4,5]<br>• Mission and system analysis<br>• Interface definition and control[4,5]<br>• Verification and testing[4,5]<br>• Design reviews[2,3,4]<br>• Trade studies[4,5]<br>• Design optimization and system concept definition[4,5]<br>• Customer support[2]<br>• Operational concept formulation[4,5]<br>• Specialty engineering and specialty integration[2,3]<br>• System engineering and program planning[3,4]<br>• Configuration control[2,3]<br>• Production / manufacturing process[4,5]<br>• Risk assessment and management[4,5] |
| Systems thinking and basic analytical knowledge | • Probability and statistics[1]<br>• Control theory[2]<br>• Operations research methodology[1]<br>• Engineering economics[1]<br>• Model building[1]<br>• Simulation[1]<br>• Computer science (database structures, information management, information / communications concepts)[4]<br>• Computer skills[2] |
| Professional effectiveness skills | • Presentations[2]<br>• Meetings[2]<br>• Teamwork and team building[3]<br>• Facilitation[2]<br>• Problem solving and decision making[1]<br>• Organizational dynamics[2]<br>• Career development[2]<br>• Listening[1]<br>• Overview of management and supervision[2] |

TABLE 13.2 CONTINUED

| Space systems knowledge[5,6] (refer to Wertz and Larson 1992 for a good top-level treatment of these areas) | • Space mission design and analysis process<br>• Mission and requirements definition.<br>• Orbital geometry and design<br>• Space environment (natural and survivability)<br>• Defining and sizing space payloads<br>• Spacecraft design and sizing<br>• Spacecraft subsystems (communications, power, thermal, structures and mechanisms command and data handling, guidance, navigation and control)<br>• Communications architecture<br>• Mission operations<br>• Contingency planning and safe modes<br>• Ground-system design and sizing<br>• Spacecraft computer systems<br>• Space propulsion systems<br>• Launch systems<br>• Space logistics and reliability[2,3]<br>• Cost modeling[2,3]<br>• Performance, cost, schedule, and and balance in design<br>• Limits and constraints on mission design<br>• Space vehicle design experience |
|---|---|

NOTES:

[1] Skill obtained from Stanford OR

[2] Skill obtained from engineering consulting firm

[3] Skill obtained from specialty engineering and system engineering planning lead job at large aerospace firm

[4] Skill obtained from system engineering and management consulting job at NASA

[5] Skill obtained from system engineer job on Earth Observation System

[6] Skills being picked up gradually over working several projects. Not necessary to be an expert in these areas, just understand the basics and driving issues to the level needed to meaningfully discuss them with experts in each field and balance considerations in all areas.

## 2.4. Why System Engineering Knowledge Is Important

System engineering is important to one's becoming a good manager in a company having a technically complex product because it provides the technical skills necessary to effectively understand all system-level issues and decisions relating to the product, what it must do, its development, and its constraints (e.g., cost, schedule, and finite resources such as mass or power). Separation of personnel performing technical and business operations is the "easy out" for a company since it lets engineers do engineering and business people do business. This is definitely not the most efficient development process and generally leads to two "independent operations" without the capability of communicating with each other.

Neither the "business-only" manager nor the "engineer-only" manager has all the skills needed to be an effective leader. If the team members are all experienced in their disciplines, either manager might get by, but problems can occur when there are major disagreements involving technical approach. Of course, the manager can simply hire a good deputy to cover weak areas (administrative or technical), but proliferation of this behavior only adds to the management bureaucracy. There are often natural conflicts between design, verification, doing what the customer wants, and doing it within cost and schedule constraints. A good program manager must be able to arbitrate effectively in such cases. Having versatile knowledgeable management reduces dependence on politics in decision making. When decision making occurs at a level where decisionmakers do not understand the issues and implications, politics or issues the decisionmakers do understand often drive the result.

The value of system engineering is apparent only to a person who has been a system engineer, or who has worked with good ones on a successful project. SE capability is easily lost at a company whose top management does not appreciate that capability.

## 3. Career History

Table 13.3 summarizes my career development over a fifteen-year period from a specialized mathematical modeler and analyst to a broad-based OR practitioner / system engineer contributing to mainstream decisions made on both the business and the technical operations side of a company. My operations research education, practice in the engineering consulting industry, and evolution into a system engineer at a large aerospace company are discussed in detail in this section.

TABLE 13.3

*Career Path Summary*

| Job assignment | Primary skills performed or gained |
|---|---|
| Stanford (education) | OR methodology, mathematical modeling, analytical "systems" thinking |
| Engineering consulting assignments (modeling evolving to application in the reliability area) | Professional effectiveness / communications, Customer support and consultation, working with cross-functional teams, application of operations research models (especially in reliability and statistics) |
| Specialty engineering and system engineering planning lead for SDI program (early project phases) | Project planning (long-and-short term), specialty engineering and integration, cost modeling and control, general management and supervision |
| NASA system engineering / management consulting | overall system development process, system engineering and business management processes, strategic planning |
| Earth Observation System, system engineer | Space system and subsystem knowledge and execution of system engineering tasks, broad-based knowledge of major program issues from a technical standpoint (requirements, technical risk analysis, technology insertion, etc.) |

## 3.1. Operations Research Education and Training

I participated in the Stanford Operations Research Ph.D. program from 1975 through 1979, having entered with a B.S. in Applied Mathematics. My primary course of study was the basic theoretical OR curriculum, which included deterministic modeling (mathematical programming, graph and network theory), and probabilistic modeling (inventory, reliability theory, queueing theory, game theory). I also took a significant number of statistics courses (time series analysis, mathematical statistics, applied statistics, stochastic processes) and energy modeling. I did not take any computer science, other engineering, engineering-economic systems, or business school courses (i.e., applications or systems-related courses). My Ph.D. thesis (Fleming 1980) was done in the area of system reliability and maintenance modeling. Jerry Lieberman served as my advisor.

## 3.2. Operations Research Practice in a Small Engineering Consulting Firm

My first job, which lasted nine years, was in a small engineering consulting firm (200–400 employees). When I joined the company, it was highly regarded in applied research in the area of controls. Some highly regarded people were on the payroll including a fair number holding Ph.D.s (though none in operations research). I was hired for my statistics degree (M.S. 1979) and my work in reliability modeling.

I spent my first five years there primarily developing and applying models in the areas of missile impact accuracy prediction and RMA (reliability, maintainability, and availability) modeling. I worked with Kalman filters, multivariate statistical estimation, Monte Carlo simulations, and closed-form stochastic predictive models. Surprisingly, I was able to apply the work performed in my Ph.D. thesis. This involved developing a Markov model for predicting the system reliability of a full authority fault-tolerant electronic engine controller given component failure data, a system configuration, and failure modes. I obtained a research contract from the Office of Naval Research (the same sponsor as the one for Jerry's research grant) as part of a five-year initiative to improve reliability in the Navy. The primary focus was research on improving the Markov reliability modeling techniques and their applications to complex systems (Fleming et al. 1985). I was able to attend two ORSA / TIMS meetings during these early years and presented two papers there, but this participation stopped after the first two years on the job, when it was no longer possible to convince my company of the business value of attending. My research contract supported attendance at conferences with more direct relevance to reliability modeling and software tools, such as the Annual Reliability and Maintainability Symposium (RAMS). After four years, my research contract with the reliability initiative ran out, and we were unable to replace it, owing to our company's high overhead rates in comparison to those of universities and to the fact that research was less and less within the mainstream of our company.

During these five years, I gradually learned basic but critical "work environment" skills not learned in an academic environment. These skills included oral communications (briefings, interpersonal communications, marketing, etc.) with people of all types of backgrounds; written communications (good clear technical writing, etc. in proposals, technical reports, etc.); computer literacy; focus on customer and deliverables rather than self; and working in an environment with deadlines. I also gained confidence that I could be good at something in which I had not written a thesis and that I had something unique to offer the world (a feeling not always obtained when attending schools with people of similar background).

My last four years at this company were spent enhancing our modeling capabilities to support the practice of RMA and supportability (defined as the properties a system must possess to be successfully supported following deployment into the field for operations) in two primary applications areas: the FAA Air Traffic Control System Upgrade and the Advanced System Avionics (ASA) architecture. Our company, in the role of a small subcontractor to Martin Marietta, obtained the Air Traffic Control System availability-modeling-and-analysis job on the basis of our reliability modeling experience. We refined our reliability algorithms and software to predict availability for each of the major air-traffic-control functions versus that required on the basis of the criticality of the function (see Fleming et al. 1986). Requirements were 0.99999 for critical functions, 0.999 for essential, and 0.99 for routine. Since the reliability function was part of Martin's system-design group, this was my first introduction to system engineering, even though I was buried deep in the details of reliability.

The ASA consulting job (see Fleming 1987) was obtained again through our reliability modeling capability. We were sought out after a demonstration of our reliability model at the Reliability & Maintainability Symposium (RAMS) in January of 1986. Hired on to support the reliability group, we ended up as consultants to the program manager by listening to everyone on the program during the first week and responding to a need for putting a project focus on a group of specialties: reliability, maintainability, logistics, and so on. In retrospect, we became necessary because of the lack of an effective system-engineering function on this particular project and the inability of matrix organizations providing support to the program to focus on the system requirements rather than on their own area of specialty. We were not doing real system engineering, but it was a lot more system-oriented than what anyone else was doing and so pleased the program manager.

After critical design reviews (CDR) for air traffic control and ASA were performed, the need for our services diminished, and this work ended. We tried to replace these contracts with others but were unsuccessful, owing to: the relative low importance of reliability (providing a far-term rather than a near-term benefit) compared with performance; competition with potential customers' in-house reliability organizations; and our company's high labor rates and large size.

During my tenure the company had gradually shifted from a young, dynamic organization full of high-tech researchers to a more mature, service contract-organization whose primary business was to provide certain specialized expertise as part of large, government-agency-support contractor teams. In 1981, the company was bought out by a very large business and was no longer able to compete effectively for small research contracts. Business focus gradually moved away from applied research and into participation in large support contracts or development efforts teamed with large aerospace companies. The direction in which the company was heading no longer required the services of people like me, so I left.

## 3.3. System Engineering in a Large Aerospace Company

My career development since starting work at a large aerospace company falls into three stages. The first was work performed for the Strategic Defense Initiative (SDI) project that hired me. I was assigned to be the group leader for specialty engineering (reliability, maintainability, logistics, system effectiveness) because of skills in logistics / supportability learned as part of the ASA work. I worked for the chief system engineer on the program.

This was my first real experience being part of the engineering development process. Previous work had instead involved off-line analyses (although with management visibility) and had not really required me to get involved with the product development itself. In an engineering development effort, everything evolves in parallel; there is no time "get everything perfect" before allowing the people who need your results to start using them. The "just-get-something-out-there-to shoot-holes-at-and-upgrade-from-there" engineering approach I learned here improved my OR skills permanently. Also, I discovered that in an environment where there is responsibility for a product that must perform to a set of requirements and must be developed within a set cost and schedule, there is a clearer definition of a right or a wrong answer than there is in a front-end-study consulting environment. This was also the first time I really appreciated the fact that products produced by a team added as much value if not more than ones produced individually.

I was able to keep expanding my responsibilities on the project because of my effectiveness at coordination, organization, planning, and so on. I was able to be effective without having a good understanding of the spacecraft development process and product because I was relatively more product-oriented than the other specialty engineering personnel at the company; because the system-engineering team were all relatively inexperienced since the company was at a period of peak expansion; and because the program was at an early stage where analysis and trades were of great importance. This job ended when the program was recycled by the government under another name.

The second career-development stage involved being a management and system engineering consultant for the National Aeronautics and Space Administration (NASA). For two and a half years, I helped NASA define and improve their system engineering and product development processes, develop long- and short-term plans for programs and organizations, and execute large in-house projects. In performing these jobs, I was forced to learn my own company's processes as examples and was given the opportunity to work with some of its best system engineers.

In the process area, I worked with a NASA-wide process-improvement team and the NCOSE National Process Subcommittee to develop a project life-cycle model, control-gate standard (describing what level of system maturity and product are expected at design reviews), data requirement descriptions (for contractor deliverables), and lexicon (SE terminology)

(Fragomeni et al. 1993). One of the lessons learned was that terminology differences are one of the primary barriers to system engineers' communicating. Everyone has learned differently, and there is no better way to upset someone than to argue with them over choice of terminology!

In the project planning and management consulting area, I performed a more traditional OR function and even got to work with another OR person (from NASA). I used network-based project management tools to develop integrated-program master schedules and bottoms-up costing for several spacecraft development projects (Graves, Morgan, Fleming, and Scheffer 1992). The same tools and processes were also used to develop multiyear budget plans for large organizations. At the more micro level, I supported (and provided vision to) the chief engineer and project manager in execution of a structured-requirements-and-concept-development phase of a project with people who had never done it before. We were needed because the particular NASA organization involved had lost the capability of doing the work themselves (an engineering-business separation problem). We also trained NASA personnel to do specific system engineering jobs, and I brought in experts as needed to support solutions to specific problems. This job ended because the customer ran out of money.

The third (and current) career stage involves practicing SE and acquiring space-system knowledge on a satellite development team. Areas of primary focus for me are: risk management (which includes identification, assessment and mitigation); technology insertion (the process for identifying candidate future technologies for insertion, insertion rationale, design accommodation, etc.); and system engineering approach (the integration of the system or technical aspects of the product). An overall system engineering approach shows not just what SE does at each phase of a program but the significance of what SE means to this particular product.

Going into depth in each area above has made me understand that all the areas of SE interrelate at a detail level and that it is impossible to know only the tools in or specialize in only one area and be truly effective as a system engineer. For example, a thorough treatment of technical risk on a program requires understanding of the driving requirements on design, contingencies and margins, design components, and definitions of risk levels based on technology readiness and the design engineering difficulty and breadboard / brassboard development programs to mitigate these risks.

Also, going into depth in each area forces an increased understanding of what goes on in all the other areas.

## 4. The Peace Dividend, Corporate Downsizing, and an Uncertain Future

Aerospace systems have historically been among the most interesting to work on (and still are if you can get the right job). This has been one of the reasons that people have wanted to work in aerospace industries. Unfortunately, opportunities to follow a product through its life cycle are now extremely limited (we are becoming "vuegraph engineers"). This is a sign of the times in the industry, given downsizing, cost constraints, and lack of stability of the needs and desires of the nation (compared to the "glory days" in the 1960's or 1980's). Job security, another reason people historically chose to work in aerospace industries, is clearly shaky at best. Declining budgets and economic hard times dictate more direct "applicability" of science and engineering that is funded. Companies had become overspecialized during good times mirroring the government bureaucracy. Now, fewer people producing the same type of products means on the average that each person needs to have broader-based skills.

Working in a downsizing environment is a two-edged sword. On the negative side are decreased job security, increased stress in the work environment, and limited opportunity for promotion and growth in responsibility and salary. On the positive side are the facts that people with real skills mean more than bureaucrats in this environment and it is one that can be a great opportunity to diversify skills, work with good people, and become more valuable for the future. Unfortunately, there is also a short-term risk associated with diversification in that one increases the risk of layoff by filling a job at which one is no longer one of the company-recognized "experts." I have taken the risk and am trying to diversify.

Some key factors which will impact my eventual decision to stay or leave the aerospace industry are the expected downsizing rate and duration, the rate of increase of new skills being acquired in the current environment, and other opportunities. Clearly, once downsizing is completed, opportunities for promotion and to augment one's value to one's current company could increase dramatically. If the "bottom" occurs too late or is too deep, one either gets laid off or misses the personal opportunities that come with working in a growth environment. This bottom will be difficult to predict, given the uncertain nature of government business and future politics. If or when it becomes necessary to act, I expect that my operations research skills, enhanced by system engineering, will be a key in performing "defense conversion".

# 5. Operations Research Ph.D. Benefits and Traps

I have found three general (independent of my field of specialization) benefits of holding a Ph.D., especially from Stanford. These are: first, the Stanford name in getting my initial and subsequent job; second, a tendency to receive more challenging and interesting assignments than someone without a Ph.D. (even if we are technically equivalent); and third, being viewed as an expert. Once I have come up to speed on a job, there are fewer people who question my results or challenge me. Of course, hard work may be needed each time during the "proving period" of a new job, and it is necessary to keep coming up with the right answers.

It is the general skills, however, rather than the specific tools and methods that have proven the most valuable to me from the Operations Research program. Such skills include: (1) analytical thinking and decision processes; (2) innovation, initiative, and self-discipline to work and produce on my own; (3) the ability to be a good listener (to understand the problem before acting) and to keep my mouth shut until I know where the audience is coming from and where I stand; and (4) the ability to gather information from a wide variety of sources, assimilate it, and draw important conclusions from the essential facts.

These skills have given me an ability to ease my way into new jobs and perform to the best of my abilities. I am good at starting from scratch in a chaotic environment filled with strangers. A deputy division chief at NASA once told me that I should put on my business card: "Makes order out of chaos." One of my great skills is the ability to always work in an environment where all my known tasks are prioritized in my head and I can work within that prioritization, even accounting for frequent dynamic reconfigurations of tasks. This skill makes me incredibly productive and focused at whatever I do. I am good at prioritizing things, getting to the heart of a complex problem. This includes the ability not to "jump to conclusions" but to gather all information possible, making decisions when necessary with the best available data.

Some of the dangers of being an OR Ph.D. in a workplace without those of like background are:

1. getting viewed as too specialized;

2. being viewed as "well qualified" but just too mathematical and not practical or "system-wise" enough to contribute to the mainstream in the company. This is especially true for an OR or mathematical-type person in an engineering company. One must be willing to get one's "hands dirty" over a period of time and to prove oneself several times over in a variety of assignments;

3. moving into middle management or a series of jobs where one no longer has the opportunity to apply real value-added skills. This can lead to a layoff during downsizing or a loss of opportunity to be given Ph.D.-level assignments due to technical obsolescence or lack of practice. One should always have one or more skills that are unique and valuable to one's employer. One's degree and education recede in importance with the passage of time;

4. being viewed as a "solution looking for a problem." A colleague from NASA once told me his view of the difference between operations researchers and industrial engineers: industrial engineers look for solutions to fit problems whereas operations researchers look for problems to fit their solutions.

# 6. Lessons Learned and Recommendations

I close with some lessons learned and recommendations to make it easier to succeed in the industrial workplace. For OR graduate students, I suggest taking a few courses in engineering, economics and / or computer science to gain or broaden knowledge of common products produced by companies you may work for as a modeler, analyst, or system engineer; taking a summer job in the workplace instead of thesis or course work to provide better workplace preparation; and making sure you have good personal computing equipment, software, and skills.

Once in the industrial workplace, get a good understanding of the products and processes produced at the company you work for. Otherwise, you may be limited to finance, off-line analytical support roles, or management consultant / support. Even in the last role, you are much more valuable with product knowledge and focus. I believe product and process knowledge, though not directly transferable across industries, is indirectly transferable at the system level. Having gone into depth on one system, you will find that it is much easier to do it again than never to have done it at all! Do not be just a "facilitator."

If you are going to make it in an environment without OR role models, you need to be a self starter, good at relating to people, figuring out what is needed, and deciding where best to fit in. People tend to relate to (and hire) people like themselves, so if, there is no one like you, you must take charge of your own direction, figure out where you can add value, and persuade your management to let you do the work.

Do not get overly specialized unless your goal is to be a world-renowned expert in a particular field, in which case academia would be a more appropriate choice of careers. Exceptions are in disciplines that are essential to the success and innovation of a major company's product line, for example, biology in pharmaceuticals or spacecraft designers in the aerospace industry. OR is tricky; it is always the "process" people who get laid off before the ones who can directly produce or sell the products that make money.

In regarding changes in your responsibilities, do not expect to be doing the same thing throughout your career in industry. If you are, you probably will not be working on the most important problems and will not be advancing your career. Do not be afraid of change; look upon it as an opportunity. Each time I have jumped to a new job, I have looked back one or two years later and have thought how much worse off I would have been without the change. The good news is that operations research skills can be used in almost any industry, but you must work harder than most people to find the right places!

# Acknowledgment

I would like to acknowledge Jerry Lieberman, my Ph.D. thesis advisor who gave me my start in operations research, recognized my talents before I did, and provided guidance when needed while allowing me to find my own way.

# References

Fleming, R. E. 1980. "Coherent System Repair Models," Ph.D. diss., Department of Operations Research, Stanford University.

Fleming, R. E., R. L. De Hoff and J. Josselyn. 1985. "Complex System RMA&T, Using Markov Models," *Proceedings 1985 Reliability and Maintainability Symposium*, pp. 125–130.

Fleming, R. E., J. Josselyn and J. Frenster. 1986. "Application of Markov Models for RMA Assessment," in *Proceedings 1986 Reliability & Maintainability Symposium*, pp. 427–432.

Fleming, R.E., J. Josselyn and P. Boyle. 1987. "Integrated Design of Modular Avionics for Performance and Supportability," *Proceedings NAECON 1987*, pp. 1296–1303. Dayton, Ohio, May 18-22, 1987.

Fragomeni, A. D., M. Ryschkewitsch, R. Fleming, B. Bain, L. Pieniazek and R. Pettis. 1993. "The NASA SEPIT Life Cycle," *Proceedings of the National Council of System Engineers (NCOSE)*, Washington, D.C. July, 1993.

Graves, C., W. Morgan, R. Fleming, and B. Scheffer. 1992. "Project Planning in an Empowered Team Environment," *Proceedings of the National Council of System Engineers (NCOSE)*, Seattle, Wash., July 1992.

Pettis, R., and J. Khouri. 1994. Space Systems Division (SSD). *Systems Engineering Manual.* Lockheed Missiles and Space Company (LMSC), Space Systems Division.

Wertz, W. J., and J. R. Larson. 1992. *Space Mission Analysis and Design*, Torrance, Calif.: Microcosm Inc.

# Chapter 14

# Teaching a Computing-Intensive Statistics Course

David A. Butler

## 1. Introduction

As in many other aspects of modern life, computers have had a large impact in the classroom. There have been many recent advances in computer-aided teaching, such as multimedia and hypermedia presentations, interactive learning programs, and authoring software. Courses that rely heavily on these teaching aids are often described as computer-intensive classes. Computer-intensive classes have been developed for a wide variety of subjects, including many nonquantitative ones such as art, English literature and foreign languages. Unlike these nonquantitative disciplines, which can benefit from computers but are not inherently dependent upon them, most quantitative disciplines, including statistics and operations research, are inextricably linked to computers and computing. Computing-intensive courses provide a means of training students how to use the computer-based analytic tools that are so prevalent in such disciplines.

This chapter discusses the author's experience in developing and teaching a computing-intensive course intended for first-term graduate students in statistics and operations research. The goal of this course is to provide a foundation of computing experience upon which subsequent courses can build. We begin the first section of this chapter by reviewing the literature on the role of computing in statistics and operations research and the integration of computers and computing into their curricula. The second section discusses why and how a computing-intensive course for first-term graduate statistics students came into being at Oregon State University. The section begins with a discussion of student backgrounds and the computing environment in my department, and a description of the forces that instigated the course. It then reviews the choices that were made in developing the course, including the computing environment, software, and prerequisites, and discusses the various means by which computing skills were taught in the course. The chapter's final section attempts to draw some general conclusions about the teaching of computing-intensive courses, based on my experience with this course.

## 2.  Computing in Statistics and Operations Research

Rapid improvements in computers and the advent of the personal computer (PC) have had, and will continue to have, profound effects on both statistics and operations research (Geoffrion 1992; Harris, 1992; Harris and Jackson 1992; Lindley 1984; Thisted 1981). The effects are not limited solely to practice but include theory as well (Efron and Gong 1981). It is widely acknowledged that computer skills are essential for practitioners in both fields. Two studies, one on the training of statisticians for industry (Snee et al. 1980) and the other on the training of statisticians for government (Eldridge et al. 1982), were conducted by the American Statistical Association (ASA) Section on Statistical Education in the early 1980's. Both studies cite knowledge of computer programming and familiarity with statistical software packages as important skills. As the latter report notes, "A statistician without such capabilities is not prepared to assume most statistical positions in the labor market—either in government ... or in private industry." Although somewhat outdated, these two reports accurately foresee "the growing significance of the computer in statistical work" (Eldridge et al. 1982). A survey (Dyer et al. 1993) conducted by the Operations Research Society of America / The Institute of Management Sciences (ORSA / TIMS) Committee for a Review of the OR / MS Master's Degree Curriculum queried approximately two thousand operations research (OR) or management science (MS) practitioners about the technical skills and knowledge they deemed most important to recent graduates in the discipline. "Computer use skills" was rated the most important of fifteen technical skills. "Information technology: applications software" ranked first among twelve knowledge areas, and "information technology: hardware and operating systems" ranked fourth.

Computing is steadily becoming a part of the curriculum of statistics and of operations research. Much, if not all, of the interface between computer science and statistics has come to be known as "statistical computing" (Kennedy 1982; Mann 1978; McNulty 1986). Kennedy (1983) considered whether or not statistical computing should be taught as a separate curriculum. He concluded that the profession will be better served if it is not, but is instead made an integral part of the general statistics curriculum. Statistical computing is a significant component of many existing and proposed statistics curricula. Eddy et al. (1986, 1987) stated that computing is an integral part of all levels of the statistics curriculum at Carnegie-Mellon University. Bates (1983) discussed topics, software development tools, and teaching methods for a statistical computing course. Makuch, Hahn, and Tucker (1990) included two three-credit, computer-oriented courses in their proposal for a graduate-level curriculum for statisticians training for a career in industry, one on statistical computing algorithms and one on statistical computing languages.

The importance of computers and computing to operations research is also evident. According to Harris and Jackson (1992), "the ubiquitous computer has made us totally rethink how we in MS/OR conduct our business and has even redefined the very nature of our solution procedures." Geoffrion (1992) listed the revolution in microcomputers and communications as the first among four major forces acting on OR/MS. Harris (1992) argued that "much of the future success of OR will depend on its ability to ... marry its approaches to computer technology."

Although the necessity of computers and computing skills is widely acknowledged in both statistics and OR, differences of opinion exist about

their place in the academic curriculum. For example, professors disagree on
the appropriateness of teaching the use of statistical software packages in
an academic curriculum. Some have argued, as did Searle (1989), that the
topic is not sufficiently intellectual to warrant academic credit; others have
argued, as did Dallal (1990), that the profession cannot afford to leave the
teaching of statistical computing packages to nonstatisticians. Whatever
the arguments for or against the merits of teaching any one computer skill,
it seems inevitable that in a computer age the integration of computers
into the curriculum will steadily increase, especially in computer-oriented
disciplines.

# 3. Teaching a Computing-Intensive Statistics Course

In any academic program, students start with different backgrounds and
experiences. The Oregon State University (OSU) Statistics Department offers graduate degrees in both statistics and operations research. There is
a broad variety of undergraduate majors among students applying to the
department, thus, the range of computer-use and computer-programming
skills among entering students is very wide. The department has entrance
requirements that ensure a given minimum level of competence in mathematics and statistics but has no requirements for computing experience.
Most domestic students are familiar with PCs, but many international students have had very little experience with them. Entering students are generally less experienced as computer programmers than as computer users.
Although most have had some exposure to computer programming, many
are not comfortable with the idea of writing a program to help solve a
statistical or OR problem. This wide disparity in student computing backgrounds has resulted in a tendency among statistics faculty to avoid assigning computer-oriented problems. Graduate students in the department
have been, for the most part, free to learn as much or as little about computers and scientific computer programming as they wish. Consequently,
graduating students have often exhibited a wider range of computer skills
than entering students. In 1993 a new course, titled Probability, Computing, and Simulation in Statistics was introduced as a one-term required

course for all entering graduate students in the department. There were several goals in instituting this course: to provide a brief review of probability theory to entering students; to introduce students at the start of their graduate studies to the role of computing in statistics and operations research; to provide remedial instruction to those students who enter without much computing background; and to provide a foundation of scientific computer programming experience upon which subsequent courses could build.

The rather all-encompassing course title reflects the desire of the department to allow a broad range of computer-oriented topics to be potentially included in the course. There is no intention to cover any one of the three topics cited in the course title extensively, let alone all three. The main principles in selecting topics are that they should be of interest to statisticians or operations researchers; they should also be understandable by first-year graduate students; and they should serve to broaden the student's familiarity and expertise with computing and computer programming. Unlike some courses with similar sounding titles, the course is not intended to serve as an introduction or survey of statistical/OR software packages.

Probability, Computing, and Simulation in Statistics covers many of the same topics as a standard course on simulation: pseudorandom number generation and testing; random-variable generation; Monte Carlo and discrete-event simulation; analyzing simulation data; and variance-reduction techniques. However, it differs from conventional simulation courses in many respects. Instead of utilizing a specialized simulation language or a conventional general-purpose, high-level programming language, it uses MATLAB (MathWorks 1992), a special-purpose, scientific, matrix-oriented language. The course attempts to make students aware of the broad role of computers in statistics and to make them intelligent consumers of computer hardware and software. Course topics include the history of computers and their use in statistics; current computer hardware and graphical user interfaces; comparisons between compilers, interpreters, and computing "environments"; a survey of statistical software packages; and an introduction to the wide variety of information sources (e-mail, ftp archives, LISTSERV, Usenet, mail servers, Gopher servers) available via the Internet (Krol 1992; Sodhi 1994).

## 3.1. Hardware Selection

The instructor of a computing-intensive course faces many more constraints than does an instructor in a more traditional class setting, because the existing campus computing environment often imposes many restrictions. Both instructor and students may need to use computers in class, in labs, in their offices, or at home, and ensuring such broad access further complicates the situation. Usually, considerations other than academic ones are the most relevant in making intelligent decisions about the computer platform for a course.

In many situations, there may be only one or two feasible choices. For example, the OSU Statistics Department owns both SUN SparcStations (SUNs) and IBM PC-compatible microcomputers (PCs). Either type of computer is sufficient for the needs of Probability, Computing, and Simulation in Statistics, but access considerations clearly favor PCs over SUNs. PCs are much more readily available to the students in the department. Every student office contains at least one (80386 or better) PC, and many contain two. Also, many statistics students own their own PCs. Availability of computer-lab facilities and access by "nonmajors", that is, students from other departments on campus, similarly favor PCs.

Classroom facilities are another issue with which the instructor of a computing-intensive course must contend. Anyone who regularly attempts to conduct in-class computer demonstrations quickly becomes involved with such mundane matters as how large and clear the computer display is, how much it is affected by ambient light, and how much it interferes with other communications media, such as chalkboards and overhead projectors. Having access to a specialized, computer-oriented classroom can be a godsend. Fortunately, OSU maintains several specialized classrooms that contain network connections, lighting controls, and overhead-projection computer-display units to which a laptop computer can be easily connected.

## 3.2. Software Selection

Just as the choice of a computer platform is driven by many nonacademic considerations, the issues involved in selecting appropriate software for a computing-intensive class are largely nonacademic and quite different from those, for example, involved in selecting a class text. Some software is available on many hardware platforms, some only on one or two. Some packages come with very liberal license agreements, allowing students and faculty to use the software at home or to consider a collection of computers in different locations as a single lab. Some software runs readily on a network; some runs poorly or not at all. Attractive educational pricing and volume discounts are available for some packages and not for others. Some software, such as compilers for popular computer languages like C or Pascal, is available from multiple vendors; other software, such as most matrix-oriented programming languages and statistical computing packages, is available from only a single vendor.

The software choices can be categorized as follows (in roughly increasing order of complexity and computer-resource requirements): (a) a general-purpose language, such as C, C++, or Pascal; (b) a special-purpose matrix-oriented language, such as GAUSS (Aptech 1992) or MATLAB (Math-Works, 1992); (c) a statistical computing package, such as S (Becker, Chambers, and Wilks 1988) or SAS (SAS Institute 1989); (d) a symbolic-math package, such as Maple (Heck 1993) or Mathematica (Wolfram 1988).

Although it is possible to expose students to more than one language in a single term, the goal of giving them a substantial experience in writing scientific computer programs effectively precludes significant coverage of multiple software packages. Thus, a single, matrix-oriented computer language, MATLAB, was used in the course. Several considerations favor a matrix-oriented language. Matrix operations are very common in both statistical and OR calculations, and a matrix-oriented language dramatically reduces the effort needed to code them. Matrix-oriented languages often include powerful built-in mathematical facilities, such as functions for numerical integration, Fourier analysis, nonlinear optimization, graphics, numerical linear algebra, polynomial and interpolation functions, sparse-matrix operations, and functions for evaluating common probability distributions and densities. Unlike larger symbolic-math or statistical packages, matrix-oriented packages generally require fewer computer resources, are simpler, and are easier to learn. Although MATLAB was chosen over competing matrix-oriented languages mainly on the basis of its technical merits, it was favored in part because its vendor, The MathWorks, Inc. offered very attractive licensing arrangements.

## 3.3. Prerequisites / Assumed Skills

Prerequisites for a computing-intensive course such as Probability, Computing, and Simulation in Statistics can be difficult to enunciate and to rely on. In learning probability theory, perhaps 70% to 80% of the material is unchanged from one book or one course to another. In learning a computing language, perhaps only 20% to 30% is independent of the particular language being learned. Thus, one can cite "probability theory" as a prerequisite and immediately use probability in the class material with little or no review. However, requiring "some experience with a high-level computer programming language" does not relieve the instructor of having to spend significant amounts of time introducing the particular language to be used in the class. The course prerequisites were "some knowledge of ... personal computers, including how to edit ASCII files and some experience with computer programming." This prerequisite was stated but not enforced, and so it did not serve to screen out students. It merely served as a warning to students without such backgrounds that they faced additional work. The first time that the course was taught some (mostly international) class members began with little or no experience with PCs. Many in the class were familiar with word processors but unfamiliar with editing ASCII files. When asked to rate their computer-programming experience on a scale of 0 (no experience) to 4 (very experienced), most students rated themselves at 2 or below. Most students' prior programming experiences were largely divorced from the rest of their scientific/technical learning experiences. That is, they had little experience in writing programs to solve technical problems in their own discipline.

## 3.4. Teaching Computer Skills

There are many means by which one can teach the use and roles of computing in statistics and OR. They include traditional ones as well as ones that use computer-aided means, such as multimedia, interactive learning programs, and so on. These computer-aided teaching tools were consciously avoided in the course because one objective of the course was to make the inner workings of every computer-related demo and program accessible to and understandable by the student. To date, the course has relied on traditional teaching settings: in-class demonstrations, computer laboratories, homework assignments, projects, and examinations. Each setting offers unique opportunities and constraints.

In-class computer-based demonstrations were effective means of conveying fundamental concepts of probability, statistics, and operations research. One obvious example from statistics was a program to simulate and display the concepts behind the Law of Large Numbers or the Central Limit Theorem. This simple program proved very effective in helping students visualize what happens as the number of observations in an average increases and how quickly its distribution approaches a normal distribution. Although one can obtain ready-to-run demo programs from a variety of commercial and public-domain sources, there are several advantages to an instructor's developing his or her own demo programs. Such programs are inevitably more flexible and more easily modified, and if a sufficiently high-level language is used, they need not be lengthy or complex. Providing students with the source-code for demo programs in the language they are using for the class makes it easy for them to modify the demos; in doing so they have the opportunity both to strengthen their programming skills and to better understand the theoretical concepts they illustrate.

Two cautions should be noted. First, instructors who enjoy programming can easily spend considerable amounts of time creating demo programs, only to find their demos too complex to be effective. Simpler demos are inevitably more effective and easier to conduct in a limited amount of time. Second, it is usually a mistake to attempt to explain how a demo program does its work. That is, reviewing a demo program's code is better left as an after-class exercise for students.

### 3.4.1 Computer Laboratories

A major goal in developing Probability, Computing, and Simulation in Statistics was to introduce students to the use of computers and computer programs as analytical tools. Homework assignments and computer laboratories were probably the most successful means of doing this. As in any programming-oriented class, the homework assignments proved to be very time-consuming for most students. Many students with little programming experience often spent hours trying to overcome simple, yet difficult to identify, bugs in their programs. A computer lab proved to be an ideal setting where students could make mistakes, puzzle over them, yet not waste hours in overcoming their difficulties. The lab was held once per week for three hours; attendance was optional. Most students attended at least the first hour of each lab, but many left before the full three hours had passed.

Although the lab contained equipment to facilitate computer-oriented lectures by the instructor (e.g., an instructor's workstation tied to a large, projection computer-display unit.), no formal lectures were given during the lab. Instead, it proved more effective for the instructor to simply walk around the room from one student group to the next. (Each student had his or her own computer, but they were allowed to interact with one another in solving homework problems and so tended to work in groups.) The choice of an interpreted programming language made it simple for the instructor to quickly identify bugs and solve problems. Some of the prominent features of MATLAB are its powerful (but often confusing) mechanisms for indexing matrices and selecting submatrices. This power was the source of many student mistakes. But because MATLAB is an interpreted language, students could be told to simply evaluate an expression (or its components) involving already defined variables to check if its value was what they expected. Whenever a problem was encountered in speaking with one group that seemed likely to be experienced by other groups, the instructor could make a short announcement to the entire class that allowed the problem to be identified and avoided.

The worth of an environment that allows students to make, identify, and recover from programming mistakes may seem to be obvious. But it requires careful attention to provide a setting wherein this can be achieved. Simply assigning homework problems, then being available to answer questions is not satisfactory. Students may struggle for hours before asking for assistance, and help may not be available when they seek it. They may not be able to reproduce the problem when they finally locate someone to help, and their description of a computer problem will often be different from what really took place. Attempting to reconstruct and resolve problems after-the-fact can be supremely frustrating, both for the student and for the instructor.

The fact that the students began the course with a wide variety of computing backgrounds made for many teaching challenges. For students with weak computing backgrounds, there is no substitute for spending substantial amounts of time at the computer in a setting where help is available.

The three-hour computer lab was the most effective means for bringing those with minimal computing and programming backgrounds up to speed without slowing the rest of the class.

### 3.4.2 Homework / Projects

The out-of-class work required in the course consisted entirely of homework problems, with no projects being required. The subject area in which a project might have proven most beneficial was discrete-event simulation. However, given the other demands placed on the students, requiring them to create a credible discrete-event simulation from scratch was not feasible. In homework problems on discrete-event simulation, students were typically provided with a program to simulate a given system and were asked to modify the code in order to accommodate one or more changes in the system.

One goal of the course was to get students used to writing short computer programs to address real (or at least realistic) problems in statistics. Thus, assigning many small problems was a more appropriate choice than assigning a few large ones. The homework assignments did tend to build upon one another. For example, in one assignment students developed a MATLAB function to generate pseudorandom observations from a t-distribution and another function to generate bootstrap-samples from a set of observations. In the next assignment they used their bootstrap sample generator in developing a function that estimated the standard error of the trimmed mean by the bootstrap method. They then developed a simulation that compared the standard error of the trimmed mean to the standard error of the overall mean for an underlying population having a t-distribution. Each of the four homework problems that constituted this work were individually simple, but taken together, they allowed students to use computers to solve a problem (estimating and comparing the standard errors of the sample mean versus more robust estimators of location) that cannot be accomplished by analytic means.

### 3.4.3 Examinations

Both in-class and take-home examinations were given in the course. Given its computing-intensive nature, the course seemed to prove take-home exams much more satisfactory. They proved better as learning experiences, involved much less time pressure, and were more comprehensive. Perhaps the principal difficulties with take-home exams were that they offered more opportunity for dishonesty and they were more time-consuming to grade. At least partial remedies exist for these problems. Developing and distributing the exam electronically can facilitate individualizing each student's exam and can thus reduce cheating. Setting limits on the lengths of programs students write can temper grading difficulties.

# 4. Conclusions

Certainly degree programs vary widely from one institution to the next. They differ in the backgrounds and goals of their student populations, the experience and interests of their faculties, and the university and departmental resources that are available. Thus, much of the discussion in this chapter will not be universally applicable to statistics or OR programs at other institutions. But two general conclusions can be drawn, namely, developing a computing-intensive course can involve an imposing amount of work, and the effort can be very worthwhile.

The effort required to develop a computing-intensive statistics or OR course is much more than that required for a traditional course. A computing-intensive course involves a genuine commitment to computing and involves much more than an occasional in-class computer demo and the assignment of a few computer-oriented homework problems. The developer of such a course must contend with a number of new issues: hardware availability, software licensing, ensuring fair access to computer facilities. Poorly setup or malfunctioning equipment can easily wreak havoc on a lecture or lab session, to the embarrassment of the instructor and the detriment of students. The effort required only in programming can be substantial. In teaching Probability, Computing, and Simulation in Statistics for the first time, I wrote more than a hundred computer programs and functions. Most of them were short, but collectively they represented weeks of effort.

Another difficulty in teaching a computing-intensive course is that computers and computing environments are constantly changing as technology improves. To maintain any degree of currency, the instructor must constantly work at keeping up with the rapid pace of change. For example,

Probability, Computing, and Simulation in Statistics was developed and taught using MATLAB Version 3.5. A new version of MATLAB, 4.0, is now available. This new version offers attractive new language constructs and features, but programs must be modified to take advantage of them. Moreover, the MATLAB 4.0 language is not completely backward compatible with the MATLAB 3.5 version, so many programs must be modified anyway.

In spite of the amount of work, a computing-intensive course can be very rewarding to teach. A surprising number of students have little or no computing experience when they begin their graduate studies, and many others have never written programs to solve statistics or OR problems. A first-term course that makes students familiar with computer programming in a context where the programs are relevant to their other studies is very beneficial. It can provide a foundation of computing experience upon which subsequent courses can build and can bring students with minimal programming experience up to speed. It is easy to assign extra-credit work to keep computer "experts" challenged. A computing-intensive course can also serve to introduce students to the broader array of computer communications tools, such as e-mail, ftp, and the other resources of the Internet, that are so important to the profession.

# References

Aptech Systems. 1992. *The GAUSS System Version 3.0.* Aptech Systems, Inc., 23804 S.E. Kent-Kangley Road, Maple Valley, WA 98038.

Bates, D. M. 1983. "Teaching Statistical Computing," in *1983 Proceedings of the Statistical Computing Section,* The American Statistical Association, Washington, D.C. pp. 63-64

Becker, R. A., J. M. Chambers, and A. R. Wilks. 1988. *The New S Language.* Pacific Grove, Calif.: Wadsworth & Brooks / Cole Advanced Books & Software.

Dallal, G. E. 1990. "Statistical Computing Packages: Dare We Abandon Their Teaching to Others?" *The American Statistician* 44: 265–66.

Dyer, J. S., J. C. Bean, L. S. Dewald, A. H. Gepfert, and A. Odoni. 1993. "Suggestions for an MS/OR Master's Degree Curriculum." *OR/MS Today* 20: 16–31.

Eddy, W. F., A. C. Jones, R. E. Kass, and M. J. Schervish. 1986. "Implications of Advances in Computing for Graduate Study in Statistics," in *Computer Science and Statistics: 18th Annual Symposium on the Interface,* pp. 131–36. Amsterdam: Elsevier Science Publishers B. V. (North-Holland).

Eddy, W. F., A. C. Jones, R. E. Kass, and M. J. Schervish. 1987. "Graduate Education in Computational Statistics." *The American Statistician* 41:60–64.

Efron, B. and G. Gong. 1981. "Statistical Theory and the Computer," in *Computer Science and Statistics: 13th Annual Symposium on the Interface,* pp. 3-7. New York: Springer-Verlag.

Eldridge, M. D., K. K. Wallman, R. M. Wulfsberg, B. A. Bailar, Y. M. Bishop, W. E. Kibler, B. S. Orleans, D. P. Rice, W. Schaible, S. M. Selig, and M. G. Sirken. 1982. "Preparing Statisticians for Careers in the Federal Government: Report of the ASA Section on Statistical Education Committee on Training of Statisticians for Government." *The American Statistician* 36: 69-81.

Geoffrion, A. M. 1992. "Forces, Trends and Opportunities in MS/OR." *Operations Research* 40: 423–43.

Harris, C. M. 1992. "Computers and Operations Research: A Marriage for Growth." *Operations Research* 40: 1031–39.

Harris, C. M., and R. H. F. Jackson. 1992. "New Methodologies and Techniques: Continued Creative Use of Computers Crucial to Future OR/MS Success." *OR/MS Today* 19: 20–21.

Heck, A. 1993. *Introduction to Maple.* New York: Springer-Verlag.

Kennedy, W. J. 1982. "The Statistical Computing Portion of a Graduate Education Program in Statistics," in J. S. Rustagi and D. A. Wolfe, editors, *Teaching of Statistics and Statistical Consulting,* pp. 233–45. New York: Academic Press.

Kennedy, W. J. 1983. "A Curriculum in Statistical Computing?" in *1983 Proceedings of the Statistical Computing Section,* American Statistical Association, Washington, D.C., pp. 65–66.

Krol, E. 1992. *The Whole Internet User's Guide and Catalog.* Sebastapol, Calif.: O'Reilly and Associates.

Lindley, D. V. 1984. "Prospects for the Future: The Next 50 Years." *Journal of the Royal Statististical Society* A 147, Part 2: 359–67.

Makuch, W. M., G. J. Hahn, and W. T. Tucker. 1990. "A Statistical Computing Curriculum to Meet Industrial Needs." *The American Statistician* 44: 42–49.

Mann, N. R. 1978. "Everything You Always Wanted to Know About the History of Computer Science and Statistics: Annual Symposia on the Interface — and More," in *Computer Science and Statistics: 11th Annual Symposium on the Interface,* pp. 2-5. Institute of Statistics, North Carolina State University. Raleigh, N.C.

The MathWorks, Inc. 1992. *The Student Edition of MATLAB.* Englewood Cliffs, N.J.: Prentice-Hall.

McNulty, S. K. 1986. "A Numerical Analysis Approach to the Teaching of Statistical Computing," in *Computer Science and Statistics: 18th Annual Symposium on the Interface,* pp. 137–40. Amsterdam: Elsevier Science Publishers B. V. (North-Holland).

SAS Institute. 1989. *SAS Language and Procedures: Usage, Version 6, First Edition.* Cary, N.C.: SAS Institute Inc.

Searle, S. R. 1989. "Statistical Computing Packages: Some Words of Caution." *The American Statistician* 43: 189–90.

Snee, R. D., T. J. Boardman, G. J. Hahn, W. J. Hill, R. R. Hocking, W. G. Hunter, W. H. Lawton, R. L. Ott, and W. E. Strawderman. 1980. "Preparing Statisticians for Careers in Industry: Report of the ASA Section on Statistical Education Committee on Training of Statisticians for Industry." *The American Statistician* 34: 65–75.

Sodhi, M. S. 1994. "Global Electronic Networking Using the Internet." *OR/MS Today* 21: 34–39.

Thisted, R. A. 1981. "The Effect of Personal Computers on Statistical Practice," in *Computer Science and Statistics: 13th Annual Symposium on the Interface,* pp. 25-30. New York: Springer-Verlag.

Wolfram, S. 1988. *Mathematica: A System for Doing Mathematics by Computer.* Redwood City, Calif.: Addison-Wesley.

# Chapter 15

# My First Days' Lectures: Past and Present

### Donald L. Bentley

## 1. Introduction

It was the first day of the Summer Quarter at Stanford, and I arrived early that morning to Sequoia Hall to move into the office I knew I would be sharing with David Haley. The routine was the same as the one David and I had been through for the past several years, including the courses we were to teach. As I approached the east door of the building, David came out on his way to his first class. We had not seen each other since the previous summer, and he asked the natural polite question, "How are you?" I responded without thinking, "Nervous!" David, who had an international reputation for his excellence in teaching the master's level statistical inference course, displayed great surprise. He then replied, "I thought I was the only teacher who got nervous on the first day of class."

Since that meeting I have queried a number of my colleagues about their emotional state at the start of a semester or quarter. The vast majority of good teachers share this common nervousness. The thought of facing a new class creates a degree of fear. In fact, there are many of us who now wonder whether there are any teachers who are not, to some degree, uncomfortable on the first day.

After exchanging greetings with David, I got the key to the office and settled in, reviewed my notes for class, and at ten o'clock began my first day's lecture. It was the standard format that I used for the first lecture in every class I taught. I began by giving my name, the title of the course, my phone number, and office hours. This information was followed by the names of the required text and reference texts. The next order of business was the structure of the class. I announced the dates of the two midterm examinations and that they would each contribute one-sixth of the grade. The final examination would contribute one-third. Homework was to be turned in at the end of the next class after the assignment was made, and the homework would contribute the final third of the grade with one exception. Any student who received a failing grade on the homework would fail the course. The above comments were followed by "Any questions?"

Once this preliminary material was out of the way, I was able to turn to the subject matter in the first chapter of the text in order to prepare the students for the evening's homework assignment. Given my nervousness about facing a new class of students, I found assurance in my canned first lecture.

It was not until quite recently that I realized there was another side I was overlooking. I never considered the fact that if I was nervous, perhaps there was a degree of fear on the part of the students. And indeed if there was a fear in the students, what was the effect of my lecture on this fear? Of course there were students in the class who had a great deal of confidence in their ability to succeed and had no fear. However, those students who were less sure of their abilities would not be reassured by knowing that an easy way to fail the course was to fail the homework. They had yet to attempt to do homework and were undoubtedly quite insecure as to whether they could complete an assignment. Instead of worrying about my comfort with a new class, I needed to be concerned about the students' comfort.

As I started thinking about ways I could structure the first day of class that would make students feel more comfortable about taking a statistics course, I realized that most students sign up for the class without a good idea of what statistics is about. In particular, they have no concept of the profession of statistics. If I want them to feel comfortable, and even consider a possible career in statistics, shouldn't I give an indication of the types of activities they would be expected to be involved with? (I have since questioned how well other fields deal with this issue.) I quickly realized that by moving directly into the text on the first day, I avoided ever creating a larger context into which the material of the course fit. I completely ignored providing an overview of the field of statistics.

As a consequence of these concerns, I decided to develop a "first lecture" that would meet the following requirements: it should provide the students with an overview of the field of statistics. The student should come away with a feeling of the breadth of activities in which statisticians are involved; the students should then understand where, in the overall picture, the topics covered in the course fit. And finally, this introduction should motivate the students to want to learn more about the subject. What follows is the lecture I developed in my attempt to meet these requirements. My remarks will be obvious to the experienced statistician. However, our students are not statisticians, and we need to gear our lecture to their level, another obvious fact we sometimes forget. Perhaps this chapter will serve as a reminder.

# 2. The Lecture

## 2.1. Introduction

On the first day of a statistics course I am reminded of the freshman who took the Introductory Statistics course in which he was required to do a project. To gather some data for his experiment he asked his dorm sponsor to buy him a bottle of gin. That Saturday night he proceeded to drink an excessive number of gin and tonics. The following morning he awoke feeling quite ill and recorded the results. The next Saturday he continued the experiment, this time with rum and tonic. Again, the following morning he awoke feeling miserable and recorded the results. The third Saturday he repeated the experiment with tequila and tonic and awoke Sunday morning with a bad headache and upset stomach. Again the results were recorded. At this point he wrote up the results of his experiment with the obvious conclusion: tonic causes hangovers. I do not recommend either the experiment or the analysis.

## 2.2. What Is Statistics?

We could start with the question, "What is statistics?" But a person could equally well ask the same question about philosophy, biology, theology or art. What is art? There are many branches to art. There is the study of art history, art criticism, and the practice of art. Within each of these there are a variety of subfields such as music, painting, ceramics and sculpture. Within music there are classical, jazz, opera, and so on. Our cultural exposure to art has provided us with an understanding of the breadth of the field, and an appreciation of the fact that it would be impossible to develop a single course that would provide the student with an introduction to all of art.

In a similar vein, statistics is a very broad field and has application in a large number of disciplines. To answer the question, "What is statistics?" within a single lecture, or even within a single course is an impossible task. I will attempt to place the content of this first statistics course in a much broader context. But to do so, I paraphrase the question as "What is the role of a statistician on a research team?"

As a statistician who has had some consulting experience, primarily in the biomedical field, I suggest that there are at least five areas of a research project in which a statistician should be intimately involved. Although experimenters do not always include statisticians in all of these stages (sometimes to the experimenter's later regret), a properly prepared statistician will feel comfortable participating in every phase. These five areas are: (1) forming the question, (2) designing the experiment, (3) gathering the data, (4) analyzing the data, and (5) communicating the result.

These stages, or areas, are presented in an order in which they would naturally occur during the course of a study. However, it is important to note that they are interdependent. Certainly, it makes no sense to design an experiment without first determining what question is being addressed. But not infrequently, the question must be modified in order to allow for a feasible experimental design. Physical, ethical, or financial constraints often limit the actual question or set of questions that can be addressed in a particular study. We now turn to some examples which I have encountered and feel demonstrate the important role a statistician plays on a research team.

## 2.3. War Stories

### 2.3.1. Forming the Question

W. Edwards Deming[1] is a name recognized in industry as that of the originator of Total Quality Management (TQM). It is his methods that were adopted by the Japanese in the 1960's and which are credited with establishing Japan's leadership in quality. This high quality is responsible for the great demand for Japanese automobiles that dominated the automobile industry into the 1980's. A comparison circulating among the TQM community points out that in Japan, when a problem arose, those involved would spend 90% of their time discussing the question and 10% finding the solution. In the United States we spent 10% of our time on the question and the remaining 90% on hunting for a solution. The above story is perhaps an exaggeration, but the message is important, as is illustrated by the following examples.

### 2.3.2. California Assessment Program (CAP)

Recently, the State of California has introduced a new form of standardized testing to evaluate the proficiency of secondary school students. This testing involves open-ended questions allowing the students to demonstrate creativity.

In 1988, as the state was gearing up to administer these tests, a book containing a sample of mathematics questions and how they were to be graded was circulated to secondary school teachers (California State Department of Education 1989). Among the mathematics questions the following appeared:

> John has four place settings of dishes, with each place setting being a plate, a cup, and a saucer. He has a place setting in each of four colors: green, yellow, blue, and red. John wants to know the probability of a cup, saucer, and plate being the same color if he chooses the dishes randomly while setting the table.

> Explain to John how to determine the probability of a cup, saucer, and plate being the same color. Use a diagram or chart in your explanation.

At this point I ask the students to work individually on the problem for about five minutes before I continue with the lecture. I then proceed with the following statement to the students: Now that you have all had time to look at the question, I would like to ask you to tell me, not what your answer is, but what problem you are attempting to solve. To begin, although John has four place settings, we do not know for how many people he is setting the table. Were you solving the problem for a table set for four, or for the table set only for John? What other possible interpretations of the question can you come up with?

HOMEWORK: By adding specific conditions to the statement of the above question, create a list of the different interpretations you can generate.

As an aside, I should state that the book contained two sample graded answers. One sample solution treated the problem as setting a single place, but made a mistake in multiplying by one-half rather than one-fourth in the last step, although the student clearly had the proper idea. This student received half credit (a score of 3) for the question. The other paper received a perfect score (a score of 6), although the logic would have led to a probability of one had there only been two types of dishes, say cups and saucers, rather than the three. I cannot figure out any interpretation for the problem for which the logic of the solution would have been correct.

The point of the above example is that the question needs to be clearly defined before one starts trying to solve it. An important part of a statistician's job is to help the experimenter define the question. The statistician should strive to fully understand the reason for the experiment and the theory behind it. Frequently, this will require spending some time reading about the subject area.

### 2.3.3. Toxicology Example

I was once asked by a pharmaceutical firm to help on a toxicological problem. My introduction to the project occurred at a meeting attended by the staff of the toxicology department and several vice-presidents from the company, plus the chairman of the toxicology department from an area medical school who had also been called in as a consultant. The meeting began with one of the researchers from the company making a presentation, directed to the other consultant and me. I listened to the presentation for about five minutes and then interrupted with the statement, "I'm sorry, but you are going to have to start back at the beginning again. I have no clue as to what you are talking about."

The initial reaction of the presenter was shock, followed by a sigh of relief as he realized that he was over my head, and hence knew more about the subject than at least one of the consultants. Perhaps this would make his job more secure in the eyes of his supervisors. As he started over on a much more introductory level (which I could understand), the chairman of the toxicology department leaned over and whispered, "Thanks, I didn't understand anything either!" As a statistician, I was not required to be an expert in the field of toxicology, and could ask *stupid* questions. He, however, was an expert in the field and, I guess, felt unable to display his ignorance. What an advantage it is to be a statistician and be able to ask questions. It is this advantage that makes statisticians valuable in the question-forming stages of a research project. Frequently, the questions we ask turn out to be related to factors not considered by the experimenter. Our questions help the experimenter better understand the project and force clear definitions of the important issues of the study.

### 2.3.4. Rabbit Eyes

A number of years ago I received a call from a company doing a preliminary study of an anti-inflammatory drug for the treatment of allergic conjunctivitis. (On a personal note, my ophthalmologist unwittingly gave me a prescription for the drug that resulted from this study this past year when I had a bloodshot eye.) The head of the unit had already gathered the data from the experiment; he suggested we meet so that he could explain what had been done and I could begin the statistical analysis.

The study was performed on rabbits, since their eyes are in many respects physiologically quite close to the human eye. The rabbits to be used in the study were challenged by injecting horse serum into their conjunctiva (the membrane that lines the inner surface of the eyelid) in order to create an allergin (make the rabbit allergic to the serum). One week later the rabbits were again injected with the serum, and then treatment was begun. One eye of each rabbit was randomly assigned the treatment solution, and the other eye given the vehicle (the solution without active drug). Treatment was continued for one week.

The person in charge of the study was well aware that statisticians like lots of data, so he used the following design. Five technicians who did not know which eye had been assigned the treatment each picked the more severe (redder) eye twice a day over a seven-day period on each of two rabbits. Hence, there were a total of $5 \times 2 \times 7 \times 2 = 140$ observations available for the analysis. The results were impressive. I was able to tell the experimenter that the technicians were consistent with one another in picking the redder eye. But when he asked me what I could say about the effectiveness of the treatment I had to admit that the data would not allow me to answer that question. He had essentially flipped a coin twice (the two rabbits) and come up heads on each toss. There was not enough information to be able to demonstrate that the coin was biased (or the drug effective).

Unfortunately, the type of problem illustrated above is not uncommon in research. Too often a study is run in which the data do not address the question of interest. It is important for a statistician to be involved in the study design to make certain that the data gathered will address the important questions.

## 2.4. Conclusion

I have listed the five areas of a study in which I feel a statistician plays an important role. The examples are intended to illustrate the importance of understanding the question, designing the appropriate experiment, and gathering meaningful data. Clearly, the data must be gathered and entered into the database with accuracy. Errors in data entry can lead to grave errors later on in the analysis.

The traditional topics of an introductory statistics course come under the heading of data analysis. The analysis is the point in a research project where the statistician is in the spotlight. This is the area in which the statistician has the expertise. However, it must be kept in mind that this part of the study usually involves a relatively small percentage of the total time that the statistician will put into the project. Since the introductory course devotes the majority of its time to this area the student needs to beware of thinking that the field of statistics is limited to this one aspect.

The one area that still needs to be discussed is communication. This

TABLE 15.1

*Population at Risk, Deaths, and Death Rates for an Unusual Episode:*

### By Economic Status and Sex

| Economic Status | Population Exposed to Risk | | | Number of Deaths | | | Deaths per 100 Exposed to Risk | | |
|---|---|---|---|---|---|---|---|---|---|
| | Male | Female | Both | Male | Female | Both | Male | Female | Both |
| I (high) | 172 | 132 | 304 | 111 | 6 | 117 | 65 | 5 | 39 |
| II | 172 | 103 | 275 | 150 | 13 | 163 | 87 | 13 | 59 |
| III (low) | 504 | 208 | 712 | 419 | 107 | 526 | 83 | 51 | 74 |
| Unknown | 9 | 23 | 32 | 8 | 5 | 13 | 89 | 22 | 41 |
| Total | 857 | 466 | 1323 | 688 | 131 | 819 | 80 | 28 | 62 |

### By Economic Status and Age

| Economic Status | Population Exposed to Risk | | | Number of Deaths | | | Deaths per 100 Exposed to Risk | | |
|---|---|---|---|---|---|---|---|---|---|
| | Adult | Child | Both | Adult | Child | Both | Adult | Child | Both |
| I and II | 560 | 19 | 579 | 280 | 0 | 280 | 50 | 0 | 48 |
| III | 645 | 67 | 712 | 477 | 49 | 526 | 74 | 73 | 74 |
| Unknown | 32 | 0 | 32 | 13 | 0 | 13 | 41 | 0 | 41 |
| Total | 1237 | 86 | 1323 | 770 | 49 | 819 | 62 | 57 | 62 |

oft-ignored topic is, in my mind, as important as any of the others. There is no value in doing a study—no matter how well designed, conducted, and analyzed—if the results of that study cannot be communicated to the end user. For this reason I feel that the writing and oral components should be an important part of each introductory statistics course. If you fully understand the technique used for data analysis, you should be able to communicate, in a clear way, the results of that analysis upon the gathered data. If one cannot communicate clearly, then learning various methods of analysis has been for naught.

### 2.5. Homework

The first homework problem, which has already been discussed, is to come up with different interpretations for the CAP problem.

As a second project I want to expose you to the detective work that is involved when we look at data. In Table 15.1 are the data from an *Unusual Episode*.[2] Look at the data with the charge of trying to figure out the unusual event. For the next class prepare a list of questions you would like to ask of the data. The data are presented first by economic status and sex, and then by economic status and age. Within each set are the data for the population exposed to the risk, followed by the number of deaths, and then the death rate per hundred persons.

## 3. Summary

My "First Lecture" was created in an attempt to motivate students to want to learn about statistics. My experiences so far indicate that it does a better job than my previous approach. I conjecture that one reason for this is that I am more excited about what I am saying.

I think it is important for statisticians to bring their own personal experiences into the classroom. Students like to hear about my experiences (War Stories), and my course evaluations from students request that I include even more. These experiences become tools which make the material come alive. It is worth noting that in providing these experiences I am in line with the movement among leaders in the field of statistics education who are moving away from fictional data sets towards either realistic or real data (see Cobb 1991). Two texts that are considered on the leading edge of this movement are those by Moore and McCabe (1993), at the precalculus level, and by Rice (1988), at the postcalculus level. As an alternative to Rice's text, Witmer's (1992) can be used to support a data analysis unit to run concurrently with the traditional course entitled "Introduction to Mathematical Statistics."

The preface to Moore and McCabe lays out priorities for the introductory course based on their conception of the role of statistics as applied in practice.

> The title of the book [*Introduction to the Practice of Statistics*] expresses our intent to introduce readers to statistics as it is used in practice. Statistics in practice is concerned with gaining understanding from data; it is focused on problem solving rather than on methods that may be useful in specific settings. ... We share the emerging consensus among statisticians that statistical education should focus on data and on statistical reasoning rather than on either the presentation of as many methods as possible or the mathematical theory of inference. Understanding statistical reasoning should be the most important objective of any reader.

Rice, in his preface, gives a similar view.

> This book is a consequence of my having taught a course at this level several times, and having come away each time feeling rather dissatisfied with what had been accomplished. It seems to me that the usual approach is a low-level introduction to a graduate course on optimality theory (which most students never take). This approach does not give students an overview of what statistics is really about ... I have tried to write a book that reflects my view of what a first, and for many students last, course in statistics should be. Such a course should include some traditional topics in mathematical statistics (such as methods based on likelihood), topics in descriptive statistics and data analysis with special attention to graphical displays, aspects of experimental design, and realistic applications of some complexity. It should also reflect the quickly growing

use of computers in statistics. These themes, properly interwoven, can give students a view of the nature of modern statistics. The alternative of teaching two separate courses, one on theory and one on data analysis, seems to me artificial.

I support the move of both these texts toward more data, and in particular more real data. However, each of these texts is taking only a first small step. Both argue that the introductory course should not be restricted to topic four from my list (analysis of the data) but should branch out to expose the student to the broader field of statistics. However, each limits its discussion to, at most, topics three (gathering the data) and four. The respective tables of contents reflect the degree to which the texts reinforce such a restriction.

As with the academic disciplines of philosophy, biology, theology and art, I do not believe that it would be possible to teach an introductory course in statistics that treats, in any depth, all areas in which a statistician could (should) be involved in a study. But I do believe that it is important to indicate such breadth at some point during the semester. I have chosen the first day in the hope that the students will recognize this importance of statistics in research and, of greater importance, in their daily lives.

# Notes

[1] For a description of the career of Deming see Mann (1988).

[2] The original source of these data is unknown to me. They were suggested to me by Dr. Julie Buring of the Harvard University School of Public Health, who obtained them in a course she had taken as a graduate student.

# References

California State Department of Education. 1989. *A Question of Thinking: A First Look at Students' Performance on Open-ended Questions in Mathematics.* Sacramento, Calif.

Cobb, G. 1991. "Teaching Statistics: More Data, Less Lecturing" *UME*

*Trends: News and Reports on Undergraduate Mathematics Education*, vol. 3. no. 4. Mathematical Association of America, 1991.

Mann, N. 1988. "Why it Happened in Japan and Not in the U.S.", *Chance* vol. 1 no. 3. New York: Springer-Verlag.

Moore, D., and G. McCabe. 1993. *Introduction to the Practice of Statistics*. Pacific Grove, Calif.: Wadsworth & Brooks/Cole.

Rice, J. 1988. *Mathematical Statistics and Data Analysis*. Pacific Grove, Calif.: Wadsworth & Brooks / Cole.

Witmer, J. 1992. *Data Analysis: An Introduction*. Englewood Cliffs, N.J.: Prentice-Hall.

# Chapter 16

# Courses for Learning the Practice of Operations Research

B. Curtis Eaves

## 1. History and Beginning

Operations research (OR) or management science is about building, researching, testing, and revising a model or models of an operation with the intent of improving the operation in some way. The word *operation* means a problem, task, system, project, or opportunity in the real world, and *model* usually means a mathematical model. From one perspective and in the simplest terms, there are the mathematical models of OR and the mathematical theory thereof. Then there is a mountain of other skills required for the practice of OR. This paper is not about OR theory or even OR modeling, but rather about courses for learning the practice of OR. It describes an extended effort in the Department of Operations Research at Stanford University to develop an environment for learning the practice of OR. Over a twenty-year period this effort has explored, retreated, and grown in many dimensions, some of which have broken new ground. Our purpose here is to provide an account of these courses and of the reactions elicited from students, instructors, and problem sponsors in the hope that various features will be studied, criticized, and perhaps, developed or adopted elsewhere.

In the 1960's the interdisciplinary OR group became the Operations Research Department at Stanford and shortly thereafter began offering an M.S. degree as well as the Ph.D. Both programs in the Department consisted of an uninterrupted sequence of theory courses. The operating assumption was that if one taught students the theory, they would figure out how to apply it. In retrospect, it is clear that this assumption was incorrect for most students. With the introduction of the M.S. degree and with the changing interests of students arriving in the late 1960's, namely, toward a demand for relevance, the pressure for applications quickly reemerged. An approach for teaching the practice of OR to forty M.S. students and not just a dozen Ph.D. students was needed.

For the first time, in the spring of 1975–76, the course titled Applications of Operations Research (OR 280) was to be offered by the Department with myself as the instructor. The course was based on the cases of von Lanzenauer (1975) and was required for the M.S. degree in OR. As it happened, Leon Lasdon, who was visiting Stanford, joined me in running the course.

The course evolved. Instructors constructed new cases themselves and borrowed from other books and programs. However, the task of supplying new and broader cases on a steady basis over the years posed a genuine obstacle. This problem, as well as a host of others, were eventually solved, but as usual the solutions led to a new set of problems.

Although students were encouraged to contact case authors and principals, and they did, a full dialogue between our students and those actually experiencing the problem was missing. Furthermore, the cases did not offer the challenge of model formulation from a raw description. This was the motivation for the existence of a second course, Field Projects. In 1986–87 the Department expanded the required course titled Applications of Operations Research into two courses, now entitled Case Studies (OR 281) and Field Projects (OR 282). These two courses now form the centerpiece of the M.S. degree program. Although over the years these courses have been shepherded principally by Alan Manne (now retired) and myself, by now, most members of the Department have conducted Case Studies.

Of course, every institution teaching OR, management science, decision science, or quantitative methods has encountered similar needs for applications, and they have developed their own proposals, perspectives, and courses. Undoubtedly, there have been many shared experiences. It is my belief, however, that our courses have developed in some uniquely interesting directions, and this record will prove useful to those developing related courses elsewhere.

For the most part I will describe these applications courses as we do to our students (but more briefly), namely, through course organization materials and quotations from prior students and from project sponsors. These documents raise a multitude of issues, any one of which deserves a long analysis in itself. These courses have been modified many times in response to student feedback. My purpose here, however, is not so much to analyze the methods we have developed as to describe them and to provide a sense of how they take shape in the classroom through the testimony of the participants themselves.

As for the setting, our M.S. program is a one-year program, three or four quarters, with a requirement of fifteen courses. Typically a student takes ten theory courses (linear, network, integer, and nonlinear programming, computer programming, matrices, probability, statistics, stochastic processes and models, and simulation), two applications courses, and three electives. Case Studies and Field Projects are offered in the Winter and Spring Quarters, respectively. Appropriate course waivers are available. Now let us turn our attention to the current versions of these two courses.

## 2. Applications Course No. 1: Case Studies (OR 281)

In the first week the class is partitioned into balanced teams, the concepts of a case and a "solution" are introduced, and intrateam dynamics are discussed. A questionnaire is used to obtain profiles of the students. The Jury (two professors and two course assistants) forms the teams, balanced according to factors from the profiles. That the teams are determined by the Jury rather than by the students serves many purposes. There are typically eight teams of five students each. Videotapes from the Franz Edelman Videotape Library and from past Case Studies team presentations are shown in class, and past team reports are briefly examined, in order to convey the idea of a case or project (operation) and a "solution." It is emphasized that a "solution" is not a solution in the theory sense, but is really shorthand for "decision support" or "a decision-support system". The matter of intrateam dynamics is addressed by two readings, a writing assignment, and a class discussion. The cases are demanding, and a fully functioning team is needed to execute the volume of effort required for a successful solution. Members of a malfunctioning team experience considerable stress. Teams were emphasized in the early history of OR and remain essential to the work place today. A great deal of what follows is about teams.

In the second week each student presents a case and solution that he or she has selected from the periodical *Interfaces*. From the third week on, the course revolves around teams. Teams, two at a time, agree on a case from *Interfaces*, and then working separately, improve the solution, write a report, and prepare a presentation of the report. The presentations are followed by extensive question, answer, and critique periods.

At this point I will describe this course as we do to students, namely, through the course organization materials and excerpts from intra-team dynamics papers by previous students. In this way I hope to communicate to the reader enough about the organization and feel of the course that parts or the whole could be reproduced with a predictable outcome.

## Case Studies (OR 281): Course Organization

**Course Objectives:** The objective of this course is to initiate the process of learning and practicing the application of operations research. In particular, the aim is to integrate and enhance a variety of skills including problem identification, problem yield estimation, case selection, teamwork, task and time management, application of theory, data collection and processing, library usage, software usage, interface construction, assembling results, technical writing, presentation skills, and questioning and answering skills as they relate to the effective application of OR.

**Individual and Team Studies:** In the first phase of the course, individuals select, prepare, and make individual presentations of cases. In the second and major phase of the course, student teams select cases, improve the solution, write reports, and make presentations of the cases with the improvements.

**Case Selection and Interfaces:** Cases are selected by the students and teams. The recommended source of cases is the periodical *Interfaces*, published by The Institute for Management Sciences and The Operations Research Society of America. Articles in *Interfaces* are about "solved" problems. For individual presentations the idea is to pick an application of OR of interest to the class. For team presentations the idea is to identify a case where the solution can be improved upon; you want to maximize your results for the effort expended.

**Jury:** All grading will represent a consensus of the (entire) Jury (two professors and two course assistants), the purpose being to try to moderate individual subjective evaluation.

**Individual Presentations:** In the first phase of the course, students individually select and present a case. The goal here is a clear presentation of the problem and the proposed solution. The use of the view graph is strongly recommended. Presentations are videotaped. There are tapes of past individual and team presentations on reserve in the Terman Engineering Library that may be checked out for home viewing. The Jury will raise brief questions and comments after each presentation.

**Team and Group Determination:** With the results of the survey "Questionnaire for Team Determination" the Jury will attempt to form semirandom balanced teams of four or five persons each. The balancing is based on fluency in English, industrial and military experience, technical ability, computer ability, ethnicity, gender, age, marriage status, and distance of residence from campus. In our next meeting teams, groups, and presentation dates will be posted. There will be about four persons per team and four teams per group. Team composition will be fixed for the duration of the course, although some early adjustments may be necessary to accommodate dropouts.

**Team Guidelines:** The main idea is to improve a published solution of a case and to communicate the proposed improvement. Teams select and develop the cases as thoroughly as possible, given the myriad of constraints. Teams meet (outside of class) to read cases, identify problems, define issues, select and analyze cases, improve solutions, write reports, deliver oral presentations, respond to questions, and question presentations of others. The solution should, as a bare minimum, offer a model for the case, that is, a clear way of thinking of the problem. For both the report and the presentation, assume the audience includes various levels of management as well as qualified OR types from that company. You want to persuade the audience and readers that your team is the entity of choice to deal with the problem. Precise recommendations are important; teams are encouraged to use any available relevant software. Team presentations should be a team effort. The teams are expected to show some responsibility and initiative, and in particular, not to ask the members of the Jury to certify solutions in advance of presentations. Take solace in the fact that the cases are complicated enough to render the notions of completeness or correctness useless.

**Two Presenting Teams, Buyers, Sellers, and Gallery:** Team presentations begin on the seventh day of class. For class, two teams are designated as the Two Presenting Teams (team and counter team), and the rest of the group is affectionately designated as the Gallery. The Two Presenting Teams will agree upon and then independently prepare a single case. Each of the Two Presenting Teams prepares a written report and a presentation for the case. Before noon on the day prior to the presentations the Jury will designate one of the Two Presenting Teams as the Buying Team and the other as the Selling Team. Members of the Buying and Selling Teams are referred to as Buyers and Sellers.

**Role Playing:** The Buyers represent members of the company or institution with the problem described in the case. The Sellers represent an outside consulting team that wants to sell their talents, their time, their interpretation of the problem, and their approach to a solution to the Buyers' company. Both Buyers and Sellers have access to the case, which was written previously by a third party about the problems of the company.

**Buying Team Presentation:** The Buying Team makes a presentation to the Jury and the Gallery of their interpretation of the problem and approach to (improving) the solution. The presentation is followed by questions from the Jury and Gallery. The Sellers are not present for this presentation or the questioning.

**Selling Team Presentation:** Following the Buying Team's presentation and questioning, the Sellers enter the classroom and present their interpretation of the problem and solution. The audience consist of the Buyers, Gallery, and Jury. Be prepared to answer detailed questions from the client.

**Questions by Buyers to Sellers:** Following the short break after the Selling Team's presentation is the question-and-answer period. The break is for the Sellers to rest and for the Buyers to organize their questions. The Buyers want to challenge the problem statement and solution as presented by the Sellers. Experience indicates that it is especially during this question-and-answer period that the audience is able to discern who really understands the case and solution and who the leaders of the teams are.

**Criticism by Jury:** After the presentations by the Sellers and questioning by the Buyers, the Jury will offer an evaluation of the case selection, analysis, presentation, and the questioning.

**Gallery Criticism:** Members of the Gallery peruse the source material before class, listen to the presentations, questions and answers, ask questions, and prepare criticisms.

**Report Guidelines:** The written report and presentation should be organized from "general to detailed" and from "general to detailed to general," respectively. The first several pages of the report should contain in the plainest English possible the problem statement, considerations, conclusions, justifications, and summary. As one reads further into the report one finds the models and full justification of the methods and recommendations; technical language is most appropriate here, but not initially.

**Integration of Presentation and Report:** The "oral presentation" is a presentation of the report, but with a summary.

**Grades for Presentations, Questioning, Answers, and Report:** The reports will be studied and carefully marked by the Jury. The presentation and questioning grades will also be placed on the report, and the reports will be returned to the teams at the next meeting of the group.

**Distribution of Paper Case:** At least one week prior to the presentation date, the Liaisons of the Two Presenting Teams distribute a copy of the case source material (the paper case or article) to each team in the Gallery (4 copies), and to each member of the Jury (4 copies).

**Collaboration Rules:** The Two Presenting Teams are not permitted to agree or coordinate in any way whatsoever on the scope, nature, or specifics of the solution or questions. They are to agree only on the case, that is, choice of article only.

**Fobidden Resource:** Unless explicitly permitted by the instructors, past or present solutions of cases by other students or student teams at Stanford or elsewhere are not to be utilized in any way. Use of all other resources is encouraged.

**Intra-Team Dynamics Paper I (Beginning of Case Studies):** For the second day of class, read "Feuds in Student Groups: Coping with Whiners, Martyrs, Saboteurs, Bullies, and Deadbeats" by Jalajas and Sutton, 1985, and "Excerpts from Past Intra-Team Dynamics Papers I (Beginning of Case Studies) and II (End of Case Studies)" of which excerpts appear below in Section 3 and write a page or two on some aspect of them.

**Intra-Team Dynamics Paper II (End of Case Studies):** At the end of the course write two pages about your team. The discussion could be, for example, (a) that some member contributed more than others in some dimension and that this contribution might otherwise go unnoticed, or (b) something learned about individual or team dynamics. Names may be used or not, as suits you. This is a graded assignment and furthermore, remarks could affect the grades of others. In a year or so with names changed (to protect the innocent) they may be used as reading material in a future Case Studies class.

**Course Grades:** Grades are determined by the quality of work on the various tasks. Grading includes everything.

**Video:** All presentations will be videotaped. The operator carefully labels the recorded tape with Case Studies (OR 281) and the date and delivers the tape to the desk in Terman Library with the instructions that the tape is to be put on Case Studies (OR 281) reserve.

**Last Two Days of Course:** On the last two days of class all teams meet together for a retrospective, teaching surveys, and an orientation for the sequel to the course, Field Projects (OR 282).

**Field Projects (OR 282):** The sequel to Case Studies is Field Projects. Here again teams solve problems, but now they are real ones. Skills developed in Case Studies are assumed to be in place and ready for use in Field Projects. The very first day of Fields Projects begins immediately with presentations by project sponsors. Please arrive on time.

# 3. Case Studies: Excerpts from Intra-Team Dynamics Papers

On the first day of Case Studies students are asked to write a page, Paper I, on two readings. The purpose of this exercise is to alert students to the importance of and measures for intra-team dynamics. At the end of the course students are asked to write two pages, Paper II, about the intra-team dynamics of their own team. In addition to enhancing student awareness of intra-team matters the second paper supplies the Jury with intra-team information. Upon reading the papers from a team, the Jury obtains a pretty good idea of the internal functioning of the team; or more particularly, who contributed what. The remainder of this section consists of a brief selection of excerpts from student Papers II, which will I hope provide a sense of the course. I have edited the excerpts for readability and have tried to collect them into helpful categories.

**Readings:**

1. Without the readings at the beginning of the course, I would have become a "martyr."

2. As I was reading through my notes of Case Studies I picked up my first assignment, I read it and I smiled. In that paper it was obvious how

concerned I was about this class: the team work and the language problem. ... All my fears proved to be wrong.

**Teams:**

1. She definitely was a support for me when I was so tired (and grouchy) that I just wanted to give up on everything.

2. Our diversity allowed us to accomplish many things during the course of the quarter that probably would not have been possible if the students had picked the teams.

3. When the members of a team have a strong commitment to it, the team delivers amazing results that would be impossible for an individual to reach.

4. I learned how to compromise on issues and when to stand firm.

5. Lack of communication skill was probably the major downfall of our team.

6. I was particularly pleased with the evolution of our team. As the quarter progressed we were able to deal with more difficult issues and complexity.

7. Initially, I was opposed to many meetings, thinking that they would only be a waste of precious time, but they were quite useful in keeping up to date on what everyone was doing.

8. The most important thing learned was how much time is required to see a complex problem to the end.

**Foreign Students:**

1. Since my native language is not English, on many occasions instead of thinking the conversation topics, my brain was busy with constructing a grammatical, error-free sentence.

2. Race and personality are not the issue; communication is.

3. If this comment can be made available to the students who are going to take this course, especially foreign students, I would strongly suggest that you should take this chance to learn to speak.

4. The strong English speakers and writers typically bear the burden of writing the paper and preparing the presentations. The OR Dept. needs to address this problem.

**Individuals:**

1. However, I did change and I became more aggressive towards the end of the quarter ... much to X's dismay.

2. During this past quarter I have felt apprehension, confusion, enlightenment, anger, joy, frustration, satisfaction, depression, elation, determination, hope, fear, sadness, and happiness.

3. I can remember one time when I actually exploded.

4. Many just seemed to lose control of their feeling when under stress.

5. Case Studies was the most demanding and the most interesting course I had ever had.

**Leadership:**

1. One of my biggest insights into team dynamics is that there exist "loud" leaders and "quiet" leaders.

2. There was no leadership in our team, which meant that no one was forced into doing something. This made everyone aware of their role in the team, which is to participate.

**Modeling:**

1. There was an occasion where I put together a working model that I understood, but that was "expanded" by the team to a model I no longer understood.

2. True, the objective function was strange-looking, but we had never read anything stating that it has to necessarily reflect cost in dollars or units of blood collected.

3. The final concern was whether or not we would be able to improve on the solutions. This was actually quite possible and this gave me confidence in my ability to apply OR techniques out in the real world. This is one of the most valuable aspects of the class.

**Tools:**

1. Technically, I had the chance to learn to use many software packages like GAMS, EXCEL, MacDraw, and especially MINITAB.

2. Practically speaking, I learned about a lot of different tools which I had never been exposed to before. For instance, I now feel confident in using the GAMS software package, Excel, and Cricket Graph.

3. Our present tool kit (linear programming, dynamic programming, probability, integer programming, networks) is far too limited for the cases available.

4. In fact my first reaction to @Risk was, why use it at all? But that afternoon at the Terman cluster with X sure showed me what it was for.

**Contacts:**

1. One useful activity that we did was to contact the company. Initial phone calls to contact people were discouraging, but with persistence we found the right people.

**Presentations:**

1. The actual presentation, especially the first time, was one of the highlights of the course - I felt stressed out during the rehearsal but very confident in the actual presentation.

2. I am even glad that the first time I froze in a presentation was in a learning environment, and not in front of a client.

3. A very good job could be hidden by a poor report, and the ability to speak in a clear and precise manner are fundamental in selling the work.

4. One fact we should always keep in mind is that no matter how excellent a solution to a problem may be, it becomes mediocre if it is not well justified and explained in both the written and oral reports.

5. As a side note, my other teammate was frustrated from the fact that a good presenter can give the impression that he knows everything but in actuality he may be clue-less.

**Questions and Answers:**

1. I feel that the questions and answers were the most enjoyable part of the presentation, because it is here that you show that you understood what you did.

**Evaluation:**

1. Now I will give some specifics about my teammates.

2. I felt "he's so much smarter than I am!" As time went on, I realized that his contributions were not the only significant contributions ... our team became a little more "equal."

**_Interfaces_:**

1. I believe that the authors of our selected cases in *Interfaces* did not sufficiently substantiate their methodologies, and I am perplexed why the journal referees were not more critical of the seemingly obvious deficiencies.

2. Reading many issues of *Interfaces* allowed me to get a feeling for the broad range of problems and situations related to OR.

3. I just would like to add how interesting the case readings were. This helped us to better understand how OR can be applied in real-world problems in an impressively broad range.

**Fun:**

1. Our team met almost every day of the week. ... We had our breakfast, lunch, dinner, and even supper at Terman 4th floor. ... It may sound very bad, but I really had a great time.

**Case Studies:**

1. Being able to improve upon an already published case is a great intellectual confidence builder.

2. I realized that the work involved is similar to what I did as a Management Sciences Analyst before I came to Stanford.

3. After experiencing Case Studies, I would describe it as an intensive and substantial experience applying OR.

4. The scope of OR is much broader than what I thought; it may require backgrounds in Manufacturing, Engineering, Economics and Organizational Behavior among others.

5. This course allowed me to see, via different case studies, practical uses of OR and to practice the skills I have gained in this program.

6. I was not looking forward to this class, but as a result of it I feel much more confident about entering the job market.

7. Having worked in industry for a few years, I would like to say that Case Studies models the "real life" situation quite well.

**Jury:**

1. I can understand that the Jury's criticism was well-intended and actually constructive and is probably one of the most beneficial things I got out of this course.

2. I have never had professors, let alone course assistants, who did so thorough a job grading papers. There were comments on everything. Our team noted every comment and tried to improve each successive report.

3. Case Studies gave me a good experience and an imagination of what Field Projects is going to be. I appreciate the comments on our presentation and report which were very useful and very valuable in order to improve our analysis and writing skill.

**Field Projects:**

1. At first, Case Studies seemed pointless to me - why resolve a problem that had been solved? Now, it is clear to me that this course is really a part of the Case Studies–Field Projects series and so serves as a training ground. Make your big mistakes here!

2. My primary concern about the class relates to our Spring Quarter course: Field Projects in OR. Although I think that we, as a class, have come a long way in our preparation and presentation techniques, I am not sure that we are ready to represent Stanford.

# 4. Case Studies: Some Lessons Learned

Over the years as I have listened to and studied many teams, solutions, and presentations in Case Studies and Field Projects, I have recorded common mistakes as well as some ideas of how to avoid them. What follows in this section are samples of words of guidance or caution for future students of Case Studies (as well as Field Projects).

**Leadership:**

1. The choice of a team leader can, unfortunately, be determined by some incidental remarks in initial meetings. Use care and time in the selection, if any, of an explicit leader. The presence or absence of an explicit team leader does not seem to be, in itself, a good indicator of team success.

2. Do not take the position of team leader unless you are ready to assume full responsibility. The diversity of the team represents the diversity of the power of the team. Keep the team together, in particular, keep each teammate involved and valuable. You must protect and guide the consensus.

**Teams:**

1. Esprit de corps is delicate. Show up late and unprepared to a few meetings and you will demoralize your team.

2. Another more subtle way to destroy a team's morale is the following: Study the case extensively alone, thoroughly analyze the case alone, develop a careful solution alone, and then arrive at the meeting with the purpose of persuading your teammates to adopt your concepts.

**Modeling:**

1. A model is a formal simplified representation of (a piece of) the real domain of study. There is always a trade-off between simple models and more comprehensive models.

2. Distinguish between the real world and the assumptions you need for your model and your algorithm. There are three categories here: the real world, the model, and the algorithm.

3. Different models may permit different aspects of the problem to be

analyzed. Confirmation of a conclusion by a second model is very compelling.

4. If you have a different objective function than that which is currently used, give an argument for why it is more appropriate for the application.

**Analysis and Development:**

1. Call the principals and authors of a case. A few words with them can be invaluable. The more homework you have done when you approach them, the better the response you can expect.

2. Any recommendation should be analyzed enough so that you can bring out its merits in commonsense language.

3. Be "problem solvers," not OR technicians. Do not be concerned with using fancy tools, rather be concerned with solving the problem.

4. It may be that during your research, you find that the solution presented in the article is no longer used, which is a problem in itself. How does one install a system so that it stays installed?

**Presentations:**

1. The final speaker could briefly reshow, say, three key slides from the presentation.

2. Number and title each slide so it can be referred to unambiguously.

3. In exhibits, tables, and charts, label axes carefully and include an example to show how to use the information. Graphs are easier to read than tables (for slides anyway).

4. Organize slides until the flow is natural, use large print, and keep illustrative materials visually simple.

5. Master the terminology of the problem. Do not change the context. If the case is stated in terms of trains, talk about trains, not some generic abstract unit such as the traveling salesman.

6. Be practical about your achievements. Speak to your audience in their terms.

7. If there are no data, show how you could use them if you had them.

8. Mention but do not dwell on technical differences like quadratic programming versus linear programming. Focus on results.

**Questions and Answers:**

1. A clear, crisp question has an important merit: it is easy to learn from a good response.

2. Organize questions so as to challenge the proposals on a broad front.

3. Buyers should not hesitate to present their own slides in clarifying or reinforcing their questions.

4. Have backup slides prepared to show the mathematical formulation of the "problem."

*Interfaces.*

1. A comprehensive operation (larger scope, multi-objective, longer to describe, etc.) is relatively harder to solve and the solution is relatively easier to challenge than a small operation.

2. Some of the published models and solutions in *Interfaces* are narrow and weak. Also, we have observed that many solutions did not stick. Yet, such cases offer more opportunity for improvement.

# 5. Course No. 2: Field Projects (OR 282)

We turn our attention now to the second course of the sequence, Field Projects. Essential to the second course is recruiting good project sponsors from local industry, business, government, institutions, and so on. Sources of project sponsors include personal contacts, faculty contacts, current student contacts, graduate contacts, the Department's affiliates program, repeat sponsors, and now some volunteers out of nowhere (because they have heard of the course through the grapevine). Also, there are spreadsheet workshops, the Stanford School of Engineering university-industry consortiums Energy Modeling Forum (EMF), Center for Integrated Facility Engineering (CIFE), and Stanford Integrated Manufacturing Association (SIMA), which we are just learning to use. Also let me not forget participants in the biennial two-day event "Achieving Global Competitiveness through Manufacturing Partnerships," sponsored by the Graduate School of Business and the School of Engineering. The possibilities are endless. Each year we use some repeats and develop some new sponsors. A representative list of past problem sponsors is given later. We ask sponsors to explain their problem as they understand it rather than to try to define the problem in our terminology. We do not want make-work problems.

The domains of some past projects follow: Tanker scheduling at Decision Focus Institute; tanker routing at Standard Oil of California; container shipping at Stolt-Nielson; partitioning mortgage pools at Bank of America; hedge fund risk evaluation with Manager's Fund; production, inventory, and delivery of feeds with Nutrena Feeds; router maintenance depot location at Cisco Systems; evaluation of Smart Talk appointment reminders at Stanford Hospital; patient referrals, authorizations, records, and billing flows at Stanford Hospital; materials inventory and delivery at Stanford Hospital and Owens and Minor; emergency assembly-line adjustment at Ford Electronics; power-demand management at Palo Alto Utilities; long-term water planning at Palo Alto Utilities; balancing service and obsolescence in inventories at Hewlett Packard; integrated-circuit fabrication facility at Hewlett-Packard; pension-fund management at Applied Decision Analysis; inventory and supply of eye lenses at R. B. Webber; inventory and shipping problems of computers and parts at R. B. Webber; hiring strategies at Radio Shack; incorporating crew scheduling in fleet scheduling at Northwest Airlines; materials management and engine-shop simulation at Northwest Airlines; inventory modeling and rework shop at United Airlines; circuit-board inventory at Varian; circuit-board repair procedures at Silicon Graphics; train makeup at Amtrak; thermo-fit hose product scheduling at Raychem; process simulation at Chevron; retirement policies at Stanford University; farmer crop planning at Shearwater Consultants; quantitative policy for awarding grants at EPRI.

I now present the essentials of the course organization material.

## Field Projects (OR 282): Course Organization

**The Course:** Eight project sponsors have been recruited. In the first four days of class, two per class, sponsors will make a presentation of a project (operation, problem, dilemma, concern, opportunity, puzzle, etc.). Each student will join a project team; there will be eight teams of about four persons each. The teams address the project as presented by the project sponsor. Teams meet, discuss, analyze, collect data, interact with project sponsors, reach conclusions, and design systems in order to assist the project sponsor with the problem. Teams give routine progress reports to the Jury, and the Jury offers guidance. At the end of the quarter teams write a report and make a presentation of the report to the project sponsor. The project sponsors will be asked to critique and evaluate the report and presentation. Finally, each student prepares two pages on his or her intra-team dynamics.

**Team Preferences:** After the last presentation by sponsors, each student submits to the Jury a ranking of his or her project preferences. The Jury will attempt to form balanced teams while simultaneously trying to respect the preferences of individuals.

**Confidentiality:** A project sponsor may request team members to sign a confidentiality agreement.

**Quick Cases:** Each student is asked to write one page for each of the eight presentations by project sponsors. Describe the project as you see it, and outline your ideas or recommendations for proceeding to a solution. Questioning the project sponsor during the presentation might ease this writing task.

**Grading Quick Cases:** Respective Project Teams will grade the quick cases.

**Team and Project Sponsor Interaction:** The project sponsor expects a dialogue with the team. A team will get best results by preparing for these meetings. Teams may want to contact other sources as well.

**Progress Presentations:** Throughout the quarter the Jury will meet with the teams to hear progress presentations, offer criticism and guidance, and monitor team spirit. For the first meetings, teams propose project scope and statement, mathematical models, data collection, resources, model building, individual assignments, a timetable for tasks, and so on. These meetings are the primary opportunity for the teams to take advantage of the Jury's expertise. Weak progress presentations preclude quality guidance from the Jury, which further compounds the weakness.

**Final Team Presentation:** The report and final presentation should be directed to the project sponsor, and then to the Jury. This is a full presentation of the project report. Each team member must participate in the presentation.

**Attending Final Presentations:** Each student should attend at least three final presentations in addition to his or her own. However, all students are invited to all presentations unless they are otherwise instructed.

**Video:** With the project sponsor's permission, all related presentations will be videotaped. Make use of them.

**Intra-Team Malfunction:** Experience suggests that one or two of the eight teams will experience substantial internal difficulties. If a team starts to have problems, students should bring them to the attention of an instructor (not a course assistant) forthrightly.

**Intra-Team Dynamics Paper (End of Field Projects):** Toward the end of the quarter, each student begins preparing a two-page paper discussing the functioning of his or her team. The discussion can mention names or not, as the student chooses. The Jury will read these statements just prior to setting final course grades, and indeed, these statements may influence grades, so care should be taken. Only the Jury will read these statements; they will be treated most confidentially. In a year or so the statements may be stripped of identifying names and used as reading material in a future Field Projects course. Some excerpts from past students are given later in Section 6.

**OR Colloquium:** Each team will give a minipresentation of the project at the final two Department Colloquia of the quarter. Each team member participates.

**Last Day of Class:** Everyone should attend the last regularly scheduled meeting of the course, which is used for reviewing the general lessons from the course and conducting evaluations.

**Course Grades:** Grades for the course are based primarily on the progress presentations, the final report and presentation, response to questions, sponsor comments, and the team dynamics statements.

**Job Search:** Experience indicates that Case Studies and Field Projects can be helpful with resumes, explaining OR, job interviews, and evaluating and making presentations to prospective employers. Most attractive job opportunities within the field require someone who can function well on a project team. Keep a copy of quick cases, team reports, and intra-team dynamics statements for a year or two as evidence of your project experience.

# 6. Field Projects: Excerpts from Intra-Team Dynamics Papers

Aside from giving students practice in summarizing the inside functioning of their teams as well as other observations about Field Projects, the intra-team papers supply essential information to the Jury for grading purposes. By the time of the final presentations, the Jury is involved with the teams, projects, and solutions, and further, the Jury has a fairly clear idea of who contributed what. Because, however, members of the Jury do not sit in on team meetings, there is some margin for error in the Jury's assessment of individual contributions. Usually, the intra-team papers hold no surprises; however, occasionally, there are some good ones. Below are some excerpts from past intra-team papers.

**Teams:**

1. Unfortunately, my disagreements with X continued, so I even had to ask Prof. Y for help, which I would not normally do, but she threatened to do the same, and I didn't want the instructors to have a one-sided opinion. Afterwards X's behavior noticeably improved, so eventually we were happy with each other.

2. I think our success was due to an extraordinarily organized and motivated team. X set our project schedule and made sure we kept it. Y

took notes at our internal meetings and distributed them to everyone. This ensured that everyone knew what was going on, even if they couldn't make it to all the meetings.

3. X and I both made deliberate attempts not to take over the group. As it turned out though, XX and YY didn't have it in them to ever really grab the bull by the horns, so X and I were forced to dole out the responsibilities sometimes.

4. Team leader is not a position I would choose in every situation. I realize, now more than ever, that the leadership position requires a great deal more than creativity and technical skill.

**Individuals:**

1. She exploded one day after X and Y left the meeting.

2. It is amazing how working closely with a person can really change our perception of that person.

3. I feel that X should fail this course.

**Analysis and Development:**

1. We analyzed data, reconstructed ideas and rewrote the program. We repeated this procedure again and again until we all had confidence in what we were doing.

2. My Personal Lesson #1 from Field Projects: Make sure to nail the frame of the problem before charging forward in analysis.

3. If the originator of those ideas had chosen to defend them more adamantly, the team could have circumvented a lot of unnecessary confusion and work.

4. We had a different view of modeling itself. I understand modeling as an intellectual process of extracting substantial features of the problem, but X sees it as writing some kind of computer program.

5. I have learned a lot of practical things that I would not have learned in any other class at Stanford. I realize how powerful OR techniques can really be in a real business decision.

**Project Sponsor:**

1. She maintained frequent contact with XX throughout the project, ensuring that the sponsor would be a part of the process. This had a tremendous effect on their satisfaction with our work.

2. Prepare for meetings with your sponsor. We used our first meeting with our sponsor as a brain-storming session; it may have given our sponsor an unfavorable first impression.

3. The problem was that our sponsor kept changing his assumptions and as a consequence we were not very efficient.

4. I was amazed at the time our sponsor was willing to spend advising and encouraging us.

5. The client offered us jobs to work further on this problem.

6. To have eight professionals spend three hours with us asking what we needed was a truly remarkable experience.

**Progress Reports:**

1. The meetings with the Jury were useful; it allowed us to get input and stay on track.

2. The Jury was very helpful whenever we had questions, and also in giving us suggestions on how we should proceed.

3. Prepare for your progress reports. Take them seriously. If possible, complete your project in time to present preliminary results at your final progress report.

**Case Studies and Field Projects:**

1. My suggestion for this class is that every student taking Field Projects should take Case Studies as a prerequisite. He/she will then know how to cooperate with other teammates and also will have some experience in presentations and report writing.

2. Field Projects is not one more case study after Case Studies, it is much more than that. The analysis is all started from scratch, and the problem has to be defined by ourselves. Through this entire process, I have

learned how to deal with a project from a workplace, e.g. how to look at a problem from different angles, how to analyze a problem, how to do relevant research and application, and how to design an approach, etc.

3. This whole concept of having the Case Studies class and the Projects class is great. I have learned a lot from both classes and it has definitely prepared me for a career in the real world.

4. I am nonetheless proud of what we have accomplished and I believe everyone did their required share. This class, and Case Studies were by far the most rewarding and enjoyable experiences I have had in the Master's Program.

**Field Projects:**

1. Since I majored in economics during my undergraduate studies, I always lacked a sense of connecting theory with application other than the "end of chapter problems." I found this course most valuable in respect to its applicability to real world problems.

2. I think Field Projects is the most useful course I have taken at Stanford.

3. As I expected, Field Projects was my favorite course this quarter. I learned a great deal and had a lot of fun. Unfortunately, I can't say there were no team frustrations.

4. Attending other teams presentations is also a good idea, since we can learn how they solved their project. My conclusion is that collecting the data (information) is the most important part of the whole project, since without good data the results won't be any good.

# 7. Field Projects: Project Sponsor Comments

As for sponsors, over the years, all have expressed satisfaction with their yield; at a minimum, the return supplied by our team has always justified their effort. Usually, project sponsors are very complimentary of the team's contribution. For many projects, sponsors have offered jobs to members of the team. In some instances team reports were still being actively discussed by the sponsors a year later. Sponsors have told us that our teams' efforts were more careful and more complete than those they had received from professional consultants. Our teams have been written up in company newsletters, and excerpts of final reports have appeared in trade journals. In the past, projects sponsors have on occasion volunteered written evaluations of the project team's efforts. This year for the first time, we explicitly asked sponsors for a written statement. Excerpts from two follow; they are representative of our experience.

Project 1: Router Maintenance Depot Location
Project Sponsor: Cisco Systems, Inc.
Contact: Gary Mattevi
Source: Response to Questionnaire

My level of understanding of the course was increased significantly by meeting the professors personally, allowing me to get a detailed explanation of the problem and feedback about the class. I recommend a similar meeting with each of your sponsors if this is not already a part of the process. The interaction was excellent; I found the students very open to learning the practical application for the material learned in their class. In addition, I found the members of the team very flexible and creative in their approach to working on the problem and providing a solution. I believe there were two significant benefits from the final report and the presentation. First, a practical solution was provided to a real business problem in a real business environment. Secondly, the presentation provided a window to the corporate processes and the varied perspectives of company personnel. When asked by our President if this was a valuable exercise, my answer was, "Yes, I would do it again." But my advice to other sponsors is to pick the problem very carefully and recognize the time requirement.

Project 2: Materials Inventory and Delivery in a Hospital
Project Sponsor: Materials Management at Stanford Hospital and Owens
& Minor
Contacts: Nick Gaich and Jim Dillon
Source: Excerpts from article in "Sales Solutions" of Owens & Minor by
Jim Dillon

We had four Stanford graduate students (Field Projects
Team STORMM) with backgrounds in mathematics, engineering and computer science to quantify savings potential. The
students had no experience working in hospitals. Nick and his
management staff, Peggy Woods, operations manager at our
San Francisco Division, and I gave the team a crash course in
hospital and distribution operations. Different members of the
Stanford / O&M team met with the students throughout the
project.

In May, Team STORMM presented its finding to the class,
professors and the Stanford / O&M team. The students' computer math model showed that 483 deliveries could be con-
solidated from 60 to 34 daily working hours. This equaled a
cost savings of $90,000 annually, assuming the current primary
competency pay scale. Restructured pay scales for delivery only
employees only, or outsourcing this function, increased the cost
savings to $150,000 annually. Considering the time constraints
on Team STORMM's analysis, Stanford considers the findings
conservative.

The triple win of this exercise is impressive. Team STORMM
completed an exciting and challenging educational project. Stanford and O&M received 150+ hours of consulting services from
four exceptional operations researchers. Team STORMM's report will be the framework for implementing the new logistics
division of Stanford University Hospital Materials Management.

# 8. Field Projects: Some Lessons Learned

Over the years I have tried to record difficulties teams have encountered in this course and ways for teams to avoid or deal with them; samples follow. The principal new obstacles that occur in Field Projects as opposed to Case Studies are a bigger environment, the project sponsor, more data, and the unexpected. At this point, misunderstandings with sponsors, alienated team members, data matters, and failure to make the most of the progress reports are probably the main threats to the success of a project.

**Case Studies:**

1. Apply skills learned in Case Studies.

**Project:**

1. A successful project will require knowledge, cooperation, and stamina.

2. Expect data collection, correction, and processing to require at least 50% of the project effort.

3. Allocate extra time for that unexpected complication whose identity is unknown and whose arrival is assured.

**Progress Reports:**

1. Make the most of Progress Reports; it might make (and has made) the difference between moving in a good direction and moving in a flawed one.

**Sponsor:**

1. Get communication channels with the problem sponsor clear as quickly as possible. Establish contact points with the sponsor. Usually, it is best to designate a single teammate for each contact point.

2. The team should visit the project sponsor site as soon as possible, if appropriate.

3. Make sure your problem sponsor understands your time constraints. Collect data as soon as possible.

4. The sponsor must be kept involved in the development process, or

he or she will neither understand, support, nor adopt your plan. Meet regularly, explain, question, and listen.

5. The sponsor's willingness to engage the team is a good measure of his or her evaluation of the team effort.

6. Sponsors can be a source of problems for many reasons.

7. With your sponsor's approval and guidance, examine competitors to determine how they are coping with operations related to the project. Failure to do this can be embarrassing.

8. Search the relevant literature, as well as the OR literature.

# 9. Conclusions and the Future

I have tried to let these two courses, Case Studies and Field Projects, tell their own story. Are they an effective environment for learning the practice of OR? An acid test would be something like this: How much did we add to the students ability to practice OR versus what could they have gained from comparable efforts? Our most immediate indicators are the reactions of students, graduates, project sponsors and faculty.

The excerpts from the Intra-Team Dynamics Papers reflect students' thoughts. My reading of these comments is that the students are learning the practice of OR at a very effective rate. As for problem sponsors, the comments we received this year (see Section 7) fairly represent the type of feedback that I have received over the years. Project sponsors are much more easily recruited today than they were in the past. As for faculty reaction, my colleagues and I have consistently been amazed at the volume and quality of teams' efforts. We have also seen some beautiful mistakes by individuals and teams, but fortunately for all, they were executed in a learning environment. Time and time again we have been very proud of our students and felt that our teams have contributed very valuable ideas. As for myself, certainly, in every project I learn something important; the environment is intellectually rich without bounds.

Clearly, there are many features of the course that need more thought and structure. There are established disciplines that are relevant to our purposes of which we have not made sufficient use. Although there is much to be done, we are well on our way toward successful applied courses. At least for the foreseeable future we will continue to expand these courses with the aim of producing students who can better practice OR.

## This Paper and Acknowledgments

This is an abridged version of a paper that is available upon request. Samples of team final reports and video tapes of final presentations are also available upon request, for a small fee. All comments and suggestions are most welcome.

This manuscript (and the complete version) has benefited immensely from extensive comments made on earlier versions by Erika Schraner and Bob Entriken; of course, blame for all remaining anomalies rests with me. Also, it is with great pleasure that I thank my fellow instructors, my course assistants, the project sponsors, and certainly, all of the students who have made this endeavor so interesting, so informative, and so much fun over the years. Preparation of this manuscript (and the complete version) was supported by National Science Foundation Grant DMS 92-07409.

## References

Jalajas, David S., and Robert I. Sutton. 1985. "Feuds in Student Groups: Coping with Whiners, Martyrs, Saboteurs, Bullies, and Deadbeats." Department of Industrial Engineering and Engineering Management, Stanford University, Stanford, Calif.

von Lanzenauer, Christoph Haehling. 1975. *Cases in Operations Research.* London, Canada: University of Western Ontario.

# Chapter 17

# Some Lessons Learned About Textbook Writing

## Frederick S. Hillier

Successful textbook writing is an art that is largely learned from experience, and I am sure that these lessons are well known to many experienced
writers, but I have enjoyed this exercise of formalizing the lessons I have
learned. Jerry Lieberman and I are coauthors of the widely used textbook
*Introduction to Operations Research*. The book was first published in 1967
and is now entering its sixth edition. This is a highly personalized account
of some lessons I have learned about textbook writing from this experience.

## 1. Our Book and Its Spinoffs

In 1961, there were very few books available that could be used as an
introductory textbook on operations research. There was a clear need for
the development of a new textbook. Jerry and I began talking about under-
taking such a project. When I returned from a year-long leave at Cornell
in June 1963, we began our writing. After a few years of hard work and of
testing our drafts with our own students, the book was published in 1967
by a small local publisher, Holden-Day, Inc. Our timing was fortuitous
and the book immediately became a "best seller." I remember well that

at the next ORSA-TIMS meeting, as a junior faculty member who still looked like an undergraduate, I received many startled comments from people seeing my name tag, "so you are Fred Hillier." It was very helpful to have a well-known coauthor to give the book immediate credibility.

When I now look back at the first edition, I tend to cringe. Although the material was presented in a logical manner, I had not yet learned the lessons presented here. I fear that our first edition would not have fared very well in today's much more competitive operations research textbook market. It has been an enjoyable challenge to continue improving the book to meet the increased demands of the evolving market. Our subsequent editions were published in 1974, 1980, 1986, 1990, and 1995. One important event was the sale of our book by our struggling publisher to McGraw-Hill in 1988. We have been delighted with our new publisher. With our first new edition with McGraw-Hill in 1990 we also published two new spinoffs, *Introduction to Mathematical Programming* and *Introduction to Stochastic Models in Operations Research*. A second edition of *Introduction to Mathematical Programming* also came in 1995. In addition, work was begun on a new textbook, *Introduction to Management Science*, that will be aimed at business students rather than at the students in engineering and the mathematical sciences who are the primary users of our current books. The new textbook is also to have a spinoff, *Introduction to Quantitative Methods*.

One of the interesting developments in the evolution of our basic book has been its substantial increase in size over the years. The first edition was just 633 pages, with moderate height and width. The sixth edition is 998 pages, with considerably larger height and width than the first edition despite substantial omissions of outdated material over the years. This is largely a reflection of the growth of our field.

The other main development has been the steadily increasing incorporation of the lessons cited here. Because of the two developments, each new edition has been a time-consuming task, even rivalling the time required for the first edition. However, we continue to be gratified by the outstanding reception of our book. In addition to the English version, there are now perhaps a dozen translations into other languages. Several hundred thousand students around the world have used our book since its appearance in 1967. It is a privilege to have introduced so many students to our field.

# 2. Some Lessons Learned About the Overall Presentation

This section focuses on lessons learned about the overall approach to the book, and then we turn in the next section to lessons regarding the detailed presentation.

**2.1. The Empathy Lesson:** Place yourself in the shoes of a student who is being exposed to this material for the very first time.

Having lived with the field for many years, I find it difficult to remember that fundamentals, terminology, and concepts that are second nature to me are brand new for the student. I am always questioning myself about whether my terminology has been properly introduced and will be meaningful to the student. How will the student react to this sentence, this paragraph, this series of paragraphs? Am I assuming too much about their background? Am I throwing too much at them without necessary elaboration? At the same time, am I failing to highlight the main idea by going into too much detail? When reusing terms or concepts introduced previously, do I need to provide quick reminders about their meaning?

To increase my sensitivity about where students are, I have found it extremely useful to have my students turn in comments weekly about spots in the book that have given them difficulty. I ask them to turn in something even if it is only the comment that "I have no suggestions this week." I continually receive revelations about material that is unclear to them that seemed perfectly clear to me when I was writing it. However, upon further reflection after placing myself in their shoes, I am usually able to see why it was unclear to them.

All the other lessons in this section flow out of this first lesson.

**2.2. The Motivation Lesson:** Proper motivation needs to be provided to the skeptical student about why the material ahead is important and worthy of their study.

Many students take an operations research course because it is a requirement. Some of these students also have considerable math anxiety. They have no idea why operations research is important, and they enter the course with little aspiration beyond surviving it. Together with the lecturer, it is the author's job to get the students excited about the material and its relevance to their future careers.

In Chapter 1 of our sixth edition, we introduce fifteen summaries of successful applications of operations research, all of which have had a major impact on the organization involved. Frequently, savings ranging into the tens of millions of dollars per year were achieved. More information about some of these applications is given in Chapter 2, with a few detailed case studies provided in Chapter 3. By this time many skeptical students are more than ready to delve into the techniques used in these kinds of applications.

**2.3. The Perspective Lesson:** Place the upcoming material into the perspective of the Big Picture.

I always give considerable attention to the introduction to each chapter. I generally will have several paragraphs that will properly introduce the topic of that chapter, its relevance, and its role within operations research. The introduction then concludes with an overview of the specific topics. Each section begins with some additional perspective on that specific topic. Finally, each chapter ends with a short conclusions (summary) section that again puts the chapter's material into perspective.

**2.4. The Illustration Lesson:** Make heavy use of examples to introduce and illustrate material.

Feedback from the first edition helped us to learn this lesson. Although the first edition had many brief examples, they frequently were given after the fact rather than to introduce upcoming material. A key change for the second edition was to have the first section of many chapters (after the chapter introduction) focus on a full-fledged and realistic prototype example for the chapter. This example then would be carried throughout the chapter to illustrate the new material. In addition, smaller examples often would be introduced to illustrate some specific points. I have found this approach much more effective than fully developing concepts first and then illustrating them.

**2.5. The Intuition Lesson:** Help to develop the students' intuition for what is going on rather than focusing on abstract concepts.

Students will learn and remember new material better if they are developing an intuitive feeling for that material. Providing intuitive explanations, sometimes including concrete analogies that have been part of their experience, will help this process. Frequently, it is helpful to be able to visualize geometrically what is going on in an algebraic technique. Each of our new editions has included a substantial number of new figures to aid this visualization. Our current edition includes hundreds of figures, even though the bulk of the material is essentially algebraic in nature. Student feedback continues to ask for even more graphical illustrations.

**2.6. The Tutorial Software Lesson:** In this computer age, including tutorial software with the book provides a powerful teaching supplement.

Beginning with the fifth edition, we have included tutorial software called "OR Courseware" packaged with the book. Both Macintosh and IBM versions are available. The sixth edition includes routines for each chapter after the two introductory chapters. The software features three kinds of routines: demonstration examples, interactive routines, and automatic routines.

The demonstration examples (demos) supplement the examples in the book in ways that cannot be duplicated on the printed page. Each one vividly demonstrates one of the algorithms or concepts of operations research in action. Most combine an algebraic description of each step with a geometric display of what is happening. Some of these geometric displays become quite dynamic, with moving points or moving lines, to demonstrate the evolution of the algorithm. The demos also are integrated with the book, using the same notation and terminology, with references to material in the book, and so on. Students find them an enjoyable and effective learning aid.

The interactive routines also are a key tutorial feature of this software. Each one enables the student to interactively execute one of the algorithms of operations research. While viewing all relevant information on the computer screen, the student makes the decision on how the next step of the algorithm should be performed, and then the computer does all of the necessary number crunching to execute that step. A Help file always is available to guide the student through the computer mechanics. When uncertain about the logic of the algorithm for how to perform the next algorithm step, the student can switch temporarily to reviewing the corresponding demonstration example and then switch back to the same point in the interactive routine. When a previous mistake is discovered, the routine allows the student to quickly backtrack to undo the mistake. To get the student started properly, the computer points out any mistake made on the first iteration (where possible). When done, the student can print out all the work performed to turn in for homework.

In our judgment, these interactive routines provide the "right way" in this computer age for students to do homework designed to help them learn the algorithms of operations research. They enable focusing on concepts rather than on mindless number crunching, thereby making the learning process far more efficient and effective, as well as far more stimulating. They also point the student in the right direction, including organizing the work to be done. However, they do not do the thinking for the student. Like any good homework assignment, these routines allow the student to make mistakes (and to learn from those mistakes), so that hard thinking will be done to try to stay on the right path. We have been careful in designing the division of labor between the computer and the student to provide both an efficient and a complete learning process. In certain cases, the computer will take over a relatively routine task after the student has demonstrated the ability to perform it correctly on the first iteration.

The software also includes a considerable number of automatic routines to provide number crunching help. Many are for stochastic modeling problems involving complicated formulas. Several others are for algorithms that are not well suited for interactive execution. In a few cases (e.g., the simplex method), an algorithm will have both kinds of routines available. In these cases, the automatic routine can be used to check the student's answer from the interactive routine. In addition, after learning the algorithm with the help of the interactive routine, the student then can quickly apply the algorithm with the automatic routine whenever the student formulates a model that is solved in this way.

These automatic routines are not intended to compete with the corresponding routines available in powerful commercial software packages, but to introduce the student to what can be done with them. For example, the output for the automatic routine for the simplex method has been designed to emulate that in popular commercial packages.

# 3. Some Lessons Learned About the Detailed Presentation

Now we focus on some lessons about the detailed presentation within each section of a book.

**3.1. The Transparency Lesson:** Think hard about how to organize, develop, and display material so that it becomes as transparent as possible to the student.

I have learned since the first edition that just laying out material in a methodical and logical manner is far from sufficient. Most students who use this book are not strong readers who will soak up all the concepts like a sponge. They are not inclined to wade through long verbal developments or detailed mathematical material. Overcoming these obstacles can be very challenging. The following lessons provide some specific ways for doing so.

**3.2. The Single Topic Lesson:** Stick to a single, specific topic at a time.

Students find it confusing to bounce back and forth between different ideas. I try to focus on just one point at a time. Before doing any writing on that point, I spend considerable time thinking through the entire development of the point (including the detailed wording), and then I write it all out at once.

After several ideas have been developed individually, then the next topic can be how to relate these ideas to develop a broader concept. This requires a careful, detailed organization.

**3.3. The Small Doses Lesson:** Present even a specific topic in small doses, including relatively short paragraphs and (on average) relatively short sentences, with an economy of words.

One of my rules of thumb is to try to avoid sentences that are longer than five handwritten lines. Occasionally I will allow longer sentences, but only after examining them to see if they can be shortened or broken into separate sentences. To enliven the writing I try to vary the writing style, including the pattern and length of the sentences. Questions and exclamatory statements can be good. (Don't you agree? Try it!) Occasional very short sentences are a nice change of pace.

I have a similar attitude about paragraphs. I do not like paragraphs that are longer than about ten to fifteen book lines. It gives the student too much to digest. For longer developments I keep looking for appropriate places to break into separate paragraphs.

I occasionally receive feedback that my longer discussions (running over a number of paragraphs) often can be clarified by condensing them. Fewer words can highlight the key points. This is a specific lesson that I am still trying to absorb.

The small doses lesson also applies to the organization within a section. I usually will separate a section into several subsections, with occasional further division into sub-subsections. This provides the student with more digestible chunks. It also identifies the current focus of discussion and its relationship to the rest of the section. Another advantage is greater ease of referring back to desired reference material.

For textbooks in engineering or the mathematical sciences, like ours, I dislike a full unbroken page of straight text. Having this occur on both the left and right pages is even worse. This makes it very difficult for a student to find the key points or to refer back to find key material. Frequent subdivisions of sections, along with tables and figures, help to avoid this problem. So does the following lesson.

**3.4. The Highlight Lesson:** Make fairly frequent use of boldface, italics, and setting off of material to help the students spot key terms, words, and results.

To help break up a page and highlight key material, I like to set off important conclusions (indented with extra space above and below). Both within these conclusions and in the regular text, I boldface important new terms. This makes it easy later for the student to refer back to the meaning of the terms. I also use italics to emphasize certain words. (However, as the copy editor for our sixth edition kept reminding us, some selectivity in the use of italics is needed because its overuse can lead to ignoring the italics.)

All these highlighting techniques give the student useful handles for identifying key material both during the first reading and during later reviews. Surrounding text can then provide needed clarification of this material.

## 4. Conclusions

I am convinced that learning and implementing the lessons described in the preceding sections have been key ingredients for the success of our textbook.

Another important ingredient for me has been a lot of hard, meticulous work. I estimate that I have devoted at least 2,500 hours to our sixth edition. This amounts to an average of more than two hours per page, plus several hundred hours for such related work as outlining and testing new routines for the book's software. Careful attention to detail is a must.

The final important ingredient is to bring a missionary zeal to a book. I find it exciting to have been able to introduce hundreds of thousands of students to the field I love. Many of these students have used or will use operations research during their careers, and some have even gone into operations research as a career. Much of this would not have happened with a lesser book. I feel a calling to give it my best.

Successful textbook writing is a learned art that takes many forms. I hope the lessons discussed here will provide useful guidelines to other aspiring authors.

# Chapter 18

# The DNA of Decision Science

## Sam L. Savage

The decision sciences are evolving rapidly. For a curriculum of study in this area to survive, it must evolve in parallel. By considering a trait common to many evolving systems, I will explore a potential path of future evolution for the decision sciences and their teaching.

## 1. Some Issues Pertaining to Evolving Systems

### 1.1. Aggregation/Sublimation

Evolving systems are often comprised of building blocks which were once at the evolutionary forefront of the system themselves. In biology, for example, ammonia and methane were at one time the "Kings of Beasts." Later, they formed the basis of amino acids, which in turn became the components of DNA.

This may be viewed as an evolutionary process of aggregation of simple building blocks into more complex building blocks. In recent discussions I have had with B. Curtis Eaves, he has suggested the term *sublimation* to describe what happens to the components that comprise the aggregate.

271

I suspect there may be a more formal statement of this principle of aggregation in the emerging theory of complexity (for example, see Waldrop 1992).

The evolutionary building blocks of ideas are discussed by Richard Dawkins (1976). He defines a cultural analog of the gene as the "meme." Memes can mutate, evolve, or become extinct as they are passed from generation to generation. Evolutionary aggregation is often discernible in the memes associated with technologies.

For example, the ancient memes of mechanical engineering—the wheel, lever, and pump—formed the basis for the heat engines of the early 1800's. For nearly half a century, these "engines" were operated only by "engineers," in large industrial applications such as the pumping of flooded mine shafts. Eventually, as it was sublimated along with the transmission and pneumatic tire into the aggregate of the automobile, the engine was finally of direct benefit to the individual.

The memes of electronics (resistors, capacitors, coils, and vacuum tubes) were the building blocks of early computers in the 1940's. The transistor led to the aggregation of far more electronic components into the computers of the 1960's. Until the early 1980's, computers were operated only by engineers. Integrated circuitry has raised the level of aggregation to millions of components per square inch and led to computers for individual use.

For technological systems, then the aggregation principle may be restated as: Today's systems are often tomorrow's subsystems.

## 1.2. Ergonomics

Much of modern industrial design is rightly focused on ergonomics, or the ease of use of technologies. The cases of the automobile and personal computer show that complex systems are often easier to use than their simpler ancestors. Today's automobiles are far more complex than those of Henry Ford's, yet far easier to drive. The starting crank that attached directly to the engine of the early automobile and that could occasionally break the user's wrist has been replaced by the ignition key. The laptop computer is more complex than John von Neumann could have imagined in the early days of computers. Yet it is much easier to use than his first simple machine. This brings to mind a pertinent comment (attributed to Arthur C. Clarke) which says that any sufficiently advanced technology is indistinguishable from magic.

## 1.3. Standardization—The Network Externality

Another important factor in technological evolution is the establishment of standards, such as the distance between railroad tracks, or the number of threads per unit length on bolts. These are known in economics as *network externalities* and can spell the difference between the proliferation or extinction of technologies. Some technological standards evolve by design, others by chance. But whatever their origin, once established, they must not be ignored.

# 2. The Decision Sciences

## 2.1. Aggregation, Ergonomics, and Standardization

The earliest memes of decision science were the laws of arithmetic required for decisions involving the sharing and bartering of commodities. Technologies built on arithmetic, such as algebra and probability, form the building blocks of modern decision science. Because most decisionmakers in industry and government do not view their decisions in algebraic and probabilistic terms, there has traditionally been a serious ergonomic problem with these techniques. I refer to this as an "Algebraic Curtain" separating the decisionmaker from decision science. Furthermore, few standards have been established for the wide dissemination and application of the methods of decision science. This has limited their proliferation.

## 2.2. Developmental Necessities of Applications—DNA

The rapid evolution of the microcomputer has resulted in a new level of aggregation for the decision sciences. The algebraic and probabilistic building blocks of the formative years are being sublimated into computerized models containing what I refer to as the *Developmental Necessities of Applications*, or DNA. Unlike the algebraic representations of the past, this digital DNA is "alive." It contains just enough representative data so that a user can experimentally infer its structure. It is ergonomic in that a user with little mathematical understanding may expand the DNA, input data, and get results as output. Furthermore, standard formats are rapidly being established in which models may be rapidly and widely disseminated. In short, this DNA is a "seed" of knowledge from which applications may grow.

### 2.2.1. Transformation vs. Formulation

Developing an application from DNA differs dramatically from the traditional decision science approach. Instead of formulating a model from scratch, the decisionmaker merely transforms existing ones, which may be combined (recombinant DNA) to form larger applications. A couple of analogies demonstrate that the right building blocks can have a multiple order-of-magnitude effect on development times. As a biological analogy, consider, for example, the daunting task of constructing a flamingo directly from amino acids, as opposed to the trivial one of incubating a fertilized flamingo egg; or as an electronic analogy, imagine how quickly von Neumann would have developed a computer had he been able to visit one of today's electronic supply houses and fill his shopping cart with 100mhz motherboards, gigabyte disk drives, and megabyte memory chips.

### 2.2.2. An Example of Decision Science DNA: A Spreadsheet Linear Program Model

For several years, Microsoft has included limited mathematical optimization capability with its Excel spreadsheet. Roughly one million of these packages are sold annually. The package includes small worksheet examples for several applications. Figure 18.1 gives a view of the dense transportation linear programming (LP) model shipped with Excel.

| | A | B | C | D | E | F | G | H |
|---|---|---|---|---|---|---|---|---|
| 1 | **Transportation Problem.** | | | | | | | |
| 2 | Minimize the costs of shipping goods from production plants to warehouses near metropolitan demand | | | | | | | |
| 3 | centers, while not exceeding the supply available from each plant and meeting the demand from each | | | | | | | |
| 4 | metropolitan area. | | | | | | | |
| 6 | | | *Number to ship from plant x to warehouse y (at intersection):* | | | | | |
| 7 | *Plants:* | *Total* | *San Fran* | *Denver* | *Chicago* | *Dallas* | *New York* | |
| 8 | S. Carolina | 5 | 1 | 1 | 1 | 1 | 1 | |
| 9 | Tennessee | 5 | 1 | 1 | 1 | 1 | 1 | |
| 10 | Arizona | 5 | 1 | 1 | 1 | 1 | 1 | |
| 12 | Totals: | | 3 | 3 | 3 | 3 | 3 | |
| 14 | *Demands by Whse ->* | | 180 | 80 | 200 | 160 | 220 | |
| 15 | *Plants:* | *Supply* | *Shipping costs from plant x to warehouse y (at intersection):* | | | | | |
| 16 | S. Carolina | 310 | 10 | 8 | 6 | 5 | 4 | |
| 17 | Tennessee | 260 | 6 | 5 | 4 | 3 | 6 | |
| 18 | Arizona | 280 | 3 | 4 | 5 | 5 | 9 | |
| 20 | *Shipping:* | **$83** | $19 | $17 | $15 | $13 | $19 | |

Figure 18.1. View of the dense transportation problem linear programming model shipped with Microsoft Excel.

Formulas relate the various parts of the model.

| *Plants:* | *Total* | *Number to ship from plant x to warehouse y (at intersection):* | | | | |
|---|---|---|---|---|---|---|
| | | *San Fran* | *Denver* | *Chicago* | *Dallas* | *New York* |
| S. Carolina | =SUM(C8:G8) | 0 | 0 | 0 | 80 | 220 |
| Tennessee | =SUM(C9:G9) | 0 | 0 | 180 | 80 | 0 |
| Arizona | =SUM(C10:G10) | 180 | 80 | 20 | 0 | 0 |

Figure 18.2. Formulas for supply constraints.

A separate window contains specifications to Excel's built-in solver to minimize the shipping cost in cell B20, by changing the values of the amounts shipped in cells C8 through G10, while satisfying both demand and capacity constraints.

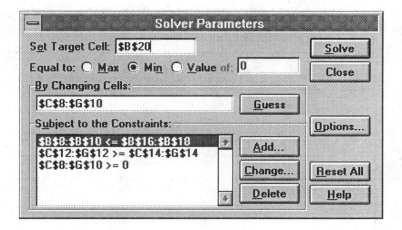

Figure 18.3. A separate window contains specifications to Excel's built-in solver.

### 2.2.3. Instantiation

Of course, no one has the exact transportation problem described above. However, this worksheet may be instantiated to create a simple application through transformations such as the addition or deletion of rows or columns and the entry of actual data. A click of the solve button then invokes the mathematical optimization routines. This addition of information and transformation of the digital DNA to create an actual application are analogous to the fertilization and incubation of biological DNA.

### 2.2.4. Replication

A measure of success in evolving systems is the degree to which they are replicated. Of course, this sort of success does not guarantee utility. Just as the DNA of the giant panda is a relative failure compared to that of the cockroach, many potentially useful applications of decision science have failed to catch on. Yet, some computer viruses represent successful forms of digital DNA with even lower utility than that of the cockroach.

### 2.2.5. Model Classes and Transformations

Geoffrion (1992) in his work on structured modeling, describes classes of mathematical models. For example, one can refer abstractly to the class of dense transportation linear programming models such as the one above without ever mentioning a particular instance of such a problem. There is great expressive power in the ability to describe model classes as opposed to model instances.

Decision science DNA serves as a representative of its model class. For DNA to be an effective modeling device, there must exist simple transformations that map it to any instance of the class. The types of transformations available in a modeling environment significantly influence the scope of this DNA mapping.

Two of the most important transformations in this regard are scaling and hyperscaling. Scaling changes the cardinality within any dimension of the DNA, for example, by adding or deleting warehouses or plants in the transportation model. Hyperscaling changes the number of dimensions themselves, for example, by creating a multiperiod transportation model by adding a time dimension.

Several readily available modeling environments exist in which DNA may be created and transformed: spreadsheets, algebraic modeling languages, and on-line analytical processing.

Electronic spreadsheets (such as Microsoft Excel and Lotus 1-2-3) are appealing, ergonomic modeling environments because of their interactivity and their ability to quickly graph results. More importantly with approximately twenty million total users, they have become the modeling vernacular among decisionmakers. This greatly increases the likelihood that spreadsheet DNA will be replicated. Because of this, spreadsheets provide a single environment in which to teach and prototype almost any sort of decision science applications. However, for industrial applications there can be drawbacks. Spreadsheet models are difficult to document, and they scale only moderately, often requiring editing or copying of formulas in the process. They are fundamentally two-dimensional but usually allow a limited third dimension. They do not hyperscale well.

Modeling languages such as AMPL, GAMS, and LINGO have been designed primarily with mathematical optimization in mind and are not suited to most other decision science applications. They are highly documentable and scalable, and they are reasonably hyperscalable. Unfortunately, they are noninteractive in the spreadsheet sense. Furthermore, they are in effect programming languages with an algebraic perspective that is not easliy used directly by most decisionmakers. As a result, they have a user base only ten thousand or so. For industrial size optimization problems they are today's best solution. For teaching, however, they present a formidable learning curve that precludes their use in courses not devoted to optimization. An expression of the transportation model DNA in LINGO follows:

```
MODEL:
  1]
  2]SETS:
  3]WAREHOUSE /SAN_FRAN, DENVER, CHICAGO, DALLAS, NEW_YORK /
    : DEMAND, RECEIVED;
  4]PLANTS / S_CAROLINA, TENNESSEE, ARIZONA /
    : CAPACITY, SUPPLIED;
  5]ROUTES(PLANTS, WAREHOUSE)  : VOLUME, COST;
  6]ENDSETS
  7]
  8]@FOR(PLANTS(J) : SUPPLIED(J) < CAPACITY(J));
  9]@FOR(WAREHOUSE(I) : RECEIVED(I) > DEMAND(I));
 10]MIN = @SUM( ROUTES(I,J): VOLUME(I,J) * COST(I, J));
 11]@FOR(WAREHOUSE(I) : RECEIVED(I) = @SUM( PLANTS(J) :
    VOLUME(J, I)));
 12]@FOR(PLANTS(J) : SUPPLIED(J) = @SUM( WAREHOUSE(I) :
    VOLUME(J, I)));
 13]DATA:
 14]CAPACITY = 310, 260, 280;
 15]COST = 10, 8, 6, 5, 4, 6, 5, 4, 3, 6, 3, 4, 5, 5, 9;
 16]DEMAND = 180, 80, 200, 160, 220;
 17]ENDDATA
 18]
END
```

New classes of data manipulating software known as On-Line Analytical Processors (OLAP) or multidimensional modelers (MDMs) have recently emerged (see New dimensions 1993; Multidimensional models 1994; and Codd, Codd, and Salley 1993). These are interactive, documentable, and scale and hyperscale smoothly. They possess some of the best features of spreadsheets, databases, and modeling languages. Because they are new, it is difficult to predict their long term future, but roughly 105 have been marketed as of 1994. They range in price from a few hundred dollars for small, standalone systems (Lotus-IMPROV) to tens of thousands dollars for client-server systems with access to gigabytes of data scattered across several databases (Ess base). These multidimensional products are currently having their greatest success in the client-server environment.

The transportation model DNA as expressed in IMPROV is shown in Figure 18.4.

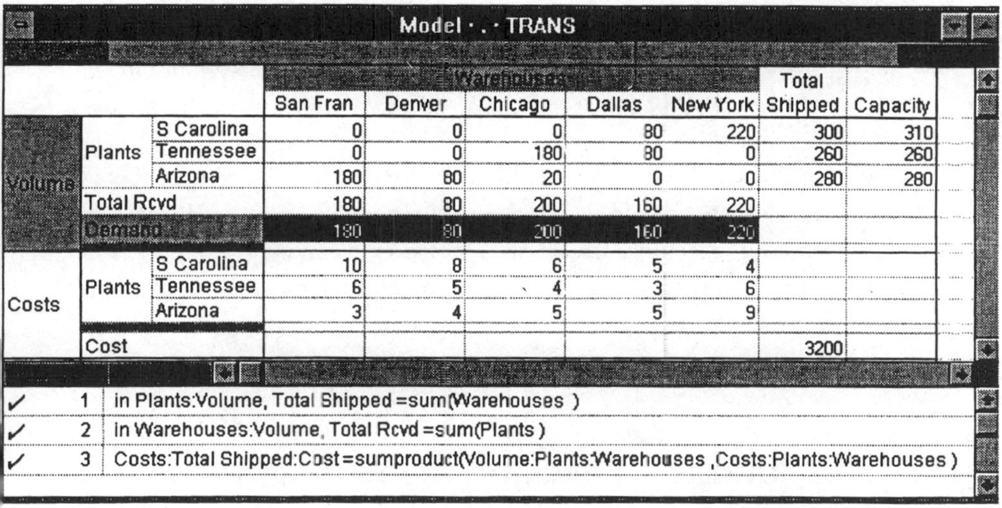

| | | | San Fran | Denver | Chicago | Dallas | New York | Total Shipped | Capacity |
|---|---|---|---|---|---|---|---|---|---|
| Volume | Plants | S Carolina | 0 | 0 | 0 | 80 | 220 | 300 | 310 |
| | | Tennessee | 0 | 0 | 180 | 80 | 0 | 260 | 260 |
| | | Arizona | 180 | 80 | 20 | 0 | 0 | 280 | 280 |
| | Total Rcvd | | 180 | 80 | 200 | 160 | 220 | | |
| | Demand | | 180 | 80 | 200 | 160 | 220 | | |
| Costs | Plants | S Carolina | 10 | 8 | 6 | 5 | 4 | | |
| | | Tennessee | 6 | 5 | 4 | 3 | 6 | | |
| | | Arizona | 3 | 4 | 5 | 5 | 9 | | |
| | Cost | | | | | | | 3200 | |

Model · . · TRANS — Warehouses

1  in Plants:Volume, Total Shipped =sum(Warehouses )
2  in Warehouses:Volume, Total Rcvd =sum(Plants )
3  Costs:Total Shipped:Cost =sumproduct(Volume:Plants:Warehouses ,Costs:Plants:Warehouses )

Figure 18.4. The transportation model DNA as expressed in IMPROV.

Although IMPROV does not provide optimization capability on its own, I have developed a system for Primal Solutions Inc., under a grant from the Air Force Office of Scientific Research, to aggregate IMPROV and an algebraic modeling language into a single system. The optimization specifications are also stored in IMPROV.

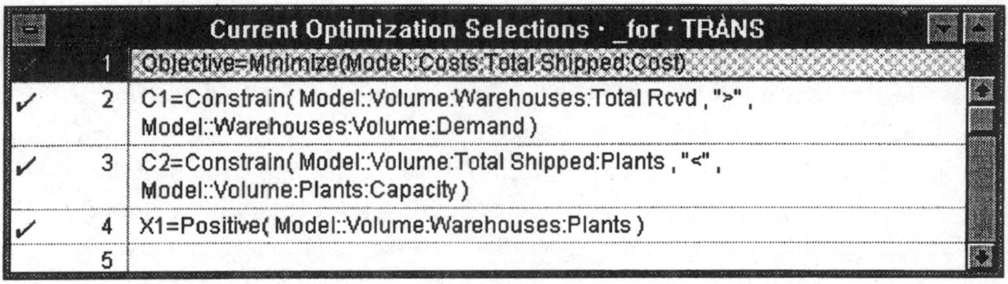

| | | |
|---|---|---|
| | | **Current Optimization Selections · _for · TRANS** |
| | 1 | Objective=Minimize(Model::Costs:Total Shipped:Cost) |
| ✓ | 2 | C1=Constrain( Model::Volume:Warehouses:Total Rcvd , ">" , Model::Warehouses:Volume:Demand ) |
| ✓ | 3 | C2=Constrain( Model::Volume:Total Shipped:Plants , "<" , Model::Volume:Plants:Capacity ) |
| ✓ | 4 | X1=Positive( Model::Volume:Warehouses:Plants ) |
| | 5 | |

Figure 18.5. Optimization specifications for the transportation model as expressed in IMPROV.

After the user invokes the optimization command, the model and the optimization specification are translated into an algebraic modeling language in which the problem may be solved directly on a PC, or in client-server mode on a remote workstation. The LINGO model shown earlier was created using this system.

I believe that the OLAP and MDM environments will be central to the future of the decision sciences, in which data manipulation and decision making become increasingly integrated. However, because these products are still in flux, it may be too soon to spend much time on them in decision science courses.

# 3. DNA and the Decision Science Curriculum

## 3.1. A Matter of Timing

How should the curriculum of the research university respond to new stages of technological evolution? Neither too quickly nor too slowly. Not too quickly, because in its early stages, a new technological standard is difficult to distinguish from a "flash in the pan." For example, one should keep an eye on OLAP and MDM environments but should not introduce them into the curriculum until they have stabilized. Not too slowly, because as technologies become obsolete or sublimated within other technologies, a curriculum becomes irrelevant. Thus, an understanding of the simplex algorithm is of no more use to someone taking a general course on the methods of decision science than an understanding of the Otto cycle of internal combustion is to someone taking driver's education.

## 3.2. We Are Overdue

There is ample evidence that curricula in the decision sciences are due for a significant change. In no particular order, that evidence is:

- Enrollment is off, especially in management science courses in business schools.

- Decision science texts and curricula have not changed fundamentally since the microcomputer revolution of fifteen years ago.

- By now it is clear that the microcomputer is not a "flash in pan."

- The two professional societies in the United States that spearhead the decision sciences, The Operations Research Society of America (ORSA) and The Institute of Management Science (TIMS), have recently sublimated themselves into a single Institute of Operations Research and the Management Sciences (INFORMS).

## 3.3. Some Directions for Change

### 3.3.1. Focus Less on Algorithms and More on Mathematical Pitfalls

As algorithms become sublimated within other technologies, such as the linear and nonlinear solvers in millions of copies of Microsoft Excel, it becomes more important to teach concepts related to using these tools than to develop new tools. Thus, efficient formulations of integer models, and convexity, convergence, and stability issues should be stressed. Algorithmists need not despair, however. In the long run, nothing should increase the demand for robust algorithms faster than the current wide dissemination of optimization.

### 3.3.2. Focus Less on Model Formulation and More on Model Classes and Data

The direct teaching of mathematical modeling is notoriously difficult and ineffective. It is more effective to introduce the DNA of important model classes and show how it may be transformed to meet individual needs. For example, in keeping with my overall theme, once the DNA of the product mix LP and dense transportation LP are presented to students, it is elementary to aggregate these to form more complex models involving both production and shipping. Furthermore, the data collection for decision science applications, which used to require specialized programming in its own right, can now be integrated with the applications themselves through dynamic data exchange (DDE) and client-server technology.

### 3.3.3. Focus Less on Statistics and More on Monte Carlo Simulation

Many people manage to make it through statistics courses without ever understanding the concept of a probability distribution. Introducing random number generators into interactive mathematical models and performing Monte Carlo simulation, can provide an intuitive link to such concepts as the central limit theorem and functions of a random variable.

### 3.3.4. Use Industry Standard Software Where Possible

Students are likely to benefit most from using software that they will see again in the workplace even if it is less suited to the task at hand than a specialized product. Do not underestimate network externalities.

### 3.3.5. Provide DNA on Disks

There is no point in taking my approach unless students leave class with a disk containing DNA (see Gardner 1992; Plane 1994; and Savage 1993, 1994). Once a number of these seeds of knowledge have germinated in the students' minds, a natural homework assignment is to ask them to create new ones.

### 3.3.6. Teach Less to More People

I have found that demonstrating DNA and providing it on disk allows a more rapid coverage of topics. Of course, all topics covered will not be absorbed immediately, but the student can easily reexamine them experimentally at a later date. The bad news, from the decision-science-faculty perspective, is that the total course hours required for a given topic have been reduced. The good news is that there is now the potential for a much larger audience of students. And the best news of all is that those who go on to become decisionmakers are more likely than ever to actually use the decision science they have been taught.

# Acknowledgment

This work was supported in part by the Air Force Office of Scientific Research, Bolling AFB (Washington, D.C.)

# References

Codd, E. F., Codd, S. B., and Salley, C. T. 1993. *Providing OLAP (On-line Analytical Processing) to User-Analysts: An IT Mandate.* San Jose, Calif.: E. F. Codd & Associates.

Dawkins, Richard. 1976. *The Selfish Gene.* Oxford: Oxford University Press.

Gardner, Everette S. 1992. *The Spreadsheet Operations Manager.* New York: McGraw-Hill.

Geoffrion, Arthur M. 1992. "The SML Language for Structured Modeling: Levels 1 and 2." *Operations Research* 40: 38–57.

Plane, Donald R. 1994. *Management Science: A Spreadsheet Approach.* Danvers Mass.: The Scientific Press.

Savage, Sam L. 1993. *Fundamental Analytic Spreadsheet Tools for Quantitative Management.* New York: McGraw-Hill.

Savage, Sam L. 1994. *Fundamental Analytic Spreadsheet Tools for Production and Operations Management.* New York: McGraw-Hill.

Stinson, Craig. 1993. "New Dimensions in Spreadsheets." *PC Magazine,* September 28, 183.

Waldrop, Mitchell M. 1992. *Complexity*. New York: Touchstone.

Williams, Christie. 1994. "Multidimensional Models Boost Viewing Options." *InfoWorld*, January 24, 69.

# Chapter 19

# Evolution of the Required Quantitative Methods Course for M.B.A.'s at Indiana University

Chris Albright

## 1. Introduction

There has been at least one required quantitative methods course for M.B.A.'s at Indiana University's Business School since I started teaching here in 1972. Through the years, the course has undergone continual changes, both because of the changing tastes and needs of the students (and other constituencies) and because of the changes in computer technology. Today, it continues to change, as we who teach the course strive to find just the right blend of theory, topics, practical examples, and computer applications. To judge from our recent experience, we may never find the perfect blend. The faculty who teach the course often disagree with each other, the M.B.A. students often disagree with the faculty, and the students often disagree among themselves. Therefore, we find ourselves being pulled in many directions during the course of the semester. It is a far cry from the days when my fellow doctoral students and I sat in Professor Lieberman's statistics classes and were content to soak up whatever knowledge he imparted to us!

In this chapter I will describe the evolution of the M.B.A. Quantitative Methods course(s) at Indiana University during the past twenty years or so. I will pay particular attention to the sweeping changes in the past few years, where two events have made a tremendous impact, the first being the widespread use of personal computers (PCs) both inside and outside of the classroom, and the second being a structural change in our M.B.A. program. Both of these changes, together with the critical M.B.A. audience, have made teaching the Quantitative Methods course a continual challenge for all involved. Usually, it is a rewarding challenge, but sometimes it is plainly frustrating.

## 2. The Early Years

Through the 1970's and even much of the 1980's, the required Quantitative Methods courses for M.B.A.'s were very traditional. We taught all the basic topics in traditional statistics textbooks, through regression and time series analysis, plus some introductory linear programming (LP) and decision making under uncertainty. (During the early to mid 1970's, we had a required calculus course for M.B.A.'s, but that was deleted as being largely irrelevant to the rest of the M.B.A. program.) Much of what we could do with "large" problems was determined by how much time we wanted to devote to teaching mainframe packages to non-computer-oriented students. For the most part, we decided to stay away from difficult programs such as SPSS and SAS. Instead, we used relatively easy-to-learn packages such as IDA and LINDO. However, data analysis on computers remained a small part of the courses. Most of the in-class lectures, the homework problems, and the examinations were devoted to small problems that could be worked by hand or on a hand calculator. In short, we taught what we had been taught—the same material that was in practically all the textbooks—and we changed gradually, at best.

It is worth noting that during these years, the faculty in my department who taught these M.B.A. quantitative courses worked virtually in a vacuum, relative to the rest of the Business School. We had some sense of what quantitative material (regression, for example) was needed in later M.B.A. courses, and we tried whenever possible to use business examples, as opposed to balls and urns or flipping coins. But we did not really coordinate the Quantitative Methods courses with other M.B.A. courses, and frankly, since most of us came from non-Business School backgrounds, we were content to teach our favorite mathematical topics and let the rest of the M.B.A. program go its own way. Surprisingly, we received little criticism from the rest of the Business School for this practice. We were regarded as a service department, and we were providing a useful service. The rest of the Business School was willing to tolerate the idiosyncratic faculty up in Decision Sciences, so long as we taught the necessary quantitative tools to the M.B.A. students.

One important aspect of these early years (that has changed with our new program) is that students were allowed to be exempted from any or all of the quantitative courses, depending on their backgrounds. For example, in the early 1980's we offered two required quantitative courses, K503 and K504, for M.B.A.'s. The first of these covered basic statistics through elementary statistical inference. The second covered more advanced statistical topics such as regression and time series analysis, plus linear programming and decision making under uncertainty. Since many students came to our program with virtually no quantitative background, we were able to place them in K503, where we could afford to be slow and basic. The students in this course did not always care for it, but they desperately needed the skills. The students with some quantitative background were able to go directly into K504. In rare cases, students could be exempted from both courses. By proceeding in this way, we taught classes of students with reasonably similar quantitative abilities. They did not all necessarily have the same interests, but at least we knew the appropriate mathematical level for each course.

## 3. The PC Arrives

By the mid to late 1980's, PCs were widely available, and user-friendly PC statistics (and LP) packages were coming along. Most of us believed that it would be negligent to ignore these in the M.B.A. Quantitative Methods courses. I felt particularly strongly that it no longer made sense to teach statistics and LP in traditional ways, where we concentrated on learning formulas and plugging into them. I could see no good pedagogical reason for teaching a student how to use the simple least squares regression formulas, for example, when they could obtain regression output easily with a PC package. Not all of my colleagues agreed with this reasoning, at least not right away, but we were definitely moving in that direction.

This movement raised several questions, however. First, which package should we use? Several textbooks came out with software packages written by the authors, some traditional mainframe packages such as Minitab came out with PC versions, and shareware of varying quality became available. Some of this software was far from user-friendly, and it frequently caused students more problems than it solved. We certainly did not want to be put in a position where we were spending most of our class time teaching software. Unfortunately, we each tended to make our own decisions about software selection; some used Minitab, some used a shareware product called B-Stat, and some used other emerging products. At best, we muddled through these years.

A second problem involved the students' use of the software. In those days we had a couple of computer labs in the building, and some of the M.B.A.'s had their own PCs. In addition, some of the lab PCs had the required software, and some of the M.B.A.'s purchased it. So it was pretty much "each person for himself or herself." This made it difficult to require PC use for every student in the class, although we attempted to do so. A related issue was exams. I believed that if we were moving away from plugging into formulas and were instead emphasizing PC solutions, it was unfair to give traditional "hand-calculation" exams. By the late 1980's I was the first to give M.B.A. exams in a PC lab. Most students appreciated the motivation behind doing this, but the technical bugs, along with the usual exam anxiety, made the experience less than entirely successful.

Finally, a problem we all faced when incorporating PC solutions into the curriculum was what to do with the freed-up time. Previously, we had spent hours of class time deriving formulas and demonstrating how to use them, usually with small numerical examples. When we decided to eliminate much of this, we had to fill up the time with something else. We were forced to look for better examples (and accompanying data sets), and we were forced to spend more time teaching the interpretation of computer output. Of course, we also had to set aside some time to show how to use the PC packages. All of this was a move in the right direction, especially for an M.B.A. audience, but it certainly required all of us to reinvent the course— and to learn a bit more about the business applications that would fit best in the course. Fortunately, this came at a time when M.B.A. programs were under attack for not being relevant, so we had an extra incentive to teach M.B.A.'s skills they could really use.

# 4. A New Structure for the M.B.A. Program

As the 1990's began, there were five of us who regularly taught the required M.B.A. Quantitative Methods course. (By now, K503 and K504 had evolved into a single course. The beginning material in K503 was now supposedly a prerequisite for the entrance into the program.) We all had our own way of doing things, we used different PC packages, we used different textbooks, and the topics in different sections of the course were only loosely coordinated. But all of this was about to change. In response to the general criticism of M.B.A. programs, our school decided to make radical changes to the program.

The most important aspects of the new program are the following:
1. The first year is a lock-step sequence of "disciplines." All students take a "foundations core" during their first semester, consisting of Quantitative Methods, Financial Accounting, Managerial Economics, and Management and Organizational Behavior. Then, in the second semester, they take a "functional core" consisting of Marketing, Finance, Cost Accounting, MIS, and Operations Management.

2. During each of these semesters, the students are divided into four cohorts, and each cohort takes classes together. Within cohorts, students are broken down into four- or five-member teams, and teamwork is emphasized much more than previously.

3. There is much more coordination among the core faculty. Usually, only two faculty members from a given department teach in the core. They work closely with one another and with core faculty from other departments. For example, the day-by-day schedule for the fall semester is worked out

jointly by the four faculty who teach a given cohort. There is a great deal of emphasis on presenting applications that cut across disciplines.

All of this has had a significant effect on the Quantitative Methods course that is part of the first-semester core. The two of us who have been involved in developing and teaching this course (Don Harnett and myself) have been forced to rethink just about everything, and to coordinate with each other and the other core faculty. We can no longer teach in a vacuum. Rather, we have to be extremely sensitive to what the rest of the M.B.A. program wants from a quantitative course, and we have to make sure that the material we teach is "relevant," as judged both by the M.B.A. students and by the rest of the faculty. We are constantly being evaluated by these constituencies, and any mistakes we make—however mistakes are defined—are magnified more than ever before. The entire process is extremely challenging, time-consuming, and rewarding as well as frustrating. I will discuss here some of the pedagogical issues we face under the new system.

The single most frustrating part of teaching this course is the huge variation in the abilities and interests of the students. As mentioned earlier, this is a lockstep program, so all first-year students are thrown together into this course, regardless of their backgrounds. In such an environment, it is impossible to satisfy everyone. Some students with quantitative backgrounds (engineering, for example) complain that we do not go fast enough, or that we do not go into enough derivations—too many concepts are treated like "black boxes." Other students, from nonquantitative backgrounds, complain continually that we are covering too much irrelevant material that they will never have to use in their jobs. These students want to get right to the exciting business cases, without ever learning the boring basics.

A second issue is the role of the computer. How much of the Quantitative Methods course should use the PC, how much should be devoted to teaching PC packages, and which packages are appropriate? We currently use two packages: Execustat for statistics and Excel for linear programming, some statistics, and a variety of other calculations. Neither of these requires a lot of time to get the students up and running, although the more computer-illiterate students in the group still require a lot of hand-holding. (In fact, we continue to be amazed at the number of entering M.B.A. students with virtually no PC experience; we hope that will change in the near future.) Execustat is easy to learn, being entirely menu-driven, and for those who need extra help, I have written a tutorial booklet that runs students through a number of typical statistical procedures. The advantages of such a package are that it is easy to learn and that it does one thing, namely, statistical procedures, very well.

By contrast, employing a spreadsheet package such as Excel has the advantage that most students will have used a spreadsheet and will use one after graduating. It also has a great deal of flexibility that is lacking in Execustat. In fact, given the continual increase in functionality of spreadsheets, there is an argument for using Excel as the sole computer package and eliminating the use of a special-purpose statistics package. We are currently evaluating the pros and cons of going in this direction. Many students would like us to move in that direction, arguing that they will certainly have access to spreadsheets when they enter the corporate world but might not ever use a statistical package again. The argument sounds good, but until Microsoft or Lotus greatly enhances the statistical capabilities of their spreadsheets, it will be difficult to give up the functionality of a statistics package such as Execustat.

A related issue is the pedagogical role of the PC. I strongly believe that the PC can be used successfully, not only to produce "answers" quickly and painlessly, but to aid in the learning process itself. An obvious example of this is the way in which we can run many regression models or many time series models on the same data set and compare results. M.B.A. students love to see real numbers, and now there is no reason to shy away from illustrating real examples with real (and often large) data sets. But there are more subtle pedagogical advantages to using today's software packages.

For example, this past semester for the first time, I taught students how to model, and then solve, linear, integer, and even nonlinear programming problems on a spreadsheet. From past experience I knew that M.B.A.'s did not take particularly well to these types of problems, at least not with the algebraic formulations we all grew up with, and they often made a mess of their formulations. This time, however, the reaction has been completely different. All at once, the formulations have become much more intuitive and interesting to them, and several students have even complained that we did not spend more time on these mathematical programming problems. In addition to their being enthusiastic, the students made far fewer mistakes in formulating the problems than I had seem them make with the algebraic method.

Computer packages, particularly spreadsheets, also enable students to solve problems and gain insights that they could never have achieved with algebraic methods. For example, when I covered decision making under uncertainty, I was able to do a sensitivity analysis on an important parameter simply by solving the problem once and then using a data table. Then a graph of the data in the data table made it immediately obvious how sensitive the optimal decision was to this particular parameter. Or as another example, on a spreadsheet it is easy to show how to convert from the Expected Marginal Value (EMV) criterion to the Expected Utility (EU) criterion (using an exponential utility function, for example) and to show how sensitive the optimal decision is to the degree of risk aversion. The point here is that when spreadsheets are used to do what they do best, namely, to make many similar calculations and to answer what-if questions, they can make a tremendous impact on the learning process.

Computer packages are not the perfect solution to everything, however. There are times when they treat the solution process too much as a black box. For example, when we used Excel's solver to solve nonlinear programming problems (portfolio problems, for instance), everything was fine when we hit upon a correct formulation. But there were times when the solver said it could not find a feasible (or optimal) solution, or when it said a solution was optimal when in fact it was not. In such cases, students typically hit a brick wall, since they have little idea of what the computer is really doing. Even in statistical applications, students sometimes feel uneasy with a package that simply spews out the results. They would sometimes like to know what is going on in there, and they have a difficult time "trusting" output when they do not know how it was produced.

I believe this is a tradeoff we are going to have to make. There is simply not enough time in a single course to derive many results or to explain detailed algorithms. Besides, most students do not want to bother with this. Therefore, I tell my most intellectually curious students to take a more advanced course if they really want to know how these methods work. Admittedly, it is a bit unsettling to consider that we are training students to use methods that they do not really understand. But given the wide variety in student abilities and interests, and given our mandate to "teach relevant information," I believe the approach we are now taking, with its strong reliance on PC packages, is the only feasible approach.

Related to this is the issue of developing mathematical skills. I still believe we have an obligation to develop basic skills in our Quantitative Methods courses. It appears that our students' mathematical abilities are decreasing each year, to the point now that a significant percentage of M.B.A. students can barely do high-school algebra. These are unfortunately the same students who want me to dispense with the basics and get right to the interesting and exciting business applications. I like to draw an analogy here with a basketball player who wants to bypass all the passing and dribbling drills and get right into the games against tough opponents. Like the passing and dribbling drills, the "pure quant" drills can be boring and tedious for some students, but I believe we are doing a disservice to the students if we do not force them to go over some of these hurdles. After all, the Quantitative Methods course is basically a "tools" course. Presumably, we are teaching students some basic quantitative skills they will need for the case-based courses in the more traditional business subjects. Certainly we in the quantitative area should use interesting business applications whenever possible, but if we do not cover basic quantitative skills in some detail, then we have not achieved an important part of our mission.

## 5. The Outlook

The teaching of statistics and other quantitative methods to M.B.A.'s is an area where change was definitely needed and where change is now occurring at a furious pace. There is no time to rest on our laurels and say that we have finally got it right. The technology keeps changing, and the students continue to demand more and more relevancy. As soon as we finish teaching one semester, we need to begin thinking about revisions for the next time around. It is a constantly moving target, and I do not see that aspect of the course changing anytime in the future. This puts a tremendous amount of pressure on the faculty. First, it requires a large time commitment to continually update teaching materials and learn new technology (such as the newest version of Excel). Second, it requires us to take risks in the classroom that do not always pay off—certainly not every teaching innovation is pedagogically effective and appreciated by the students. Third, it is not clear at all institutions whether the time and energy needed to innovate is rewarded in terms of tenure, promotions, and salary decisions. But in spite of these concerns, the field is moving rapidly in new directions, and any of us who fail to move with it will soon be considered hopelessly old-fashioned.

If we assume that we do move with the times, what can be anticipated about student learning? Will the M.B.A.'s learn as much as they used to learn, or as much as we want them to learn? I believe this depends on our objectives. If we focus on the old objectives—learning a set body of statistical concepts and formulas, say—the answer is probably that the new quantitative methods courses will not succeed as well as the old courses. However, if we concede that we are not training M.B.A. students to be professional statisticians or management scientists but are instead attempting to teach them some data analysis and modeling skills that they can really use in their jobs, then there is every reason to believe that the new teaching methods are exactly what we should be using. I, for one, am sold on the new directions and am making every effort to incorporate them into my quantitative methods M.B.A. course.

# Chapter 20

# The Challenge for Operations Research in American Graduate Business Schools

Evan L. Porteus

## 1. Introduction

The first great challenge for operations research (OR) in American graduate business schools was to have its theories and methods absorbed into their curricula and faculties. I conclude that this challenge has been met successfully. The second great challenge is to have its theories and methods absorbed into the everyday lives of the M.B.A.'s who graduate from such schools.

In the mid 1950's, studies of business schools concluded that they should become more research oriented and do so in part by infusing themselves with various research paradigms that had been developed and were being vigorously pursued in other parts of universities, such as operations research, statistics, economics, psychology, sociology, and so on. Most business schools took this advice seriously and moved to transform themselves in dramatic ways. In particular, the theories and methods of OR are now intimate parts of the theories and methods of the functional fields of business, namely, accounting, finance, marketing, and so on. There are many graduate business school faculty members with Ph.D.'s in OR. Many OR courses have been taught at such schools. However, there seems to be a national trend in such schools to de-emphasize OR and OR courses. I would like to present my interpretation of this phenomenon and elaborate on some ways to correct this trend and to meet the challenge.

## 2. The Importance of Context

Starting in the 1960's, and continuing for over twenty years, people like myself, with Ph.D.'s in OR, oriented toward theory and methods, and with relatively little practical experience, were hired, developed, and tenured at many business schools. One of the first things I discovered upon beginning teaching at a business school was that there was a culture clash between M.B.A. students and professors like myself: M.B.A.'s were interested in breadth and rapid problem solving, whereas I was interested in depth and rigor. A joke I heard from my colleague Jeffrey Moore, who ascribes it to John D. C. Little of MIT, takes this difference to the extreme to make the point: "Academics always think before they act, if they ever act. Managers always act before they think, if they ever think." Although I could safely attempt to transmit my culture and values to Ph.D. students, a different approach was required in the M.B.A. classroom. I wanted to help them prepare to become outstanding managers, and I believed that OR theories and methods should be absorbed into the daily routines of their careers. However, I was not sure how to do it.

I had been taught OR theories and methods in courses that were essentially context-free. These had been efficient vehicles for learning this material. However, I now believe that I was mistaken to teach, and support the teaching of, purposefully context-free M.B.A. courses, with titles such as "Optimization" and "Stochastic Models." Although such courses continue to be good vehicles for transmitting theories and methods to those who are eager to learn them, such as doctoral students, they were not successful in getting M.B.A.'s to apply those theories and methods. That is, I was wrong to think that M.B.A. students needed only to master the theories and methods of OR to become capable of (and inclined toward) carrying out successful applications of them.

During the 1970's, there was another trend in business schools, including Stanford's, to discontinue offering courses that emphasized the context of operations management rather than the models and techniques of OR. However, by the late 1970's, it was clear to our school that we needed to reverse this trend. In 1982, my area, called Decision Sciences, reshuffled the material in the four core courses that we taught and created a required course in "Operations."

I taught a section of that course that first year, and I have taught many sections of it over the intervening years. I was not prepared for how painful that process was going to be for me personally: I thought that since most of the applications of the models and techniques that I understood so well were to manufacturing and operations management, the transition to teaching with an emphasis on the context rather than on the methods would be stimulating and relatively smooth. It was definitely stimulating, but it was not smooth. I had not been absorbing institutional detail. I had few anecdotes to tell and practical experiences to relate, so I had trouble illustrating the relevance of the ideas I was presenting.

Indeed, I was insensitive to the desirability of conveying institutional detail in class, as the following anecdote illustrates. Shortly after I joined the Graduate School of Business, I was preparing a course examination jointly with two other professors who were teaching different sections of the same M.B.A. course. One question required a probability computation and was initially posed in terms of drawing colored balls from an urn. The senior professor, who was not a formal member of our group, suggested that the problem be rephrased in a business context. The other professor and I, both junior but formal members of our group, overruled his suggestion. It took me years to realize what a mistake we were making. I now understand that the context of an example is just as important as, if not more important than, the theory in an M.B.A. course: A good example that illustrates a meaningful way to apply a model or technique can set in students' minds the usefulness of that model or technique. An abstract example or an unrealistic application of a powerful theory often leaves students cold and makes no lasting impression.

When my students would ask me how much these theories and methods were applied in managerial practice, I could offer a number of examples but could not claim that they were as widely used as I thought they should be. For years, I hid behind the excuse that top management at the time had not been trained in OR, so they therefore would not apply it, and we had to wait for those we had trained in OR to reach the top before the situation would change. The situation should have changed by now, but it has not, and the explanation lies somewhere else. I now believe that one of the consequences of our taking a substantially context-free approach to pedagogy is that our M.B.A. students did not learn how to apply our theories. They also were not convinced that our theories were worth applying. In practice, they did not try to apply them or to sponsor their application. Years later, they would conclude that they did not learn much of value in these courses and that these would be good courses to consider for modification or deletion.

## 3. The Case for Case Analyses

The basic flaw in our pedagogy goes beyond the extent to which context is included. We have not successfully taught our M.B.A. students how to apply our theories and methods, even in courses that included a lot of institutional detail and context.

I believe that there is a dysfunctional dichotomy between theory and practice that arises in our teaching of M.B.A.'s. On the one side, we have courses that teach OR theories and methods. The applications presented in these courses are usually example problems for which there is a "right answer" using the presented methods. Sometimes very elaborate problems with piles of data are used. However, these still tend to have one "right model" and one right answer. Indeed, the philosophical beginnings of OR preach such an approach, and students of these courses are apt to attempt to find the one right model and the one right answer in practical applications. Although such course designs are efficient at presenting theories and methods, and in making initial connections to practice, I contend that they are inappropriate for M.B.A.'s. M.B.A.'s are trained and encouraged to be action oriented, to become capable of facing a wide variety of difficult practical situations, and to take appropriate actions in each. Reality is rarely so simple that there is one right model and one right answer.

In practice, there are usually many different things going on, and what kind of model should be developed, if any, is an important decision to be made. Someone trained in and oriented toward one of the disciplines, such as OR, statistics, economics, psychology, and so on, can usually formulate a model within the framework of that discipline that will address one or more of the issues being faced. However, there usually are not one right model and one right answer. Indeed, even within only the OR discipline, there are usually many possible models one can develop, from an aggregate model that can be analyzed on the back of an envelope, to a detailed Monte Carlo simulation model that attempts to capture everything that might be relevant. Each of these extremes may well be right in some situations. However, I believe that they are not the only two relevant choices. In particular, the latter approach can incur great costs to pay for the analysts conducting the study and the computer time used, and can result in fodder for the circular file because nobody really understands the model or can convince the consumers of the report that it is right or useful. (There are numerous other ways in which a big, detailed simulation study can go wrong.) Although I agree that there are practical situations in which there is, ultimately, one best model and one best answer, I believe that the way to get there is through formulation of a variety of simple models first, gaining insight from each of them, and continuing the process of making them more sophisticated and realistic. In many situations I think it will turn out that our theories are still too undeveloped to end this process at a single model and solution. Prematurely focusing on a single type of model can lead to missing the most important insights and even to misleading suggestions. I argue that in most managerial problems, anybody who tries to direct the analysis toward one right model in search of the one right answer is misguided and possibly even dangerous.

I believe that in a managerial problem to which OR models can usefully be applied, there are several, perhaps many, different models that can be usefully applied. Each yields one or more useful insights into the case and productive decisions that could be made in that context. One way to think about this is to imagine that models differ by turning up the brightness on some things and turning it down on others: some issues are modeled in detail, and others are dealt with in an aggregate way or even assumed away.

On the other side are the case courses. Good cases, for all of their numerous weaknesses, present enough of the subtlety and detail of the practical setting to make it clear that there is not one right model and not one right answer. Outstanding case method teachers with extensive experience with a particular case will know of a variety of models that can be applied to the case and the insights that can be gleaned from them. They will find ways to elicit the discussion of these different models and their insights. However, a case class is too short to formulate and analyze much in the way of sophisticated models. Students of case courses are often not trained in the methods of OR at much depth, and there is as yet no discipline that helps students determine what models to formulate and analyze in particular situations. Thus, students in case courses rarely carry out sophisticated analyses of even one model of that case. And, even if they do, the other students in the class rarely understand the analysis and derive any valuable insights from it. The professors who are able to get their students in their courses to carry out sophisticated analyses and draw a variety of insights from them have tended to dispense their magic only to the lucky few who attend their courses. The field needs their wisdom put into print in the public domain to help the rest of us do the same.

Thus, I propose that we take steps to help students learn how to formulate and apply a variety of different models in practical situations, and to gain useful insights from each. Indeed, perhaps we can develop a discipline for this process. But rather than philosophize about the form of this new discipline, I suggest that we focus on getting examples of the process of formulating and analyzing a variety of models in the context of a single practical problem, garnering useful insights from them, and getting these insights into print, both in journals and in textbooks. Perhaps after a number of examples of this process are printed, the form of the discipline will become clear. (Perhaps somebody has already specified this form, and I am unaware of it.)

I contend that there is little in print that does what I think is needed. Although case analyses are often available for cases obtained from the usual outlets, these analyses are not readibly accessible. Furthermore, these analyses tend to suggest how to manage the discussion of the case in which there is little expectation that any sophisticated model formulations and analyses will be carried out by the students.

There are numerous applications papers published in academic and professional journals. However, these tend to focus on the (one) model that was developed, the results that were obtained from it, and the practical consequences of the process. In particular, there is no description of the original problem, with all its subtle intricacies, so no insights into the process of model selection and assumption making can be obtained. They include little data that would allow for additional (or alternative) analyses to be carried out. These papers are better at showing how a particular kind of model can be useful in a certain context than at showing in how to gain different insights from different models that might be applied in that context. These papers cannot be used to ask M.B.A.'s to read about a managerial problem, try to formulate an approach to solving it, wrestle with the tradeoffs, and later learn of the depth to which analysis can be carried out.

I have made an attempt to begin this process, by arranging to have a case published in *Interfaces* (Porteus 1989), followed by a variety of analyses of that case (Porteus 1993a,b). However, at best, this is only a start, with a wealth of different perspectives yet to appear. At worst, it is so idiosyncratic that nobody else will follow up with their approaches to cases they have studied.

This process of publishing cases and analyses of them from a variety of perspectives not only can teach students how to successfully apply theories and analytical methods and to draw insights from them. It can educate practitioners in how to apply theories and methods that they may not have known how to use. It can educate theoreticians about the subtleties of real applications and sensitize them to important practical issues. Finally, it can inspire theoreticians to develop new theories and methods to deal with the important practical issues presented in these cases. Indeed, from a practitioner's perspective, there are numerous issues in practical inventory problems that are not adequately addressed by our existing inventory models, and hence, most inventory models are useless in practice. Perhaps there are simple adjustments to or ways of applying existing inventory models that can make them eminently useful in practice. Or perhaps new developments need to be made in these models to make them applicable.

# 4. The Second Great Challenge

My proposal of publishing cases and varieties of analyses of them is only a small part of the bigger mission of meeting the second great challenge of OR in American business schools, that of having its theories and methods absorbed into the everyday lives of the M.B.A.'s who graduate from such schools. This bigger mission, in my opinion, is to improve our connections between theory and practice, to get the best of both and have each benefit from the other.

There are many ways in which the OR-trained faculty in an American graduate business school can make connections with practice. Conducting field studies of companies is very valuable but is time consuming; having more journal outlets for those who wish to share the insights they gain from their field studies is desirable. Consulting can be equally valuable, except that sharing the insights gained from the experience is sometimes precluded because of confidentiality issues. Either of these activities can lead to writing cases that elucidate the managerial contexts and problems facing current organizations. Cases do and will continue to represent a critically important component of American business school curricula.

We also have a great need for richly detailed databases that researchers can access to test or illustrate their theories. And to guide the development of new theories. Doing empirical research automatically puts the researcher at the interface between theory and practice. Visiting plants and meeting with managers of the plant can take relatively little time and be productive. Attending departmental seminars in which people with pertinent practical experience report on current practices and developments and reading the popular press, such as *Business Week, Fortune,* the *Wall Street Journal,* and the business section of newspapers such as the *New York Times* can also be helpful. Insightful comments are often made in class by students with experience during discussions of contextual issues. Teaching in executive programs can provide intensive educational experiences in this regard for the faculty. Another way that may be difficult to implement is to have lecturers or others with extensive practical experience regularly attend the departmental seminars in which academic research is presented with the expectation that they will comment on the pertinence and relevance of the research that is being reported. Hearing such comments would sensitize the theoreticians of the subtleties of practice and possibly guide the development of new theories.

To remain (or become) topnotch, almost any American business school is going to require a mixture of strengths from its faculty, covering the spectrum from theory to practice. And the various people with these different strengths must be able to communicate with and learn from one another. I believe that a topnotch American business school should expect and encourage its tenured faculty to take the lead in making the connections between theory and practice—to reach out to practice and master the activities that connect to practice. I think that such a school should develop and maintain an ongoing strength in theoretical research and that its theoretical research strength should derive from its junior faculty, its newly tenured faculty, and those senior faculty who continue to be active in such research. Such a school should always have faculty members with expertise in theory and practice, and as many as possible with expertise in both. But the labeling evolves over time: As the tenured faculty become more experienced and wiser, they become the masters of practical connections. Those who were theoreticians in their younger years can continue to connect with the ongoing thrust of theoretical research and guide the younger theoreticians in their school toward more realistic, important, and relevant research.

I think that it is reasonable and desirable to expect junior faculty's initial expertise to be in theoretical research, rather than in applications and connections to practice. I think it is much more fruitful to expect a faculty member with expertise in theoretical research to learn to make connections to practice than to expect a faculty member with expertise in applications to learn how to do theoretical research. And theoretical research is too important to leave behind on the road to practical connections. Furthermore, the process of a theoretically trained faculty member gaining experience and becoming a master of practical connections will usually take many years. Indeed, it is a lifetime process. Setting a short-time deadline for this mastery is unreasonable and dysfunctional. Put bluntly, it would be a big mistake to require that all junior faculty demonstrate mastery of practical connections to qualify for tenure.

There are other dimensions to the challenge of OR in American business schools. One is the rapid development of technology, particularly digital computers. I was stunned at the impact that the electronic spreadsheet had on management. When it first appeared, I was not impressed, thinking that it did not do anything that could not already be done with simple computer languages, such as FORTRAN and BASIC. That was not the point. I did not appreciate the importance of the WYSIWYG (what you see is what you get) aspect of the software. I also did not appreciate the importance of user-friendliness. Now we have sophisticated OR techniques being connected with spreadsheets. For example, knowing little more than how to use a spreadsheet, one can push a few buttons and have a linear program automatically formulated for you, solved, and its numerical solution, including shadow prices, placed back into your spreadsheet. Our task in this regard is to transmit an understanding of when linear programs can be usefully applied, how to apply them without getting misled, and how to master the art of drawing useful insights from the process.

Another important development is the connection between databases and spreadsheets. The technological process of automatically gathering data, transmitting them to useful places, analyzing and massaging them, and converting them into inputs that go directly into one's spreadsheet, for further analysis by OR methodology is improving rapidly. If we look at the process as a technological system, we are naturally led to address questions such as what data to collect and how often, at what level of aggregation should they be saved, what kinds of analyses should be conducted with the aim of yielding what kinds of insights. The connections between OR and statistics, so important in the early days of OR, will once again cry out to be examined.

Finally, it may well turn out that the way in which OR theories and methods play a daily role in an executive's career is through their role in the preparation of new forms of accounting data. For example, the executive might examine the aggregate results of several linear programs each day, each one based on certain automatically collected and processed data, and on different sets of assumptions, such as level of aggregation, the way in which variability is treated, and so on. Each of these are answers to questions such as, "What should we be doing, and how much better off would we be, compared to our current policy, if product demands continue as projected by our forecasting model, assuming no unpredictable variability?" The numerical answers are not to be implemented but give the executive sophisticated insight into the current situation, such as the current volatility of demands.

In conclusion, the way to meet the second great challenge for OR in American graduate business schools is to foster more and better connections between theory and practice, to get the best of both, and have each benefit from the other. Some of the means of accomplishing these connections have been discussed.

# Acknowledgments

I am very grateful to Charles Holloway, James Miller, Jeffrey Moore, and Seungjin Whang for their helpful comments and suggestions.

# References

Porteus, E. 1989. "The Case Analysis Section: National Cranberry Cooperative." *Interfaces* 19: 29–39.
Porteus, E. 1993a. "The Case Analysis Section: Analyses of the National Cranberry Cooperative I. Tactical Options," *Interfaces* 23 :21–39.
Porteus, E., 1993b. "The Case Analysis Section: Analyses of the National Cranberry Cooperative II. Environmental Changes and Implementation," *Interfaces* 23: 81–92.

# Chapter 21

# Operations Research and Statistics in Manufacturing—An Educational Model

## Donald B. Rosenfield

Manufacturing has taken on a new importance in the past several years, underscoring its importance to societal welfare. Manufacturing education models have tried to address some of the perceived needs of companies competing in a global arena. This chapter describes one of these models and describes how operations research and statistics played a critical role in it. The approach of the model suggests how operations research and statistics can be a major part of educational endeavors in business, manufacturing, and other endeavors.

## 1. Introduction

In today's global environment, manufacturing capabilities are a prerequisite for adding value to and creating wealth in an economy. The myth of the postindustrial economy is that companies and societies can compete on the basis of service. The vision of a service economy has been cited as a possibility as manufacturing employment has declined. Such a vision is also based on a comparison with past industrial history, when we progressed from an agricultural to an industrial economy (see Cohen and Zysman 1987). However, the United States did not stop practicing agriculture, we automated it. We cannot choose for ours to become a service economy unless we master manufacturing. In addition, service activities such as logistics are intricately linked to manufacturing, just as certain manufacturing industries (e.g., chemicals) are linked to agriculture. Finally, manufactured goods are the primary method for developing exports. Thus, manufacturing capabilities are critical to societal welfare.

The United States has faced a series of economic challenges in the past twenty years. Indeed, a number of U.S. industries went through a period of major decline. The importance of manufacturing in these trends was often debated. Most government, academic, and industry leaders now recognize, however, that our declines in manufacturing capabilities were an important part of this series. Most of these leaders now believe that we need to have strong capabilities in manufacturing in years to come.

Actual solutions to improve manufacturing capabilities are also subject to debate. Suggested solutions encompass a range of concepts, in terms of technology, education and skill levels, macroeconomic policies, and the role of government. In assessing such solutions, it is important to understand how value can be added to manufactured goods. Competing societies and competing companies can add value and achieve advantage through various factors, including capital, labor, energy, materials, and knowledge. The global capital and labor markets of today generally cannot provide a source of competitive advantage: all corporations borrow from the same capital markets and tap the same labor markets. Although a society can compete on the basis of labor cost, any competitive advantage attributable to this factor is not sustainable: societal growth increases pressures for a rising standard of living, eroding a society's labor-cost advantage. A case in point is South Korea, where a strong growth rate recently slowed. Although energy and materials remain a source of competitive advantage, the so-called green revolution has limited their impact; few societies' wealth today is directly attributable to natural resources.

As Thurow (1992) emphasizes, historical bases of wealth, exemplified by those of Britain and the United States in the past two centuries, drew upon combinations of natural resources, capital, human resources, and technology. Today, the only remaining sustainable source of competitive advantage is implemented new knowledge: the realized capability of developing and producing, and generally doing things better. This implies continually improving generations of products, and state-of-the-art manufacturing and management processes. Not only must companies add value through knowledge, but this knowledge must now emphasize processes as well as products. In today's technologically sophisticated world, it is often feasible to identify innovations and copy them elsewhere. The competitive advantage of a new product, therefore, can be ephemeral: competitive advantage derives from manufacturing processes as well as product design. (Another form of competitive advantage derives from systems for developing new products more frequently, in itself a type of process.)

Companies will be most successful if they structure themselves to focus on knowledge. Evidence suggests that an emphasis on teamwork is the best way to do this. Teamwork is evident in most important business processes. These include multifunctional product-development teams that simultaneously develop products and processes, supply-chain teams that cut across corporations and functions, and alliances among corporations that require still other forms of teamwork.

Capabilities in manufacturing and the associated skills and knowledge constitute what I believe are the critical imperatives for the welfare of our society. The leaders of our large companies need to be proficient in both the technological and managerial aspects of their businesses. U.S. companies, many believe, rely too much on the general manager model of leadership—that one can just as easily manage a hamburger empire as a car company, or, an example taken from recent history, a computer company as easily as a beverage company.

This belief leads to some new requirements for our educational programs. Corporations' increasing focus on teams and processes requires a shift from universities' traditional role in assisting companies to one more of collaborating with them. Such collaboration is a prerequisite for developing the types of skills and processes needed for corporations. The U.S. educational system traditionally has been a "Type A" system, in that formal education has provided most skills needed in employment. In countries with "Type B" systems, such as Japan and West Germany, on-the-job training is much more extensive. (Dertouzos, Lester and Solow 1989). Because U.S. corporations rely on universities so heavily, universities need to address the particular skills and capabilities required by corporations in the near and long-term future. Teaching and research must emphasize process knowledge, including management processes relating to product development, and teamwork of all sorts.

These tenets led to a new educational program at MIT, developed in conjunction with thirteen major U.S. corporations (Aluminum Company of America, The Boeing Company, Chrysler Corporation, Digital Equipment Corporation, Eastman Kodak Company, Ford Motor Company, General Motors Company, Hewlett-Packard Company, Intel Corporation, Johnson & Johnson, Motorola Incorporated, Polaroid Corporation, and United Technologies Corporation). The program, called the Leaders for Manufacturing Program (referred to as LFM), is a two-year, dual master's program offering one degree in management and one in one of six engineering programs. The program, started in 1988, takes two full years, including two summers, and includes a six-month internship at a partner site. Several other major universities, including Stanford, have developed similar programs.

The program has undergone many experiments and certainly several changes, but it attempts to be consistent in addressing our views of societal needs in several ways: by using the structure of a dual-degree program, we incorporate the view that leaders need to be proficient in both technology and management; we focus on teamwork and integrative activities through several integrative courses, for example, product process design, and other activities such as the internship; and we focus on core methodologies with foundations in several areas.

The approach is depicted in the educational triangle of Figure 21.1. The program is based on a series of disciplinary foundations. These include mathematical foundations based on operations research and statistics. The integrating level consists of a series of activities and courses that cut across disciplines and support our view of the importance of teamwork and integration. The major integrating activity is a six-month internship at one of the partner sites. This internship consists of a challenging problem with both managerial and technical issues and serves as the basis for the dual-degree thesis. (The internship was also a vehicle for collaboration between the two schools of management and engineering, a critical and challenging

Figure 21.1.    Educational Triangle of Leaders for Manufacturing Program.

factor in the success of the program.) The top of the triangle denotes leadership. LFM, while recognizing that leadership is difficult to teach, uses a series of activities that runs the entire length of the two-year program. These include courses, seminars run by corporate executives, and practice modules in which students actually manage program activities. The leadership program, currently under the direction of a single faculty member, has been the most difficult part to develop, as we continue to develop new experimental models.

Operations research and statistics and the philosophies they embody are critical parts of the Leaders program in three ways. First, the methodologies are major parts of the curriculum foundations. In the very first summer of the two-year program, students take two rigorous courses, one in probability and statistics, and one in optimization models in manufacturing. Second, operational and statistical approaches are the heart of a large number of internship projects. Third, and most important, the underlying principles of operations research are synthesis and integration of data—bringing together a wide range of information to make the best decisions systematically. The theme of integration is the heart of the Leaders program and, in this sense, is the embodiment of operations research principles and practice.

The remainder of this chapter describes the use of operations research and statistics in some of the Leaders internships and in the curriculum, and discusses how the Leaders for Manufacturing Program represents a potential model for the use of these methodologies.

# 2. Operations Research and Statistics in Internships

As indicated by our experience with the six-month internship projects (having completed 220 at this time), the issues faced by manufacturing companies are complex ones. Operations research and statistics methods have proved very valuable and have underscored the importance in manufacturing of the skills these methods use. Table 21.1 classifies a recently completed set of past LFM thesis projects. The area most frequent chosen for projects was that of process control. The key to manufacturing success is process knowledge, and all of the thirteen LFM companies are struggling with this area. A large number of these projects involved issues of experimental design and statistical analysis. Indeed, our graduates have reiterated the belief that the most important skills in today's environment are the statistical ones. Issues in statistics (e.g., process control) and experimental design arise frequently enough so that our senior faculty member in statistics usually needs to provide guidance to a large number of students.

TABLE 21.1

*One Recent Set of Completed Theses*

| Topic | Number of Projects |
| --- | --- |
| Process Control/Optimization | 15 |
| Manufacturing Integration | |
| with Other Functions | 9 |
| Cycle-time (Flow-Time) Reduction | 4 |
| Inventory Control | 3 |
| Product Development | 3 |
| Scheduling | 3 |
| Performance Metrics | 2 |
| System Integration | 2 |
| Inspection | 1 |
| Tooling | 1 |
| Total | 43 |

A second important topic area is that of materials management and production planning. These projects have dealt with problems of inventory management within a multistage or multiechelon manufacturing and of managing production within a plant. Operations research models in inventory control and production planning were frequently applied in these situations and were often responsible for major improvements at the companies.

Three internship projects exemplify the impact of operations research and statistics in manufacturing. The first was a project on process improvement and production strategy for Hewlett-Packard's gas chromatograph products (MacDonald 1992). Gas chromatographs analyze gases by separating their components as they pass through a long, glass capillary tube. At Hewlett-Packard, capillary tubes are produced from glass rods called "preforms" in production cells called "drawing towers." Tubes are subject to randomly occurring defects that limit the length and the usability of the tubes and hence the ultimate type of product that can be sold. The internship project focused on improving the process and yield and, indirectly, on some of the strategic issues facing the business. These included a major decision about the possible procurement of a third tower, as well as decisions on whether to purchase tubes from outside vendors.

The student, in conjunction with Hewlett-Packard personnel, two advisors at MIT (the author and a professor in Electrical Engineering) and a postdoctoral fellow, developed an experimental design to optimize the factors involved in tube drawing. The design included controllable factors such as drawing speed, furnace temperature, capillary wall thickness, and the use of two prior steps (acid etching and fire polishing), as well as uncontrollable factors such as the specific operator.

The design ultimately involved 64 experiments. (Each test took nearly one full day.) The student used two experimental designs, Taguchi robust design (Phadke 1989), and an approach developed by an MIT post-doctoral fellow (Alkhairy 1991). (Part of the project was a comparison of alternative experimental design methods.) These experiments identified the effect of each controllable factor. The experiments were followed by an analysis of variance to identify significant factors and interaction, a regression to measure effects, and a set of confirmation experiments to confirm revised process parameters. The process improvement enabled Hewlett-Packard to significantly increase the capacity of the two existing drawing towers and avoid the purchase of a third.

The project also examined the strategic impact of the process improvements. An innovative model, utilizing the types of systems thinking the program tries to teach its students, led to a clear understanding of the strategic options available to Hewlett-Packard. Capillary lengths were based upon the frequency of defects. Data supported the hypothesis of a Poisson distribution of defects and hence exponential tube lengths between defects. By establishing from the experiments the average tube length before and after process improvements, we were then able to establish tube-length distributions.

We next developed the functional relationship between tube length and revenue and profit. We then computed the expected numbers of tubes of each of the possible target tube lengths. These computations were part of a strategic analysis. We concluded that the company could realize annual savings of at least $300,000.

In summary, the analytic skills manifested in the experimental design and strategic analysis, plus the systems approach through the project, represented the philosophy of the LFM program.

A second example was a project involving the management of the supply chain for a division of the Eastman Kodak Company (Hetzel 1993). The manufacturing operation consisted of three stages. The system was plagued by high and out-of-balance inventories. Again, the student worked with a company supervisor Kodak and two faculty advisors at MIT.

The approach was based upon a multiechelon inventory model (Graves, Kletter, and Hetzel 1994). Multiechelon approaches have been of interest in the operations research field since Clark and Scarf (1960) first worked on a serial system. Many of the internship projects dealt with such issues of inventory positioning and material movement.

Modeling the manufacturing system and appropriate order points and safety stocks, the student and advisors suggested increasing inventory at the upstream stage in order to decrease inventories at the downstream stages. Although the merit of such a strategy needed extensive discussion and explanation with all the stakeholders, it soon proved to be far superior to the existing system. Implementation of the recommendations for the supply chain reduced the inventory in the supply chain by 20%, with an annual savings of over $100,000 per year in holding costs without any reduction in customer service levels. Again, the approach combined analytic skills and systems thinking.

The third example arises from three LFM internships at Chrysler Motors (Drees 1991). The three interns worked on related projects in the development of a new line of automobiles, code-named LH, which became the Dodge Intrepid, Eagle Vision, and Chrysler Concorde. The development of these vehicles marked a turning point in the fortunes of Chrysler and started its recent renaissance. The roles of the students in these projects as part of Chrysler's team approach to development projects (referred to as "platform teams" in the industry) embodied our vision of integration and teamwork and systems thinking. One student whom I cosupervised studied the design and development of stamping dies by Chrysler as well as those of a number of domestic and Japanese competitors. The student studied the causes, both technological and managerial, of the significant leadtime advantages that Japanese companies held over American ones. For example, a survey and interviews by the student showed that for fourteen sets of dies from Japanese diemakers and six sets of dies from American diemakers, the Japanese companies had a lead time from first release through trial completion of 13 months, versus 22 months for U.S. companies. These data were also consistent with other surveys (e.g., Clark 1989). Because die development is a crucial part of car product development, this difference represented a major part of the car product development lead time that the Japanese manufacturers held at the time of the study, in 1990.

The student found a number of critical reasons for this time advantage, including differences in machine feed rates, excess stock in castings, differences in die lifetime that affect manufacturability, and organization of the development project. Because die design is done in job shops, the student also carefully studied congestion and work-in-process in the network of job-shop queues. Whereas other sources cited congestion and work-in-process as major reasons for the Japanese advantage, the student, using data from his surveys, showed that the U.S. diemakers held anywhere from a 33% to a 40% advantage in dies-in-process per milling machine, depending on downtime assumptions. The calculations were made by applying Little's Law (Little 1961) to the embedded queues in the system. These surprising results underscored other technological and managerial reasons for the time difference. More important, the results demonstrated the power of relatively simple operations research techniques.

# 3. Operations Research and Statistics in the Academic Program

Operations research and statistics models are currently at the heart of the Leaders for Manufacturing Program. In their very first summer, in a program developed in our second year of operation, students take a five-course, intensive program in fundamentals. The summer program focuses largely in operations research and statistics. Systems Analysis and Optimization is an operations research course, and a second course, Introduction to Operations Management, is heavily based on operations research. Engineering Probability and Statistics is a statistics course, and a fourth course, Total Quality Management, is closely related to it. In addition to the formal classwork, three major collaborative exercises that were joint class sessions were all based on operations research models.

The Systems Optimization course includes linear programming, control theory, nonlinear programming, integer programming, and simulation. Visitors from industry present applications of these approaches. In addition, students master computer techniques and complete a project using the methods they learn.

The Probability and Statistics course, co-taught by a probabilist and a statistician, includes probability spaces, distributions, statistical inference, and experimental design.

The Operations Management course includes queuing effects in manufacturing, factory floor simulation (including a computer exercise), inventory and production-planning models, and optimization applications to logistics and facility networks.

The three collaborative exercises cited earlier included:

1. A mixed integer formulation and optimization based on a multiple plant and warehouse configuration. The configuration problem encompassed transportation, manufacturing, inventory, and facilities costs. Students learn about how to formulate complex operation research models, the significance of various modeling factors, how to interpret models, and computational complexities.

2. Applications of the theory of constraints (Goldratt and Cox 1984). This theory focuses on managing bottlenecks in a production system and stipulates, for example, that non-bottleneck operations should sometimes be shut down. The collaborative exercise utilizes a sophisticated Monte Carlo simulation in which student teams seek to optimize profits in a multistage, multiproduct job shop.

3. A role-playing simulation to illustrate how to manage a sequential multi-stage distribution process. This exercise, referred to as the "Beer Game," is actually an operations research simulation model that is widely used in business schools. Within the exercise, four players representing

TABLE 21.2

*Typical Academic Program for Leaders Fellows*

| Year 1 | Year 2 |
|---|---|
| SUMMER<br>　Total Quality Management<br>　Systems Optimization & Analysis for<br>　　for Manufacturing<br>　Engineering Probability & Statistics<br>　Financial & Managerial Accounting<br>　Operations Management | SUMMER, FALL<br>　Thesis<br><br>JANUARY<br>　Organizational Leadership<br>　　& Change (conclusion) |
| FALL<br>　Economic Analysis for<br>　　Business Decisions<br>　Communication for Managers<br>　Strategic Management<br>　Proseminar in Manufacturing<br>　Two engineering electives | SPRING<br>　Manufacturing Policy<br>　Two electives |
| SPRING<br>　Introduction to Marketing<br>† Product Design & Manufacturing<br>　but not required<br>　Proseminar in Manufacturing<br>‡ Materials Processing or<br>　　engineering elective<br>　Manufacturing elective in finance,<br>　　HR management, management of<br>　　technology, or macroeconomics<br>　Information Technologies as an<br>　　Integrating Force in Manufacturing | |

† Recommended but not required.
‡ Recommended for ChE, MSE.

a retailer, a wholesaler, a distributor, and a manufacturer, order from each other without looking at system measures. When a level of demand changes, chaotic results ensue starting with multiple stockouts, followed by overordering, then excess inventory.

Systems thinking and analytic skills were at the heart of the summer program. During the remainder of the two years, students took additional management and engineering courses covering a variety of topics such as business strategy, information systems, and manufacturing processes. The other courses and activities of the program are presented in Table 21.2. Operations research is generally not an explicit part of these courses. However, related modeling approaches are used in major courses. For example, the popular course Systems Dynamics for Business Policy "uses a mixture of simulation models to develop principles for successful management of complex strategies in a dynamic world" (MIT 1994).

In addition, the approach of operations research has been a major part of the philosophy of LFM. Operations research is based on systems thinking and integration, bringing various disciplines together, and evaluating issues holistically. Courses after the first summer, and the internship as well, try to meet this goal of integration. An example of the effort is the course we developed in 1991 in product and process design. (An early assessment indicated clearly that this was an area the program needed). This course is cotaught by faculty in the School of Engineering and in the School of Management. Students learn in it to deal with the development of a new product from concept through market feasibility and process development.

# 4. Conclusion

The Leaders for Manufacturing Program represents an educational approach geared to meeting some of the challenges of our society. Similar programs have also been launched at other universities. We constantly assess our vision and the building blocks of the program and look for emerging areas of new emphasis (such as environment and global issues); the role of operations research and statistics has been very prominent in the program in the following areas: as the heart of the methodological core in the program; as the basis of many practice exercises in the research internship; and in emphasizing the concepts of systems thinking and integration.

Operations research and statistics are crucial in many of our business and management challenges in our society. LFM perhaps suggests a powerful and effective role for our disciplines. Rather than representing a single field or profession, operations research and statistics can play the lead role in a variety of professions. These include—in addition to manufacturing—logistics and transportation, service operations, and strategic planning. Our experience with Leaders for Manufacturing indeed indicates how important and effective operations research and statistics skills and thinking can be in these a professions.

# References

Alkhairy, A. 1991. "Optimal Product and Manufacturing Process Selection: Issues of Formulation and Methods of Parameter Design." Doctoral dissertation Department of Electrical Engineering and Computer Science, Massachusetts Institute of Technology.

Clark, A. J., and H. Scarf. 1960. "Optimal Policies for a Multi-echelon Inventory Problem," *Management Science* 6: 475–490.

Clark, K. 1989. "High Performance Product Development in the World Auto Industry." Working paper 90-004, Graduate School of Business, Harvard University.

Cohen, S. S., and J. Zysman. 1987. *Manufacturing Matters: The Myth of a Post-Industrial Economy*, New York: Basic Books.

Dertouzos, M., R. Lester, and R. Solow. 1989. *Made in America.* Cambridge, Mass.: MIT Press.

Drees, F. 1991. "Comparative Analysis of Best Practice in the Manufacture of Hard Dies for Automotive Stamping Operations." Master's thesis, Massachusetts Institute of Technology.

Goldratt, E. and J. Cox. 1984. *The Goal.* Croton-on Hudson, N.Y.: North River Press.

Graves, S., D. Kletter, and W. Hetzel. 1994. "A Dynamic Model for Requirements Planning with Application to Supply Chain Optimization," Working paper 3669-94, Sloan School of Management, Massachusetts Institute of Technology.

Hetzel, W. 1993. "Cycle Time Reduction and Strategic Inventory Placement Across a Multistage Process," Master's thesis, Massachusetts Institute of Technology.

Little, J. D. C. 1961. "A Proof for the Queuing Formula $L = \lambda W$ *Operations Research* 9: 383–387.

MacDonald, J., Jr. 1992. "An Integrative Approach to Process Parameter Selection in Fused-silica Capillary Manufacturing." Master's thesis, Massachusetts Institute of Technology.

MIT. 1994. *MIT Bulletin, 1994-1995*. Cambridge, Mass.: Massachusetts Institute of Technology. (Description of course 15.874.)

Phadke, S. 1989. *Quality Engineering Using Robust Design*. Englewood Cliffs, N.J.: Prentice-Hall.

Thurow, L. 1992. *Head to Head*. New York: William Morrow and Co.

# Chapter 22

# Graduate Programs in the Mathematical Sciences: The Clemson Model

## Kenneth T. Wallenius

## 1. Overview

There is general agreement within the mathematical sciences[1] community that, while there has been a dramatic increase in activity and urgency
of reform efforts at the school and undergraduate collegiate levels, "no comparable national effort or leadership has emerged as yet in the mathematics
graduate education enterprise. Despite the apparent mismatch between the
needs of the nation and much of the current practice in graduate programs,
relatively little attention has been given to post-baccalaureate education
in the mathematical sciences" (Conference Board of the Mathematical Sciences [CBMS 1992, p.1]). Calls for revision and suggested models of reform
are numerous in the mathematical sciences community (Board on Mathematical Sciences [BMS] 1990a,b; 1991, 1992; BMS/MSEB 1991; CBMS
1992) and also within the specific disciplines of statistics (Committee on
Applied and Theoretical Statistics (CATS) 1994) and operations research

(Horner 1992; Larson 1992; ORSA/TIMS 1993; White, 1991). Business, industry, and government (BIG) has never been satisfied with the training given students in traditional programs focused on academic research. "The main problem is the mismatch between graduate programs and the existing job market. The gap is even wider if we take into account potential, unexploited markets" (CBMS 1992, p.3).

This chapter focuses on the development of a program at Clemson that anticipated today's called-for reforms over twenty years ago. The chapter is not about a specific discipline such as statistics, OR, discrete mathematics, computing, and so on, but about a program melding the component areas of the mathematical sciences into programs administered within a single academic unit. Ten graduate programs in the mathematical sciences, including Clemson's, were selected for study in a recent report by the Board of Mathematical Sciences of the National Research Council (BMS 1992). These ten were examined during site visits and offered as models of "successful" programs. The Clemson program was also one of some 27 programs in departments, institutes and centers listed and described in the proceedings of a Conference on Graduate Programs in the Applied Mathematical Sciences II (Fennell and Ringeisen 1993), where ideas as to what constitutes a program in mathematical sciences were as varied as the speakers themselves. Indeed, diversity is one of the strengths of graduate education in the United States. Before describing the Clemson program itself, I will give a brief summary of events and conditions surrounding the development of programs in the mathematical sciences that borrows heavily from BMS 1992 and McClure 1993 to provide perspective. Circumstances that helped and hindered the Clemson experiment will be identified. It will be suggested that the window of opportunity for program reform that existed in the 1960's and early 1970's is open again.

# 2. Background

## 2.1. The National Scene

World War II created unprecedented opportunities for the application of mathematics and statistics to the technology of weaponry, electronics, cryptography, sampling inspection, and quality control. Urgency of the war effort shaped national priorities and gave importance to relatively new areas, such as operations research. Research in mathematical statistics grew at a phenomenal rate, aided by new sources of government support such as the Office of Naval Research (ONR) and, later, the National Science Foundation (NSF). Grant support for graduate assistants, travel, conferences, and so on changed the focus at many institutions. Academicians who could obtain grants were in great demand by the late 1950's. Increased government support for research in mathematics gave momentum to the movement emphasizing academic research at the expense of teaching and program development. Graduate assistants relieved senior faculty of considerable responsibilities related to undergraduate teaching. The 1950's and 1960's were decades of growth. Annual production of Ph.D.'s went from about 200 in 1950–51 to 1070 in 1968–69. Employment opportunities were unlimited during this period of expansion.

The situation turned around in the 1970's and a decade of contraction followed the twenty years of growth. Overall Ph.D. production fell to about 791 in 1979–80. The decline was concentrated in the pure areas which experienced a decrease of 55%, whereas statistics and operations research actually increased slightly. The decline was amplified by the emergence of computer science as a separate discipline with it own identity, drawing students and resources in the process. Market conditions forced graduates trained for academic research to seek employment in educational institutions where teaching was stressed and in nonacademic positions. These were jobs for which graduates were ill-prepared. Paradoxically, the declining demand in the 1970's for graduates trained for academic research was accompanied by a new respect for and reliance upon mathematical methods for solving problems in an increasingly technological society. One might have expected some serendipitous balance to result from the two offsetting trends. But this was not so.

BIG employers were reluctant to hire the traditionally trained mathematician whom they viewed as an awkward luxury. Academic training, admittedly excellent by traditional standards, did not prepare graduates to communicate with clients, with coworkers trained in science and engineering, or with management. Many expected to be allowed to do independent research often irrelevant to company interests (Gaskell and Klamkin 1974). This may not be entirely fair—no one would deny that there were many exceptions—but the image was widespread. "Much of industry and business still regards mathematicians with suspicion. Few industries have career paths for mathematicians; contributions of a mathematical nature are often not recognized as such because they are made by physicists, engineers and computer scientists" (CBMS 1992, p.4).

The 1980's were relatively stable compared to the previous three decades of ups and downs. Ph.D. production continued to decline slowly, reaching a low of 726 in 1984–85 and then climbed again to 929 in 1989–90. Although Ph.D. production was increasing, the number of degrees awarded to U.S. citizens actually decreased due to a dramatic change in the mix of international and U.S. students. The proportion of Ph.D.'s awarded to U.S. students dropped from 68% in 1980–81 to 43% ten years later. This trend was and still is a source of concern throughout the mathematical sciences community, especially in major research institutions where graduate students are used to teach undergraduate service courses. Employment patterns and unemployment rates are also a sources of concern. Although the number of new Ph.D.'s employed in the United States went up, most of the increase was in non-doctoral-granting academic institutions and in nonacademic positions. The percentage of new Ph.D.'s still looking for jobs six months or more after receiving the degree averaged nearly 10% in the late 1980's.

The slow upward trend of Ph.D. production of the 1980's accelerated into the 1990's reaching 1202 in 1992–93, an all-time high. But a majority of these, 56% were foreign nationals. Employment patterns of the late 1980's also continued into the early 1990's. Among those whose employment status was known as of late September 1993, 12.4% were still seeking employment. This rate nearly equals 1992's 12.7% record. Only 252, or 21% of new Ph.D.'s, obtained positions in doctoral-granting institutions. It can be argued that some of the problems are due to a national economy in recession. But there is a general agreement that national needs are not reflected in our graduate programs and that revision of traditional training is long overdue. In short, we are producing too many square pegs in a market dominated by round holes. More will be said about this issue in the section titled "Challenges and Opportunities for the Future."

## 2.2 The Clemson Scene

There is not much to report about the scene at Clemson Agricultural College in 1960. The small land grant college in rural South Carolina was emerging from its all-male military "A&M" background (to become Clemson University in 1964). A first-year graduate student in statistics at Stanford at the time, I knew nothing of Clemson beyond a vague perception that it had a good football team. It was at Stanford in 1960 that I met Clayton Aucoin, who was visiting on an NSF Science Faculty Fellowship.

A stint in industry after earning his Ph.D. in algebraic topology had convinced Aucoin that an alternative to traditional training in pure mathematics was needed. He recognized that even those trained in the applied mathematics of the day were seriously deficient in solving problems involving modeling and analyzing real data, constrained optimization, and computing. He foresaw the impending overproduction of mathematicians being trained for careers in academic research and envisioned a program oriented toward filling BIG needs. This prophetic viewpoint was not given much credibility in national forums and probably would have been branded there as heretical in the face of unprecedented activity, growth, and support for academic research at that time. Aucoin chose to broaden his own training at Stanford because of its established reputation in statistics and its emerging graduate program in operations research. In addition, Stanford was experimenting with a cooperative undergraduate program involving the departments of Statistics, Mathematics, and Industrial Engineering that Aucoin thought might provide a model for what he had in mind. He came to Clemson in 1963 and became head of a small, service-oriented department.

In a short period of time, Aucoin was able to sell his concept to a rather forward-looking administration willing to commit resources and take chances. I joined the Clemson faculty in 1968, when Aucoin had already begun implementing his ideas by assembling a faculty, mostly mathematicians, who shared his philosophy and who would play key roles in developing the program. Diminished academic job opportunities in the 1970's made it possible to be rather selective. Despite heavy recruiting competition in the key areas of operations research, computational mathematics, and statistics, the novelty of the program concept and the enthusiasm of the faculty seemed to infect visitors. We were able to attract the people we wanted. Primarily through Aucoin's efforts, an innovative undergraduate major that required courses in computing, operations research, probability, and statistics in addition to the more typical undergraduate fare had been put in place. That program also required students to select an "option" (e.g., biology, communications, computing, statistics, etc.) which consisted of specialized training in designated courses. More traditional M.A. and Ph.D. programs were created to get a foothold in the graduate degree business in South Carolina making it possible to justify the hiring of additional faculty as the envisioned program evolved.

The award of an NSF grant in the "Alternatives in Higher Education" program in 1975 gave visibility, legitimacy, and support to our plans to create an applied M.S. program to prepare graduates for BIG careers. A distinguished Board of Advisors, Thomas Banks (Brown University), Stuart Hunter (Princeton University), Robert Lundegard (Office of Naval Research), Donald McArthur (Milliken Corporation), James Ortega (Institute for Computer Applications in Science and Engineering), and Robert Thrall, chairman (Rice University), provided valuable guidance during the planning phase of the applied master's program. Many others contributed ideas and encouragement, notably Jack Borsting (Naval Postgraduate School), William Boyce (Rensselaer Polytechnic Institute), Donald Bushaw (Washington State University), Gerald Lieberman (Stanford University), William Lucas (Cornell University), and Jerome Spanier (Claremont Graduate School). The consensus opinion was that a level of training between the baccalaureate and the Ph.D., something more ambitious than the traditional master's degree, would be attractive to students and fill a significant national need. The applied master's program was formally created in December 1975. The NSF Alternatives grant also called for the development of a Ph.D. program that would build on the breadth-and-depth philosophy of the M.S. degree. The resulting Ph.D. program was approved by the faculty in the spring of 1979.

# 3. The Clemson Graduate Degree Programs in the Mathematical Sciences

Of the four graduate degree programs offered by the Department of Mathematical Sciences at Clemson University, the first two are administered wholly within the department, and the second two are jointly administered with other academic units. These programs involve roughly 50 faculty members and 100 graduate students in the Department of Mathematical Sciences, plus an assortment of colleagues and students from the College of Commerce and Industry (pertaining to the doctoral program in Management Science) and from the College of Education (pertaining to the master's program in Mathematics Education). There have been some measures of success. Elements of the programs prepare graduates for careers in teaching in colleges and universities and for careers in business, industry, and government.

The applied M.S. program in mathematical sciences was inaugurated in 1975. It was based on the following premises as stated in (Proctor 1973, p.9): (1) The major source of employment for mathematical scientists in the future will be nonacademic agencies. (2) Most such employers will require more than a B.S. degree but less than a Ph D. degree in the mathematical sciences. (3) Employers will prefer personnel who possess not only a concentration in a particular area of the mathematical sciences, but also a diversified training in most of the other areas. (4) Graduates should have more than superficial education in applying mathematical techniques to solve problems in areas other than the mathematical sciences. Inherent in such training is the ability to communicate, both orally and in writing, with persons from these areas. (5) It is desirable to obtain such broad-based education in the mathematical sciences prior to specializing for the Ph.D. degree.

The initial plan called for fourteen 3-hour courses (42 semester hours) plus a 1-hour paper to be completed over two academic years and an intervening summer. This was a substantial increase from typical requirements in which the master's degree was often regarded as a consolation prize to Ph.D. candidates unable to pass their qualifying examinations. Requirements for the M.S. degree were broken down into two categories: breadth and concentration. The breadth requirements consisted of eight courses:

- Two "core" courses (e.g., an analysis and an advanced linear algebra course)

- Two computing courses (e.g., digital modeling and scientific computing)

- One statistics course (e.g., data analysis)

- One OR course (e.g., mathematical programming)

- One additional statistics/OR course (e.g., applied multivariate analysis, linear statistical models, network flows, advanced linear programming, stochastic processes, etc.)

- One applied models course taught outside the department (a course in science/engineering/economics/ ... employing mathematical models to study various system behaviors)

The seven departmental breadth courses and the external applied models course were designed to meet the requirements of premises (3) and (4), respectively. With the aid of a faculty advisor, each student selects six additional courses in one of five areas of concentration: applied algebra, applied analysis, computational mathematics, operations research, and statistics. A concentration could be a blend of advanced courses in more than one area and could include courses taught in other departments, if such a blend achieves sufficient depth and better meets a student's objective.

As might be expected, the initial program requirements described earlier have undergone minor changes over the years. For example, after many successful "external models" courses, a few bad experiences led to the abandonment of this requirement in favor of the inclusion of more modeling content in the breadth courses. The one-hour paper requirement was replaced by a variable-credit master's project culminating with both written and oral presentations in conjunction with the master's examination. Despite these minor changes, the guiding philosophy of breadth and depth remains intact.

The present Ph.D. program, inaugurated in 1979, was developed after experience was gained with the master's program. It was fashioned along the same general philosophy of breadth and depth. Breadth requirements are met by taking at least two graduate courses in each of five areas: algebra/combinatorics, analysis, scientific computing, operations research, and statistics. Breadth is assessed by performance on three preliminary examinations selected from six areas: algebra, analysis, computational mathematics, operations research, statistics, and stochastic processes. These three prelims plus a fourth comprehensive examination administered by the student's advisory committee comprise the Ph.D. qualifying examination required for formal admission to degree candidacy. The comprehensive examination addresses depth of understanding and serves three purposes: to assess the student's readiness to perform independent research; to assess the student's competency in advanced graduate material relevant to the student's chosen research area and to provide a forum for members of the committee to learn about and provide input into the student's proposed research program. A thesis proposal is not a required part of this fourth examination, although such a proposal is frequently discussed during the oral part of the examination. Weaknesses identified during the comprehensive examination can be remedied through additional course work and directed reading. A successful thesis defense is the final requirement.

A second Ph.D. program, in management science, was created in 1971 through a joint effort of the faculties of the Departments of Management and Mathematical Sciences. Predating the applied master's program by four years, its genesis is discussed later. Program requirements consist of twelve courses considered fundamental (called "core" courses), plus an additional six advanced courses (called "concentration" courses) approved by the student's advisory committee. Core courses include training in both departments whereas the concentration might be in a single area, such as production/operations management, stochastic models, applied statistics, and so on. Admission to candidacy is based on successful completion of a comprehensive examination composed of one-day written examinations in applied statistics (statistical inference and data analysis) and in operations research (mathematical programming, stochastic models, and operations management), plus a weeklong case study requiring a definitive analysis and evaluation of a management science application, including financial and mathematical modeling, formulation, analysis, and final recommendations in the form of a written study citing appropriate references. The program culminates with a defense of the student's dissertation.

A Master of Education degree in mathematics education is offered by the College of Education. It is administered by a joint committee and re-

quires a minimum of eighteen hours of graduate credit in the mathematical
sciences. The mathematical sciences community views the decline in mathematics preparation of incoming freshmen with considerable concern. We
share in that concern and view our participation in the training of mathematics teachers for elementary and secondary education as an extremely
important professional service. However, the training of school teachers is
outside the focus of this paper and will not be discussed further.

It is to be hoped that these descriptions give a general idea of the nature
of these graduate programs without getting lost in details about specific
courses. Interested readers will be furnished with details upon request.
Additional information on the faculty, departmental governance, guidelines
for tenure and promotion, faculty evaluation and reward policies, and so
on is also available through the Clemson University GOPHER system.

It is difficult to define "success," let alone quantify the degree to which
success has been achieved by these programs. In July 1990 the National Research Council's Board on Mathematical Sciences appointed a Committee
on Doctoral and Postdoctoral Study in the United States. In preparation
for the study reported in BMS 1992 the committee defined a "successful"
Ph.D. program. The Clemson program satisfied that definition and was
among the ten models chosen for study. The master's program has received
national recognition and attracts outstanding students who have had great
success competing with graduates trained in traditional programs at pres-
tigious universities. Counter to national trends in which U.S. citizens comprise a minority of the candidates for graduate degrees in the mathematical
sciences, of the 82 graduate students enrolled in the Clemson program in
the spring of 1994, 70 were U.S. citizens. Of these, 26 were females and
5 were black or Hispanic. International students in the program represent
China (5), Germany, India (2), Mexico, Poland, Turkey, and Togo. The
uniqueness of the program, the quality and enthusiasm of the faculty, and
the success of graduates in obtaining exciting employment goes a long way
in attracting high-quality applicants, many of whom come from small, elite
four-year colleges. Another measure of success, one the most gratifying, is
follow-on applications from institutions after one of their former students
completes the program. For example, the first student from St. Olaf College in Northfield, Minnesota, enrolled in the master's program in 1985.
She had an outstanding undergraduate education and was well qualified

in the mathematical sciences. Since then, there has been a steady flow of excellent students from St. Olaf College, eight in all, several of whom have completed the Ph.D. program. Besides the success of graduates in finding good initial positions, return visits by BIG recruiters after having hired a previous graduate indicates the customer is happy with the product. Contact with former students is maintained and helps the department keep abreast of changing conditions.

In addition to breadth of academic training, virtually every study and paper dealing with graduate student preparation for today's job market stresses the importance of communication skills and preparation for college teaching. Various opportunities to acquire and improve these skills exist on all campuses. Examples include the passive observation by the student of what makes for good teaching by his or her professors, the requirement to orally defend a dissertation and, for some, the opportunity to consult, tutor, or teach. These opportunities are often not thoroughly exploited because of the emphasis placed on learning subject matter. One cannot expect communication skills to be absorbed by osmosis but must facilitate their acquisition through conscious planning.

The most obvious opportunity for absorbing these skills is in the classroom since, at most graduate institutions, teaching assistants (T.A.'s) must be used to shoulder some of the heavy undergraduate service teaching load. The necessity to take on this kind of responsibility is viewed as an opportunity for students to gain poise and self-confidence in front of an audience, whether it be a group of students in the classroom or a future group of clients or business associates in a board room. The ability to prepare and deliver an organized lecture and to think on one's feet in response to questions in the classroom is extremely valuable. The importance of these skills is taken seriously at Clemson, as made manifest by specific requirements.

All new graduate teaching assistants are required to attend an intensive, weeklong orientation prior to commencement of classes. They attend lectures on "The Role and Responsibilities of the Graduate Teaching Assistant," "Methods for Active Teaching and Learning," "Questioning and Discussion Techniques," "Planning for Instruction: The First Day", "Dealing with Potential Problems in the Classroom and Office," and so on. They are given a 92-page "Guidebook for Clemson University Teaching Assistants" containing sections on preparation and teaching techniques along with other information on the use of audio-visual aids, computing facilities, administrative information, cheating, plagiarism, sexual harassment, and so on. Students are divided into groups of four or five for practice teaching sessions. Each student is required to prepare a five-minute lecture on an assigned topic. The lecture is given to members of the group and recorded on video tape. After listening to the lecture and reviewing the tape, group members and a faculty advisor critique the lecturer's performance. During the course of actual classroom teaching, a faculty mentor is assigned to each T.A. The mentor is required to visit the classroom on several occasions and make a written evaluation of teaching performance after each visit. The mentor also checks on test preparation and evaluation and, in general, is a source of experience and support. Teaching assistants understand the importance of good recommendations by faculty mentors in letters of reference accompanying job applications.

In addition to the initial training and mentoring given all teaching assistants, special requirements have been established for all advanced Ph.D. students (i.e., students who have passed prelims). With support from the Fund for the Improvement of Post Secondary Education (FIPSE), Clemson was one of eight universities cooperating with a joint committee of the American Mathematical Society, the Mathematical Association of America, and the Society for Industrial and Applied Mathematics on Preparation for College Teaching in developing specific practices aimed at advanced graduate students. The other participants were the University of Cincinnati, Dartmouth College, the University of Delaware, Harvard University, Oregon State University, the University of Tennessee, and Washington University. Directed by a faculty member who had been recognized for excellence in research and teaching with an Alumni Professorship, activities at Clemson focused on helping students become more effective teachers; helping students become more aware of the components and expectations of the profession; broadening the student's mathematical sciences perspectives; and accomplishing this with minimum expense (time and money) to the students. These goals were met through the careful design of a professional seminar carrying three semester hours of graduate credit, the purchase of a small amount of video equipment, and the establishment of a special departmental library for the project. Details on all eight projects plus interesting survey statistics, are listed in CPCT 1994.

# 4. Program Operation

Although there seems to be a consensus on the importance of breadth in graduate training in the mathematical sciences, there is no consensus on how to achieve it. The two most obvious approaches are either to bring together, in a single academic unit, a faculty each of whom has depth in one or more of the areas comprising the program to be delivered (the Clemson approach used in the development of the applied M.S. and the Ph.D. programs); or to build a cooperative program involving several traditional departments (a more common approach, used to develop the Clemson programs in management science and mathematics education). To be successful, both approaches require cooperation, one intra- and the other interdepartmental. Since this chapter is about programs developed using the first approach, I will discuss some special problems and benefits involved with operating such a program.

Implementing and operating a program requiring a diverse faculty that typically reside in separate academic units is a challenging administrative problem. People in the mathematical sciences are notoriously parochial and are sometimes accused of lacking an abundance of interpersonal skills. It is natural for each faculty member to feel his or her specific area of expertise should occupy a place of prominence among the component disciplines. Governance, tenure and promotion policies, procedures for determining raises, defining and filling new faculty positions, and so on, are all potentially divisive issues when real or perceived inequities exist between component areas. Since differences in opinion are bound to occur within any organizational structure, it is important to have clearly stated and effective departmental governance practices in place.

A structure built around "subfaculties" has been found to work reasonably well at Clemson. Subfaculties have developmental responsibilities relative to academic matters associated with interest areas. The subfaculties are Analysis, Computational Mathematics, Discrete Mathematics, Operations Research, Statistics and Probability, and Undergraduate Education. Each faculty member is encouraged to join several subfaculties but can be a voting member of only one. Subfaculties elect a representative to the Mathematical Sciences Council (MSC) and to each of three rather standard standing committees (Research, Graduate Affairs, Undergraduate Affairs). The MSC advises the department head on long-range planning, curricular issues, and all matters brought before it by the faculty or the department head. The MSC also functions as the Personnel Committee relative to recruitment of new faculty members. The department head serves at the pleasure of the Dean of the College of Sciences and bears the ultimate responsibility for all administrative decisions. In practice, however, decisions counter to the counsel of the MSC would probably generate serious discussions between the faculty and the Dean. The department head, although not a chairperson elected by the faculty, cannot be effective in a confidence vacuum. This is an extremely important and delicate aspect of departmental governance. The department head is professionally associated with one of the component disciplines and must assiduously avoid showing favoritism toward that subfaculty for obvious reasons.

The Graduate Affairs Committee makes recommendations to the MSC on curricula and course offerings. Many new courses had to be developed and existing courses modified to implement these programs. Course coverage had to be coordinated across areas. For example, students in a statistical computing course or in a linear statistical models course may need to know about matrix decompositions and generalized inverses. Including these topics in a linear algebra breadth course taken early in the program saves valuable time in subsequent depth courses and demonstrates to students the interdependence of the various areas. Persuading the algebraists to adjust the coverage in their course is easier in an integrated department than it would be if the decision involved separate academic units with different goals. Cooperation, mutual respect, and collegiality, more easily discussed than achieved among strong-willed academicians, is at least possible within a single, integrated administrative unit composed of scholars attracted to that unit by a common philosophy.

It could be argued that the subfaculty structure emphasizes disparity and hence might hamper cooperation and synergism in an integrated department. In view of the realities of extant recognition-and-rewards practices in the mathematical sciences (CPRR 1994) and in academia in general (NSF 1992), individual faculty members must still travel along traditional academic research routes to tenure, promotion, and mobility destinations. (More will be said about the need to reform recognition-and-reward systems in the next section.) The subfaculty structure reflects the reality of this situation by encouraging collaboration within specific disciplines. Subfaculties plan and run their own research seminar series as well as a unique Distinguished Visitors Program (DVP). The opportunity to plan a DVP rotates among the subfaculties on a yearly basis. Although arrangements can vary greatly with details left up to the cognizant subfaculty, the nominal year consists of six to ten week-long visits during which distinguished visitors deliver survey and special-topics lectures, consult with faculty members on research interests, meet with students, and are generally available during the day. The subfaculty structure thus facilitates both area-specific autonomy for professional growth and a workable, representative system for departmental governance.

There are some notable examples of subfaculty research synergism. The department was successful in competing for NSF funding under the Experimental Program to Stimulate Competitive Research (EPSCoR). The five-year program was entitled "Research in Discrete Structures" and involved faculty members in algebra, OR, and computational mathematics. (The algebra subfaculty subsequently adopted the name "Discrete Mathematics" reflecting the broadened interest in combinatorics, graph theory, and computing. A Discrete Mathematics Miniconference sponsored by ONR is held annually at Clemson, and so on.) Another successful joint effort, this entitled "Distributed Computing" and funded for three years by ONR, involved the analysis, OR and computational mathematics subfaculties.

# 5. Challenges and Opportunities for the Future

The challenge seems clear. Look at the bibliography. Every professional society is calling for reform in graduate education. Opposing viewpoints, if they exist, have not been aired. There seems to be no rebuttal. We do not need more studies: "The amount of national attention now given to educational reform in mathematics is staggering." (CMBS 1992, p.2) But school and "undergraduate mathematics education [are] the focus of major programs in the National Science Foundation and in many of the mathematics professional societies. In contrast to this, no comparable national effort or leadership has emerged as yet in the graduate education enterprise" (CBMS 1992, p.1). The quoted report concludes by listing nineteen recommendations broken down into five cognizance categories: departments, universities, professional societies, government, and industry. Although it is useful to have these recommendations catalogued, it is discouraging to read in the same report that without reform in graduate education, no lasting change in school or undergraduate education is likely, and that leadership and effort are lacking in the important enterprise of graduate education.

In the concluding paragraph entitled "The Key to Action," the burden of effecting reform is clearly placed on the faculty: "But action, if it starts at all, will start from the faculty." (BMS 1992, p.51.) Should we expect the tenured full professors to initiate the action? Perhaps the main reason that no leadership has emerged from the faculty bench is that those in positions of control, the tenured professors, are largely content with the status quo. And why not? Even though our graduate students have been unable to obtain employment in academic research, we ourselves have enjoyed low teaching loads, summer research support, travel, conferences, and, in general, the freedom to pursue whatever is intellectually stimulating. Even in a tight economy, we are less vulnerable than our recently graduated students, most of whom are either untenured in non-doctoral-granting institutions or are feeling the crunch in a firm associated with the shrinking business of national defense. "We are doing quite well, thank you! What crisis?" There is little motivation to abandon that which has been so rewarding in order to spend time and effort worrying about programs, national needs, and the like.

If not the senior faculty, then the job falls on the junior faculty. With an academic reward system "which places a premium on published theoretical research" (Geoffrion 1992) and success in obtaining funding for that research, untenured faculty cannot afford the risk of expending time and energy in program reform activities, even if they had the leverage to effect such revisions. Academic programs rooted in tradition are like supertankers of the sea, an analogy borrowed from Horner (1992). They have so much inertia it takes a tremendous coordinated effort to change course, let alone turn one around. What chance is there if the captains are content with steady-as-she-goes and the crews will not risk mutiny?

The "Key to Action" offered in BMS 1992 is naive. Slightly closer to the answer are the two National Research Council reports, BMS 1990a and BMS/MSEB 1991, which state that the recognition-and-rewards system in mathematics must change if renewal and revitalization are to take place. But who can change these well-entrenched systems? A definitive study of *Recognition and Rewards in the Mathematical Sciences* published in 1994 by the Joint Policy Board for Mathematics of the AMS (CPRR 1994) lists ten findings and six guiding principles. Although acknowledging the roles of government, professional societies, and university administrations in influencing the mathematical sciences community, the report asserts that "The main responsibility [for changing the recognition-and-rewards system] rests with individual departments of mathematical sciences" (CPRR 1994, p.2). This view ascribes some sort of organic identity to a department. But a department is a collection of individuals with momentum, as in the tanker analogy given earlier.

We live in a capitalist society where change is effected by some combination of foresight, ingenuity, energy, and the willingness to invest resources in risky ventures. Those were the ingredients that made Aucoin's experiment of the 1960's successful: He had foresight and ingenuity; the National Science Foundation had the capital; NSF and the administration at Clemson University took a calculated risk; and the faculty provided the energy. It was a team effort, and it paid off.

Today, the "government sees leadership in science and mathematics as a critical element to regain American competitiveness in the international arena" (CBMS 1992). Reform in graduate education in the mathematical sciences is a prerequisite to regaining that leadership. It seems inescapable, therefore, that it is government policy and funding priorities that should influence the recognition and reward system that will then influence the faculty to get the job done. The NSF has called on universities to change the recognition-and-rewards system by encouraging and rewarding teaching excellence, instructional scholarship, and public service as well as research (NSF 1992). Yet the NSF perpetuates the extant recognition-and-rewards system by continuing to place funding emphasis within the mathematical sciences budget on basic research. Programs like the NSF "Alternatives in Higher Education" which helped make reform at Clemson a reality, do not exist any more. The NSF and other major federal funding agencies must take the helm if the ship is to be turned. A strong message would be sent if that agency were to shift some funds from traditional areas to support innovative graduate curricular development.

At this time the NSF seems to be the pivotal key to effecting change in the recognition-and-rewards system. Reform is at the same time easier and more difficult now than it was when the Clemson experiment started over 25 years ago. Aucoin is now retired, but his program, described in this chapter, and other successful ones described in BMS 1992 and Fennell and Ringeisen 1993, can serve as models for future programs. Departments are more mature, and boundaries may be less flexible now than they were in the 1960's. Departmental leaders are less likely to take chances and challenge the status quo in this time of economic uncertainty. Planning on how to survive the next budget cut has a higher priority than long-range planning and contemplation of major program revisions. Yet there are some opportunities on the horizon. The economy seems to be emerging from recession. Senior faculty members hired in the expansion decade of the 1960's are entering the retirement zone, thus allowing departments to increase breadth by hiring replacement faculty from specialty areas such as statistics or OR. Besides new Ph.D.'s, downsizing in BIG should bring applicants with diverse experience into the job market. The many calls for reform from the highest levels of government, from funding agencies, and from professional societies provide the challenge. As the little red hen said, "Now, who will help me pick the grain?"

# Note

1  For the purposes of this paper, the definition of "mathematical sciences" given by the Board of the Mathematical Sciences of the National Research Council in BMS 1992 will be adopted: "pure mathematics, applied mathematics, statistics and probability, operations research and scientific computing." Although we agree with most statisticians that "statistics is not a subset of mathematics" (Fennell and Ringeisen 1993; see discussions by James R. Thompson), such distinctions will not be addressed. Similar arguments about OR/MS, and so on, will also be avoided.

# References

Board on Mathematical Sciences (BMS). 1990a. ιRenewing U.S. Mathematics: A Plan for the 1990's. National Research Council. Washington, D.C.: National Academy Press.

Board on Mathematical Sciences (BMS). 1990b. *Actions for Renewing U.S. Mathematical Sciences Departments.* National Research Council. Washington, D.C.: National Academy Press.

Board on Mathematical Sciences (BMS). 1991. *Mathematical Sciences, Technology and Economic Competitiveness.* James Glimm, Editor, National Research Council. Washington, D.C.: National Academy Press.

Board on Mathematical Sciences (BMS). 1992. *Educating Mathematical Scientists: Doctoral Study and the Postdoctoral Experience in the*

*United States.* National Research Council. Washington, D.C.: National Academy Press.

Board on Mathematical Sciences and Mathematical Sciences Education Board (BMS/MSEB). 1991. *Moving Beyond Myths: Revitalizing Undergraduate Mathematics.* National Research Council. Washington, D.C.: National Academy Press.

Committee on Applied and Theoretical Statistics of the Board on Mathematical Sciences (CATS). 1994. *Proceedings of a Symposium on Modern University Statistics Education.* National Research Council. Washington, D.C.: National Academy Press.

Committee on Preparation for College Teaching (CPCT). AMS/IMS/MAA. 1994. *You're the Professor, What Next: Ideas and Resources for Preparing College Teachers.* Betty Anne Case, Editor. MAA Notes Number 35. Washington, D.C.: Mathematical Association of America.

Committee on Professional Recognition and Rewards (CPRR). 1994. *Recognition and Rewards in the Mathematical Sciences.* Report of the Joint Policy Board for Mathematics. Washington, D.C.: American Mathematical Society.

Conference Board of the Mathematical Sciences (CBMS). 1992. Graduate Education in Transition: Report of a Conference. Washington, D.C.: Conference Board of the Mathematical Sciences.

Fennell, Robert E., and Richard D. Ringeisen. 1993. *Conference on Graduate Programs in the Applied Mathematical Sciences II.* Clemson University, Clemson, S.C.

Gaskell, R. E., and M. S. Klamkin. 1974. "The Industrial Mathematician Views His Profession: A Report of the Committee on Corporate Members." *American Mathematical Monthly* 81: 699–715.

Geoffrion, Arthur M. 1992. Forces, Trends, and Opportunities in MS/OR. *Operations Research* 40: 423–445.

Horner, Peter. 1992. "Where Do We Go From Here?" *OR/MS Today* 19(2) April 1992: 36–40.

Larson, Richard. 1992. "Curriculum Corrections: Teaching Operations Research as Research on Operations." *OR/MS Today* 19(2) April 1992: 36–40.

McClure, Donald E. 1993. "Report on the 1993 Survey of New Doctorates." *Notices of AMS* 40(9): 1164–96.

National Science Foundation (NSF). 1992. *America's Academic Future: A Report of the Presidential Young Investigator Colloquium on U.S. Engineering, Mathematics, and Science Education for the Year 2010 and Beyond.* NSF Publication 91–150, Washington, D.C.

ORSA/TIMS Committee for a Review of the OR/MS Master's Degree Curriculum. 1993. Suggestions for an MS/OR Master's Degree Curriculum. *OR/MS Today,* February 1993: 16–31.

Proctor, T. G. 1973. *Graduate Programs in the Applied Mathematical Sciences: Perspectives and Prospects.* Technical Report no. 274, Department of Mathematical Sciences, Clemson University, Clemson, S.C.

White, J. 1991. "An Existence Theorem for OR/MS." *Operations Research* 39: 183–93.

# Chapter 23

# Analysis and Judgment in Policymaking

## Alexander George

In the early days of the RAND Corporation, Charles Hitch, who organized the Economics Department there, made an observation about the role
of analysis in policymaking that intrigued me. Hitch, one of the founders
of modern systems analysis, emphasized that the results of even the best
systems analysis study should be regarded as an aid to the preparation
of policy decisions, and not as a substitute for the judgment of the policymaker. His statement tantalized me. Deeply convinced that scholarly
analysis can make important contributions to policymaking, I have tried
ever since to understand what "judgment" means in this context and how
good analysis can aid the judgment of decisionmakers. I know that psychologists have written a great deal about judgment and how it can be
influenced and distorted by cognitive dynamics. I am also conversant with
the literature on the impact that small-group dynamics and organizational
and bureaucratic behavior can have on the quality of decisions. I need not
attempt to summarize or comment on these important literatures except to
say that I have not found a complete or satisfactory answer to the question
of what constitutes the elusive "judgment" of policymakers.

After studying presidential decision making over a period of many years,
my conclusion, not novel to be sure, is that policymakers typically take into

account various factors—such as domestic political considerations, international opinion, the need to prioritize values embedded in an issue, and so on—that cannot be properly anticipated and dealt with in policy analysis. Thus, whereas scholars and policy analysts inside and outside the government can and should preoccupy themselves with the task of identifying high-quality policy options (i.e., that meet the special criterion of "analytical rationality"), high-level policymakers must exercise broader judgments that take into account a variety of additional considerations. To reflect this broader judgment I have coined the term "political rationality" to distinguish it from "analytical rationality."

One way to proceed with this task is to replace the global notion of "judgment" with an identification of specific aspects of decisional problems about which policymakers exercise some kind of judgment, whether or not it is aided by available policy analysis. Elsewhere I have identified and briefly discussed seven different types of judgment that enter into high-level decision making.[1] (See George 1993, chapter 2. That publication and the present article draw on George, 1980.) Here, given the limitations of space, I will discuss only one type of judgment which I believe to be particularly important in foreign policy decisions.

One of the most important judgments high-level policymakers are often obliged to make concerns the trade-off between seeking to maximize the analytical quality of the policy to be chosen (i.e., which option is most likely to achieve given policy objectives at acceptable levels of cost and risk), and the need to obtain sufficient support for the policy option that is finally chosen. Another familiar, often difficult trade-off problem arises from having to decide how much time and policymaking resources to allocate to the effort to identify the best possible policy option. A third trade-off problem arises from having to decide how much political capital, influence resources, and time to expend in an effort to increase the level of support for the option to be chosen. The three trade-off problems discussed here are depicted in Figure 23.1.

Academic specialists can easily fall into the error of thinking about high-quality policy decisions in too narrow a framework. Policymakers have to deal with the tension that often exists between policy quality and the need to choose a policy that commands enough support. Very often a measure of quality has to be sacrificed in favor of a decision that will get the kind of political support within and outside the administration that is necessary if the policy is to have a chance of being sustained.

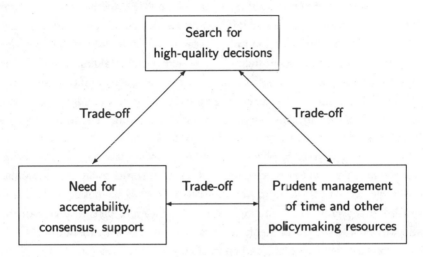

Figure 23.1.     Three Trade-off Problems.

Another trade-off in political policymaking is the one between the quality of the decision and the policymaker's sensible use of time and of analytical and political resources. A policymaker who spends a tremendous amount of time trying to arrive at a policy decision of superior quality may incur considerable costs; time is not free. And if policymakers tie up all the analytical resources at their disposal in order to achieve a higher quality decision, the analysis of other policy issues may be neglected or shortchanged. (This trade-off is said to have been a problem with Kissinger's style when he dominated foreign policymaking in the Nixon administration.) Policymakers also face the practical question of deciding how much of the political capital and influence resources at their disposal they should expend in order to gain support for a higher quality decision. They may decide to adopt a lesser policy option for which potential support is more easily gained.

Dealing with these trade-off problems requires policymakers to exercise ad hoc judgments, since well-defined rules are lacking. When such dilemmas arise, how, if at all, can policy-relevant theories and generic knowledge about the type of foreign policy issue in question assist in exercising judgment? This question is all the more difficult to answer because theory and generic knowledge are most directly relevant in the search for policy options of high analytical quality. This is also the focus and objective of prescriptive models of "rational' policymaking, which pay little, if any, attention to the trade-off dilemmas identified here. In fact, I know of no theory or model of decisionmaking that tells policymakers how best to manage trade-offs among quality, consensus, and management of time and policymaking resources. What is needed and lacking is what may be called a broader theory of *effective* decisionmaking which would subsume in some way models of analytically rational decisionmaking.

Nonetheless, several ideas can be put forward regarding the relevance of theory and generic knowledge for dealing with some trade-off problems. Knowledge can be developed about strategies such as deterrence, coercive diplomacy, and crisis management; for example, distinctions can be made between strong and weak variants of these strategies and between conditions that favor success and conditions that are likely to hamper success. Generic knowledge of this kind should be helpful in deciding whether the trade-off of policy quality for enhanced support would be acceptable or whether it would jeopardize the success of the weaker variant of the strategy chosen in order to gain additional support. Of course, the need for support may sometimes push the policymaker in the other direction— toward adopting a stronger variant of a strategy when a milder one would be more appropriate.

There is another way theory and generic knowledge can contribute to a better understanding of the costs and risks of trade-offs between quality and consensus. As is well known, bargaining often takes place among advocates of different policy options, and at times the dynamics of bargaining weaken the role of objective analysis during the course of a search for an option that different members of the policymaking group can agree on. However, good analysis of a policy problem can equip policymakers to anticipate what kinds and degrees of effectiveness a high-quality option is likely to lose if trade-offs are made during the bargaining in order to gain broader support. In this view, analysis is not a substitute for bargaining but serves to inform and discipline the bargaining process in a way that helps prevent ending up with a compromised policy that is likely to prove ineffectual.

Perhaps this brief discussion of basic trade-off judgments policymakers often (though not always) must make suffices to provide a richer framework, albeit a more complicated one, for considering the extent to which general knowledge of foreign policy problems and policy analysis within government can contribute to the decisions of policymakers. Quite obviously, scholarly knowledge and policy analysis can contribute more to some of the judgments policymakers make than others. And, certainly, some types of judgments take precedence over—or are relatively insensitive to—the professional knowledge base that is analytically relevant for policymaking. In other words, there can be no assurance that even a well-developed knowledge base and competent policy analysis will have impact when policymakers are impelled to make judgments in reaction to other considerations. Whereas scholars and policy analysts can and should concern themselves with identifying a high-quality policy option, top policymakers have to deal with the difficult trade-off between doing what they can to enhance the quality of a policy and the need for obtaining sufficient consensus and support for the policy option they eventually choose. Also, top policymakers have to decide how much time and how much of the limited pool of resources to allocate to each of these efforts.

In other words, a distinction can be made between *effective* and *rational* decisionmaking. Decisionmaking is effective when the policymaker deals reasonably well with trade-offs between quality, support, and time and other resources. Rational decisionmaking, on the other hand, reflects the scholar's and the policy analyst's effort to come up with a high-quality policy decision without reference to these trade-offs or to various political considerations with which the policymaker must deal. Although scholars have provided a number of models of rational decisionmaking, I know of no theory of "effective" decisionmaking that seeks to improve the ad hoc judgments top policymakers often feel obliged to make.

Kenneth Arrow, one of the editors of this volume, discussed with me some of the implications of this chapter for university education. He posed two questions: "How does one teach the role of judgment in public decision making?" and "How does one convey the feeling of judgment either for general education (undergraduate or graduate) or for future policymaking?" The following thoughts, obviously of a highly provisional character, may provide a starting point for addressing these questions.

It should come as no surprise to the reader if I emphasize that much more research is needed on this difficult, largely neglected aspect of decision making. Cognitive psychologists have produced an impressive body of experimental research on various attribution errors and biases but do not seem to have given much attention to the types of judgment problems discussed here. It surely will not tax their ingenuity and research methods to devise useful studies of this kind. Several suggestions are offered here as possible useful starting points. First, as noted at the outset of the chapter, it will probably be necessary to disaggregate the global concept of "judgment" and develop a typology of different types of judgment that often enter into high-level decision making. (See also footnote 1 for a brief listing of different types of trade-offs encountered in policy making.)

Second, it will be necessary to treat the level of support thought to be necessary or desirable by a policymaker as a variable, one that will be sensitive to the type of policy being addressed. For example, in making decisions in diplomatic crises that carry large risks, policymakers may feel it necessary to give greater weight to choosing a high-quality option rather than one of lower quality that will gain more support. For other types of policy problems, the trade-off may be weighted in favor of gaining more solid support. Moreover, the concept of "support," in a democracy such as ours, itself needs to be disaggregated: Whose support is particularly needed by a president for different types of policies in different situations? Also, the amount of support judged to be necessary or at least desirable can vary for different policies and in different situations. Not to be over- looked is that in some foreign policy situations, presidents can muster more support after they act decisively—that is, the well-known "rally-around-the-flag" phenomenon. Nonetheless, they must also be sensitive to the possibility that initial support may decline over a period of time if the policy chosen runs into difficulties and mounting costs.

A third factor that future research on questions of judgment may want to take into account is personality variables which probably affect how different individuals diagnose and deal with trade-off problems.

Experimental-type research on these questions can probably usefully be supplemented by interviews with executives who have accumulated a great deal of experience in exercising various types of judgment. Do such persons operate with implicit or explicit criteria, rules of thumb, maxims, guidelines in making different types of judgment? Do they believe that they learn better judgment through personal experience or from the experience of others?  Notwithstanding the limitations of self-reports in research of this kind, interviews of executives (and participant-observers of executive decision making) may yield useful hypotheses for additional examination. One possible research design: request executives to identify an instance of what he or she considers to have been an example of his or her exercise of good judgment, and another example of what he or she considers to have been bad judgment.  The interviewer might probe to have the executive describe his or her understanding of the trade-off faced, what it consisted of, how the trade-off was analyzed and evaluated with the benefit of what kind of information and advice, and why he/she dealt with it in the way described.[2]

I will turn now to the question of how one might introduce the judgmental aspect of decision making into educational curricula.  One possibility: public policy schools and business schools might generate case studies that report how experienced executives have tried to deal with different types of judgmental problems by making use of available policy analysis or working in the absence of such analytical studies. (Such case studies might be drawn from research based on interviews with executives to which reference has already been made.)

The objective of having students read and discuss these case studies would be to sensitize them to the complexity and different types of judgment executives are called upon to make and, whenever possible, to call attention to the role that analytical studies of the problem played or might have played. A related question: what kinds of factual information would have been relevant and of some use?

Another pedagogical technique would make use of well-designed simulations. A variety of decisional problems that pose trade-off dilemmas would be developed. Each student would be asked a series of questions about each case designed to bring out their understanding of the nature of the trade-off dilemma, their identification of different ways in which it might be dealt with, their judgment as to how best to deal with it, and why. After each student completed the exercise, classroom discussion would follow, and an effort might be made to reach some consensus as to these questions or at least to identify the major preferred solutions. At the end of a series of such exercises, students would be asked to address the question whether guidelines for assisting judgment can be formulated and how they might be used. As a follow-up, experienced executives might be asked to evaluate the students' guidelines and, perhaps, some of the judgments they had expressed in the simulated cases.

## Acknowledgments

The author expresses appreciation for helpful comments from Kenneth Arrow, Philip Zelikow and Deborah Larson. In a personal communication (August 10, 1994), Herman Leonard, Academic Dean for Teaching Programs at the Kennedy School of Government, Harvard University, provided information on how the relationship between analysis and judgment is conceptualized and taught at the Kennedy School. Paul Brest, Dean of the Law School, provided material from a seminar he teaches which touches upon problems of judgment.

## Notes

[1] The six other types of judgments, discussed briefly in George (1993, pp. 25–28), are: (1) judgment of political side-effects and opportunity costs of choosing a particular policy option; (2) judgment of the utility and costs/risks of different policy options that are acceptable; (3) judgment of possible trade-offs between short-term and long-term payoffs; (4) judgment whether to "satisfice" or "optimize"—that is, whether to settle for a limited payoff in a particular situation or strive for a substantially greater one; (5) judging which of several ways to deal with the "value complexity" of a policy problem—that is, when the problem is laden with competing values and interests that cannot be reduced to a single utility criterion; (6) judging *when* to make a policy decision—whether, how long, and why to delay or not to delay.

[2] A doctoral dissertation at the Stanford Graduate School of Business employing a method similar to that described here was undertaken by Alan Rush (1981) in order to study how executives take advice.

# References

George, A. L. 1980. *Presidential Decisionmaking in Foreign Policy: The Effective Use of Information and Advice.* Boulder: Westview Press.

George, A. L. 1993. *Bridging the Gap: Theory and Practice in Foreign Policy.* Washington, D.C.: United States Institute of Peace.

Rush, A. 1981. "Advice and Counsel in Management: Effective and Ineffective Use by Top Executives." Doctoral dissertation, Stanford University.

# Chapter 24

# The Impact of Operations Research and Decision Theory on Teaching and Research in Microeconomics

Kenneth J. Arrow

## 1. Historical Background to 1940

Operations research, decision theory, and the "marginalist" branch of economic theory have been three intellectual currents that have interacted over the postwar period. They have indeed common roots going back to the eighteenth century, when the rational aspects of behavior were both described and extolled as guides for action and policy.

In the study of games of chance, which initiated probability theory, a kind of rationality assumption was inherent; a game was worth playing if it gave an expected value of at least zero. The famous "St. Petersburg" paradox created doubts about the meaning of rationality in this context. This was a game with a fee, say $F$, for entering. A fair coin was tossed until a head turned up, say, at the $n$th toss, when a payment of $2^n$ was made. The expected payment was therefore infinite, so that, if expected net payoff were the criterion, the player should enter the game no matter how large $F$

is. This is clearly absurd. Daniel Bernoulli (1738) proposed a resolution, which may be thought of as the first paper in decision theory. The value of a payoff is measured, not by money payment, but by its "moral worth" or, in modern terms, its utility. Utility is a function of the payment, but its derivative is decreasing (the utility function is concave). The player chooses among games (including abstention from games) on the basis of the expected value of utility. Not only does this resolve the St. Petersburg paradox (so-called from the place of publication of Bernoulli's paper), but Bernoulli showed that it also explained taking out insurance, even though typically the insured has a negative expected payoff (because of the profits and expenses of the insurer).

Thus, Bernoulli not only resolved a paradox posed by a thought-experiment (of dubious realism but considerable intellectual provocation) but also explained a real-life phenomenon. The first can be thought of as a major step in the creation of decision theory, the second as an example of economic theory. The first clarifies how decisions are or ought to be made; the duality of purpose persists into modern decision theory. The second is the use of the hypothesis that individuals behave rationally (in some sense) to explain the existence and working of a market.

What was not present in Bernoulli was the problem of using rational analysis in a concrete way to improve the performance of some social or economic activity. Condorcet (1785) developed a theory of juries, and Jeremy Bentham and his followers had a powerful influence on English law in seeking to make it more useful. Jules Dupuit (1844) developed rational criteria for deciding on public works, particularly bridges, highways, and railroads, and this work had some influence on practice. It was this strand of activity that might be regarded as the precursor of operations research, the third of our intellectual currents.

In the 1870's, the idea of explaining economic activity as the outcome of rationally maximizing agents was developed independently by W. Stanley Jevons (1871) in Great Britain, Léon Walras (1874, 1877)) in France, and Carl Menger (1871) in Austria, the so-called marginalist economists. Among other developments, this led to an elaboration of the meaning and detailed implications of optimization for firms and for consumers. The rough outlines were developed by the end of the nineteenth century, but fully developed models are the work of Eugen Slutsky (1915), John R.

Hicks and Roy G. D. Allen (1933), and Harold Hotelling (1932, 1935). These models were in principle capable also of providing a basis for operations research, that is, for giving advice to a firm as to how to maximize profits, but no economist took that step, as far as I know.

Choice under uncertainty, the Bernoulli problem, was referred to by economists only distantly and with little analytic development, even though Bernoulli's work was very well known. However, decision theory under uncertainty was stimulated from another direction, that of mathematical statistics. Various elements of statistical theory and practice had been developing over the nineteenth century and were sharply advanced by Karl Pearson, "Student" (the pseudonym of W. C. Gossett), and especially Ronald A. Fisher (1922). But the logic of hypothesis testing, though intuitively understood in many applications, was unclear until the pioneering work of Jerzy Neyman and Egon S. Pearson (1933), which was then given more systematic and general formulation by Abraham Wald (1939, 1950).

Statistical inference can be thought of as a decision problem, in the sense that the statistician has to choose one among a number of hypotheses on the basis of data. The assumption is that the data have a random distribution which, however, depends on the true hypothesis. Neyman, Pearson, and Wald tried to avoid assigning prior probabilities to the hypotheses, but this left either some indeterminacy in the choice of statistical method or an arbitrariness in the choice of a selection principle (minimax in the case of Wald, which certainly appears to yield very unreasonable results in some cases).

Another school of thought held that coherence in decisions under uncertainty demanded that the decisionmaker have some choice of probabilities in mind, though they might be personal to the chooser. This view, sometimes called the Bayesian approach, had been expressed and the theory articulated by Frank P. Ramsey (1931b), but his paper seems to have gone unnoticed. Something similar was developed by Bruno de Finetti (1937).

Finally, in this survey, we must mention the beginning of what has turned out to be one of the most decisive steps in the history of decision theory, the development of the theory of games. In a game, the payoff to any one player depends not merely on his or her actions but on those of all the players. Actually, the concept, though not the name, of games had already appeared in nineteenth-century economics. Auguste-Antoine

Cournot (1838) had analyzed competition among a small number of firms. Clearly, the profit to be made by any one firm depends on the production decisions made by its competitors as well as itself, since the market price depends on the total quantity offered. Cournot took as a solution the outputs, one for each firm, such that each firm was maximizing profits given the outputs of all other firms. Cournot was thoroughly neglected in his day, but the marginalists recognized him. The standard works on microeconomic theory always had a chapter on Cournot's theory of competition by few firms, "oligopoly," as it later became known. But the literature more or less repeated Cournot's original analysis and made little improvement.

Edgeworth (1881) had considered the outcome of unrestricted bargaining, where again the outcome depends on the actions of all parties, in this case, on the terms on which each is willing to conclude a bargain. Here the central idea was that a set of bargains could be upset if any subset of the parties could make a deal using only their own resources which could make all of them better off. What was sought (and found under the typical assumptions of a market) was a set of bargains which could not be so upset. Edgeworth's work, unlike Cournot's, was well reviewed. Yet it had little influence on subsequent work in economics and was hardly mentioned, at least until 1959.

Suitable generalizations of the concepts of Cournot and Edgeworth have turned out to be the most influential in modern game theory; they are now called the "equilibrium point" of a noncooperative game and the "core" of a game, respectively. But when game theory was first given recognition, in the magisterial work of von Neumann and Morgenstern (1944), neither concept played a significant role. The educational part of the book was, in many ways, the sheer concept of the game, the formalization of interactive decisionmaking, and the reduction of multistage games of varying complexity to a simple "normal form." But all this would not have made much impression without an array of interesting theorems. A great deal of attention was paid to the special class of zero-sum, two-person games. Here, there was shown to be a natural solution concept, the maximin strategies of the two players, and the universal existence of this solution (by use of mixed strategies) was striking and powerful. This was what later came to be known as the equilibrium point applied to this special class of games, but von Neumann and Morgenstern did not have the general concept.

The rest of von Neumann and Morgenstern's analysis was devoted to cooperative games, a generalization of the unrestricted bargaining of Edgeworth. But they did not use Edgeworth's definition of a solution. However, that did occur in a number of the examples they worked in developing their own more complicated notion. Their work made no reference to either Cournot or Edgeworth.

# 2.  The Teaching of Microeconomics About 1940

Specifically, I will here be discussing microeconomics (the economic theory of the firm, the household, and the formation of prices in the market) as taught at the graduate level. In about 1940, the course was usually referred to as "price theory"; the term "macroeconomics" was just coming into use for the study of unemployment and inflation, and "microeconomics" was coined as a contrast.

A course in price theory had been a staple of the American graduate curriculum for a long time (just how long I have not tried to trace). It was not entirely universal. There was a good deal of reaction, especially in the United States, against what was considered the excessive abstraction and unreality of the assumptions of rational behavior. There were those who emphasized the importance of economic institutions in the study of economics, and there were others who emphasized the collection of data. These groups occasionally overlapped. At Columbia University, when I was a graduate student there in 1940–42, there was literally no basic course in microeconomics (or price theory). But this was unusual, even then; the leading centers for economic research and graduate study, Harvard, Chicago, and Yale, all had such courses.

The content was marginal economics, but developed, as had been the norm in the literature, in a literary and graphical form, rather than with much use of mathematics. Although the extensive use of mathematics in marginalist analysis dates from Cournot's work (1838), its use was sporadic, although there were such great names as Walras and Vilfredo Pareto associated with its use. But in the 1930's there was an increasing economic literature using mathematical methods, with scholars both from within eco-

nomics proper and from branches of applied mathematics. Ragnar Frisch
in Norway, Harold Hotelling in the United States, and John R. Hicks in
Great Britain were among the pioneers. They were joined by younger scholars, most especially Paul Samuelson and Tjalling Koopmans, who arrived
in the United States in 1940, with a background of econometric research.
The publication of John R. Hicks's *Value and Capital* (1939) and Samuelson's *Foundations of Economic Analysis* (1947) meant that books were now
available for the student. Personally, I can testify how the reading of Hicks's
book and the papers that later went into Samuelson's book supplied the
education I could get only to a very limited extent from courses.

Institutionally, this area of scholarship was organized in the Econometric Society, an international organization founded in 1932 that combined
the interests of mathematically oriented economists with those of econome-
tricians (those using or developing statistical methods for economic data).
It had and has a journal, *Econometrica*. I do not know how many courses in
mathematical economics there were at this time, probably very few; Harold
Hotelling gave one at Columbia.

As a result of these developments, there was a growing number of
economists with mathematical training who were capable of understanding the coming developments in operations research and in decision theory.
In particular, since maximization of utility or profit was a key concept,
the mathematics of unconstrained and constrained optimization, including
second-order conditions, became a staple of knowledge. Dynamic systems
also became a tool of analysis, under the influence of Frisch, Hicks, and
Samuelson, so that stability theory became known. In particular, matrix
theory was needed for studying the local stability conditions. The level
of mathematics used in advanced work in price theory in the late 1930's
is well expressed in Roy G. D. Allen's much-used and still useful volume
(1938).

# 3. Operations Research and Its Influence on Economic Research

Operations research developed during World War II to serve the needs
of the British and United States armed services. The idea of improving per-

formance by modelling a situation (military, especially logistic) and then optimizing or at least improving it according to some criterion proved remarkably useful. Analytically, much of the most useful work was very simple. But gradually, more sophisticated problems began to be attacked. Queuing theory became a major tool, and the need for it became a great stimulus to research. But it never had much influence on economic theory.

What did excite economists was the development of linear programming. Here was an optimization problem of exactly the sort that micro-economists had talked of for a long while but stated in a form sufficiently concrete to raise the possibility that actual numerical solutions to particular problems could be envisaged. The first work was indeed taken in a specific industrial context. The brilliant, then young, Soviet mathematician, Leonid Vital'evich Kantorovich, was approached by a plywood plant for advice on scheduling operations. He promptly formulated the problem as maximization of a linear function subject to linear equalities and inequalities and made a number of observations that characterized the solution. His methods were first published in a short monograph (1937). His methods did not constitute a true algorithm and would not help in solving large problems, but his introduction of what we now call dual variables permitted at least some problems to be solved by trial and error. He saw quickly enough that the planning of a whole economy could be formulated the same way. But now it became clear that his formulation had much in common with bourgeois marginalist economics, and subsequent publication was held up for a long while (1959), by which time it had become irrelevant.

Kantorovich's work was unknown outside of the Soviet Union. Meanwhile, Marshall K. Wood and George B. Dantzig formulated some of the Air Force's war and postwar needs as a series of interdependent activities (1949a, b). Under the assumption of linearity, this gave rise, as in Kantorovich, to the problem of maximizing a linear function subject to linear inequalities.

What was still needed was an effective way of solving linear programming problems. Here, the great breakthrough was Dantzig's development of the simplex method. Koopmans, in particular, was quick to recognize the importance of both linear programming in general and the simplex method in particular. He organized a conference of economists and operations researchers on what the economists called activity analysis; the proceedings were published under his editorship (1951a). The volume contained a number of very influential papers. One was Dantzig's presentation of the simplex method (1951). Another was Koopmans' own development of the theory of production (1951b), which showed how optimization by the firm in an activity analysis model led to something like the usual marginalist assumptions. In fact, the results gave a good deal more insight and deeper results.

The creation of linear programming as a tool coincided with a great interest in economic planning. Postwar Europe was interested for the most part in guided economies. The Marshall Plan created additional incentives, for the United States government, acting much like a bank, demanded some evidence about how the borrowing countries were going to use the loans and grants to improve their economies. At the same time, there was a growing interest in improving the lot of the less-developed countries, many of which were newly created in the postwar decolonization that ended most of the old empires. Again, among other currents, the idea that central planning could speed the process of development led to the employment of linear programming as a tool in diagnosis and policy formation. Hollis Chenery at Stanford and then at Harvard and as Chief Economist of the World Bank was central in urging these methods and in getting young scholars to apply them. An early and influential exposition of this work is to be found in Chenery and Paul Clark's book (1959).

Research to improve the policies of firms in the holding of inventories exemplifies a different history; in this case, the direction of influence was from engineers and economists to operations researchers. Although there has been some mathematical modelling of inventory holdings since the 1920's (and, in some special cases, even earlier), the first large-scale study seems to have been that of the French engineer-economist, Pierre Massé, who studied the optimal holding of water reserves for hydroelectricity (1946). This work was not known in the United States, and a somewhat different dynamic model of inventory holding was developed independently by Kenneth J. Arrow, Theodore E. Harris, and Jacob Marschak (1951). A thorough review and development of the more static models was also developed independently by Thomson Whitin (1953). Although Arrow, Marschak, and Whitin were all economists, the subsequent research on the theory of optimal inventory holdings was largely conducted by operations researchers.

The principle behind the study of inventories was generalized by Richard Bellman (1957) into the general method of dynamic programming for solving problems of optimization over time where there is a recursive structure. Because problems of economic planning are intrinsically dynamic, dynamic programming methods also came to be used in applied work, more particularly for policies relating to individual projects or sectors rather than for the economy as a whole. An alternative approach to the same range of problems was developed by the Soviet mathematician, L. S. Pontryagin, and his associates (1962). It is called "optimal control theory," and it was more stimulating in theoretical work, whereas dynamic programming was more useful in numerical work. Control theory in particular turned out to be a much used tool, not merely in economic planning, but in the theory of intertemporal optimization by firms and households and in fact became the basis of much empirical work in understanding such topics as economic fluctuations, savings, and variations in labor supply over a lifetime.

# 4. Decision Theory and Its Impact on Economic Research

The developments in decision theory were of the utmost importance in themselves and also had a very considerable influence in refining the theory of the market. There were two parallel movements. One was a wide acceptance of the Bayesian approach after its rediscovery and amplification by Leonard J. Savage (1954). One fairly straightforward consequence was the revival of Bernoulli's expected-utility theory. For the first time, it was seriously used for the analysis of economic behavior under uncertainty in several areas: the development of general equilibrium theory with uncertainty (for general equilibrium theory, see the discussion later), the choice of securities portfolios (which has become a very large area of research, no doubt stimulated by its practical value), and the study of real investments. This work dominates much of current research.

Game theory and, more generally, what has come to be known as interactive decisionmaking, the recognition that actual outcomes depend on

the choices made by several individuals, has become a large area of study
in itself and has also found many applications in microeconomics. As indicated earlier, the actual results in von Neumann and Morgenstern's great
work were not very useful in economic analysis. The book received major
reviews in the leading economic journals but not much followed in the way
of economic research. Later developments had more applications, though
in fact it took twenty years or more for them to appear in large numbers.

The first of these developments was John Nash's (1950) introduction of
the equilibrium of a game, a choice of strategies by all players such that
each one is maximizing his or her payoff, given the strategies of the other
players. As can be seen from the discussion in section 1, this is simply
the same as the concept Cournot expressed in 1838. Nash stated the definition for all games, not merely the specific oligopoly games discussed by
Cournot. What is more, he proved the existence of equilibrium under certain conditions, generalizing the results of von Neumann and Morgenstern
for the zero-sum, two-person case. The immediate direct impact of his paper on economic theory was moderate. Since the obvious application was
to oligopoly, where economists already knew about it, the chief novelty was
the ability to restate more complicated kinds of interactions among firms
with the use of the notions of game theory. Valuable results of this type
appeared in the works of Martin Shubik (1959b) and James W. Friedman
(1977); the latter in particular began to appear on the reading lists of
microeconomics courses.

Nash's work had one indirect effect. In the proof of existence of equilibrium, he used a generalized fixed-point theorem, referred to as Kakutani's
theorem but essentially the same as one proved by von Neumann in proving the existence of economic equilibrium in a rather strange model. This
theorem turned out to be the key tool in proving the existence of general
equilibrium in a competitive economic system (see McKenzie 1954; Arrow
and Debreu 1954).

To return to the applications of Nash equilibrium, it took two more
important developments before game theory became a central tool of microeconomics. The more important was the development of the theory
of games under conditions of incomplete information, that is, where some
players do not completely know the payoffs or strategy domains of others.
The basic theory was first presented by John Harsanyi (1967–68). This

has given rise to an enormous literature in application as well as to further basic research.

The second development in fundamentals is the idea of refinement of equilibrium. Consider, for example, a multistage game in which at each stage all the relevant information in the past play is known to both parties. Then it is reasonable to demand that the original equilibrium strategies still be equilibrium strategies in a game starting at any stage. This requirement, called subgame perfection of equilibrium, does not follow from the general definition but is an additional requirement. It reduces the possible set of equilibria. Subgame perfection was introduced by Selten (1965), in the context of a dynamic oligopoly model. Subsequently, there has been an explosion of additional refinements of Nash equilibrium appropriate to different contexts, and these have been used to reduce the set of possible equilibria in multistage games.

As noted earlier, cooperative game theory, which goes back to Edgeworth, had been discussed at great length by von Neumann and Morgenstern. The Edgeworth solution concept, which had been developed for marketlike situations, was generalized to games in general by D. B. Gillies (1959) and given the name of the core. The original Edgeworth program had included the attempt to show that in a marketlike economy, the core approximated the competitive equilibria as the number of participants became indefinitely large. This was indeed demonstrated in models of increasing generality by Shubik (1959a) and Debreu and Scarf (1963).

# 5. The Evolution of the Microeconomics Curriculum

I will sketch the changes in the basic graduate course in microeconomics over the period from 1945 induced by the developments in operations research and in game theory. My sketch is based largely on my recollections, together with some examination of the course outlines and readings for Economics 202–204, the basic microeconomics courses at Stanford for the academic years 1985–6, 1990–1, and 1991–2.

Not surprisingly, the courses in 1945 were much the same in general style as they had been before the war. The detailed content changed over

time in reflection both of the leading economic issues of the day and of
new developments in the literature, but it remained largely literary and
graphic in exposition, with some admixture of elementary calculus. Linear
programming was deemed too difficult and anyway was not understood
by most of those teaching the course. However, the new developments
did begin to appear gradually in the form of more advanced courses, on
subjects such as welfare economics, the economics of uncertainty (which
reflected the theory of decisions under uncertainty), and, after a while,
general equilibrium theory. I can personally remember asking to teach
the basic course in 1957, when one of the senior professors left, and being
refused on the grounds that my teaching would be too difficult for the
average student.

By the middle 1960's there had been considerable change. The mathematical preparation of both students and faculty had considerably improved, and it was now standard to require calculus, sometimes even advanced calculus, for the Ph.D. in Economics. The parts of the course dealing with imperfect competition were frequently introduced with a statement of the concept of Nash equilibrium, which at least supplied a uniform
framework with which to discuss oligopoly. The theory of production now
included a section on activity analysis in which the linear programming
theory and at least the principles of the simplex method were presented.
In some places, even simple expositions of the existence theorem for competitive equilibrium appeared. Dynamic programming was referred to only
occasionally.

Useful textbooks and expositions began to appear. Especially used
were those of Robert Dorfman, Paul Samuelson, and Robert Solow (1958),
Michael Intriligator (1971), and William Baumol (1972). Linear programming and its implications for economic theory, including the interpretation
of the dual variables as prices, became available, at least to a wide spectrum of students. Nonlinear programming, which included elements of
the calculus, was strongly emphasized. Koopmans's (1957) Essay 1 was a
very important exposition of competitive economic theory based on activity
analysis and eventually made its way onto the reading lists of the basic microeconomics courses. Along with the use of activity analysis in economic
planning for developed and developing countries, it appeared that there

would be a greater tendency for the role of operations research in the economics curriculum to grow.

Not all textbooks are equally open to operations research elements. Two of the best graduate textbooks in microeconomics in the last quarter-century, Malinvaud 1972 and Kreps 1990, both of which use mathematics freely, are quite innocent of any reference to either linear and nonlinear programming or dynamic optimization.

There have been tendencies that worked against the use of operations research techniques in the teaching of microeconomics. For one thing, operations research began to appear as a separate discipline. Thus a Committee on Operations Research was started at Stanford in 1963 and became a full-fledged department by 1967, with Jerry Lieberman as Chairman. Under his leadership, there was a rich set of courses, which were available to economics students among others and reduced the need for supplying the corresponding course work in the Economics Department. For another, the enthusiasm for planning began to wane and in any case was never consequential in the United States. Developing countries in some cases saw planning as a form of imperialism. In other cases, the emphasis on the market reduced the importance of operations research as an economy-wide tool, though it increased its role in guiding individual firms. Thus, the operations research departments gained a market, whereas the economics departments lost one.

The one area in which operations research elements have increased in the economics curriculum is dynamic optimization. Investment policy for individuals and for the economy as a whole, models of growing economies, and, more recently, the economics of exhaustible resources, have made the previously esoteric tools of dynamic programming and optimal control theory widely dispersed. These are now staple parts of the microeconomics curriculum.

Linear programming is still taught, under some such heading as "activity analysis of production," but it occupies perhaps a week of the course's time. Dynamic optimization takes several weeks; today it includes some simple examples of optimization under uncertainty. A comparison of the courses of 1985–6 with those of the last two years does not reveal any important change.

By contrast, decision theory has had a profound and still increasing effect. In the first place, the economics of uncertainty, firmly based on the expected-utility theory, has become standard and important; by now, critiques of the expected-utility theory, based on the works of psychologists such as Amos Tversky and Daniel Kahneman (1982) have also entered the reading lists.

But the most dramatic change has been in the importance of game theory, especially in the form of games of incomplete information. Since the early 1970's, many applications of this branch of game theory have been found in the literature, and it is necessary to develop the basic theory in the microeconomics course. Kreps 1990 has no reference to linear programming but devotes most of its pages to game theory. By now, game theory occupies nearly a third of the time of the microeconomics course at Stanford and is the one topic to have grown in coverage even in the last seven years.

No doubt there will be further changes. In many ways, though, the implications of this history are that economics as a form of social engineering is not in high repute today and that economics courses are more concerned with understanding the economy than with solving highly specific problems. Only in the environmental field do we find some element of the engineering viewpoint. By and large, the present orientation is closer to the long history of the subject than was the emphasis on directly implementable models. No doubt, we will see further swings and oscillations in the future.

# References

Allen, R. G. D. 1938. *Mathematical Analysis for Economists.* London: Macmillan.

Arrow, K. J., and G. Debreu. 1954. "Existence of an Equilibrium for a Competitive Economy." *Econometrica* 22: 265-90.

Arrow, K. J., T. E. Harris, and J. Marschak. 1951. "Optimal Inventory Policy." *Econometrica* 29: 250-72.

Baumol, W. J. 1972. *Economic Theory and Operations Analysis.* Englewood Cliffs, N.J.: Prentice-Hall.

Bellman, R. 1957. *Dynamic Programming.* Princeton, N.J.: Princeton University Press.

Bernoulli, D. 1738. "Specimen Theoriae Novae de Mensura Sortis." *Commentarii academiae imperiales Petropolitanae* 5: 175-92.

Chenery, H. B., and P. G. Clark. 1959. *Interindustry Economics.* New York: John Wiley & Sons.

Condorcet, M. J. A. N. Caritat, Marquis de. 1785. *Essai sur l'application de l'analyse à la probabilité et décisions rendues à la pluralité des voix.* Paris: Imprimerie Royale.

Cournot, A.-A. 1838. *Recherches sur les principes mathématiques de la théorie des richesses.* Paris: Rivière.

Dantzig, G. B. 1951. "Maximization of a Linear Function of Variables Subject to Linear Inequalities. In Koopmans 1951a, pp. 331-47.

Debreu, G. 1959. *Theory of Values.* New York: John Wiley & Sons.

Debreu, G., and H. Scarf. 1963. "A Limit Theorem on the Core of an Economy." *International Economic Review* 4: 235-46.

De Finetti, B. 1937. "La prévision: Ses lois logiques, ses sources subjectives." *Annales de l'Institut Henri Poincaré* 7: 1-68.

Dorfman, R., P. A. Samuelson, and R. Solow. 1958. *Linear Programming and Economic Analysis.* New York: McGraw-Hill.

Dupuit, J. 1844. "De la Mesure de l'Utilité des Travaux Publics." *Annales des Ponts et Chausées,* 2ᵉ *Série,* Vol. 8. Translated by R. H. Barback as "On the Measurement of the Utility of Public Works." *International Economic Papers,* No. 2 (1952): 83-110.

Edgeworth, F. Y. 1881. *Mathematical Psychics.* London: C. Kegan Paul.

Fisher, R. A. 1922. "On the Mathematical Foundations of Theoretical Statistics." *Philosophical Transactions of the Royal Society of London, Part A* 22: 309-68.

Friedman, J. W. 1977. *Oligopoly and the Theory of Games.* Amsterdam: North-Holland.

Gillies, D. B. 1959. "Solutions to General Non-Zero-Sum Games." In A. W. Tucker and R. D. Luce 1959, pp. 47-85.

Harsanyi, J. C. 1967-8. "Games with Incomplete Information Played by Bayesian Players." *Management Science* 14: 159-82, 320-34, 486-502.

Hicks, J. R. 1939. *Value and Capital.* Oxford: Clarendon Press.

Hicks, J. R., and R. G. D. Allen. 1934. "A Reconsideration of the Theory of Value." *Economica,* 1: 52-76, 196-219.

Hotelling, H. 1932. "Edgeworth's Taxation Paradox and the Nature of Demand and Supply Functions." *Journal of Political Economy* 40: 577–616.

Hotelling, H. 1935. "Demand Functions with Limited Budgets." *Econometrica* 3: 66–75.

Intriligator, M. 1971. *Mathematical Optimization and Economic Theory.* Englewood Cliffs, N.J.: Prentice-Hall.

Jevons, W. S. 1871. *The Theory of Political Economy.* London: Macmillan.

Kantorovich, L. V. 1937. *Matematicheskie metody organizatsii i planirovaniia proizvodstkia.* Leningrad: Leningrad University Press.

Kantorovich, L. V. 1959. Ekonomicheskii raschet nailuchshego izpel'zouzniia resursor. Moscow: AN SSSR. Translated by G. Morton under the title *The Best Use of Resources.* (Cambridge, Mass.: Harvard University Press 1965.)

Koopmans, T. C. 1951a. *Activity Analysis of Production and Allocation.* New York: Wiley.

Koopmans, T. C. 1951b. "Analysis of Production as an Efficient Combination of Activities." In Koopmans 1951a, pp. 33–97.

Koopmans, T. C. 1957. *Three Essays on the State of Economic Science.* New York: McGraw-Hill.

Kreps, D. 1990. *A Course in Microeconomics.* Princeton, N.J.: Princeton University Press.

Malinvaud, E. 1972. *Lectures on Microeconomic Theory.* Amsterdam: North-Holland.

Massé, P. 1946. *Les réserves et la régulation de l'avenir dans la vie économique.* 2 vol. Paris: Hermann.

McKenzie, L. W. 1954. "On Equilibrium in Graham's Model of World Trade and Other Competitive Systems." *Econometrica* 22: 147–61.

Menger, C. 1871. *Grundzüge der Nationalökonomie.* Wien: A. Holder.

Nash, J. F. 1950. "Equilibrium Points in N-person Games." *Proceedings of the National Academy of Sciences* 36: 48–49.

Neumann, J., von, and O. Morgenstern. 1944. *Theory of Games and Economic Behavior.* Princeton, N.J.: Princeton University Press.

Neyman, J. and E. S. Pearson. 1933. "The Testing of Statistical Hypotheses in Relation to Probabilities A Priori." *Proceedings of the Cambridge Philosophical Society* 29: 492–510.

Pontryagin, L. S., V. G. Boltyanskii, R. V. Gamkrelidze, and E. F. Mischenko 1962. *The Mathematical Theory of Optimal Processes.* New York: Interscience.

Ramsey, F. P. 1931a. *The Foundations of Mathematics and Other Logical Essays.* London: K. Paul, Trench, Trubner and Co.

Ramsey, F. P. 1931b. "Truth and Probability." In Ramsey 1931a.

Samuelson, P. A. 1947. *Foundations of Economic Analysis.* Cambridge, Mass.: Harvard University Press.

Savage, L. J. 1954. *The Foundations of Statistics.* New York: John Wiley & Sons.

Selten, R. 1965. "Spieltheoretische Behandlung eines Oliogopolmodells mit Nachfrageträgheit." *Zeitschrift für die Gesamte Staatswissenschaft* 12: 301–24.

Shubik, M. 1959a. "Edgeworth Market Games." In A. W. Tucker and R. D. Luce (1959), pp. 267–78.

Shubik, M. 1959b. *Strategy and Market Structure.* New York: John Wiley & Sons.

Slutsky, E. 1915. "Sul teoria del bilancio della consommatore." *Giornale degli economisti* 51: 1–26.

Tucker, A. W., and R. D. Luce. 1959. *Contributions to the Theory of Games, Vol. 4.* Princeton, N.J.: Princeton University Press.

Tversky, A., and D. Kahneman. 1982. *Judgment Under Uncertainty.* Cambridge, Eng.: Cambridge University Press.

Wald, A. 1939. "Contributions to the Theory of Statistical Estimation and Testing Hypotheses." *Annals of Mathematical Statistics* 10: 299–326.

Wald, A. 1950. *Statistical Decision Functions.* New York: John Wiley & Sons.

Walras, L. 1874, 1877. *Élements d'économie politique pure.* Lausanne: L. Corbaz.

Whitin, T. 1953. *The Theory of Inventory Management.* Princeton, N.J.: Princeton University Press.

Wood, M. K., and G. B. Dantzig. 1949a. "The Programming of Interdependent Activities: General Discussion." *Econometrica* 17: 193–99.

Wood, M. K., and G. B. Dantzig. 1949b. "The Programming of Interdependent Activities: Mathematical Models." *Econometrica* 17: 200–11.

# C.    Research Reaching Society

# Chapter 25

# Linear Programming

*The story about how it began: Some legends, a little about its historical significance, and comments about where its many mathematical programming extensions may be headed*

### George B. Dantzig

Industrial production, the flow of resources in the economy, the exertion of military effort in a war, the management of finances—all require the coordination of interrelated activities. What these complex undertakings share in common is the task of constructing a statement of actions to be performed, their timing and quantity (called a program or schedule), which, if implemented, would move the system from a given initial status as much as possible toward some defined goal.

Although differences may exist in the goals to be achieved, in the particular processes to be used, and in the magnitudes of effort involved, when modeled in mathematical terms these seemingly disparate systems often have a remarkably similar mathematical structure. The computational task is then to devise for these systems an algorithm for choosing the best schedule of actions from among the possible alternatives.

The observation, in particular, that a number of economic, industrial, financial, and military systems can be modeled (or reasonably approximated) by mathematical systems of *linear inequalities and equations* has given rise to the development of the *linear programming* field.

The first and most fruitful industrial applications of linear programming were to the petroleum industry, including oil extraction, refining, blending, and distribution. Perhaps the second most active user of linear programming is the food processing industry where it was first used to determine the best flow of shipping of ketchup from a few plants to many warehouses. Food packers use linear programming to determine the most economical mixture of ingredients for sausages and animal feeds.

In the iron and steel industry, linear programming has been used for evaluating various iron ores, what mix of low-grade ores to pelletize and how much of different ingredients should be added to coke ovens are additional applications. Linear programming is also used to decide what products rolling mills should make in order to maximize profit. Determining the proper blend of iron ore and scrap to produce steel is another area where it has been used. Metalworking industries use linear programming for shop loading and for determining the choice between producing and buying a part.

Other applications of linear programming suggest its utility. Paper mills use it to decrease the amount of trim losses. The optimal design of a communication network and the routing of messages over it, the awarding of contracts, and the routing of aircraft and ships are other examples where linear programming methods are applied. The best program of investment in electric power plants and transmission lines has been developed using linear programming methods.

More recently, linear programming (and its extensions) has found its way into financial management, and Wall Street firms have been hiring mathematical programmers whom they call "rocket scientists," for a variety of applications, especially for lease analysis and portfolio analysis.

Linear programming can be viewed as part of a great revolutionary development that has given mankind the ability to state general goals and to lay out a path of detailed decisions to take in order to "best" achieve its goals when faced with practical situations of great complexity. Our tools for doing this are ways to formulate real-world problems in detailed mathematical terms (models), techniques for solving the models (algorithms), and engines for executing the steps of algorithms (computers and software).

This ability began in 1947, shortly after World War II, and has been keeping pace ever since with the extraordinary growth of computing power.

So rapid have been the advances in decision science that few remember the contributions of the great pioneers that started it all, among them John von Neumann, Leonid V. Kantorovich, Wassily Leontief, and Tjalling C. Koopmans. The first two were famous mathematicians; Kantorovich and Koopmans received the Nobel Prize in economics for their work.

In the years since I first proposed it in 1947 (in connection with the planning activities of the military), linear programming and its many extensions have come into wide use. In academic circles decision scientists (operations researchers and management scientists), as well as numerical analysts, mathematicians, and economists have written hundreds of books and an uncountable number of articles on the subject.

# 1. Developments Prior to 1947

Curiously, in spite of its wide applicability today to everyday problems, linear programming was unknown prior to 1947, with some isolated exceptions: J. B. J. Fourier (of Fourier series fame), in 1823, and the well-known Belgian mathematician Charles de la Vallée Poussin in 1911, each wrote a paper about it, but that was all. Their work had as much influence on post-1947 developments as would the discovery in an Egyptian tomb of an electronic computer built in 3000 B.C. Leonid Kantorovich's remarkable 1939 monograph on the subject was shelved by the communists in the U.S.S.R. for ideological reasons. It was resurrected two decades later after the major developments in linear programming had already taken place in the West. An excellent paper by Frank L. Hitchcock in 1941 on the transportation problem went unnoticed until after others in the late 1940's and early 1950's had independently rediscovered its properties.

What seems to characterize the pre-1947 era was a lack of any interest in trying to optimize. Theodore S. Motzkin, in his scholarly thesis written in 1936, cites only 42 papers on linear inequality systems, none of which mentioned an objective function.

The major influences of the pre-1947 era were Leontief's work on the input-output model of the economy (1933), an important paper by von Neumann on game theory (1928), and another by him on steady economic growth (1937).

My own contributions grew out of my World War II experience in the

Pentagon. During the war period (1941–45) I had become an expert on programs and planning methods using desk calculators. In 1946 I was Mathematical Advisor to the U.S. Air Force Comptroller in the Pentagon. I had just received my Ph.D. (for research I had done mostly before the war) and was looking for an academic position that would pay better than a low offer I had received from Berkeley. In order to induce me not to take another job, my Pentagon colleagues, Dale Hitchcock and Marshall K. Wood, challenged me to see what I could do to mechanize the air force planning process. I was asked to find a way to more rapidly compute a time-staged deployment, training, and logistical supply program. In those days "mechanizing" planning meant using analog devices or punch-card equipment. There were no electronic computers.

Consistent with my training as a mathematician, I set out to formulate a model. I was fascinated by the work of Wassily Leontief, who proposed in 1932 a large but simple matrix structure which he called the "interindustry input-output model of the American economy." It was simple in concept and could be implemented in sufficient detail to be useful for practical planning. I greatly admired Leontief for having taken the three steps necessary to achieve a successful application: (1) formulating the inter-industry model; (2) collecting the input data during the Great Depression; and (3) convincing policy makers to use the output. Leontief received the Nobel Prize in 1976 for developing the input-output model.

For the purpose I had in mind, however, I saw that Leontief's model had to be generalized. His was a steady-state model and what the Air Force wanted was a highly dynamic model, one that could change over time. In Leontief's model there was a one-to-one correspondence between the production processes and the items being produced by these processes. What was needed was a model with many alternative activities. Finally a model had to be computable. Once the model was formulated, there had to be a practical way to compute what quantities of these activities to engage in that were consistent with their respective input-output characteristics and with given resources. This would be no mean task since the military application had to be on a large scale, with hundreds and hundreds of items and activities.

The *activity analysis* model I formulated would be described today as a time-staged, dynamic linear program with a staircase matrix structure.

Initially there was no objective function; broad goals were never stated explicitly in those days because practical planners simply had no way to implement such a concept. Noncomputability was the chief reason, I believe, for the total lack of interest in optimization prior to 1947.

A simple example may serve to illustrate the fundamental difficulty of finding an optimal solution to a planning problem once it is formulated. Consider the problem of assigning 70 men to 70 jobs. Suppose a known value or benefit $v_{ij}$ would result if the $i$th man is assigned to the $j$th job. An *activity* consists in assigning the $i$th man to the $j$th job. The restrictions are: (1) each man must be assigned a job (there are 70 such), and (2) each job must be filled (also 70). The level of an activity is either 1, meaning it will be used, or 0, meaning it will not. Thus, there are $2 \times 70$ or 140 restrictions, and $70 \times 70$, or 4900, activities with 4900 corresponding zero-one decision variables $x_{ij}$. Unfortunately, there are $70! = 70 \times 69 \times 68 \cdots \times 2 \times 1$ different possible solutions or ways to make the assignments $x_{ij}$. The problem is to compare the 70! solutions with one another and to select the one that results in the largest sum of benefits from the assignments.

Now 70! is a big number, greater than $10^{100}$. Suppose we had had available at the time of the big bang 15 billion years ago a computer capable of doing a million calculations per second. Would it have been able to look at all the 70! combinations by now? The answer is no! Suppose instead it could perform at nano-second speed and make one billion complete assignments per second? The answer is still no. Even if the earth were filled solid with such computers all working in parallel, the answer would still be no. If, however, there were $10^{40}$ earths circling the sun, each filled solid with nano-second-speed computers all programmed in parallel from the time of the Big Bang until the sun grows cold, then perhaps there would be enough time to examine all the combinations.

This easy-to-state example illustrates why up to 1947, and for the most part even to this day, a great gulf exists between man's aspirations and his actions. Man may wish to state his wants in complex situations in terms of some general objective to be optimized, but there are so many different ways to go about it, each with its advantages and disadvantages, that it would be impossible to compare all the cases and choose which among them would be the best. Invariably, man in the past has left the decision of which way is best to a leader whose so-called experience and mature judgment would guide the way. Those in charge like to lead by issuing a series of ground rules (edicts) to be executed by those developing the plan.

This was the situation in 1946 before I formulated a model. In place of an explicit goal or objective function, there were a large number of ad hoc ground rules issued by those in authority in the Air Force to guide the selection. Without such rules, there would have been, in most cases, an astronomical number of feasible solutions to choose from. Incidentally, Expert System software, a software tool currently used in artificial intelligence, which is very much in vogue, makes use of this ad hoc ground rule approach.

## 2. Impact of L.P. on Computers

All that I have related up to now about the early development of linear programming (L.P.) took place in late 1946 before the advent of the computer, or more precisely, before we were aware that it was going to exist. But once we were aware, the computer became a vital tool for our mechanization of the planning process. So vital was the computer going to be for our future progress that (in the late 1940's) our group successfully persuaded the Pentagon to fund the development of computers.

To digress for a moment, I would like to say a few words about the electronic computer itself. To me, and I suppose to all of us, one of the most startling developments of all time has been the penetration of the computer into almost every phase of human activity. Before a computer can be intelligently used to solve a problem, a model must be formulated and good algorithms developed. To build a model, however, requires the axiomatization of a field of knowledge. In time this axiomatization gives rise to a whole new mathematical discipline which is then studied for its own sake. Thus, with each new penetration of the computer, a new science is born. Von Neumann noted this tendency to axiomatize in his 1948 talk "The General and Logical Theory of Automata" (see Taub 1963, pp. 228–328). In it he states that automata have been playing a continuously increasing role in science. He goes on to say:

> Automata have begun to invade certain parts of mathematics
> too, particularly but not exclusively mathematical physics or

applied mathematics. The natural systems (e.g., central nervous system) are of enormous complexity and it is clearly necessary first to subdivide what they represent into several parts which to a certain extent are independent, elementary units. The problem then consists of understanding how these elements are organized as a whole. It is the latter problem which is likely to attract those who have the background and tastes of the mathematician or a logician. With this attitude, he will be inclined to forget the origins and then, after the process of axiomatization is complete, concentrate on the mathematical aspects.

By mid-1947, I had formulated a model that satisfactorily represented the technological relations usually encountered in practice. I decided that the myriad of ad hoc ground rules had to be discarded and replaced by an explicit objective function. I formulated the planning problem in mathematical terms in the form of axioms which stated that (1) the total amount of each type of item produced or consumed by the system as a whole is the algebraic sum of the amounts inputted or outputted by the individual activities of the system; (2) the amounts of these items consumed or produced by an activity are proportional to the level of an activity; and (3) these levels are nonnegative. The resulting mathematical system to be solved was the minimization of a linear form subject to linear equations and inequalities. The use (at the time it was proposed) of a linear form as the objective function to be maximized was a novel feature of the model.

Now came the nontrivial question: Can one solve such systems? At first I assumed the economists had worked on this problem since it was an important special case of the central problem of economics, namely, the optimal allocation of scarce resources. I visited T. C. Koopmans in June 1947 at the Cowles Foundation (which at that time was at the University of Chicago) to learn what I could from the mathematical economists. Koopmans became quite excited. During World War II he had worked for the Allied Shipping Board on a transportation model and so had the theoretical as well as the practical planning background necessary to appreciate what I was presenting. He saw immediately the implications for general economic planning. From that time on, Koopmans took the lead in bringing the potentialities of linear programming models to the attention of other young economists who were just starting their careers, among them Kenneth Arrow, Paul Samuelson, Herbert Simon, Robert Dorfman, Leonid Hurwicz, and Herbert Scarf, to name but a few. Some 30 to 40 years later, the first three also received the Nobel Prize.

Seeing that economists did not have a method of solution, I next decided to try my own luck at finding an algorithm. I owe a great debt to Jerzy Neyman, the leading mathematical statistician of his day, who guided my graduate work at Berkeley. My thesis was on two famous unsolved problems in mathematical statistics, which I mistakenly thought were a homework assignment and solved. One of the results, published jointly with Abraham Wald, was on the Neyman-Pearson Lemma. In today's terminology, this part of my thesis was on the existence of Lagrange multipliers (or dual variables) for a semi-infinite linear program whose variables were bounded between zero and one and satisfied linear constraints expressed in the form of Lebesgue integrals. There was also a linear objective to be maximized.

Luckily, the particular geometry used in my thesis was the one associated with the columns of the matrix instead of its rows. This column geometry gave me the insight that led me to believe that the *simplex method* would be a very efficient solution technique. I earlier had rejected the method when I viewed it in the row geometry because running around the outside edges seemed so unpromising.

I proposed the simplex method in the summer of 1947. But it took nearly a year of experimentation before my colleagues and I in the Pentagon realized just how powerful the method really was. In the meantime, I decided to consult with the "great" Johnny von Neumann to see what he could suggest in the way of solution techniques. He was considered by many as the leading mathematician in the world. On October 3, 1947, I met him for the first time at the Institute for Advanced Study at Princeton.

John Von Neumann made a strong impression on everyone. People came to him for help with their problems because of his great insight. In the initial stages of the development of a new field like linear programming, atomic physics, computers, or whatever, his advice proved to be invaluable. Later, after these fields were developed in greater depth, however, it became much more difficult for him to make the same spectacular contributions. I guess everyone has a finite capacity, and Johnny was no exception.

I remember trying to describe to von Neumann (as I would to an ordi-

nary mortal) the Air Force problem. I began with the formulation of the
linear programming model in terms of activities and items, and so on. He
did something which I believe was not characteristic of him. "Get to the
point," he snapped at me impatiently. Having at times, a somewhat low
kindling point, I said to myself, "O.K., if he wants a *quickie*, then that's
what he'll get." In under one minute I slapped on the blackboard a geometric and algebraic version of the problem. Von Neumann stood up and
said, "Oh, that!" Then, for the next hour and a half, he proceeded to give
me a lecture on the mathematical theory of linear programs.

At one point, seeing me sitting there with my eyes popping and my
mouth open (after all I had searched the literature and found nothing),
von Neumann said:

> I don't want you to think I am pulling all this out of my sleeve
> on the spur of the moment like a magician. I have recently
> completed a book with Oscar Morgenstern on the theory of
> games. What I am doing is conjecturing that the two problems
> are equivalent. The theory that I am outlining is an analogue
> to the one we have developed for games.

Thus, I learned about the *Farkas Lemma* and about *duality* for the first
time. Von Neumann promised to give my computational problem some
thought and to contact me in a few weeks, which he did. He proposed an
iterative nonlinear interior scheme. Later (around 1952) Alan Hoffman and
his group at the National Bureau of Standards tried it out on a number
of test problems. They also compared it to the simplex method and with
some interior proposals of Motzkin. The simplex method came out a clear
winner.

As a result of another visit in June 1948, I met Albert Tucker, who later
became head of the mathematics department at Princeton. Soon Tucker
and his students Harold Kuhn and David Gale and others, such as Lloyd
Shapley, began their historic work on game theory, nonlinear programming,
and duality theory. The Princeton group became the focal point among
mathematicians doing research in these fields.

The early days were full of intense excitement. Scientists, free at last
from wartime pressures, entered the postwar period hungry for new areas of research. The computer came on the scene at just the right time.

Economists and mathematicians were intrigued with the possibility that the fundamental problem of optimal allocation of scarce resources could be numerically solved. Not too long after my first meeting with Tucker there was a meeting of the Econometric Society in Wisconsin attended by well-known statisticians and mathematicians such as Harold Hotelling and von Neumann, and economists such as Koopmans. I was a young unknown, and I remember how frightened I was with the idea of presenting for the first time the concept of linear programming to such a distinguished audience.

After my talk, the chairman called for discussion. For a moment there was the usual dead silence; then a hand was raised. It was Hotelling's. I must hasten to explain that Hotelling was huge. He loved swimming in the ocean; when he did, it was said that the level of the ocean rose perceptibly. This huge whale of a man stood up in the back of the room; his expressive round face took on one of those all-knowing smiles we all know so well. He said: "But we all know the world is nonlinear." Having uttered this devastating criticism of my model, he majestically sat down. And there I was, a virtual unknown, frantically trying to compose a proper reply.

Suddenly another hand in the audience was raised. It was von Neumann. "Mr. Chairman, Mr. Chairman," he said, "if the speaker doesn't mind, I would like to reply for him." Naturally, I agreed. Von Neumann said: "The speaker titled his talk 'linear programming' and carefully stated his axioms. If you have an application that satisfies the axioms, well, use it. If it does not, then don't," and he sat down. In the final analysis, of course, Hotelling was correct in that the world is highly nonlinear. Fortunately, systems of linear inequalities (as opposed to equalities) permit us to approximate most of the kinds of nonlinear relations encountered in practical planning.

In 1949, exactly two years from the time linear programming was first conceived of, the first conference (sometimes referred to as the Zeroth Symposium) on mathematical programming was held at the University of Chicago. Tjalling Koopmans, the organizer, later titled the proceedings of the conference *Activity Analysis of Production and Allocation*. Economists such as Koopmans, Arrow, Samuelson, Hurwitz, Robert Dorfman, N. Georgescu-Roegen, and Herbert Simon, academic mathematicians such as Albert Tucker, Harold Kuhn, and David Gale, and Air Force types such as Marshall Wood, Murray Geisler, and myself all made contributions.

The advent of the electronic computer (or rather the promise that it would soon exist), the exposure of theoretical mathematicians and economists to real problems during the war, the interest in mechanizing the planning process, and last but not least, the availability of money for such applied research, all converged during the period 1947–49. The time was ripe. The research accomplished in exactly two years is, in my opinion, one of the remarkable events of scientific development. The proceedings of the conference remain to this very day an important basic reference, a classic!

The simplex method turned out to be a powerful theoretical tool for proving theorems as well as a powerful computational tool. To prove theorems it is essential that the algorithm include a way of avoiding degeneracy. Therefore, much of the early research around 1950 by Alex Orden, Philip Wolfe, and myself at the Pentagon, by Jack H. Edmondson as a class exercise in 1951, and by Abraham Charnes in 1952 was concerned with what to do if a degenerate solution is encountered.

# 3. Extensions of Linear Programming

In the early 1950's, many areas that we call collectively "Mathematical Programming" began to emerge. These subfields grew rapidly, with linear programming playing a fundamental role in their development. A few words will now be said about each of these.

*Nonlinear programming* began around 1951 with the famous Karush, Kuhn-Tucker Conditions, which are related to the Fritz John Conditions (1948). In 1954, Ragnar Frisch (who later received the first Nobel prize in economics) proposed a nonlinear interior point method for solving linear programs. Earlier proposals such as those of von Neumann and Theodore Motzkin can also be viewed as interior methods. Later in the 1960's, G. Zoutendijk, R. T. Rockafellar, P. Wolfe, R. W. Cottle, A. V. Fiacco, and G. P. McCormick, and others developed the theory of nonlinear programming and extended the notions of duality.

*Commercial applications* were begun in 1952 by A. Charnes, W. W. Cooper, and B. Mellon with their (now classical) optimal blending of petroleum products to make gasoline. Applications quickly spread to other commercial areas and soon eclipsed the military applications that started the field.

*Software development* started in 1954 when William Orchard-Hays of the RAND Corporation wrote the first commercial-grade software for solving linear programs. Many theoretical ideas, such as ways to compactify the inverse, take advantage of sparsity, and guarantee numerical stability, were first implemented in his codes. As a result his software ideas dominated the field for many decades and made commercial applications possible. The importance of Orchard-Hays's contributions cannot be overstated for they stimulated the entire development of the field and transformed linear programming and its extensions from an interesting mathematical theory into a powerful tool that changed the way practical planning is done.

*Network flow theory* began to evolve in the early 1950's with the work of Merrill Flood and a little later with that of Lester Ford and D. Ray Fulkerson in 1954. Alan Hoffman and Harold Kuhn in 1956 developed its connections to graph theory. Recent research on combinatorial optimization has benefited from this early research.

*Large-scale methods* began in 1955 with my paper "Upper Bounds, Block Triangular Systems, and Secondary Constraints." Later, Wolfe and I (1960-61) published our papers on the *decomposition principle*. Its dual form was discovered by J. F. Benders in 1962 and applied to the solution of mixed integer programs. It is now extensively used to solve optimization problems under uncertainty.

*Stochastic programming* began in 1955 with my paper "Linear Programming under Uncertainty" (an approach which was greatly extended by Roger Wets in the 1960's and by John Birge in the 1980's). Independently, at almost the same time in 1955, E. M. L. Beale proposed ways to solve stochastic programs. Important contributions to this field have been made by Charnes and Cooper in the late 1950's using chance constraints, that is, constraints that hold with a stated probability. Stochastic programming is one of the most promising fields for future research, one closely tied to large-scale methods. One approach that Peter Glynn, Gerd Infanger, and I began in 1989 combines Benders's decomposition principle with ideas based on Monte Carlo techniques such as importance sampling and control variables, and on the use of parallel processors.

*Integer programming* was begun in 1958 by Ralph Gomory. Unlike the earlier work on the traveling salesman problem by D. Ray Fulkerson, Selmer Johnson and Dantzig, Gomory's work showed how to systematically generate the "cutting" planes. Cuts are extra necessary conditions which, when added to an existing system of inequalities, guarantee that the optimization solution will solve in integers. Ellis Johnson of I.B.M. and the Georgia Institute of Technology extended the ideas of Gomory. Egon Balas and many others have developed clever elimination schemes for solving 0–1 covering problems. Branch-and-bound has turned out to be one of the most successful ways to solve practical integer programs. The most efficient techniques appear to be those that combine cutting planes with branch-and-bound.

*Complementary pivot theory* was started around 1962–63 by Cottle and Dantzig and greatly extended by Cottle. The pivot-type algorithm was an outgrowth of Wolfe's method for solving quadratic programs. In 1964 Carleton Lemke and Joseph T. Howson, Jr., applied the approach to bimatrix games. In 1965 Lemke extended it to other nonconvex programs. Lemke's results represent a historic breakthrough into the nonconvex domain. In the 1970's, Herbert Scarf, Harold Kuhn, and Curtis Eaves extended this approach once again to the solving of fixed-point problems.

*Computational complexity.* Many classes of computational problems, although they arise from different sources and appear to have quite different mathematical statements can be "reduced" to one another by a sequence of not-too-costly computational steps. Those that can be so reduced are said to belong to the same *equivalence class*. This means that an algorithm that can solve one member of a class can be modified to solve any other in the same equivalence class. The *computational complexity* of an equivalence class is a quantity that measures the amount of computational effort required to solve the most difficult problem belonging to the class, that is, its worst case. A non-polynomial algorithm would be one that requires in the worst case a number of steps not less than some exponential expression like $Ln^m$, $n!$, or $100^n$, where $n$ and $m$ refer to the row and column dimensions of the problem and $L$ to the number of bits needed to store the input data.

*Polynomial time algorithms.* For a long time it was not known whether or not linear programs belonged to a non-polynomial class called "hard" (such as the one the traveling salesman problem belongs to) or to an "easy" polynomial class (like the one that the shortest path problem belongs to). In 1970, Victor Klee and George Minty created a worst-case example that showed that the classical simplex algorithm would require an "exponential" number of steps to solve a worst-case linear program. In 1978, the Russian mathematician, L. G. Khachian developed a polynomial time algorithm for solving linear programs. It is an interior method using ellipsoids inscribed in the feasible region. He proved that the computational time is guaranteed to be less than a polynomial expression in the dimensions of the problem and the number of digits of input data. Although polynomial, the bound he established turned out to be too high for his algorithm to be used to solve practical problems. N. Karmarkar in 1984 made an important improvement on the theoretical result of Khachian. Moreover his algorithm turned out to be one that could be used to solve practical linear programs. As of this writing, interior algorithms are in open competition with variants of the simplex method. It appears likely that commercial software for solving linear programs will eventually combine pivot type moves used in the simplex methods with interior moves, especially for those problems having very few polyhedral facets in the neighborhood of the optimum.

## 4. Origins of Certain Terms

Here are some stories about how various linear-programming terms arose. The military refer to their various plans or proposed schedules of training, logistical supply, and deployment of combat units as a *program*. When I had first analyzed the Air Force planning problem and saw that it could be formulated as a system of linear inequalities, I called my first paper "Programming in a Linear Structure." Note that the term "program" was used for linear programs long before it was used for the set of instructions used by a computer to solve problems. In the early days, computer instructions were called *codes*. In the summer of 1948, Koopmans and I visited the RAND Corporation. One day we took a stroll along the Santa Monica beach. Koopmans said: "Why not shorten 'Programming in a Linear Structure' to 'Linear Programming'" I agreed: "That's it! From now on that will be its name." That same day I gave a talk at RAND, entitled "Linear Programming". Years later, Tucker shortened the expression "Linear Programming Problem" to "Linear Program." The term *mathematical programming* is due to Robert Dorfman, of Harvard, who felt as early as 1949 that the term *linear programming* was too restrictive. The term *simplex method* arose out of a discussion with T. Motzkin, who felt that the approach I was using, when viewed in the geometry of the columns, was best described as a movement from one simplex to a neighboring one. A simplex is the generalization of a pyramidlike geometric figure to a higher dimension. Mathematical programming is also responsible for many terms that are now standard in mathematical literature—like *Arg-Min, Arg-Max, Lexico-Max, Lexico-Min.* The term *dual* is an old mathematical term. But surprisingly, the term *primal* is new and was first proposed by my father Tobias Dantzig around 1954, after William Orchard-Hays stated the need for a shorter phrase to call the "original problem whose dual is ... "

# 5. Summary of My Own Early Contributions

If I were asked to summarize my early and perhaps my most important contributions to linear programming, I would say they are three:

1. Recognizing (as a result of my wartime years as a practical program planner) that most practical planning relations could be reformulated as a system of linear inequalities.

2. Replacing ground rules for selecting good plans by general objective functions. (Ground rules typically are statements by those in authority of the means for carrying out the objective, not the objective itself.)

3. Inventing the simplex method, which transformed the rather unsophisticated linear-programming model for expressing economic theory into a powerful basis for practical planning of large complex systems.

The tremendous power of the simplex method is a constant surprise to me. To solve by brute force the assignment problem that I mentioned earlier would require a solar system full of nano-second electronic computers running from the time of the Big Bang until the time the universe grows cold to scan all the permutations in order to select the one which is best. Yet it takes only a moment to find the optimum solution using a personal computer and standard simplex-method software.

In retrospect it is interesting to note that the original class of problems that started my research—namely the problem of planning or scheduling dynamically over time, particularly when there is uncertainty about the values of coefficients in the equations—are just now in 1995 beginning to be solved. If such problems could be successfully solved, their resolution could eventually produce better and better plans and thereby contribute to the well-being and stability of the world.

The area of planning under uncertainty or stochastic programming has become a very exciting field of research and application, with research taking place in many countries. Some important long-term planning problems have already been solved. Progress in this field depends on ideas drawn from many fields. For example, our group at Stanford is working on a solution method that combines the nested decomposition principle, importance sampling, and the use of parallel processors.

## 6. Conclusion

Prior to linear programming, it was not of any use to explicitly state general goals for planning systems (since such systems could not be solved), and so objectives were often confused with the ground rules in order to have a way of solving such systems. Ask a military commander what the goal is and he probably will say, "The goal is to win the war." Upon being pressed to be more explicit, a Navy man might say, "The way to win the war is to build battleships," or, if he is an Air Force general, he might say, "The way to win is to build a great fleet of bombers." Thus, the means to attain the objective becomes an objective in itself, which in turn spawns new ground rules for how to go about attaining the means, such as how best to go about building bombers or space shuttles. These means in turn become confused with goals, and so on, down the line.

Since 1947 the notion of what is meant by a goal has been adjusting to our increasing ability to solve complex problems. As we near the end of the twentieth century, planners are becoming more and more aware that it is possible to optimize a specific objective while at the same time hedging against a great variety of unfavorable contingencies that might occur and taking advantage of any favorable opportunity that might arise.

The ability to state general objectives and then be able to find optimal policy solutions to practical decision problems of great complexity is the revolutionary development I spoke of earlier. We have come a long way down the road to achieving this goal, but much work remains to be done, particularly in the area of uncertainty. The final test will come when we can solve the practical problems under uncertainty that led to the origins of the field back in 1947.

# Acknowledgment

The material for this article has been adapted with permission from the forthcoming book "Linear Programming, Extensions and Software"— authored by George B. Dantzig and Mukund N. Thapa, Copyright © GBD/MNT, 1987–1994.

# References

Dantzig, George B. 1955a. "Upper Bounds, Secondary Constraints, and Block Triangularity in Linear Programming." *Econometrica* 23: 174–83.

Dantzig, George B. 1955b. "Linear Programming Under Uncertainty." *Management Science* 1: 197–206.

Dantzig, George B. and Philip Wolfe. 1960. "The Decomposition Principle for Linear Programming." *Operations Research* 8: 101–11.

Dantzig, George B. and Philip Wolfe. 1961. "The Decomposition Algorithm for Linear Programming." *Econometrica* 29: 767–78.

Fourier, Jean Baptiste Joseph. 1826. "Solution d'une question particulière du calcul des inegailtés." Extracts from "Histoire de l'Acaémie" 1823, 1824. *Oeuvres* II, pp. 317–28.

Hitchcock, Frank L. 1941. "The Distribution of a Product from Several Sources to Numerous Localities." *Journal of Mathematics and Physics* 20: 224–30.

John, F. 1948. "Extremum Problems with Inequalities as Side Conditions." In K. O. Friedrichs, O. E. Neugebauer, and J. J. Stoker, eds., *Studies and Essays, Courant Anniversary Volume*, pp. 187–204. New York: Interscience.

Kantorovich, L.V. 1939. "Mathematical Methods in the Organization and Planning of Production." Publication House of the Leningrad State University. 68 pp. English translation in *Management Science* 6: 366–422.

Kantorovich, L.V. 1942. "On the Translocation of Masses." *Comptes Rendus de l'Académie des Sciences de l'U.R.S.S.* 37 199–201.

Koopmans, T. C. 1947. "Optimum Utilization of the Transportation System." In D. H. Leavens, ed., *Proceedings of the International Statistical Conferences* Volume V.

Koopmans, T. C., ed. 1951. *Activity Analysis of Production and Allocation.* New York: John Wiley & Sons.

Leontief, W. 1951. *The Structure of the American Economy, 1919–1939.* New York: Oxford University Press.

Leontief, W., H. B. Chenery, P. C. Clark, J. S. Duesenberry, A. R. Ferguson, A. P. Grosse, R. N. Grosse, M. Holzman, W. Isard, and H. Kistin 1953. *Studies in the Structure of the American Economy.* New York: Oxford University Press.

Motzkin, T. S. 1936. *Beiträge zur Theorie der Linearen Ungleichungen.* (Inaugural Dissertation, Basel, 1933.) Jerusalem: Azriel.

von Neumann, J. 1928. "Zur Theorie der Gesellschaftsspiele." *Mathematische Annalen* 100: 295–320.

von Neumann, J. 1937. "Über ein ökonomisches Gleichungssystem und ein Verallgemeinerung des Brouwerschen Fixpunktsatzes." *Ergebnisse eines mathematischen Kolloquiums* (Vienna) 8: 73–83. An English translation by G. Morgenstern appears in *Review of Economic Studies* 13: 1–9.

Taub, A. H., ed. 1963. *John von Neumann: Collected Works*, Volume V, pp. 288–328. Oxford: Pergamon Press.

# Chapter 26

# Greenhouse Gas Abatement: Toward Pareto-Optimality in Integrated Assessments

Alan S. Manne

## 1. Introduction

Ten years ago, the prospect of global warming was considered a remote scientific hypothesis. Today it is headline news. Numerous proposals have been advanced for international cooperation in reducing greenhouse-gas emissions. This chapter examines the economic logic of integrated assessment balancing the costs against the benefits of greenhouse-gas abatement. Pioneering work in this area has been undertaken by Nordhaus (1991), Peck and Teisberg (1992), and others. In order to identify optimal control policies, these authors have adopted a one-world paradigm as though there were a single decisionmaker for the world as a whole. This assumption provides a useful starting point but does not address the difficult issue of how the abatement costs might be divided up among different regions of the world. It is as though friends were to share a meal in a restaurant, simultaneously deciding what to order and how much each individual is to pay.

A multiregion, computable, general equilibrium model is employed here. The analysis is confined to Pareto-optimal (cooperative) solutions. One region's welfare cannot be improved without a reduction in the welfare of another. Gaming situations and threats are excluded. To obtain analytical results, the model is static rather than intertemporal. There are no technological details on the mix of conservation and supply-side abatement activities. The level of emissions (or abatement) is determined endogenously, but the cost-sharing rule is specified exogenously.

Two simple cases are contrasted. In one, the benefits of abatement enter directly into the utility functions of the individual regions. In the other, the benefits enter into their production functions. In the second case (but not the first), it is possible to separate the issues of equity from those of economic efficiency. One may then speak of an optimal level of global abatement. This type of analysis is essential if we are to clarify what is meant by hedging strategies and the sequential resolution of uncertainties.

Greenhouse-gas abatement represents a prime example of a "public-good" problem. There is no way for a rich nation to buy a level of atmospheric concentrations different from that of a poor one. We all live in the same greenhouse. For public finance issues within individual nations, there is a long tradition of determining economically efficient principles for cost-sharing, taxation, and the level of provision of public goods (see Lindahl 1919; Bowen 1948; Samuelson 1954, 1955; and Musgrave 1959. For an application of these principles to greenhouse issues, see Chichilnisky 1993).

There are public-good aspects in any type of international greenhouse-gas agreement. Typically, one supposes that there is a collective decision on the global level of emissions. One explores alternative cases, for example, business-as-usual, stabilization of emissions, or stabilization of concentrations (For an example of such comparisons, see Manne, Mendelsohn and Richels 1995). By contrast, this chapter attempts to show how one might calculate a Pareto-optimal emissions policy. A sharp distinction is drawn between the global level of abatement (the public good) and the cost-sharing rules. Each region's share of global emissions might be based, for example, on its historical level, on its population, or on the skill of its international negotiators. To ensure economic efficiency, it will be supposed that emission quota rights are tradable on an international market. Other institutions are conceivable but would not necessarily be efficient.

# 2. Abatement Benefits Enter into the Utility Functions

To clarify the basic issues, suppose that there are just two regions: North and South. North has a low population, high per capita incomes, and it owns 60% of the world's wealth as measured conventionally in terms of private goods. The remainder of the world's wealth is owned by the South. Let the regional subscripts $N$ and $S$ refer, respectively, to North and South, and let $w_r$ denote the share of total wealth owned by region $r$. Thus, $w_N = .6$, and $w_S = .4$. The unit cost of abatement is identical in both regions, and so there would be no incentive to trade emission quota rights.

Let the decision variable $x_r$ denote the consumption of the private good in region $r$. Let the decision variable $y$ denote the consumption of the public good (emissions abatement) in each region. This unknown does not have a regional subscript. Assume that both regions' preferences are expressed in terms of Cobb-Douglas utility functions. There is a unitary elasticity of substitution between private and public consumption. For illustrative purposes, the two regions have markedly different preferences with respect to nonmarket (ecological) benefits such as biodiversity. If North were the only region in the world, it would allocate 40% of its wealth to public consumption. If South were the only region, it would allocate just 5%. Alternatively, one may interpret these assumptions as though they were the consequence of a high income elasticity of demand for the public good.

Rutherford (1992) has shown how general equilibrium problems may be solved numerically by his sequential joint maximization (SJM) algorithm. In order to apply this approach, Negishi weights must be determined for each of the regions. These are chosen so that each region's outlays do not exceed the value of its wealth. In equilibrium, the weights must equal each region's share of the world's wealth.

Denote the Negishi weight for region $r$ by $nw_r$. These weights must be positive and sum to unity. In this first example, they are chosen so that each region's private consumption plus its share of the cost of the public good just add up to the value of its wealth endowment. With the Negishi weights as parameters and taking the logarithm of each region's utility function, the model may be written as the problem of choosing values of

$x_r$ and $y$ so as to maximize the following joint utility function:

$$(2.1) \qquad nw_N[.6\log(x_N) + .4\log(y)] + nw_S[.95\log(x_S) + .05\log(y)]$$

subject to the following constraint governing the allocation of their joint wealth between private consumption and the acquisition of the public good:

$$(2.2) \qquad x_N + x_S + y = w_N + w_S = 1.$$

In (2.2) the costs of abatement have been normalized so that it would take the world's entire wealth to purchase one unit of the public good. Provided that we know the values of the Negishi weights $nw_r$, it is straightforward to maximize (2.1) subject to constraint (2.2). Because of the logarithmic form of (2.1), note that positive values must be assigned to each of the three decision variables. The only remaining difficulty is the determination of the Negishi weights. Recall that these are determined so that each region satisfies its individual budget constraint.

There is only a single price to be determined here, the one associated with equation (2.2). Without loss of generality, the price of this composite consumption good may be taken as the numeraire and arbitrarily set to unity. The Negishi weights may be interpreted as each region's dollar voting rights in the allocation of the world's resources. They are determined so as to be proportional to each region's wealth available for expenditures on private and public goods after making allowances for sharing in the cost of the public good. Let the exogenously determined abatement cost shares be $sh_r$. Then the Negishi weight for region $r$ would be proportional to the following expression:

$$(2.3) \qquad w_r - y(sh_r - w_r).$$

For the special case in which the public good is financed by means of proportional taxation on each region's wealth, $sh_r = w_r$. The solution is immediate. According to (2.3), the Negishi weights would then be identical to the regional wealth shares, $w_r$. Otherwise, we apply Rutherford's SJM algorithm iteratively. An arbitrary initial value is chosen for the Negishi weights. Expression (2.1) is maximized subject to constraint (2.2). The resulting value of $y$ (the quantity of the public good) is inserted into expression (2.3), and this determines a revised value of the Negishi weights, $nw_r$. Typically, this leads to convergence after just a few iterations.

With the public good entering the utility functions, note that the cost-sharing parameters may affect the level of provision of this public good. According to expression (2.1), North is willing to spend 40% of its resources on the public good, but South only 5%. Figure 26.1 shows how the allocation variables $x_N$, $x_S$ and $y$ are then affected by the sharing rule. If North bears a high share of global abatement costs, wealth is reallocated from North to South. South's level of private consumption is raised, and more weight is placed upon South's tastes with respect to the level of provision of the public good. There is a lower allocation of the world's resources to this good than if wealth were transferred in the reverse direction.

There are two special cases in which there is no interaction between the sharing rule and the quantity of the public good. First, this can occur when both regions have identical exponents in their Cobb-Douglas utility functions. Second, it can occur when these exponents differ from one another, but are each quite small. In both cases, it is clear that the value of the collective decision variable $y$ will be independent of the numerical value of the abatement cost shares, $sh_r$. Wealth transfers will then have a negligible effect on the level of the public good.

Let us make one concluding observation. Thomas Rutherford has suggested that it would be more appropriate to determine the Negishi weights by employing a variant of the Lindahl rule in place of expression (2.3). He has proposed that regional "wealth" be defined to equal the value of private endowments less the cost of abatement plus the imputed dollar value of the marginal utility of public goods consumption. In qualitative terms, this leads to results similar to those shown in Figure 26.1. The higher the share of the costs that are assigned to the North, the lower will be the level of provision of the public good.

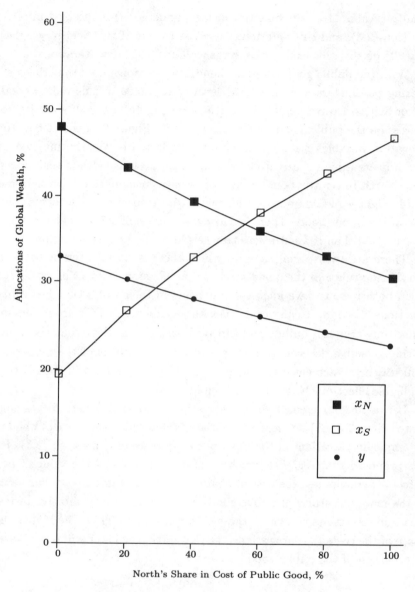

Figure 26.1. Impact of North's cost share on quantities of public goods $y$ and private goods $x_N$ and $x_S$.

# 3. Abatement Benefits Enter into the Production Functions

In the greenhouse model formulations proposed by Nordhaus (1991), Peck and Teisberg (1992), and others, the benefits of abatement enter directly into the economywide production functions. The public good is usually described in terms of its complement: a public "bad" such as cumulative emissions or mean global temperature change. As a simplification, this undesirable quantity will be described hereafter as "cumulative emissions of greenhouse gases."

To remind the reader that this model involves multiple decisionmakers and is intended as an economic equilibrium analysis, it is convenient to refer to it by the name of PARETO. Unlike expression (2.1), the global maximand depends only on the quantities of consumption of the private good. Again let $x_r$ be the quantity of consumption of the private good in region $r$, and let $nw_r$ be the Negishi weight for region. The global maximand is written:

$$(3.1) \qquad\qquad \sum_r nw_r \log(x_r).$$

This is to be maximized subject to the three following constraints. The right-hand side of expression (3.2) describes what may be termed "green" Gross Domestic Product (GDP). For each region, this is the product of $w_r$ and a new type of decision variable, $elf_r$. The parameter $w_r$ indicates the share of the world's conventional wealth that is available to region $r$. The variable $elf_r$ (economic loss factor) measures the fraction of this wealth that is available for disposal as green GDP. In turn, $elf_r$ depends upon the decision variable $z$. This represents the quantity of emissions, the public "bad." The higher the value of $z$, the lower is the value of $elf_r$, and the lower will be the fraction of the region's conventional wealth that is available for consumption and for abatement activities. The left-hand side of expression (3.2) describes the allocation of the world's green GDP between $x_r$ (private consumption) and the costs of abatement.

The decision variables $y_r$ describe the quantity of abatement undertaken in region $r$. In order to illustrate the potential gains from trade in carbon emission rights, it will now be supposed that the abatement activities in each region are characterized by linearly increasing marginal costs, and that the marginal and total costs of zero abatement are zero. Accordingly, the total abatement-cost function is a pure quadratic. It has neither a linear nor a constant term. Assume that if region $r$ were to undertake the abatement of all of the world's emissions, its total cost would be $ac_r$. Without loss of generality, units may be chosen so that if no abatement is undertaken, the global level of emissions is 1. Accordingly, the green GDP global allocation equation is written:

$$(3.2) \qquad \sum_r x_r + \sum_r ac_r y_r^2 = \sum_r w_r(elf_r).$$

The economic loss functions are region-specific. Each region may have a different perception of what would constitute a catastrophic level of global emissions. This is the level at which its entire conventional wealth would be worthless. Denote this level by $ct_r$. To translate from conventional wealth into its "green" equivalent, we assume that the economic loss rate is a quadratic function of $z$ (the global level of emissions) and is inversely proportional to a region-specific catastrophe level, $ct_r$. The economic loss factor, the second constraint, is the complement of the loss rate shown below in square brackets:

$$(3.3) \qquad elf_r = 1 - [z/(ct_r)]^2.$$

Note that the form of expression (3.3) is chosen so that $elf_r$ is unity when $z = 0$, and it drops rapidly to zero as $z$ approaches the catastrophe level $ct_r$. As $elf_r$ approaches zero, equation (3.2) implies that total private consumption must approach zero in region $r$. By expression (3.1), this means that the marginal utility of consumption will increase without limit. According to PARETO, global emissions must therefore remain well below the catastrophic level.

The third constraint describes the interdependence between global emissions and regional abatement activities. By definition, the business-as-usual (BAU) level of emissions equals the sum of emissions plus abatement. We then have:

(3.4) $$1 = z + \sum_r y_r.$$

In each successive iteration, PARETO is solved as a nonlinear optimization in which nonnegative values are to be assigned to $x_r$, $y_r$, $z$, and $elf_r$ so as to maximize (3.1) subject to constraints (3.2)–(3.4). To recapitulate the meaning of these four types of decision variables:

$x_r$ = fraction of the world's conventional wealth used for private consumption, region $r$;

$y_r$ = fraction of the world's BAU emissions level abated in region $r$;

$z$ = fraction of the world's BAU emissions level that is not abated; and

$elf_r$ = fraction of conventional wealth in region $r$ that is not lost as a result of emissions level $z$.

There is an immediate analytical result of this formulation. The optimal values of the production system variables ($y_r$, $z$, and $elf_r$) are independent of the values assigned to the Negishi weights. Because of the logarithmic form of the utility function, the parameters $nw_r$ define the optimal share of $x_r$ (each region's private consumption) in the global total, but they have no other impact on the system. This differs markedly from the structure of the model described by expressions (2.1)–(2.3), and this is why the equity conflict (who gets what) is separable here from the issue of productive efficiency. With tradable emission rights, the equity debate may then be focused over the principles governing the allocation of the global abatement shares. As in expression (2.3), these shares will be denoted by $sh_r$. They play a critical role in the determination of the Negishi weights but not in the choice of global levels of emissions and abatement.

Suppose that PARETO has been solved for an arbitrary set of Negishi weights. The primal and dual solution values may then be applied in an iterative process for the revision of these weights. Each region's private consumption is governed by its conventional wealth and by the economic loss factor determined by the global level of emissions. These two factors are described by the first term in expression (3.5). Private consumption is reduced by the second term (abatement costs). Private consumption is also reduced by the third term, the net value of tradable emission rights that are purchased from other regions.

The symbol $\pi$ denotes the marginal value of each unit traded. It is calculated by taking as the numeraire the dual variable of the green GDP equation, (3.2). When the dual variable of (3.3) is divided by this numeraire, the ratio may be described as $\pi$, the value of emission rights. Each region's net purchases are determined by the expression in square brackets. This quantity may be positive or negative depending upon whether emission rights are bought or sold. It represents the difference between the region's share in global abatement obligations and its actual abatement level. To summarize, the Negishi weights are revised during each iteration so as to be proportional to the following:

$$(3.5) \qquad w_r(elf_r) - ac_r y_r^2 - \pi[(sh_r)(1-z) - y_r].$$

For solving this type of model when there are a large number of goods, regions, and time periods, it is convenient to use GAMS software. (See Brooke, Kendrick, and Meeraus 1988. A GAMS file of PARETO is included in an appendix available upon request to the author.)

# 4. The PARETO Model—Numerical Examples

The following examples are purely illustrative, and are not intended directly for policy purposes. For more realistic cases, it remains to be seen whether the equity and efficiency issues can be separated as clearly as in PARETO. In addition to the abatement shares $sh_r$, the following parameters must be specified for the North and South regions, respectively:

| region $r$ | North | South |
|---|---|---|
| $w_r$, conventional wealth, shares of global endowment | 60% | 40% |
| $ct_r$, catastrophic levels of cumulative global emissions | 2.0 | 1.0 |
| $ac_r$, abatement cost parameters | 1.0 | 1.5 |

The absolute levels of these parameters have been chosen, not for realism, but primarily so that the results can be graphed and compared on the same scale. Their relative levels are designed to reflect several "stylized facts." For example, South is more dependent on agriculture and other climate-sensitive sectors than North. This is why a higher catastrophe parameter is assigned to the North than to the South. The abatement-cost coefficients are chosen so as to be inversely proportional to the levels of conventional wealth. With these numerical values, it is optimal for each region to assign the same ratio of its wealth to abatement.

Figure 26.2 shows which variables are sensitive and which are insensitive to the abatement-share parameters, $sh_r$. The higher is North's share, the greater are its obligations for transfers to South. Accordingly, the lower is its consumption of private goods, $x_N$, the higher is $x_S$. To this extent, PARETO is a constant-sum game. Note that the abatement levels, $y_N$ and $y_S$, are independent of the cost-sharing arrangements. It turns out that the same insensitivity applies to a many-region extension of PARETO.

The model's results are data-driven. Different numerical assumptions will lead to different levels of emissions and abatement. Suppose, for example, that South's catastrophe parameter $ct_S$ is doubled, tripled, or raised even further above its base level of 1.0 (the BAU level of emissions). Further, suppose that North's parameter $ct_N$ is also doubled, tripled, and so on in the same proportion. The higher the values of these parameters, the lower will be the economic losses from emissions. From the definition of $elf_r$ in equation (3.3), recall that damages are inversely proportional to the catastrophe parameter. Accordingly, the higher are the levels of $ct_r$, the higher will be the Pareto-optimal value of global emissions, the decision variable $z$. Figure 26.3 shows how this level is affected by alternative levels of South's catastrophe parameter.

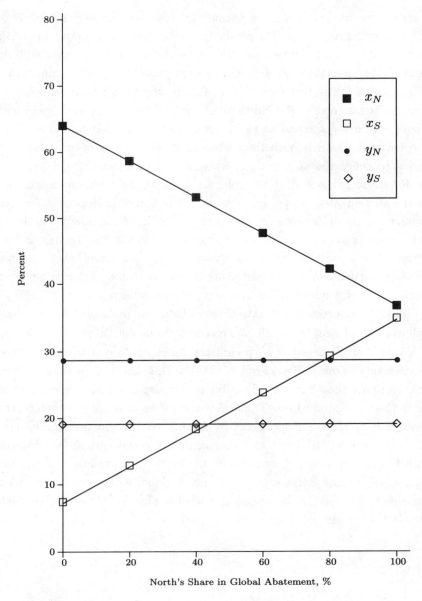

Figure 26.2. Impact of North's abatement share on quantities of private goods; $x_N$ and $x_S$ and abatement levels $y_N$ and $y_S$.

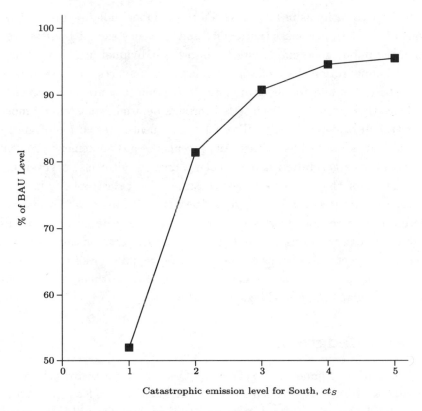

Figure 26.3. Pareto-optimal level of global emissions, $z$.

# 5. Where Do We Go From Here?

What are the next steps after these thought-experiments? First, it is essential to introduce dynamics explicitly. Abatement costs are high in the short run, but the benefits of avoiding climate change will not accrue until the distant future. It will also be important to translate emissions into climate-related variables such as mean global temperature change, and to provide a more realistic technological description of emission-abatement activities. Assuming that the climate variables can be translated through damage models into some such concept as green GDP, we will find it instructive to see whether equity and efficiency issues can be separated from each other as easily as in PARETO. From the model described by expressions (2.1)–(2.3), it is clear that equity and efficiency cannot be separated when the public good enters directly into the individual utility functions, the individual regions have distinctly different preferences, and the costs of both abatement and emissions are large in relation to conventional wealth.

Once these ideas have been tested through deterministic scenario modeling, the next step will be to allow for the sequential resolution of uncertainties. It is misleading to pose the greenhouse-gas-abatement problem as though this generation had to make a once-for-all decision governing emissions over the next one or two centuries. No catastrophe is in sight during the next few decades. There will be time to gather new information. During this period our task is to prepare wisely for whatever transitions may be necessary during the middle or end of the 21st century. For the economic aspects of integrated assessment, we would do well to define alternative scenarios, attach reasonable probabilities to them, and do our best to calculate an optimal hedging strategy.

# Acknowledgments

The author is indebted to Timothy Olsen and Susan Swinehart for research assistance. He has benefited from discussions with Kenneth Arrow, Graciela Chichilnisky, Robert Dorfman, Geoffrey Heal, David Montgomery, Richard Richels, John Rowse, Thomas Rutherford, and David Starrett.

This paper was presented at The Conference on Market Instruments for International Environmental Policy, Stanford University, November 29–December 1, 1993. This research was funded by the Electric Power Research Institute (EPRI). The views presented here are solely those of the individual author, and do not necessarily represent the views of EPRI or its members.

# References

Bowen, H. 1948. *Toward Social Economy*. New York: Rinehart & Company.

Brooke, A., D. Kendrick, and A. Meeraus. 1988. *GAMS: A User's Guide.* Redwood City, Calif.: Scientific Press.

Chichilnisky, G. 1993. "The Abatement of Carbon Emissions in Industrial and Developing Countries." Paper presented at the International Conference on "The Economics of Climate Change," OECD/IEA, Paris, June.

Lindahl, E. 1919. *Die Gerechtigkeit der Besteuerung*, Lund. English excerpts reprinted in R.A. Musgrave and A.T. Peacock, eds. *Classics in the Theory of Public Finance*, pp. 168-176. New York-London: Macmillan. 1958.

Manne, A., R. Mendelson, and R. Richels. 1995. "MERGE—A Model for Evaluating Regional and Global Effects of GHG Reduction Policies." *Energy Policy* 23: 17-34.

Musgrave, R. 1959. *The Theory of Public Finance*. New York: McGraw-Hill.

Nordhaus, W. 1991. "To Slow or Not to Slow: The Economics of the Greenhouse Effect." *Economic Journal* 101: 920-37.

Peck, S., and T. Teisberg. 1992. "CETA: A Model for Carbon Emissions Trajectory Assessment." *Energy Journal* 13: 55-77.

Rutherford, T. 1992. "Sequential Joint Maximization." Working paper, University of Colorado, September.

Samuelson, P. 1954. "The Pure Theory of Public Expenditure." *Review of Economics and Statistics* 36: 387-89.

Samuelson, P. 1955. "Diagrammatic Exposition of a Theory of Public Expenditure." *Review of Economics and Statistics* 37: 350-56.

# Chapter 27

# New Directions in Education: Computational Tools for the Molecular Biologist and Biological Sources for the Mathematician

Samuel Karlin and Volker Brendel

## 1. Introduction

The dramatic advances in biology and medicine in the second half of the twentieth century, in part relying on new mathematical, statistical, and computer science methods, has been the source and stimulation of much of our research endeavors over the past years. We describe in this chapter a number of simple models of mathematical biology revealing this amalgam in a spirit of interdisciplinary research, teaching, and scholarship.

The unprecedented increase in molecular sequence data in the last two decades has fundamentally changed the way biological sciences are viewed and applied. What began with the discovery of the structure of DNA by Watson and Crick in 1953 is leading to the deciphering of the entire human genome as well as the genomes of several other model organisms. The Human Genome Project entails determination of the exact linear array of the DNA sequence in each of the 22 human autosomes and two sex chromosomes, totaling roughly three billion base pairs. The listing of the human genome sequence would take as much printed space as 13 sets of the *Encyclopedia Britannica*, containing within it the coding sequences of some 100,000 proteins and, to a much larger extent (about 95% of the genome), DNA sequences of unknown function. For comparison, the sizes of other model genomes that are being sequenced are about 160 million base pairs in the case of the fruit fly *Drosophila melanogaster*, 100 million base pairs for the nematode *Caenorhabditis elegans*, 14 million base pairs for baker's yeast, and 4.7 million base pairs for the bacterium *Escherichia coli*. DNA is the universal carrier of genetic information, and thus, knowledge of DNA sequences and their gene products underpins all biological research, be it concerned with medical, developmental, ecological, or evolutionary questions. The ability to manipulate DNA has tremendous impact on fields like preventive medicine, drug design, industry, and agriculture.

The necessity to organize and analyze the large amount of sequence data already available has brought about a proportionate development of mathematical, statistical, and computational tools. Both DNA and protein sequences are compiled and annotated in internationally maintained databases, available to researchers around the world on-line via the Internet. Efficient algorithms have been designed to compare newly derived sequences against all entries in the current databases. Other programs attempt to predict the location of genes or the possible structure and function of gene products. Molecular biologists will need to become more at home with the use of these tools. Already an essential part of the evaluation of any study involving sequence determination, use of theoretical tools will also increasingly precede biological investigations as the available sequence information suggests specific testable hypotheses. In the words of Walter Gilbert, one of the pioneers of modern molecular biology, "The new paradigm, now emerging, is that all the 'genes' will be known (in the sense of being resident in databases available electronically), and that the starting point of a biological investigation will be theoretical" (Gilbert 1991).

The implication of these developments for the education of students of (molecular and mathematical) biology is the need for interdisciplinary courses that familiarize the students with the concepts, techniques, and tools of mathematical and computational molecular biology. At Stanford we have offered a pilot course on these topics since 1985, and a seminar series on current research has been held on a consistent basis for the last several years. We hope to see this part of the educational innovations at our university develop into a broad interdisciplinary program, possibly also involving interested faculty in computer science and statistics. We discuss in what follows a few typical, simple examples of how mathematical and statistical methods are being used in the interpretation of sequence data. All the examples can be read independently of one another.

# 2. Background

Deoxyribonucleic acid (DNA), the molecule of heredity, is a thread-like molecule made of "nucleotides" or "bases" strung together like beads on a string. There are four DNA bases: $A$ (adenine), $T$ (thymine), $G$ (guanine), and $C$ (cytosine). Specific pairs are "complementary," forming stable, hydrogen-bonded pairs: $A$ is complementary to $T$, $G$ is complementary to $C$. DNA is most often double-stranded and exists stably in a helical conformation. Strands have directionality. Double-stranded DNA consists of two oppositely directed single strands held together by complementary base pairings.

A structural gene in the DNA is "transcribed" to RNA (ribonucleic acid) as follows: DNA base on template strand: $A, T, G, C$; complementary base on (pre-) "messenger RNA" (mRNA): $U, A, C, G$, respectively. RNA is similar to DNA except for its sugar moiety, is generally single stranded, and uses $U$ (uracil) in the place of $T$. The processed mRNA strand is then "translated" to protein. Each RNA "triplet" or "codon," beginning with a special "start codon" (AUG), codes specifically for one of 20 amino acids. The amino acids are attached consecutively to form a protein until a "stop codon" is reached. In higher eukaryotes (organisms with cells having a separated nucleus) most genes are "split genes": after the DNA has been transcribed into RNA, certain parts of the RNA transcript ("introns") are spliced out such that the resulting mRNA consists only of the remaining "exons." The origins and mechanisms of split genes and splicing are under intense investigation, and the problem of accurately predicting exons and introns in a DNA sequence is largely unresolved. Proteins fold into a

3-D (three-dimensional) structure. How proteins fold is largely unknown (protein-folding problem). More than 35,000 amino acid sequences of proteins from many organisms are known, whereas distinct (nonhomologous) 3-D structures are adequately resolved for only about 400 of them, due to the laborious experimental process of structure determination.

Chromosomes are large segments of DNA that contain many genes. Chromosome size, structure, and number vary among different organisms. For example, the bacterium *E. coli* has one circular chromosome, humans have 23 pairs of linear chromosomes, fruit fly 4, and plants on average 40. Chromosome size varies within genomes. For example, the smallest human chromosome is about 50 Mb ($50 \times 10^6$ base pairs), whereas the largest is about 300 Mb.

Taken together, all of an organism's chromosomes make up the genome. The size of the genome varies widely among organisms. Some genome size data follow: Hepatitis-B virus, 0.003 Mb; Epstein-Barr virus (associated with mononucleosis), 0.172 Mb; *E. coli*, 4.7 Mb; yeast, 14 Mb; *Drosophila* (fruit fly), 150 Mb; human, 3000 Mb; toad, 9000 Mb; newt 30,000 Mb. Intriguingly, the toad's genome size is greater than the human by a factor of three and the newt's (salamander's), by a factor of 10. Newts, however, may not have more genes than humans. In general, amphibians have enormous quantities of satellite DNA (many tandem repeats of simple sequence) and other variegated repeats that do not code for protein.

The fields of molecular genetics and medicine are accumulating DNA and protein sequence data at an accelerating rate. Discovering and interpreting sequence patterns can contribute to understanding molecular mechanisms and evolutionary processes.

# 3. Locating Genes

The human genome initiative is rapidly producing huge volumes of long DNA sequences. A penultimate objective of large scale sequencing is to map all genes of a genome. A gene starts with the start codon ($ATG$) and terminates with a stop codon ($TAA$, $TAG$, or $TGA$). A relevant problem is to find the average and distribution properties of the distance (number of bases) along a sequence until a start codon is first reached. In the simplest model we assume the sequence of bases are generated independently with respective probabilities $p_A, p_C, p_G, p_T$. The first passage time (number of bases) until reaching the start codon can be obtained by calculating the absorption time in the four-state Markov chain with transition matrix

(1)
$$M = \begin{array}{c} \\ A \\ \overline{A} \\ AT \\ ATG \end{array} \begin{array}{cccc} A & \overline{A} & AT & ATG \\ \left[ \begin{array}{cccc} p_A & p_C + p_G & p_T & 0 \\ p_A & 1 - p_A & 0 & 0 \\ p_A & p_C + p_T & 0 & p_G \\ 0 & 0 & 0 & 1 \end{array} \right] \end{array},$$

where $\overline{A}$ refers to any of the states $C$, $G$, or $T$, but $T$ not preceded by $A$. The absorption times (number of bases) starting from $A$, $\overline{A}$, or $AT$, respectively, satisfy the linear equations

(2)
$$\begin{aligned} u_A &= 1 + p_A\, u_A + (p_C + p_G)u_{\overline{A}} - p_T\, u_{AT}, \\ u_{\overline{A}} &= 1 + p_A\, u_A + (1 - p_A)u_{\overline{A}}, \\ u_{AT} &= 1 + p_A\, u_A + (p_C + p_T)u_{\overline{A}}, \end{aligned}$$

which gives

(3)
$$u_A = \frac{1 - p_T\, p_G}{p_A\, p_T\, p_G},$$

$$u_{\overline{A}} = \frac{1}{p_A\, p_T\, p_G},$$

$$u_{AT} = \frac{1 - p_G}{p_A\, p_T\, p_G}.$$

If $L$ is the random variable of the first passage time and $\underline{w}^{(k)}$ is the vector

(4)
$$\begin{aligned} w_A^{(k)} &= \Pr\{L \geq k \mid \text{initial state is } A\}, \\ w_{\overline{A}}^{(k)} &= \Pr\{L \geq k \mid \text{initial state is } \overline{A}\}, \\ w_{AT}^{(k)} &= \Pr\{L \geq k \mid \text{initial state is } AT\}, \end{aligned}$$

then $\underline{w}^{(k)} = \overline{M}\underline{w}^{(k-1)}, k \geq 2$, where $\overline{M}$ is the matrix $M$ restricted to the first three rows and columns. The largest characteristic root $\overline{\lambda}$ of $\overline{M}$ satisfies $\frac{2}{3} < \overline{\lambda} < 1$, so that $\underline{w}^{(k)}$ decreases to zero exponentially fast of the order $\overline{\lambda}^{k}$.

If the sequence is generated as a first-order Markov chain, then the analogous calculations are based on the six-state matrix

$$
(5) \quad
\begin{array}{c}
\\ \\ \\ \\ \\ \\
\end{array}
\begin{array}{c}
A \\ C \\ (\text{not } ATG)\ G \\ (\text{not } AT)\ T \\ AT \\ ATG
\end{array}
\begin{array}{cccccc}
A & C & G & T & AT & ATG \\
\left[\begin{array}{cccccc}
p_{AA} & p_{AC} & p_{AG} & 0 & p_{AT} & 0 \\
p_{CA} & p_{CC} & p_{CG} & p_{CT} & 0 & 0 \\
p_{GA} & p_{GC} & p_{GG} & p_{GT} & 0 & 0 \\
p_{TA} & p_{TC} & p_{TG} & p_{TT} & 0 & 0 \\
p_{TA} & p_{TC} & 0 & p_{TT} & 0 & p_{TG} \\
0 & 0 & 0 & 0 & 0 & 1
\end{array}\right]
\end{array} .
$$

The first passage to a stop codon in any frame can be obtained using the Markov matrix:

$$
(6) \quad
\begin{array}{c}
T \\ \overline{T} \\ TA \\ TG \\ \text{stop}
\end{array}
\begin{array}{ccccc}
T & \overline{T} & TA & TG & \text{stop} \\
\left[\begin{array}{ccccc}
p_T & p_C & p_A & p_G & 0 \\
p_T & 1 - p_T & 0 & 0 & 0 \\
p_T & p_C & 0 & 0 & p_A + p_G \\
p_T & p_C + p_G & 0 & 0 & p_A \\
0 & 0 & 0 & 0 & 1
\end{array}\right]
\end{array} ,
$$

where $\overline{T}$ is the state "$C$, $A$ not preceded by $T$, or $G$ not preceded by $T$." The expected times for reaching a stop codon in any frame starting from the different states are

$$
(7) \quad
\begin{aligned}
u_T &= \frac{1 - p_A^2 - 2p_A p_G}{p^*}, \\
u_{\overline{T}} &= \frac{1}{p^*}, \\
u_{TA} &= \frac{p_C + p_T}{p^*}, \\
u_{TG} &= \frac{1 - p_A}{p^*},
\end{aligned}
$$

where $p^* = p_T p_A^2 + 2p_T p_A p_G$ is the probability of stopping. If $K$ is the random variable of first reaching a stop codon in any frame, then for $k$ large, $\Pr\{K \geq k\} \approx (\lambda^*)^k$, where $\lambda^*$ is the largest positive solution of the equation $\lambda^3 - \lambda^2 + p^* = 0$.

We now investigate the variable of the first time until reaching a stop codon in all three frames. There is a vague speculation that split genes developed in nature in order to circumvent randomly occurring stop codons. This hypothesis is supported by some studies that claim that the size of exons in DNA corresponds quite well to the distance between stop codons that would be observed in randomly generated sequences (assuming that if a sequence gets blocked by a stop codon in one frame it can still continue in the two other frames). It is therefore of some interest to investigate the length of sequence segments that are blocked by stop codons in all three frames.

The calculation includes three steps, $K_1 =$ first time until a stop codon is reached in any frame, $K_2 =$ first time until a stop codon is reached in one of the two remaining frames, and $K_3 =$ first time until a stop codon is reached in a fixed frame. It is easy to see, with $K$ measured in codon units, that $\Pr\{K_3 = k\} = (1 - p^*)^{k-1} p^*$. The analysis of $K_1$ relies on the matrix (6). The analysis of $K_2$ is based on the 10-state matrix (10) displayed overleaf. In this transition matrix, $T^{(2)}$ denotes $T$ appearing in the second frame, $T^{(3)}$ denotes $T$ appearing in the third frame, $X$ signifies any base not part of a stop codon in the first frame, and the other states are designated similarly.

In an independence model, let $L_i$ be the length in frame $i$ ($i = 1, 2, 3$) until reaching a stop codon in the three frames, respectively. Let $L = \max(L_1, L_2, L_3)$. Assuming independence,

$$(8) \qquad \Pr\{L \geq k\} = 1 - (1 - (1 - p^*)^k)^3 \,,$$

where $k$ is measured in units of codons. The expectation for $L$ is

$$(9) \qquad E[L] = \frac{3}{p} - \frac{3}{p(2 - p)} + \frac{1}{p(2 - p + (1 - p)^2)} - 1 \,,$$

which for $p = \frac{3}{64}$ is about 40. Data comparisons show that this is about the average size of an exon.

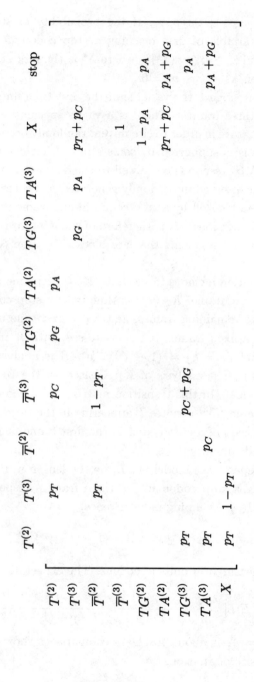

$$
\begin{array}{c|cccccccccc}
 & T^{(2)} & T^{(3)} & \overline{T}^{(2)} & \overline{T}^{(3)} & TG^{(2)} & TA^{(2)} & TG^{(3)} & TA^{(3)} & X & \text{stop} \\
\hline
T^{(2)} & & p_T & & p_C & p_G & p_A & & & & \\
T^{(3)} & & p_T & & p_C & & & p_G & p_A & & \\
\overline{T}^{(2)} & & & p_C & 1-p_T & & & & & & \\
\overline{T}^{(3)} & & & & p_C+p_G & & & & & 1 & \\
TG^{(2)} & & & & & & & & & 1-p_A & p_A \\
TA^{(2)} & & & & & & & & & p_T+p_C & p_A+p_G \\
TG^{(3)} & p_T & & & & & & & & & p_A \\
TA^{(3)} & p_T & & & & & & & p_A & & p_A+p_G \\
X & 1-p_T & & & & & & & & p_T+p_C & \\
\end{array}
\tag{10}
$$

# 4. Evaluation of Pattern Occurrence Counts

Many important signal sites or structural motifs in DNA and protein sequences are described by specific residue preferences in given locations along the primary sequences. For example, most dyad-symmetrical hexamers in DNA are recognized by sequence-specific restriction/methylation enzymes that cut the DNA double-strand or methylate certain bases in the site, respectively; transcription factors bind to sites upstream of genes; DNA-dependent RNA polymerase recognizes promoters and terminators (sites where to start and end the process of transcribing DNA into RNA). Enzymes often display specific residues in fixed positions within their active sites. Particular residue patterns may be associated with certain structures, as for example the periodic repeat $LX_6LX_6LX_6L$ (where $L$ is leucine, and $X$ is any amino acid) that is associated with a particular type of coiled-coil structure termed "leucine zipper" (Landschulz, Johnson, and McKnight 1988; O'Shea, Rutkowski, and Kim 1989).

Given the inherent redundancy in biological systems (with many alternative solutions to selective pressures in the course of evolution), one is often faced with the formidable challenge of having to distinguish chance matches from "true" (biologically meaningful) matches against any particular pattern when searching other sequences for possible occurrences of the corresponding signal or structure. For example, the leucine heptad repeat may occur in leucine zipper structures but also in other contexts. The problem is confounded by the aforementioned redundancy which, for example, may allow a leucine to methionine substitution in a leucine zipper structure while maintaining its functionality. Establishment of such allowed substitutions is, however, a laborious experimental process, and until the experimental evidence is obtained, speculation can be as misleading in some cases as it is helpful in others. The process of speculation is often reminiscent of Abraham's negotiations with the Lord with respect to the destruction of Sodom and Gomorrah (Gen. 18:23–32): "Wilt thou also destroy the righteous with the wicked? Peradventure there be fifty righteous within the city: wilt thou also destroy and not spare the place for the fifty righteous that are therein?" and as the Lord concedes, "Peradventure there shall lack five of the fifty righteous: wilt thou destroy all the city for lack of five?" and on it goes until the Lord agrees "I will not destroy it for ten's sake." In this purview, for some time leucine zippers were proposed abundantly in many a new sequence, some of which were based upon patterns in which only two of the leucines remained, with the two other positions featuring instead serine, an amino acid with biochemical properties quite different from those of leucine.

Mathematical considerations can help by setting benchmarks for speculations in such situations. In the case of the leucine zipper motif one would like to know the probability of occurrence of a leucine heptad repeat in random sequences of similar length and composition as protein sequences. The purpose of such considerations would not be to model natural sequences (which are clearly nonrandom) but rather to set some guidelines for one's intuition. Following the classical theory of recurrent events, the probability of observing a success run of length $r$ in a sequence of length $n$ for a given success probability $f$ is closely approximated by

$$(11) \qquad 1 - \frac{(1 - fx)}{(r + 1 - rx)(1 - f)x^{n+1}},$$

where $x$ solves $(1 - f)x(1 + fx + \cdots + f^{r-1}x^{r-1}) = 1$ (e.g., Feller 1968, p. 325). When $f$ represents the observed frequency of leucine in a protein sequence of length $n$ the following probabilities of repeats of length 4 and 5 are obtained (Table 27.1):

TABLE 27.1

*Probabilities of Repeats of Length 4 and 5*

| $n\backslash f^a$ | $r = 4$ | | | $r = 5$ | | |
|---|---|---|---|---|---|---|
| | 6.5% | 10.0% | 13.5% | 6.5% | 10.0% | 13.5% |
| 200 | 0.003 | 0.020 | 0.060 | 0.001 | 0.002 | 0.008 |
| 300 | 0.005 | 0.030 | 0.080 | 0.001 | 0.003 | 0.010 |
| 500 | 0.008 | 0.040 | 0.130 | 0.001 | 0.004 | 0.020 |
| 1000 | 0.020 | 0.090 | 0.250 | 0.001 | 0.009 | 0.040 |

[a] $f$ represents the frequency of the repeated letter in a sequence of length $n$.

A lower bound for the probability of observing an $r$-repeat of *any* (not predetermined) amino acid is given by the same formula with values $r - 1$ and $f = 5\%$ (0.03–0.06 for $r = 4$ and $n = 300$–500). It is seen, for example, that a repeat of length 4 in a 300–500 residue sequence of average leucine content (10%) occurs with only 3–4% probability, but that this probability is considerably increased for sequences of higher leucine content or greater length.

In a screening of some 450 distinct mammalian proteins of mean length 450 residues and average leucine content 9.7% for occurrences of the motif $LX_6LX_6LX_6L$ it was found in more than 30 (or about 7%) of the sequences, but in only about half of these cases were the intervening residues free of helix-breaking prolines (Brendel and Karlin 1989). Heptad repeats of other amino acids occurred much less than half as frequently as the leucine heptads, in agreement with the fact that leucine is by far the most common amino acid over all the proteins analyzed. For the same set of proteins leucine repeats of length 4 with spacing 5 or 7 (rather than 6) were found in only about 20 proteins each. Also, spacings 3 and 6 were preferred over spacings 4, 5, 7, and 8 between (not necessarily nearest) neighboring leucines. This relative excess of leucine heptad repeats is consistent with the role of leucines in establishing hydrophobic faces of $\alpha$-helices, including those involved in coiled-coil interactions. Interestingly, the same preference for spacing 6 also holds for glutamic acid residues, possibly reflecting their role in establishing hydrophilic faces of $\alpha$-helices.

These considerations showed that the leucine repeat by itself occurs widely on both probabilistic and empirical grounds. Whereas this abundance undoubtedly reflects the particular structural role of this motif, it also warrants a cautioning note with respect to the prolific citation of leucine zippers. Such caution particularly applies in view of the aforementioned tendency in pattern search applications to relax the matching conditions (e.g., allow for substitutions in the leucine positions). Although one might rightly want to accommodate true variations in primary sequence yielding equivalent three-dimensional structures, attention ought to be given to the concomitant increase in the level of false positive occurrences for which the observed sequence motif will likely serve other purposes unrelated to those hypothesized.

# 5. Rare and Frequent Words

Consider a long, random letter sequence sampled from an alphabet of size $a$ (e.g., $a = 4$ for DNA, $a = 20$ for proteins). Consider an $s$-word to be a contiguous array of $s$ letters in the sequence. There are then $a^s$ urns corresponding to all possible $s$-words ($a^s$ would generally be large). For a given sequence length $N$, each position $i = 1, \ldots, N - s + 1$ determines an $s$-word (therefore, a ball in an appropriate urn). Overlapping words are certainly dependent, but to an approximation the balls (i.e., the collection of $s$-words in the sequence) may be considered independently generated ($N \gg s$).

In this setting we have $a^s$ possible words (urns) and essentially $N$ (actually $N - s + 1$) independent tosses. As $N \to \infty$, $a^s \to \infty$

$$\Pr\{\text{urn 1 contains } \geq r \text{ balls}\} = \sum_{k=r}^{N} \binom{N}{k} \left(\frac{1}{a^s}\right)^k \left(1 - \frac{1}{a^s}\right)^{N-k}$$

$$(12) \qquad\qquad \approx \binom{N}{r} \left(\frac{1}{a^s}\right)^r$$

for moderate $r$ and $a^s \gg N$.

Let us consider a word of size $s$ "frequent" if it occurs at least $r$ times in the sequence. The expected number of such frequent words is approximately

$$(13) \qquad a^s \binom{N}{r} \left(\frac{1}{a^s}\right)^r \approx \frac{N}{r!} \left(\frac{N}{a^s}\right)^{r-1} = \lambda,$$

and in the case where $\lambda$ is small, the number of frequent words is approximately Poisson distributed with parameter $\lambda$ (see Karlin and Leung 1991 for elaborations). Guided by these formulas, the definition of a *frequent word* is now formalized. For a given sequence of length $N$, we determine $s$ to satisfy

$$(14) \qquad\qquad s - 1 \leq \frac{\log N}{\log a} < s,$$

(such that (12) holds) and then we determine $r$ to satisfy

(15)
$$\frac{r-2}{r-1} < \frac{\log N}{\log a^s} \le \frac{r-1}{r};$$

(i.e., $r$ is the smallest integer such that $a^s \left(\frac{N}{a^s}\right)^r \le 1$ and, by (13), $\lambda$ is small). Accordingly, few $s$-words are expected to occur at least $r$ times in the sequence and may be considered *frequent words*.

We characterize *rare words* as follows. Set the word size $s$ obeying the inequalities

(16)
$$a^s \log a^s \le N < a^{s+1} \log a^{s+1},$$

and then determine $r$ satisfying

(17)   $a^s (\log a^s + r \log \log a^s) < N \le a^s (\log a^s + (r+1) \log \log a^s).$

Following these prescriptions, $s$-words occurring at most $r$ times are categorized as *rare words*. See Karlin and Leung 1991 for the rationale underlying equations (16) and (17).

For variable probabilities $p_1, p_2, \ldots p_a$ generating the letters and a word $w$ of size $s$, set $p(w) = \prod_{i=1}^{s} p_{k_i}$. The probability of at least $r$ occurrences is then $\approx \binom{N}{r} (p(w))^r$. The minimal copy number $r$ for a particular word $w$ to be considered a *frequent word* is calculated from the equation

(18)
$$\binom{N}{r} (p(w))^r = \binom{N}{r_0} \left(\frac{1}{a^{s_0}}\right)^{r_0},$$

where $s_0$ and $r_0$ are determined from equations (14) and (15), respectively. A corresponding formulation is available for rare words allowing variable letter probabilities.

We turn now to some biological examples of frequent words and rare words. We examined the *E. coli* DNA database (a total of 1.68 Mb, Rudd et al. 1991) for DNA frequent words. For this sequence, the relevant frequent-word size according to formulas (14) and (15) is $s = 11$, requiring at least $r = 16$ copies. Our search uncovered 129 frequent words. The most abundant word (49 occurrences) was *TGCCGGATGCG*, a part of a REP (repeated extragenic palindromic) element (Krawiec and Riley 1990). In fact, all of the frequent words exhibiting at least 27 copies were related to the REP motif. Many of the frequent words occurring 16 to 25 times contained the pentamer $GCTGG$ or its inverted complement $CCAGC$. This is part of the *Chi* motif ($GCTGGTGG$), which is a hot spot for recombination (a point of exchange of genetic material between different DNA strings, ibid.).

A random sampling of human DNA sequences of aggregate 1.41 Mb, and therefore $s = 11$, $r = 13$, revealed 1314 frequent words predominantly composed from short iterations exemplified by $X_{11}$ ($X = A$, $C$, $G$, or $T$); $(XY)_5$ $X$ ($XY = GT$, $AC$, $AG$); $(TGC)_3TG$, and so on. The contrasts between *frequent* words in the human genome and the *E. coli* genome emphasize the iterative character of these words in human sequences and multiple occurrences in the same sequence versus less structured and more dispersed repeats in the *E. coli* genome, the latter phenomena putatively implying functional importance.

We further ascertained all *frequent* words in a database of 1734 nonredundant *E. coli* proteins with an aggregate length $N = 595,254$ amino acids. According to the conditions of equations (14) and (15), with $a = 20$ as the alphabet size, frequent words have size $s = 5$ with copy number at least $r = 8$. Copies of frequent words in all available nonredundant human protein sequences (1741 in number) of aggregate 788,580 amino acids correspond to word size $s = 5$ showing at least $r = 10$ occurrences. We do not display the actual frequent words, but the following striking contrasts emerge (see Karlin and Cardon 1994 for explicit cases). Copies of frequent words in the *E. coli* protein collection (the highest word count is 26) occur mostly in distinct protein sequences, whereas in the human collection, there are many copies (often tandem repeats) in relatively few sequences. Many of the frequent words of the human set are homopeptides, that is, iterations on one or two amino acid types.

An alternative approach in deciding whether a prescribed DNA word is frequent in a sequence of length $\tau$ is to count the number $N(\tau)$ of its occurrences in the sequence and compare it to the expected count $E[N(\tau)]$ postulating independent identically distributed (or Markov-generated) sequence letters. Let $\sigma^2$ be the variance of the length $L$ between successive occurrences of $w$. For the independence model, using standard renewal theory (see, e.g., Karlin and Taylor 1975, chapter 5), we have

(19)     $E[N(\tau)] \approx \dfrac{\tau}{E[L]} + \text{constant}, \qquad \text{Var}[N(\tau)] \approx \tau \dfrac{\sigma^2}{E[L]^3},$

and

(20)                 $c(\tau) = \dfrac{N(\tau) - (\tau/E[L])}{\sqrt{\tau}\sigma/(E[L])^{3/2}}$

approximately follows a standard normal distribution as $\tau \to \infty$. Here $E[L]$ and $\sigma$ may be calculated following standard procedures similar to the calculations in the section on locating genes (see also Kleffe and Borodovsky 1992). The tails of the normal distribution can be used to define *rare* and *frequent* applied to each individual word. The Poisson approximation implicit in equations (12)–(17) embodies an intrinsically different formulation where the relevant word size and copy number depend on the length of the sequence under scrutiny.

The concept and identification of rare and frequent words in a letter sequence provides a perspective on sequence heterogeneity. A comparison of such words with sets of sequences from different organisms may suggest evolutionary tendencies or constraints in different organisms. Comparisons with sequences grouped into functional classes can distinguish features of particular groups or indicate new relationships.

# 6. Evaluation of Spacings Between Sequence Markers

A frequent problem in molecular sequence analysis concerns assessment of heterogeneity in terms of sequence composition and the distribution of certain markers along the sequence. These issues arise, for example, in attempts to derive physical genome maps that display the location of particular markers (restriction sites, genes, sequence-tagged sites) on a chromosome. Are different chromosome parts unusually dense or sparse in markers? Are the markers distributed excessively even? These questions may be addressed by a statistical consideration of the cumulative lengths of $r$ consecutive fragments (called $r$-fragments or $r$-scans; for example, $r = 1, 2, 3, 5, 7, 10$), where a (single) fragment length is the distance between two consecutive marker sites. In particular, the lengths of the $k$

longest and the $k$ shortest $r$-fragments (e.g., $k = 1, 2, 3$) can serve as appropriate statistics for detecting cases of significant clumping, significant overdispersion, or excessive regularity in the spacings of the marker.

Consider a sequence of length $N$ and a specified array of $n$ markers randomly distributed in the sequence. These occurrences induce $n+1$ spacings $(U_0, U_1, \ldots, U_n)$, where $U_0$ is the distance before the first occurrence, $U_i$ is the distance from the $i^{\text{th}}$ occurrence of the marker to the $i+1^{\text{st}}$ occurrence, and $U_n$ is the distance after the last occurrence. Let the extremal spacings be $m^* = \min\{U_0, U_1, \ldots, U_n\}$ and $M^* = \max\{U_0, U_1, \ldots, U_n\}$. The following classical exact probability calculations for independent uniformly distributed sites on the unit interval apply (e.g., Karlin and Taylor 1981, chapter 13 exercises):

$$(21) \qquad F(a) = \Pr\{m^* < a\} = 1 - [1 - (n+1)a]^n,$$

for $0 < a \le 1/(n+1)$, and

$$(22) \qquad G(b) = \Pr\{M^* \ge b\} = 1 - \sum_{i=0}^{n+1} \binom{n+1}{i} (-1)^i [\delta(1 - ib)]^n,$$

for $1 > b \ge 1/(n+1)$, where in the $i$-th term of the sum $\delta = 1$ if $ib < 1$ and $\delta = 0$ otherwise. More generally, let $P_k(x)$ denote the probability that $k$ of the $n+1$ fragments are of lengths less than $x$; then

$$(23) \qquad P_k(x) = \binom{n+1}{k} \sum_{i=0}^{k} \binom{k}{i} (-1)^i [\delta(1 - (n+1+i-k)x)]^n,$$

where $\delta = 1$ if $(n+1+i-k)x < 1$ and $\delta = 0$ otherwise.

The evaluation of an extremal minimum at the 1% significance level rests on the determination of $a^*$ such that $F(a^*) = 0.01$. For an observed $m^*$ smaller than $a^*$ the minimum spacing is considered significantly small. Similarly, the largest gap is considered statistically significant if the observed $M^*$ exceeds $b^*$, where $b^*$ satisfies $G(b^*) = 0.01$. For an observed $m^*$ too large ($m^* \ge c^*$ where $F(c^*) = 0.99$) or an observed $M^*$ too small ($M^* < d^*$ where $G(d^*) = 0.99$) or both, the spacings are considered to be overly regular.

The above formulas are practical for $n$ small or of moderate size. For $n$ large, one may use the following asymptotic probability calculations. For a given set of single spacings $\{U_0, U_1, \ldots, U_n\}$, $r$-scans are formed according to $R_i = \sum_{j=i}^{i+r-1} U_j$, $i = 0, 1, \ldots, n - r + 1$. To study the distribution of the markers in a sequence, we compare the distribution of $\{R_i\}$ calculated under a theoretical model with the observed distribution of $r$-fragment lengths. The extreme-valued $r$-scans (largest and smallest) are of particular use: $M_k^{(r)}$ = length of $k^{\text{th}}$ largest $r$-fragment and $m_k^{(r)}$ = length of $k^{\text{th}}$ smallest $r$-fragment. To detect clustering among markers, we examine all $r$-scans and ascertain whether the minimum is especially small with respect to the postulated theoretical distribution of markers. Similarly, in deciding whether some successive markers are excessively dispersed, we check the maximum length among $r$-scans to see whether it is especially large. Conversely, when the minimum $r$-scan length is especially large or the maximum $r$-scan length is especially small or both, then the spacings of the marker are assessed to be excessively regular.

To assess clustering, we use the theoretical probability that the $k^{\text{th}}$-smallest $r$-fragment (length $m_k^{(r)}$) would be as small or smaller than those observed if markers were distributed randomly (for example, sampled uniformly over the long sequence). The following asymptotic formula holds for $n$ large (Cressie 1977; Holst, 1980; Karlin and Macken 1991; Dembo and Karlin 1992):

$$(24) \qquad \Pr\left\{ m_k^{(r)} < \frac{x}{n^{1+1/r}} \right\} \approx 1 - \sum_{i=0}^{k-1} \frac{\lambda^i}{i!} e^{-\lambda}, \qquad \lambda = \frac{x^r}{r!}.$$

With $x$ chosen so that the right side is equal to 0.01, we declare the observed $m_k^{(r)}$ too small if it is less than $x/n^{1+1/r}$.

To assess overdispersion, we use the theoretical probability that the $k^{\text{th}}$ largest $r$-fragment (length $M_k^{(r)}$) would be as large or larger than those observed if markers were in fact located randomly. The asymptotic formula in this case is

$$(25) \quad \Pr\left\{ M_k^{(r)} > \frac{1}{n}[\log n + (r-1)\log\log n + x] \right\} \approx 1 - \sum_{i=0}^{k-1} \frac{\mu^i}{i!} e^{-\mu},$$

where $\mu = e^{-x}/(r-1)!$. With $x$ chosen so that the right side is equal to 0.01, we declare the observed $M_k^{(r)}$ too large at the 1% significance level when it exceeds $[\log n + (r-1)\log\log n + x]/n$.

As an example of application we review the distribution of the tetranucleotide $CTAG$ in human herpes virus genomes (Karlin and Brendel 1992). The frequency of $CTAG$ is significantly low in most bacterial sequences and substantially low in many eukaryotic DNA sequence sets—including *Drosophila*, chicken, *C. elegans*, CMV (cytomegalovirus), HSV1 (herpes simplex virus type 1), and adenovirus—and below average in virtually all sequence collections examined. The reasons are unknown. We speculate on some possible contributing factors. The stop codon $TAG$ embedded in $CTAG$ in both orientations may be selected against. However, the tetranucleotide $TTAA$ (with the same property of embedding a stop codon in both orientations) has normal representations in most organisms. The DCM methylase/short-patch repair system could also be involved in some cases (enterobacteria). The DCM methylase targets the second $C$ of the pentanucleotide $CCAGG$, which can then mutate by deamination to $CTAGG$. The repair system corrects $T/G$ mismatches of this kind back to $C/G$. If the repair system lacked perfect specificity and sometimes "corrected" legitimate occurrences of $CTAG$, that might operate to some extent in limiting $CTAG$ representations (Burge, Campbell and Karlin 1992). The perfect 14-bp dyad symmetry $A\underline{CTAG}TTAA\underline{CTAG}T$ is the consensus binding site for the *E. coli* trpR-encoded repressor, and this regulatory activity might require sufficient rarity of $CTAG$. The almost universal rarity of $CTAG$ may implicate a structural role or defect. In this context, there is some evidence from the crystal structure of the trp-repressor/operator complex that the two $CTAG$ tetranucleotides "kink" when bound by trpR, which may, under conditions of supercoiling, be structurally deleterious (Otwinowski et al. 1988).

Application of the r-scan statistics ($r = 1, 3, 5, 10$) to study the distribution of $CTAG$ sites in the major human herpes viruses gave the following results: (1) CMV (genome size $\sim$ 230 kb) contains a total of 341 $CTAG$ sites (frequency = 0.0015). A significant cluster of $CTAG$ occurs starting at position 91832 with 11 copies (10-scan) of $CTAG$ over a stretch of 1064 bp (probability < 0.01). It is noteworthy that the region 91800 to 93500 is distinguished as the lytic origin of replication of CMV. Is it possible that these sites help in suitable protein binding for the formation of the preinitiation complex effecting replication? (2) The Epstein-Barr virus (EBV B-95 strain; genome size $\sim$ 172 kb) contains 342 $CTAG$ sites (frequency

= 0.0020). The most significant cluster of *CTAG* sites in EBV measured by 5-scans occurs at position 53082, extending for 255 bp. This region overlaps the EBV lytic origin of replication. (3) The neurotropic herpes viruses HSV1 and VZV (varicella-zoster virus), both substantially low in *CTAG* counts, have no significant clusters or gaps of *CTAG* as measured by *r*-scans. (4) In the CMV genome, a 1% significantly long (overdispersed) 5-scan of *CTAG* sites occurs at position 133865 stretching 10039 bp, that is, only 6 *CTAG* sites occur in a segment longer that 10 kbp. This region of CMV contains the genes UL91, UL92, UL93, UL94, UL95, which are well-conserved among the major human herpes viruses. The stretch 160449–174296 contains only 11 *CTAG* sites, a highly significant long 10-scan value that also involves several conserved genes, suggesting that *CTAG* sites are selectively avoided in these regions. (5) A significant overdispersion of *CTAG* sites in EBV occurs (with respect to both 5- and 10-scans) over the region 62376–74265, which includes two important transactivator genes involved in the productive growth of EBV.

# 7. Perspective

The foregoing examples illustrate how mathematical considerations may aid in interpreting molecular sequence data. Although biologists are not necessarily expert in developing such analytical tools, in view of the vast amount of sequence information currently being compiled, active researchers must become familiar with the principles and applications of these techniques. It is hoped that our efforts to design and develop a new course in mathematical and computational molecular biology will prepare Stanford students well for the exciting research opportunities in modern molecular biology and bioinformatics.

# Acknowledgment

This research was supported in part by NIH grants 2R01HG0033XS5-06, 5R0GM10452-30 and NSF Grant DMS91-06974.

# References

Brendel, V., and S. Karlin. 1989. "Too Many Leucine Zippers?" *Nature* 341: 574–75.

Burge, C., A. M. Campbell, and S. Karlin. 1992. "Over- and Under-representation of Short Oligonucleotides in DNA Sequences." *Proceedings of the National Academy of Sciences, USA* 89: 1358–62.

Cressie, N. 1977. "The Minimum of Higher Order Gaps." *Australian Journal of Statistics* 19: 132–43.

Dembo, A., and S. Karlin. 1992. "Poisson Approximations for *r*-scan Processes." *Annals of Applied Probability* 2: 329–57.

Feller, W. 1968. *An Introduction to Probability Theory and Its Applications*, 3rd ed. Vol. 1 New York: John Wiley & Sons.

Gilbert, W. 1991. "Towards a Paradigm Shift in Biology." *Nature* 349: 99.

Holst, L. 1980. "On Multiple Covering of a Circle with Random Arcs." *Journal of Applied Probability* 17: 284–90.

Karlin, S. and V. Brendel. 1992. "Chance and Statistical Significance in Protein and DNA Sequence Analysis." *Science* 257: 39–49.

Karlin, S., and L. R. Cardon. 1994. "Computational DNA Sequence Analysis." *Annual Review of Microbiology* 44: 619–54.

Karlin, S., and M.-Y. Leung. 1991. "Some Limit Theorems on distributional Patterns of Balls in Urns." *Annals of Applied Probability* 86: 513–38.

Karlin, S., and C. A. Macken. 1991. "Some Statistical Problems in the Assessment of Inhomogeneities of DNA Sequence Data." *Journal of the American Statistical Association* 86: 27-35.

Karlin, S., and H. Taylor. 1981. *A First Course in Stochastic Processes*, 2nd edition, New York: Academic Press.

Karlin, S., and H. Taylor. 1981. *A Second Course in Stochastic Processes*. New York: Academic Press.

Kleffe, J., and M. Borodovsky. 1992. "First and Second Moments of Counts of Words in Random Texts Generated by Markov Chains." *Computer Applications in the Biosciences* 8: 433–41.

Krawiec, S., and M. Riley. 1990. "Organization of the Bacterial Chromosome." *Microbiological Review* 54: 502–39.

Landschulz, W. H., P. F. Johnson, and S. L. McKnight. 1988. "The Leucine Zipper: A Hypothetical Structure Common to a New Class of DNA Binding Proteins." *Science* 240: 1759–64.

O'Shea, E. K., R. Rutkowski, and P. S. Kim. 1989. "Evidence That the Leucine Zipper is a Coiled Coil." *Science* 243: 538–42.

Otwinowski, Z., R. W. Schevitz, R.-G. Zhang, C. L. Lawson, A. Joachimiak, R. Q. Marmorstein, B. F. Luisi, and P. B. Sigler. 1988. "Crystal Structure of *trp* Repressor/Operator at Atomic Resolution. *Nature* 335: 321–29.

Rudd, K. E., W. Miller, C. Werner, J. Ostell, C. Tolstoshev, and S. G. Satterfield. 1991. "Mapping Sequenced *E. coli* Genes by Computer: Software, Strategies, and Examples." *Nucleic Acids Research* 19: 636–47.

# Chapter 28

# Phase II—Some Advanced Applications in Statistical Quality Control

Gary C. McDonald

There have been substantial advances in statistical quality-control methodology since the seminal work of Walter Shewhart in the 1920's and 1930's. However, many of these advances have not found their way into the standard operating procedures within quality and process control. With the increasing emphasis on quality programs and the increasing use of personal computers the benefits of advanced quantitative techniques are realizable today. Here I describe some of these methods and computer programs and illustrate them with examples I have encountered within General Motors.

## 1. Introduction

A Phase II application in quality control presupposes that there is a Phase I, and indeed there is one! In my terminology Phase I is the large-scale training that has taken place over the last decade and is still taking place in many industrial plants and facilities. It consists of training people in many of the rudimentary or basic applications of statistical quality and process control. Phase II is the natural evolution from this basic or rudimentary approach to quality control to one that is more sophisticated and, in a very defined sense, better than the rudimentary approach. In this chapter I provide an overview of some specific instances where the "Phase II" approach has been used in General Motors and has resulted in continuous improvement.

I served on the National Research Council Panel on Applied Mathematics Research Alternatives for the Navy (PAMRAN) with Professor Gerald Lieberman during the 1980's. As part of our activities we organized a very exciting two-day workshop entitled, "Quality Control: New Developments and Practice for Sampling Inspection." The formal proceedings of that workshop consisted of fifteen papers published as a group in the February 1985 issue of the *Naval Research Logistics Quarterly*. This Phase II discussion is based on several talks I undertook, in part, as a follow-up to the workshop activities.

Motivation for quality control is really not needed today. Dr. W. Edwards Deming and Dr. Joseph Juran deserve much of the credit for the current emphasis on quantitative quality control in American industries today. It is very unusual to pick up a magazine, a newspaper, or an auto report and not find somewhere in that material an article or a notation related to the impact of quality on consumer purchasing. It may not be a direct article. For example, it may appear in the advertising of a given product or service. In 1926 the first Pontiac was introduced by Oakland, and it was priced at $825.00. It was advertised as "Chief of the Sixes, the lowest price high quality 6-cylinder automobile." Quality, even in 1926, was a prime ingredient in the advertising of automotive products. Pontiac at that time was an immediate success. In 1931 Oakland was discontinued, and the company became known as the Pontiac Motor Division. The vintage of quality control charting is identical to the vintage of the first Pontiac. Indeed, Dr. Walter A. Shewhart was developing control-chart methodology in the mid 1920's, and one of his seminal articles appeared in 1926.

In contrast to the 1926 era of control methodology, today we have access to advanced computing equipment and data collection technology. Just as better and more advanced higher quality products are needed in the marketplace to remain competitive, better analytical tools, process-control tools, and quantitative tools are needed to remain competitive in the areas of analysis and quality control.

This chapter provides an overview of five areas in which Phase II of quality control can be carried out today on a routine basis: inspection sampling at minimum cost, computer-aided experimental design, control charts (CUSUM and multivariate), and analysis of customer satisfaction data. There is little new methodology here. Rather, the emphasis is on illustrating and motivating the use of what is already readily available.[1]

## 2. Inspection Sampling

Let us now turn to inspection sampling. This portion of the chapter[2] is addressed specifically to the question: When receiving material, how much should be inspected? This is a simple question, but a good answer requires additional aspects that are not explicitly stated in the question.

More specifically, we would like to determine a sampling plan that minimizes the costs involved with: (1) sampling the item, that is, how much do we pay to generate information on the quality of an item; (2) the cost that is incurred by either rejecting or accepting shipments; and finally, (3) the cost of a nonacceptable item entering the manufacturing system. The cost involved in allowing a nonacceptable item to enter the manufacturing system is complex. It frequently is difficult to delineate costs precisely, but approximate figures that are sufficient to run the program and determine the cost consequences of the sampling procedures that will be presented can usually be derived.

The sampling procedure determined by the computer program (described in Lorenzen 1985) prescribes that a random sample of items drawn from the lot are to be inspected or tested. On the basis of the results of the testing, the remainder of the lot is decided to be of such a quality that it can be accepted and incorporated into the production process, or the remainder of the lot is of questionable quality and hence should be rejected. Rejection may imply that the remainder of the lot needs to be screened—thoroughly checked, thoroughly tested—before placing any item into the production process, or it may imply that the whole lot should be returned to the vendor to be screened, reworked, or replaced.

Finally, additional information that is required by the computer program is related to the quality of goods supplied. That additional information may come from one's knowledge and judgment about a particular supplier, it may come from quality control charts that the supplier provides, or it may come from past testing on the product. The program that we have developed asks specifically for the most likely percentage of nonacceptable items shipped, and for the optimistic and pessimistic values of the percentage nonacceptable items shipped by that supplier.

Placing these values into the computer program called ACCEPT generates the optimal sampling plan. Once again the user input includes the cost figures and three characteristics of supplier quality. As an example, suppose the cost of sampling an item is $1 (regardless whether the item is acceptable or not); the cost of accepting an item is $10 if it is not acceptable (otherwise it is $0); and the cost of rejecting an item is 60¢. Moreover, the most likely supplier quality for this item is 6% nonacceptable; the worst case is 14%, and the best case is 1% nonacceptable. Based on this input, ACCEPT determines the optimal sample size, rejection criteria, and minimum expected cost by lot size. It determines that for a lot size of 10,000 items, a sample of 252 is optimal. The lot should be rejected if more than 14 items are tested and determined to be nonacceptable. The expected cost associated with the sampling strategy and the subsequent decision strategy is $5,655.

Let us turn our attention to a question that has generated some concern and attention: When is all-or-nothing sampling optimal? W. Edwards Deming (1982, chapter 13) provides a cost model that indicates under a fairly restricted set of circumstances that sampling everything (that is, total testing of the lot) or sampling nothing (that is immediate acceptance of the lot) is the optimal strategy—optimal depending on what the cost consequences are. When prior quality is known, never varies, and rejection means the inspection of each item, then one should not sample. Instead, you should accept the entire lot immediately or reject the entire lot immediately. There is no need to take a sample upon which to base one's decision.

How does the all-or-nothing sampling strategy compare with the example given previously for a lot of 10,000 items? The cost for accepting the lot without sampling can be shown to be $6,500. The cost for inspecting the entire lot is $10,000. Remember, the cost of inspection in this example was $1 independent of the condition of the part. The minimum (expected) cost possible using the sampling plan determined by the program ACCEPT incurred a cost of $5,655. In this particular example with this particular choice of cost data, no sampling and inspecting the entire lot do not provide the lowest cost strategy to inspection sampling, which is the plan that is derived by the program ACCEPT. An important point to note here is, not these particular numbers, but that some savings will always occur by using the minimum cost sampling plan as determined by ACCEPT. The savings may be small or large depending on the particular circumstances of the problem.[3]

There are many uses for acceptance sampling plans of this type: improving the quality of vendor's products, evaluating the usefulness of line inspectors, trade-off between quality and cost, and so forth. The main idea here is that a determination of an optimum inspection procedure can be made by specifying costs and quantifying characteristics of the supplier. There is no need to use a rule-of-thumb or other simplified procedures when the optimal ones can be obtained readily.

# 3. Computer-aided Experimental Design

A computer-aided experimental design program is driven by a desire to relate experimentally one or more variables to an output. The question specifically to be addressed is: How should the experiment be run to minimize the time required to generate the information or to minimize the amount of data required to obtain an acceptable relationship between the output and the input? Specifically, how many data points are needed? To answer this question a reasonable criterion needs to be established so that the effect of the data used to verify or to estimate the model can be calculated (see Vance 1986).

In a simple example one variable $x$ is related to a variable $y$, and for the sake of this discussion, let us assume that $y$ is linearly related to the $x$ plus an error component added onto the linear relationship. The question of interest here is: Where should we set the dial on $x$ in order to measure the $y$'s? For convenience assume the $x$ values fall within a finite interval. One good criterion upon which to base the answer is the variance of the estimated slope of the regression line. The slope relates the effect of $x$ on

$y$ and is one coefficient that is estimated with the data. The data should be chosen in such a fashion that the variance of the estimated slope will be as small as possible. Ideally we would like it to be zero, but nature is not usually that kind. The variance of the estimated slope can be expressed as a function that involves explicitly the $x$'s at which the data are actually measured. To minimize the variance , the $x$'s should be set at the end points of the interval with equal frequency. No time should be spent taking data between the endpoints.

This conclusion comes as a surprise to some readers, and I suspect that the surprise is related to the degree of belief in the model that is specified. Minimizing the variance of the estimated slope is based on the assumption that the model is truly representative of the relationship between $y$ and $x$. However, an experimenter who does not believe that model to be representative of the relationship between $x$ and $y$ may well choose to set the $x$ dial at a few points between the endpoints as a check on the linearity of that relationship. The choice of where to set the $x$ dial does affect how well the relationship between $y$ and $x$ can be estimated. That choice ought to be made in a fashion that optimizes the inference about the process.

Once the best spacing of the $x$ variable has been determined, a related and equally important question is: How many data points are actually needed? Should we put two at the endpoints? Should we put five? To answer that question a criterion relating the number of data points to a measure of goodness is required. We now turn to one measure of goodness to see how it relates to the number of data points required (i.e., sample size).

Often the desire or need to relate $y$ to $x$ is driven by a need to predict. That is, we would like to predict the value of $y$ at some point $x$ in the experimental region and have that prediction to be as good as possible. A good prediction often means a prediction that has low statistical variability as well as a value reasonably close to what the expected value should be. Obviously, if the prediction is to be based on a sample of information, zero variance on the predicted value is not an achievable target, but a minimum variance is possible. So, the number of needed data points is related to the variance of a predicted $y$ value. Since there are many $y$ values that can be predicted, we simplify by minimizing the largest variance over a class of predicted $y$ values. For the optimal strategy, discussed earlier in this section, within the data points the variance of a predicted value of $y$ over the experimental region is always bounded above by $(2/n)\sigma^2$, where $\sigma^2$ is the variance of the additive error component and $n$ is the sample size. The upper bound decreases as $n$ increases.

We have linked the original question of how many data points are needed to the closely related question: What kind of accuracy is required for the predicted value of $y$? If the predicted value of $y$ should have a variance no greater than $(0.1)\sigma^2$, then a sample size of 20 would be the optimal choice. Taking larger values of $n$ serves to reduce the maximum variance. A smaller value of $n$ will not guarantee that the maximum variance on the predicted values of $y$ is below $(0.1)\sigma^2$.

In addition to a tool that allows one to determine where the $x$ dial should be set in order to generate data, we have a criterion that explicitly relates the effect of sample size on the accuracy of the predicted values of $y$. Although the focus has been on a simple example relating one value of $x$ to a value of $y$, the approach and the ideas carry over to more complicated models.

A general approach to the problem of experimental design—one that is computer-aided—can be described simply. The approach is to first specify the model and an experimental region. In the previous example, the model is a linear model, and the experimental region corresponded to values of $x$ in a finite interval. Then set control variables at values that minimize a measure of variability of the estimated parameter(s). In the previous example the control variable was set at values that minimized the variance of the estimated slope of the linear relationship between $y$ and $x$. Finally, we choose the sample size so that the predicted response is sufficiently good. All of these items are imbedded in a computer program called D-OPT. (For a good review discussion of experimental design, including references to computer algorithms, see Steinberg and Hunter 1984.)

We illustrate a more complicated application of these ideas with two examples. The first one, dealing with estimating the deterioration factors that relate automotive emissions to accumulated mileage, is taken from McDonald (1981, 1988).[4] Currently emissions measurements are taken every 5,000 to 50,000 miles (the endpoint) in order to estimate the regression model. If the upper endpoint is lowered (i.e., if testing is stopped earlier) and repeated measurements are taken at both endpoints—very much the same way as in the example illustrated earlier—it can be done in such a fashion that there is no loss in the statistical accuracy compared to the current procedure for estimating vehicle deterioration factors (a function of the regression model).[5] In fact, the estimated deterioration factors can be improved in a statistical sense not by accumulating as many miles, but perhaps by being a bit smarter about where the emission tests are actually taken. The current procedure takes one measurement at every 5,000 mile increment from 5,000 to 50,000 miles requiring eleven total measurements (a repeat measurement is taken before and after vehicle maintenance, usually at 25,000 miles). If two measurements were taken at the left boundary, and two measurements at the 45,000 mile point, and the same testing pattern in between were maintained, twelve measurements would be required but would yield an estimated deterioration factor at least as good as the one obtained from the current procedure. Termination could occur at 30,000 miles if six repeated measurements were taken on the endpoints of that design space. It would require a total of seventeen measurements, but again, the statistical accuracy would be at least as good as that achieved with the current procedure.

Another example, taken from the report by Dr. Lonnie Vance (1986), has to do with an engine mapping problem—modeling fuel consumption or emissions (HC, CO, or NOx) as a function of three control variables. The controls in this case were Air/Fuel (A/F) ratio, Exhaust Gas Recirculation (EGR), and Spark Advance (SA). The design space is a discrete design space (4 levels of AF, 6 of EGR, and 8 of SA) generating a total of 192 possible design points, that is, combinations of the three control variables. The model used for this particular response is a full quadratic model. It includes all the linear terms and all the quadratic terms of the three control variables as well as the products of these control variables. The program D-OPT takes as input the information on the design space, that is, the number of variables and the levels of those variables. It also takes into consideration the model specified for the relationship between the control variables and the response variables.

The output provides information on the variability of the predicted values of $y$ at points in the design space. These are indicated by the maximum of the variances and an average variance. The maximum and average are taken over all candidate points. The design matrix indicates the best combination of design points that are obtainable in this particular context. In this particular example D-OPT was asked to specify 100 points in which to run this particular experiment and of all possible choices of 100 points to find the selection that was best in the sense discussed. Out of the 100 points so selected, 33 of those points were distinct.

The computer program D-OPT does provide a quick and inexpensive mechanism for generating a design that gives some guarantee of covering the entire response region and, moreover, for doing it in an economical fashion with as few observations as possible to guarantee a bound on the variance of predicted values.

# 4. Control Charts

## 4.1. CUSUM Charts

Control charting is perhaps the most popular statistical quality (or process) control method in use today. Control charts are simple to use, effective, easy to understand, and provide a consistent ongoing quantitative basis for monitoring the quality of products progressing through a manufacturing or production environment. Shewhart control charts, although extremely effective and worthwhile in their own right, do not necessarily represent the best approach to identifying out-of-control situations rapidly as will be illustrated. Most of this material is taken from Duncan 1974, which includes more detailed references.

We begin by constructing a control chart based on twenty groups of numbers where each group consists of five measurements which are then averaged. For this illustrative case the overall average, say, is 0.8312 and the overall standard deviation of the twenty averages is 0.006169.

Now consider some additional groups, 21 through 29, whose averages over five observations are displayed on the control chart, Figure 28.1. The first 20 groups of numbers are used to generate the displayed control limits. The usual three standard deviation limits for the upper and lower control limits[6] are used here. Does this chart indicate the process to be out-of-control? No one point is explicitly out of the control limits, but suspicion might be piqued because there are seven data points that do lie above the central line. There may be suspicion that something is amiss, and a statistical test, such as the number of runs test, might confirm that there may be a problem.

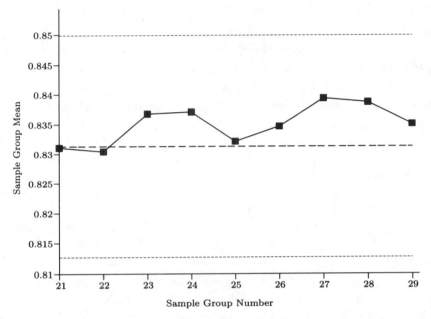

Figure 28.1 Shewhart control chart.

We now consider a slightly different rule, a CUSUM rule (i.e., a cumulative sum rule), and see how the view of these data might change if they are presented in a slightly different fashion. For the sake of illustration, suppose that in each period an average of three observations are taken—not five, as previously indicated. Track the value of the sum $S$ of the deviation of the group averages from the value 0.83465. If the value of $S$ is less than 0, then discard the negative value and start a new sum. If the value exceeds 0.01069, then assert that the process is out-of-control.

In laying out this CUSUM rule, three "magic" numbers have been used. Those numbers are the sample size (3), the value from which $S$'s are deviated (0.83465), and the critical value (0.01069). These three values are constructed in a well-defined way as described, for example, in Duncan 1974. We illustrate the implication of this rule and how it compares with the standard Shewhart control chart.

The CUSUM calculations are summarized in Table 28.1. The means ($\bar{x}$'s) listed here are those indicated previously from groups 21–29. (They cannot really be exactly those values since I have taken the liberty of asserting that the data are based on a sample of three, not five.) For the sake of illustration, assume those observations did indeed yield the same averages. Note in Table 28.1 that the first two cumulative values are negative, and according to the CUSUM rules stated earlier, those values would be zeroed out. The accumulation does not start until the third group and continues until the second from last value, in which case we accumulated 0.01120 exceeding the critical point 0.01069. At that point we stop and assert that the process is out-of-control.

The arithmetic is quite straightforward. It can be displayed graphically in a chart somewhat similar to a Shewhart control chart. Are the conclusions better or worse than, or any different than those we might have derived with the Shewhart control chart? The answer is that the conclusions are dramatically better! But it is dramatic only if the intent in implementing a control chart is to detect rapidly "out-of-control" situations and to leave "in-control" situations alone as long as possible.

TABLE 28.1

*Example of CUSUM Calculations*

| $\bar{x}$ | $\bar{x} - 0.83465$ | $S$ |
|-----------|---------------------|-----------|
| 0.8310 | −0.00365 | — |
| 0.8304 | −0.00425 | — |
| 0.8368 | 0.00215 | 0.00215 |
| 0.8372 | 0.00255 | 0.00470 |
| 0.8322 | −0.00245 | 0.00225 |
| 0.8346 | −0.00005 | 0.00220 |
| 0.8394 | 0.00475 | 0.00695 |
| 0.8389 | 0.00425 | 0.01120* |
| 0.8352 | 0.00055 | 0.01175* |

* Exceeds 0.01069; process out-of-control.

The comparison between the Shewhart chart and the CUSUM chart is given in Table 28.2. If the process mean is actually 0.8312, when in control, a Shewhart control chart will run about 740 groups before falsely indicating an out-of-control situation. For the CUSUM chart, the average run-length, the ARL, will be over 1,000, that is, it will run over 1,000 groups on the average before indicating falsely that the process is out-of-control.

TABLE 28.2

*Control Chart Comparisons of ARL's*

| Process Mean | Shewhart ($n = 5$) | CUSUM ($n = 3$) |
|---|---|---|
| 0.8312 (in-control) | 740 | 1000+ |
| 0.8381 (out-of-control) | 4 | 4 |

For an out-of-control situation, say at a value of 0.8381, a Shewhart control chart will run about 4 groups before it correctly indicates the process is out-of-control. The CUSUM chart will also run about 4 groups before it indicates correctly that the process is out-of-control. So the gain lies primarily in the fact that the CUSUM chart will run longer when the process is in-control before falsely detecting an out-of-control situation, and that translates into less risk of looking for trouble when there is none. There is also a 40% reduction of sampling required in this instance.

TABLE 28.3

*Ratio of the Sample Size Required for a Shewhart Chart*
*to that Required for a CUSUM Chart with*
*Equal Run-Lengths at AQL ($L_a$) and RQL ($L_n$)*

| | $L_a$ | | |
|---|---|---|---|
| $L_r$ | 250 | 500 | 1,000 |
| 2.50 | 1.3 | 1.3 | 1.3 |
| 5.00 | 1.8 | 1.9 | 2.0 |
| 7.50 | 2.2 | 2.4 | 2.5 |
| 10.00 | 2.5 | 2.8 | 3.0 |

SOURCE: Table 22.3, Duncan 1974, 426.

In fact there is much broader applicability of the CUSUM chart as indicated in Table 28.3 which compares the sample size required for a Shewhart scheme to that required for a CUSUM with equivalent run-length at an acceptable quality level (AQL) or at a rejectable quality level (RQL). The run-lengths of the two schemes are fixed so that they match when the process is out-of-control. The sample sizes required by each of the two schemes to achieve those goals are then determined. An examination of the ratio of these sample sizes is one good way to compare the procedures. For example, assume that a run length of approximately 500 is desired when the process is in-control and a run length of about 5 groups when out-of-control. To achieve that with a Shewhart control scheme would require a sample size per group of about 1.9 times that of the CUSUM scheme. The Shewhart schemes may be appropriate in some cases, and in other cases it may be advantageous to use other more advanced methods, such as CUSUM charting.[7]

## 4.2. Multivariate Control Charts

Because of the many characteristics that reflect the quality of a component or a product, it is difficult to assess the total quality of a product with only one index, one measurement, or one response. How should quality be monitored if it involves several characteristics? One approach is to examine each characteristic individually. A second approach is to combine the characteristics into one composite index. A third approach is to explicitly exploit the multivariate structure of the total ensemble of the quality characteristics.

Each of these three approaches has some merit and is worth considering in its own right. However, I would like to focus on the third approach here, namely, exploiting the multivariate structure and seeing what can be done in that context. Again, the points will be illustrated with an example to carry the thrust of the argument.

Suppose quality is assessed with two characteristics, say $x$ and $y$. They may be height and weight, inside and outside diameter, or length and width. In the spirit of the Shewhart control charts we can examine the group means ($\bar{x}$ and $\bar{y}$) over the $k$ groups. Calculate the overall mean (denoted with a double bar), the standard deviations of those two columns of mean values, and the correlation between the $\bar{x}$ and $\bar{y}$ values. Now, in the process-control structure, we can exploit this information and calculate and monitor the statistic called Hotelling's $T^2$, which is a function of the group averages as well as of the standard deviations and correlations that are indicated above.[8]

Just as with the Shewhart control charts, the $T^2$ statistic lends itself to suitable limits so that if the statistic exceeds that limit, then the process is deemed out-of-control. However, the $T^2$ statistic is a positive quantity so there is an algebraic lower bound of zero for its value, and usually, small values are not of concern. Large values are critical and indicate that the current group may not be of the same nature as the calibration group. An upper control limit is specified, and if the $T^2$ statistic exceeds that value, then an out-of-control situation exists, and perhaps remedial action is required.

The effect of correlation can be illustrated quite effectively in scatter plots. The bulk of the data is captured in an elliptical region. A few points may be outside that region (see, for example Figure 28.3 bottom left scatter plot). If we project those points down, say on the $\bar{x}$ abscissa, it appears that at least three of the possible five points falling outside of the elliptical cluster would be within the bulk of the data as viewed on the projection. The same would be true of all five points if they were projected on the $\bar{y}$ ordinate. Thus individually most points outside of the ellipse would not appear as atypical in the $\bar{x}$ data or the $\bar{y}$ data separately. On the bivariate plot, those points are readily seen to be different. That visual appearance is captured quantitatively in the $T^2$ statistic.

Figure 28.2 is a compendium of all of these ideas for a particular set of data. In this chart the $\bar{x}$ and the $\bar{y}$ data are highly correlated. The correlation coefficient is 0.99. This may not be atypical of many of the quality indices in use. The group averages are based on a sample of ten, and the sample means for the $\bar{x}$, variable 1, and the $\bar{y}$, variable 2, are displayed in the top two control charts. The scatter plot of the $\bar{x}$ and $\bar{y}$ data is in the lower left control chart. The pattern is very tight and highly elliptical. This is a characteristic of the high correlation of the $\bar{x}$ and $\bar{y}$. The $T^2$ statistic with its corresponding upper limit is displayed in the lower right-hand chart. These data are generated as an in-control process, and indeed, none of the individual control charts appear out-of-control—nor does the $T^2$.

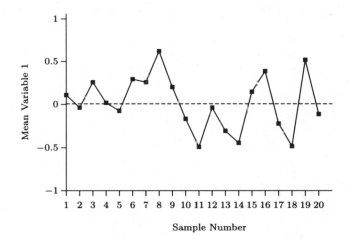

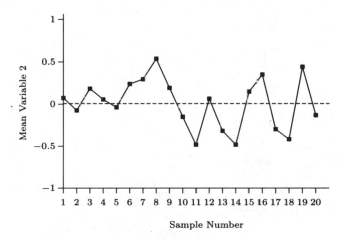

Figure 28.2. Bivariate control chart: in-control case. (Correlation = 0.99; sample size = 10.) Upper, sample mean for the $\bar{x}$ variable 1; lower, sample mean for the $\bar{y}$ variable 2.

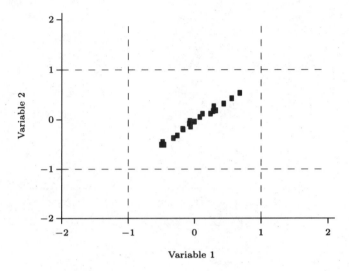

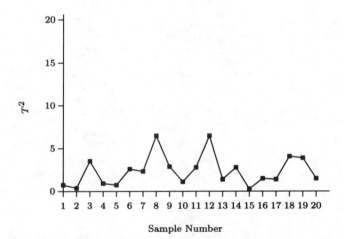

Figure 28.2 (continued). Bivariate control chart: in-control case. (Correlation = 0.99; sample size = 10.) Scatter plot of the $\bar{x}$ and $\bar{y}$ data; lower, $T^2$ statistic with its corresponding upper limit.

Now consider a variation in the process by changing variable 1 from sample 11 to sample 16 by increasing the mean of the process by 0.2 units successively. In sample 17 we return the mean to 0, which is the in-control situation. The resultant data and chart are displayed in Figure 28.3. In the lower left-hand corner, note that there are at least 5 values that are outside the elliptical pattern that was representative of the in-control situation. Those represent the points or the groups in that process where variable 1 was perturbed by increasing the mean 0.2 units successively. The upper left-hand corner, the Shewhart control chart for that first variable, indicates an out-of-control situation at sample 15. That is the first point that goes above the upper control limit. Point 16 does also. Recall in the generation process here that group 17 was returned to an in-control situation, and that is pretty well reflected on the Shewhart control chart for that variable, so that group 17 is among the pack of "good guys" that were generated in the first 10 samples.

Variable 2 looks fine, and it should. We have done nothing to variable 2 by itself. It is still generated with zero mean, the same standard deviation, and the averages here appear as though they are just random fluctuations.

The $T^2$ chart explicitly takes into consideration the pattern of the data as indicated on the bivariate plot. It utilizes the correlation as well as the means and the variances of the data. Step 11 falls close to the control limit, sample 12 is above the control limit detecting an out-of-control situation. For this particular deviation from control a Shewhart control chart detects the deviation for variable 1 at step 15, whereas the $T^2$ statistic detects the deviation at least by sample 12 and maybe by sample 11. So the $T^2$ chart does indeed detect the out-of-control situation more quickly than does a combination of the Shewhart control charts. Of course this is just one process realization. The true long-run properties of the procedures need to be established on the basis of many realizations.

Information from all of these graphs is really needed. The $T^2$ statistic may detect an out-of-control situation, but it does not explicitly indicate if it is the first variable or the second, or both. That information needs to be garnered from either the individual Shewhart control charts or the scatter plots of the data.

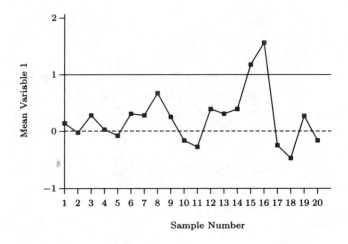

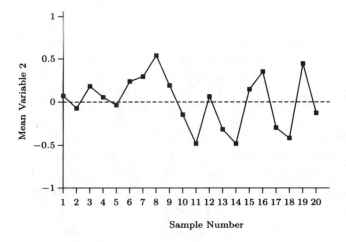

Figure 28.3. Bivariate control chart: shift in variable 1. (Correlation = 0.99; sample size = 10.) Upper, Shewhart control chart for variable 1; lower, Shewhart control chart for variable 2.

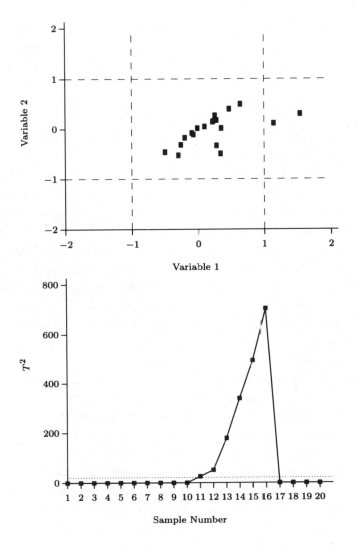

Figure 28.3 (continued). Bivariate control chart: shift in variable 1. (Correlation = 0.99; sample size = 10.) Upper, scatter plot of the $\bar{x}$ and $\bar{y}$ data; lower, $T^2$ statistic with its corresponding upper limit.

Now, make the same changes as indicated in the previous example, but do it for both variables. That is, for group 11 increase the mean by 0.2 units successively through group 16, and for group 17 return both variables to their process in-control value of zero. Figure 28.4 summarizes the relevant findings. All the data points on the scatter plot, with one exception, fall within that elliptical region. Despite the fact that the process in some sense has been placed in an out-of-control situation, there is a difference from the previous example. Both variables have moved in a direction that is consistent with the in-control pattern. Recall that the in-control situation has a correlation between the $\bar{x}$ and the $\bar{y}$ of 0.99. What we have done in this second change is increase both variables simultaneously and in exactly the same proportions, that is quite consistent with the correlation structure of the in-control situation. The scatter plot may indicate some high values, but it does not indicate a deviation from the elliptical pattern. The Shewhar' control chart on the first variable indicates an out-of-control situation at step 15 which is about the same point as was indicated in the previous example. An out-of-control situation is also indicated on the second control chart for the second variable at step 15. Finally, the $T^2$ chart indicates an out-of-control situation at group 16.

In this particular case the multivariate approach to the problem of control charting does not seem to indicate an out-of-control situation earlier than that indicated by either of the univariate Shewhart control charts. This points out a very important facet in control-chart methodology. There are instances where out-of-control situations can be rapidly detected using multivariate methods, and there may be instances where the out-of-control situation is not quite so susceptible to rapid detection. Each application and situation should be looked at individually. If the type of out-of-control situations that may occur in a given process are of the type that the multivariate chart can immediately detect then the multivariate approach should be used. If the out-of-control situation tends to follow a pattern that is consistent with the scatter plot of the data in the in-control situation, then multivariate structure and the multivariate approach may not be needed.

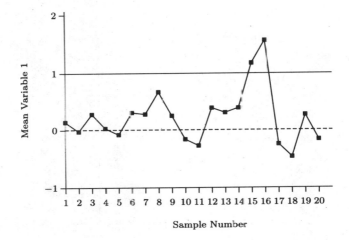

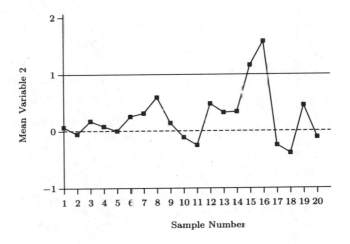

Figure 28.4. Bivariate control chart: shift in both variables. (Correlation = 0.99; sample size = 10.) Upper, Shewhart control chart for variable 1; lower, Shewhart control chart for variable 2.

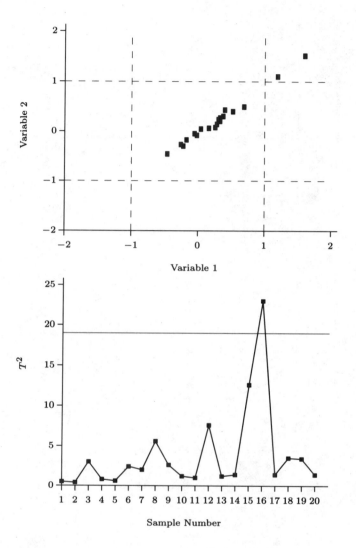

Figure 28.4 (continued). Bivariate control chart: shift in both variables. (Correlation = 0.99; sample size = 10.) Upper, scatter plot of the $\bar{x}$ and $\bar{y}$ data; lower, $T^2$ statistic with its corresponding upper limit.

One application that we have made of these multivariate techniques arose from a problem brought to our attention by Pontiac Engineering concerning quality characteristics of connecting rods. There are several critical dimensions that characterize the quality of the connecting rod. In particular, we will focus on the maximum and minimum diameter on the connecting rod hole on both the top and the bottom sides. That focus generates four characteristics on the quality of a connecting rod with respect to the roundness of the hole. These characteristics are very highly correlated.

The control chart for the individual variables are noted on the top four charts of Figure 28.5. The bottom chart is the $T^2$ statistic. Displays such as this can be used first to determine quickly if there is an out-of-control situation. If there appears to be an out-of-control situation, as with sample 3, then the individual control charts can be examined to see if there is a specific variable or a specific characteristic that appears to be giving difficulty. In this case there are several characteristics that appear to be out-of-control at sample 3, thus suggesting target areas for remedial action.

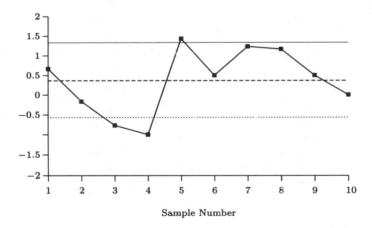

Sample Number

Figure 28.5. Multivariate control chart: connecting rod assembly. (Sample mean units = 0.0001 inches; sample size = 10.) Quality characteristics of maximum diameter on top connecting rod hole.

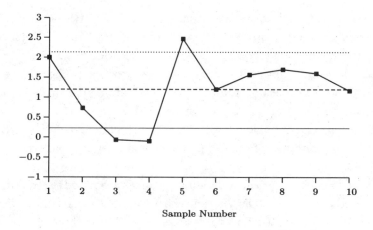

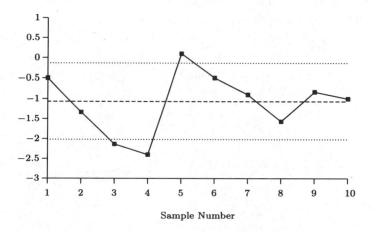

Figure 28.5 (continued). Multivariate control chart: connecting rod assembly. (Sample mean units = 0.0001 inches; sample size = 10.) Upper, quality characteristics of maximum diameter on bottom connecting rod hole; lower, quality characteristics of minimum diameter on top connecting rod hole.

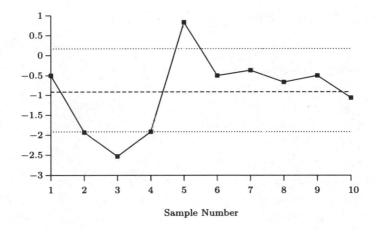

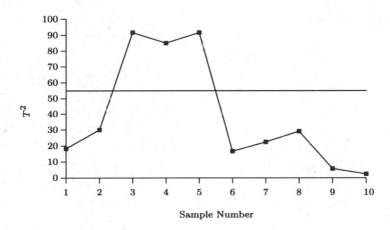

Figure 28.5 (continued). Multivariate control chart: connecting rod assembly. (Sample mean units = 0.0001 inches; sample size = 10.) Upper, quality characteristics of minimum diameter on bottom connecting rod hole; lower $T^2$ statistic.

# 5. Customer Satisfaction

An important and challenging area of quality management is the interpretation of customer satisfaction data. In this particular instance an example of satisfaction with a car-selling dealer will be used. This is representative of customer satisfaction survey data that is now collected by most automotive manufacturers covering both the product and service segments of their business.

The approach to assessing customer satisfaction with the dealer can be summarized as follows: survey a random sample of customers from a dealer and ask how satisfied they have been with the dealer. An approach to the problem is to allow a response on a 5-point scale ranging from very satisfied to very dissatisfied. Superimposed on those responses is a numerical scoring from 0 to 100 in increments of 25. These values are then averaged (though not necessarily given uniform weighting) over the respondents for a particular dealer.

Table 28.4 presents data from nine selected dealers covering the fourth quarter of 1979 through the fourth quarter of 1981. The overall averages of those dealers are displayed in the right column. Indeed one will note a great deal of variability in those overall averages ranging, in particular, from a low of 37.4 to a high of 75.8. This table indicates the averages, standard deviations, and the sample sizes by year and quarter.

It is easier to examine responses displayed in a graphical format, as indicated in Figure 28.6 where the average values are displayed by quarter and dealer. Without trying to assess statistical variability or the statistical representativeness of the sample, some items clearly can be highlighted. Dealer 1 is consistently lowest for all but the last quarter. From the third quarter of 1980 through the third quarter of 1981 the average response of dealer 5 has consistently improved, but at the fourth quarter of 1981 there was a dramatic drop for that particular dealer which may be the most interesting point on the chart. Perhaps there was a dramatic shift in the mix of vehicles that were sold and serviced in that period of time, or perhaps there were other extenuating circumstances, such as dealership modification in the physical facilities, that would help explain that particular data point. Let us ask a few questions and see if we are in a position to answer them using some statistical methodology.

TABLE 28.4

*Customer Satisfaction Survey Results from 9 Dealers*

|  | 79Q4 | 80Q1 | 80Q2 | 80Q3 | 80Q4 | 81Q1 | 81Q2 | 81Q3 | 81Q4 | avg $\bar{y}$ |
|---|---|---|---|---|---|---|---|---|---|---|
| $n_1$ | 49 | 49 | 41 | 49 | 33 | 45 | 53 | 55 | 10 | |
| $\bar{y}_1$ | 38 | 30 | 44 | 35 | 42 | 37 | 41 | 35 | 36 | 37.4 |
| $s_1$ | 36.8 | 34.3 | 37.0 | 38.6 | 37.3 | 34.7 | 36.3 | 35.8 | 41.7 | |
| $n_2$ | 69 | 61 | 56 | 54 | 68 | 54 | 72 | 52 | 41 | |
| $\bar{y}_2$ | 61 | 59 | 60 | 61 | 65 | 65 | 69 | 70 | 62 | 63.6 |
| $s_2$ | 32.7 | 28.7 | 35.1 | 33.4 | 35.2 | 33.0 | 30.4 | 31.5 | 36.6 | |
| $n_3$ | 69 | 60 | 60 | 53 | 44 | 51 | 47 | 45 | 20 | |
| $\bar{y}_3$ | 75 | 76 | 74 | 73 | 61 | 70 | 70 | 73 | 64 | 71.6 |
| $s_3$ | 30.9 | 28.7 | 33.7 | 35.1 | 35.5 | 29.0 | 36.0 | 30.6 | 40.9 | |
| $n_4$ | 67 | 70 | 64 | 50 | 52 | 57 | 59 | 56 | 21 | |
| $\bar{y}_4$ | 64 | 70 | 68 | 64 | 76 | 62 | 66 | 76 | 64 | 68.0 |
| $s_4$ | 32.7 | 31.6 | 29.6 | 33.7 | 26.0 | 33.4 | 32.0 | 27.8 | 34.9 | |
| $n_5$ | 46 | 46 | 39 | 35 | 41 | 51 | 45 | 37 | 19 | |
| $\bar{y}_5$ | 60 | 49 | 54 | 45 | 48 | 51 | 55 | 58 | 34 | 51.6 |
| $s_5$ | 37.4 | 37.2 | 35.6 | 38.3 | 37.4 | 36.1 | 39.3 | 37.3 | 27.9 | |
| $n_6$ | 40 | 41 | 43 | 41 | 44 | 38 | 49 | 37 | 19 | |
| $\bar{y}_6$ | 67 | 53 | 67 | 68 | 63 | 62 | 67 | 63 | 63 | 63.8 |
| $s_6$ | 28.5 | 37.2 | 34.7 | 30.5 | 33.3 | 36.6 | 32.7 | 39.0 | 33.7 | |
| $n_7$ | 67 | 55 | 56 | 58 | 55 | 59 | 60 | 63 | 14 | |
| $\bar{y}_7$ | 74 | 75 | 67 | 81 | 75 | 79 | 77 | 79 | 71 | 75.8 |
| $s_7$ | 31.6 | 31.0 | 31.9 | 27.1 | 28.2 | 28.8 | 28.1 | 26.2 | 23.4 | |
| $n_8$ | 61 | 52 | 56 | 52 | 62 | 50 | 59 | 69 | 55 | |
| $\bar{y}_8$ | 63 | 71 | 67 | 71 | 61 | 77 | 73 | 75 | 76 | 70.3 |
| $s_8$ | 37.8 | 34.8 | 37.2 | 32.3 | 35.5 | 32.5 | 32.7 | 28.1 | 30.1 | |
| $n_9$ | 58 | 66 | 54 | 68 | 49 | 55 | 66 | 63 | 21 | |
| $\bar{y}_9$ | 69 | 72 | 78 | 76 | 69 | 71 | 72 | 72 | 65 | 72.1 |
| $s_9$ | 28.0 | 33.1 | 33.2 | 29.9 | 34.7 | 33.2 | 33.8 | 31.4 | 37.6 | |
| $\bar{\bar{y}}$ | 64.2 | 63.1 | 65.4 | 65.2 | 63.5 | 64.5 | 66.2 | 67.7 | 63.2 | 64.9 |

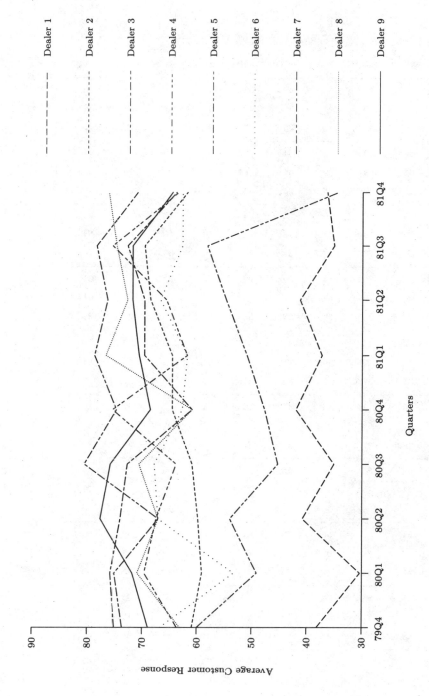

Figure 28.6. Average customer response to satisfaction survey for 9 dealers, 1979–1981.

Are there differences between two specified dealers? There is a way to answer that question using Duncan's multiple-range procedure, which is both intuitive and simple.[9] The overall averages of the dealers are ordered according to magnitude. Dealer 7 has the highest average, namely, 75.8; dealer 1 has the lowest average, 37.4. If the difference between two averages is sufficiently small, less than or equal to some constant denoted by $C_{ij}$, then we assert there is no evidence to indicate a real difference between the overall means of those two dealerships. If the difference is larger than $C_{ij}$ we assert, based on the statistical evidence, there appears to be a statistical difference between those mean values.

Applying this procedure with the dealership data, we can conveniently place together dealerships so that those appearing within the same parentheses can be asserted to show no difference; and dealerships that are in different collections of parentheses can be asserted to show a statistical difference. In this example those groupings would be: (7,9,3), (9,3,8,4), (4,6,2), (5), and (1). So, for example, we cannot assert a difference between dealers 7 and 9, dealers 9 and 3, and dealers 7 and 3. However, we can assert a difference between dealer 8 and dealer 6 because 8 appears in the second parenthetical collection and 6 appears in the third. They are not members of a common contained grouping of dealerships.

The critical statistical issue in this particular exercise is determining how close is close, namely, how do you determine the constants $C_{ij}$? The role of statistics is to address how close is close by calculating what those $C_{ij}$'s are. The mechanics of that calculation is referred to as Duncan's multiple-range procedure, and it does provide a basis for answering the question: Are there differences between two specified dealers?

A second question that we might wish to ask is: Which dealer(s) can be asserted to have the lowest average response? Obviously, dealer 1 is a prime candidate here, having consistently attained the lowest average in all but the last quarter and hence the lowest overall average. But, it may be that other dealers might be sufficiently close so that we cannot state with a great deal of assurance that dealer 1 unquestionably has the lowest average response in the whole population of customers.

A procedure used to address that question can be stated as follows: Select that dealer or collection of dealers for which their average is less than or equal to the minimum average plus some constant, $C$. Now, applying that procedure to this set of data, indeed, we would select dealer 1 and only dealer 1 to assert with a high degree of confidence that he or she has the lowest average response among all the dealers involved there—average in the population sense, not the sample sense. The class of procedures that are used to answer this type of question is referred to as ranking and selection procedures.[10]  The statistical contribution in formulating an answer to that question is in determining how to calculate the value of $C$ used in this procedure, and that has been done for many sets of assumptions.[11]

A very important question in these survey problems is: How many people should be sampled? In order to answer that question we must have a goal—one to which sample size can be related. One goal might be to tag that dealer with the lowest response with 95% confidence, if the dealer is low by a suitable margin, say by at least 5 units. What we would like to do is take a sample of individuals that is sufficiently large so that if there were really a 5-unit difference between the lowest and the next lowest dealership, it could indeed be tagged with a probability of 0.95.

Using the relationship between sample size and the ability to detect statistically a difference of that magnitude, we can calculate that a sample of size 56 is required—a sample of size 56 per quarter, and we would have to generate data for about two years in order to make that kind of an assessment. Now, if a sharper assessment is needed, that is, if we want to get the dealer with the lowest response when the difference is smaller than 5 units, then either the sample size or response rate must increase, or a longer period of time is required to generate that degree of assurance. This approach provides a way to trade off the expense and intensity of a survey, with the ability to answer a sharp question.

Has the response for a dealer changed? In many cases this is a very meaningful question. It is certainly stimulated, for example, by looking at dealer 5, where the average response dropped off remarkably in the last quarter of 1981. Another way of stating that in a control setting is: Is the response of a dealer out-of-control? Well, in that case, control-chart methods can be very useful. In using the standard rules for control-chart limits, we would have a plus or minus 15-unit limit on the control chart; applying that limit to the dealerships displayed on that chart, we would assert that dealer 5 at point 81Q4 would be out-of-control. The pattern of response is not what it has been in the previous time periods.

In this section I have attempted to present a series of questions which, depending on one's interest, are meaningful to the topic of customer satisfaction. In this case it was customer satisfaction with the dealership rather than with the product. We asked questions and indicated what areas of statistics are relevant to answering those questions in a quantitative sense.

# 6. Conclusion

The spirit of Phase II—advanced applications in quality control—is enhanced and stimulated by formulating sharp questions about the processes and products. Asking sharp questions should drive both the answers and the tools that are used to answer those questions. Where appropriate, statistical methods should be used to provide insights about our processes and products. The question should motivate the methods and techniques used to answer the question, not the reverse.

Phase II involves using and building on the very basic methods. It does not depend on exclusively using methods that were developed in 1926. This does not mean that rudimentary application of statistical quality control and statistical methods are necessarily inappropriate. A 1926 Pontiac is not a bad means of transportation compared to lots of other methods. If we are taking a serious look at doing our job as best we can, then we ought to exploit the modern approaches to quality control and use methods that are developed and are available today[12] to best address the questions and the problems we have today. Companies state frequently that quality is their highest operating priority. We need to apply that same quality priority to the methods and techniques that are used in analyzing the problems of assembly, of manufacturing, and of process control.

# Acknowledgments

The author gratefully acknowledges the expert assistance of Darlene Wilson, Donna Kirka, and David Gonsalvez in preparation of the text and figures.

# Notes

[1] An extensive and controversial survey and discussion of industrial statistics is given in Banks 1993.

[2] This discussion is extracted from Lorenzen 1985.

[3] For an in-depth discussion of the all-or-nothing sampling issue, see Vander Wiel and Vardeman 1994.

[4] There are several other articles that delve into statistical design issues in this particular area. See McDonald 1988.

[5] The vehicle-deterioration factor is a ratio of regression points and thus is nonlinear in the regression parameters. For a discussion of the statistical issues, see McDonald and Studden 1990.

[6] There are, in fact, cost-based methods for determining these control limits together with sample size and sample frequency. Such determination should be strongly emphasized over rule-of-thumb guidelines. See Lorenzen and Vance 1986.

[7] For an approach to comparing Shewhart charts and CUSUM charts based on cost consequences, see Lorenzen and Vance 1986.

[8] The material of this section and the definition of the statistics are taken from Hatton 1983.

[9] Miller 1966 gives a comprehensive description of this and other simultaneous inference procedures.

[10] For references and an application of this methodology to binomial models, see Gupta and McDonald 1986.

[11] Two excellent references on such methodology are Gibbons, Olkin, and Sobel 1977, and Gupta and Pachapakesan 1979.

[12] A bibliography on control charting techniques is given in Vance 1983.

# References

Banks, D. 1993. "Is Industrial Statistics Out of Control?" *Statistical Science* 8: 356–409.

Deming, W. Edwards. 1982. *Quality, Productivity and Competitive Position.* Cambridge, Mass.: Massachusetts Institute of Technology, Center for Advanced Engineering Study.

Duncan, A. J. 1979. *Quality Control and Industrial Statistics,* 4th ed. Homewood, Ill.: Richard D. Irwin, Inc.

Gibbons, J. D., I. Olkin, and M. Sobel. 1977. *Selecting and Ordering Populations: A New Statistical Methodology.* New York: John Wiley & Sons.

Gupta, S. S., and S. Panchapakesan. 1979. *Multiple Decision Procedures: Theory and Methodology of Selecting and Ranking Populations.* New York: John Wiley & Sons.

Gupta, S. S., and G. C. McDonald. 1986. "A Statistical Selection Approach to Binomial Models." *Journal of Quality Technology* 18: 103–15.

Hatton, M. B. 1983. "Effective Use of Multivariate Quality Control Charts." Presented at the 17th Annual Fall Technical Conference, October 13–14, 1983, Midland, Mich. General Motors Research Publication GMR-4513. General Motors Research and Development Center, Warren, Mich.

Lorenzen, T. J. 1985. "Minimum Cost Sampling Plans Using Bayesian Methods." *Naval Research Logistics Quarterly* 32: 57–70.

Lorenzen, T. J., and Vance, L. C. 1986. "Economic Comparisons of Control Charts." ASQC 40th Annual Quality Congress Transactions. Anaheim, Calif., May 19–21, 1986.

McDonald, G. C. 1981. "Confidence Intervals for Vehicle Emission Deterioration Factors." *Technometrics* 23: 239–42.

McDonald, G. C. 1988. "Some Statistical Design Aspects of Estimating Automotive Emission Deterioration Factors." In S. S. Gupta and J. O. Berger, eds., *Statistical Decision Theory and Related Topics IV.* (Volume 2) pp. 363–71. New York: Springer-Verlag.

McDonald, G. C., and W. J. Studden. 1990. "Design Aspects of Regression Based Ratio Estimation." *Technometrics* 32: 417–24.

Miller, R. G. Jr. 1966. *Simultaneous Statistical Inference.* New York: McGraw-Hill Book Co.

Steinberg, D. M., and W. G. Hunter. 1984. "Experimental Design: Review and Comment." *Technometrics* 26: 71–97.

Vance, L. C. 1983. "A Bibliography of Statistical Quality Control Chart Techniques, 1970-1980." *Journal of Quality Technology* 15: 59–62.

Vance, L. C. 1986. "Computer Construction of Experimental Designs." General Motors Research Publication GMR-5411. General Motors Research and Development Center, Warren, Mich.

Vander Wiel, S. A., and S. B. Vardeman. 1994. "A Discussion of All-or-None Inspection Policies." *Technometrics* 36: 102–9.

# Chapter 29

# The Use of Statistics in Judicial Decisions

## Kenneth E. Scott

The proper role of statistical techniques and statistical evidence in litigation has never been free from controversy. For example, Harvard law professor Laurence Tribe, in an article titled "Trial By Mathematics," (1971), argued on behalf of "proof of a more individualized character"[1] and concluded that, with very limited exceptions, "I think it fair to say that the costs of attempting to integrate mathematics into the factfinding process of a legal trial outweigh the benefits" (Tribe 1971, p. 1377). "Individualized" evidence, it has been contended, offers proof of causation or occurrence in a way that statistical probabilities do not (Thomson 1986).[2]

Of course, the propriety and contribution of statistical methodology to legal decisionmaking have had their proponents as well as their critics. Interest in the topic seems to have increased considerably over the last quarter century, perhaps under the impetus of books such as Howard Raiffa's *Decision Analysis* (1968) and celebrated cases such as *People v. Collins* (68 Cal.2d 319, 438 P.2d 33) in California in 1968.[3] The lame use of probability theory in *Collins*, for example, promptly led to more sophisticated analyses such as Finkelstein and Fairley 1970.

But it is not my purpose to add to the debate about the proper methods of mathematical inference or whether juries are overawed by statistical evidence and expert testimony.[4] Instead, I wish simply to make a statistical examination of the use of statistical tools in judicial decisions. How often are they employed? Is there a discernible trend? If so, what may account for it? Do the proponents or opponents of statistical techniques in legal analysis seem to have the upper hand?

# 1. Methodology

The methodology for this inquiry is sufficiently primitive that it should allay the forebodings of even the most fearful critics of statistical evidence. A search was made of the Lexis database of state and federal cases for signs of reliance on statistical concepts in the courts' opinions. The Lexis general federal database covers all reported district court, appellate court and Supreme Court decisions from 1789 to date. The state database includes time periods more unevenly. State supreme courts are generally covered for at least the last 50 years, with the oldest decisions going back to 1821 (Ohio). State intermediate appellate courts' and trial courts' decisions do not go back as far, with some going back only to the 1980's.

As to what constitutes the use of statistical techniques, there is of course a definitional question. Some might include any use of arithmetic and numerical data, and others any form of mathematics from algebra on. For my purposes, it seemed sufficient to use as illustrative a set of ten statistical terms:

1. Regression analysis (or regression equation)

2. Event study or abnormal return

3. Logistic regression or logit or probit

4. Poisson distribution

5. Sampling error

6. Type I error or Type II error

7. Bayes' theorem or Bayesian

8. Chi-square

9. Probability distribution

10. Discriminant analysis

Obviously, the list could be expanded, and with it the numbers generated, but as will be seen shortly, I doubt that the overall pattern would be materially altered.

It is clear that this search is not an accurate measure, even by proxy, of the use of statistical evidence in litigation. Many lawsuits are settled and never result in reported decisions; much of the evidence in trials does not figure in the judges' opinions. What surfaces in the opinions each year may be only the tips of the icebergs but may nonetheless help give a sense of what is taking place in the larger world of litigation.

## 2. Results

The basic results of the search are set forth in Figure 29.1 for federal courts and Figure 29.2 for state courts. A few comments may be in order. Prior to 1970 the search found only three federal and two state cases (not shown) employing the listed terms. In the 1980's the yearly numbers move into double digits on the federal level, and become at least visible on the state level. It should be pointed out that the two categories are not really comparable; trial court decisions are reported frequently in federal cases and rarely in state cases. Federal district court decisions account for most of the federal cases, as can be seen from Figure 29.3.

The upward trend after 1970 is apparent; case references averaged about 8 per year in the 1970's, 35 per year in the 1980's, and 41 per year so far in the 1990's. The graph in Figure 29.4 depicts this trend. To put these numbers into better perspective, account should be taken of the fact that the number of judges and the volume of reported decisions from the court system were also growing. For example, reported cases for federal district courts went from 3287 in 1971 to 11,020 in 1993, and from 18,180 to 44,719 for state courts in the database. The pattern when adjusted for growth in decided cases is shown in Figures 29.5 and 29.6, in terms of the number of cases referring to the statistical terms per 10,000 decisions.

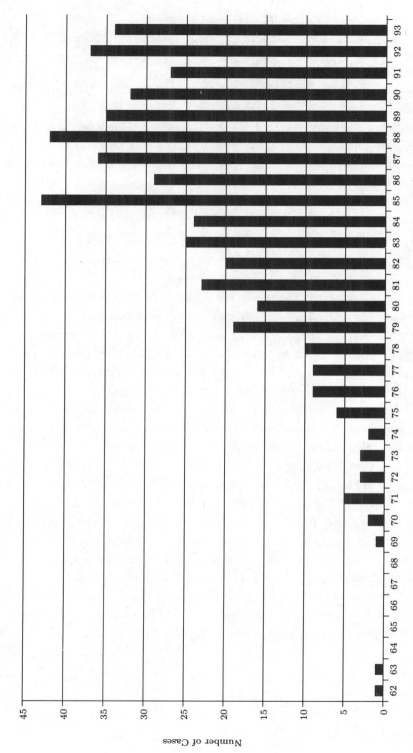

Figure 29.1. Number of cases in all federal courts where the courts' opinions show signs of reliance on statistical concepts; derived from search of Lexis database.

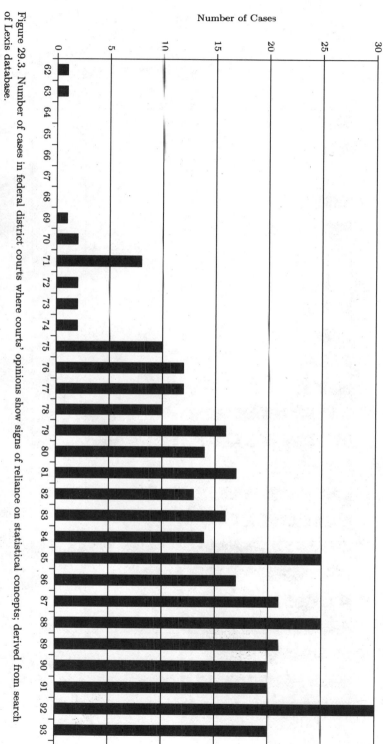

Number of Cases

Figure 29.3. Number of cases in federal district courts where courts' opinions show signs of reliance on statistical concepts; derived from search of Lexis database.

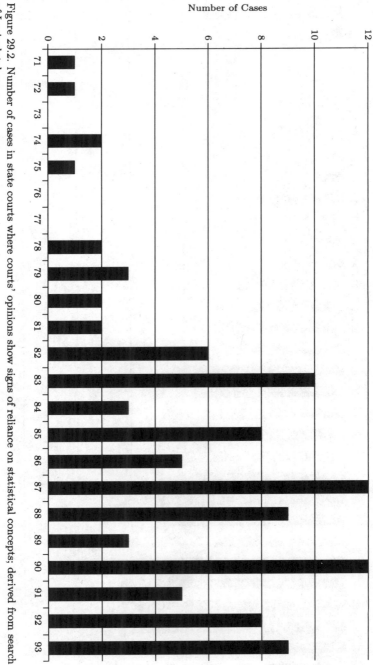

Number of Cases

Figure 29.2. Number of cases in state courts where courts' opinions show signs of reliance on statistical concepts; derived from search of Lexis database.

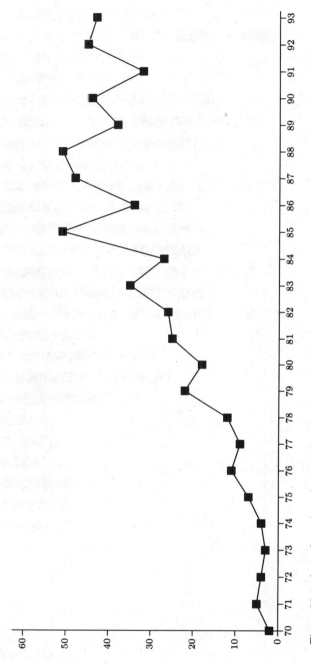

Figure 29·4. Annual number of cases referring to statistical terms.

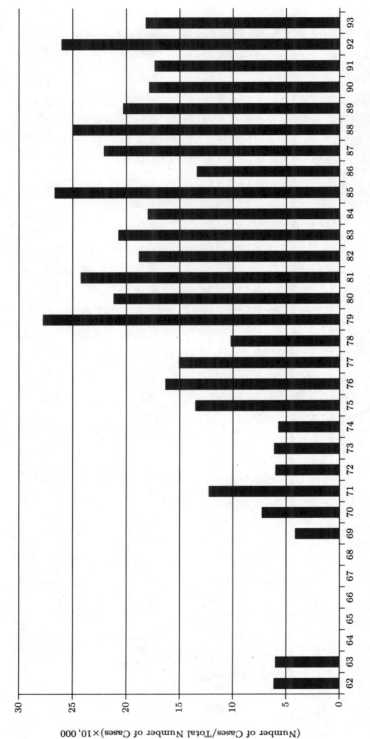

Figure 29.5. Pattern of cases in federal district courts where courts' opinions show signs of reference to statistical terms; adjusted for growth in decided cases and shown in terms of number of cases per 10,000 decisions.

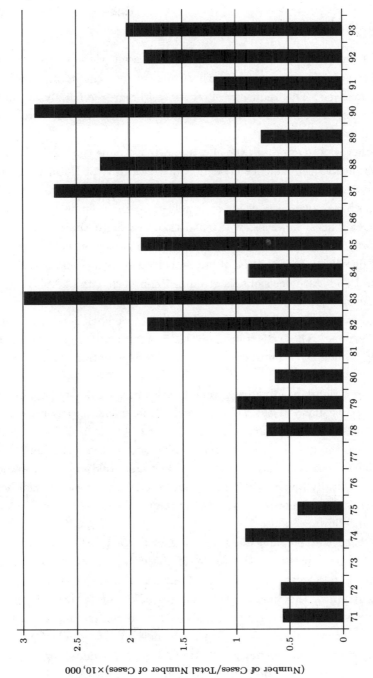

Figure 29.6. Pattern of cases in state courts where courts' opinions show signs of reference to statistical terms; adjusted for growth in decided cases and shown in terms of number of cases per 10,000 decisions.

# 3. Trend

What has produced the upward trend? In terms of the statistical tools being surveyed, it has come primarily from an increase in the use of regression analysis. The frequency of reference to regression analysis and the other statistical concepts is shown in Table 29.1 and, for the three most common, in Figure 29.7.

Another way to approach the question is to examine the legal context in which the statistical evidence is being utilized. The West Publishing Company indexes statements in legal opinions under an elaborate Key Number System, which can be searched separately from the opinion text. Not all textual references, however, will make their way into the index system, particularly when (as in this case) the reference is to nonlegal concepts.

The distribution of the set of statistical terms across index headings, for federal and state decisions, is given in Figures 29.8 and 29.9. The concentration of statistical references in the civil rights heading for federal cases and in the criminal law and children-out-of-wedlock headings in state cases is striking. Those cases have not all been individually examined, but browsing among them produces suggestions of explanations of the concentration.

The civil rights heading cases mainly arise under the Civil Rights Act of 1964, particularly Title VII on equal employment opportunity,[5] and under the Age Discrimination in Employment Act of 1967.[6] Typically, they involve the use of regression analyses to prove discrimination.

In the state cases, both the criminal law and children-out-of-wedlock headings typically involve the issue of paternity. The statistical tool being employed is Bayes' Theorem, and the opinions display considerable wariness about allowing its use.[7]

For those with a particular interest in rulings by the U.S. Supreme Court, it should be noted that eight of the citations are to opinions in decisions of the Court. In only four of the cases, however, was there any real discussion of the validity or usefulness of the statistical techniques. Three involved multiple regression analysis[8], in the context of proving racial discrimination or the deterrent effect of the death penalty. The fourth was a discussion of the minimum Constitutional size of a criminal jury, in terms of optimizing between type I and type II errors.[9]

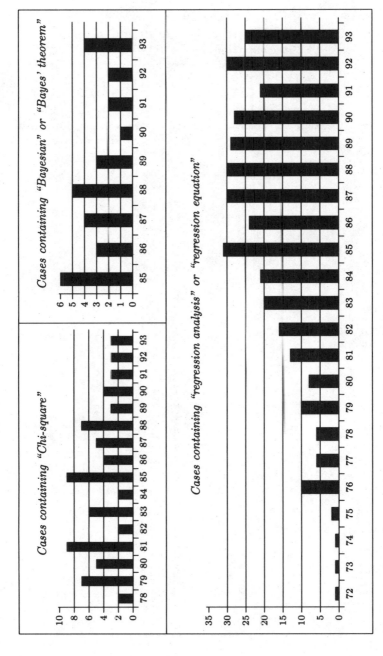

Figure 29.7. Annual number of cases containing the most commonly occurring statistical terms.

TABLE 29.1
*Frequency of References to Statistical Concepts
in Court Opinions, 1962–1993*

| Date | "Event Study" "Abnormal Return" | Bayesian or Bayes' theorem | Chi-square | Logistic regression | Poisson distribution |
|---|---|---|---|---|---|
| 1962 | | | | | |
| 1963 | | | | | |
| 1969 | | | | | |
| 1970 | | 2 | | | |
| 1971 | | 3 | | | |
| 1972 | | 1 | 2 | | |
| 1973 | | | 1 | | |
| 1974 | | | 3 | | |
| 1975 | | | 4 | | |
| 1976 | | | 1 | | |
| 1977 | | | | | |
| 1978 | | 1 | 2 | | |
| 1979 | | 2 | 7 | | 1 |
| 1980 | | | 5 | | |
| 1981 | | | 9 | | |
| 1982 | | 4 | 2 | | |
| 1983 | | 7 | 6 | | |
| 1984 | | | 2 | 3 | |
| 1985 | | 6 | 9 | 3 | |
| 1986 | | 3 | 4 | | |
| 1987 | | 4 | 5 | 1 | |
| 1988 | | 5 | 7 | | |
| 1989 | | 3 | 3 | | 1 |
| 1990 | | 1 | 4 | 1 | |
| 1991 | | 2 | 3 | | 1 |
| 1992 | | 2 | 3 | 2 | |
| 1993 | 1 | 4 | 3 | | |
| TOTAL | 1 | 50 | 85 | 10 | 3 |

| Regression (analysis or equation) | Sampling error | Type I error or type II error | Probability distribution | Discriminant analysis | Total | Total without repetition |
|---|---|---|---|---|---|---|
| 1 | | | | | 1 | 1 |
| | 1 | | | | 1 | 1 |
| 1 | | | | | 1 | 1 |
| | | | | | 2 | 2 |
| | 1 | | | 1 | 5 | 4 |
| 1 | | | | | 4 | 3 |
| 1 | 1 | | | | 3 | 2 |
| 1 | | | | | 4 | 4 |
| 2 | 1 | | | | 7 | 7 |
| 10 | | | | | 11 | 9 |
| 6 | 2 | | | 1 | 9 | 9 |
| 6 | | 2 | 1 | | 12 | 12 |
| 10 | 1 | 1 | | | 22 | 22 |
| 8 | 2 | | 2 | 1 | 18 | 16 |
| 13 | 2 | | 1 | | 25 | 24 |
| 16 | 4 | | | | 26 | 25 |
| 20 | 1 | 1 | | | 35 | 33 |
| 21 | 1 | | | | 27 | 27 |
| 31 | 1 | | 1 | | 51 | 49 |
| 24 | 2 | | 1 | | 34 | 33 |
| 30 | 5 | | 3 | | 48 | 48 |
| 30 | 5 | | 3 | | 51 | 50 |
| 29 | 2 | | 1 | | 38 | 38 |
| 28 | 7 | 1 | 2 | | 44 | 43 |
| 21 | 4 | | 1 | | 32 | 32 |
| 30 | 7 | 1 | | | 45 | 44 |
| 25 | 8 | 2 | | | 43 | 40 |
| 365 | 58 | 8 | 16 | 3 | 599 | 579 |

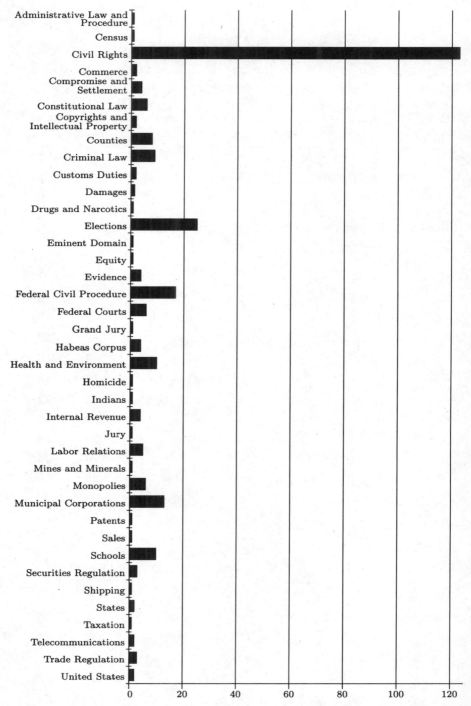

Figure 29.8. Distribution of the set of statistical terms across West Publishing Company index headings for federal court decisions.

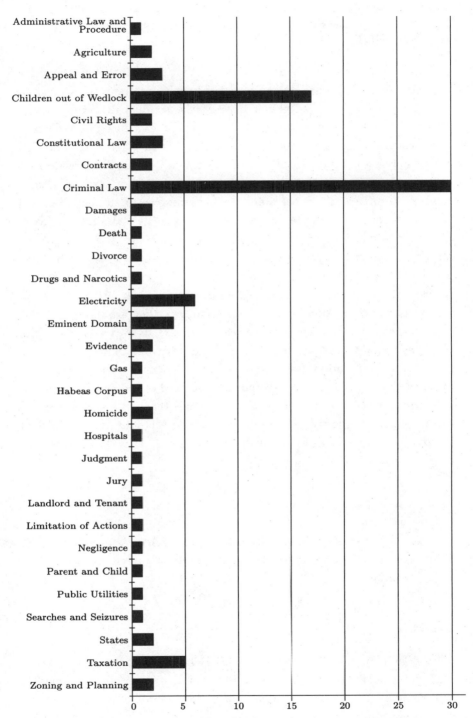

Figure 29.9. Distribution of the set of statistical terms across West Publishing Company index headings for state court decisions.

## 4. Interpretation

The interpretations, however tentative, that one might place on these data depend significantly on one's prior expectations about what such an inquiry might show. Fienberg and Straf, who conducted a study in the 1980's for the Panel on Statistical Assessments as Evidence in the Courts, of the National Research Council, commented that the "extent to which US courts now allow expert statistical testimony may surprise the reader..." (Fienberg and Straf 1991).[10] My own reaction is one of surprise at how modest an impact statistical proof and reasoning seem to have made on the courts, at least as reflected in their opinions. The absolute numbers of reference citations are low, and the flavor of court discussion about statistical evidence seems even more skeptical than that accorded other forms of expert testimony.[11]

No doubt lawyers are in general more comfortable with verbal than mathematical expression, and perhaps as judges, they are more resistant to statistical than to other experts. But there are signs that the world is changing. Law schools are introducing quantitative methods courses into their curriculum, and professors are integrating them into their analyses of legal rules. Practitioners are becoming accustomed to presenting statistical evidence, and treatises are being written to guide them.[12] A similar inquiry in ten years, I fearlessly predict—that is, being a lawyer, on the basis of limited data and no theory—will show a much greater willingness to rely on statistical science.

## Acknowledgment

I wish to express my appreciation to my research assistant, Daniel Ko, for invaluable assistance in executing the database analysis on which this article is based.

## Notes

[1] Tribe 1971, p. 1361; see also ibid. at 1341 at n. 37.
[2] There are also issues as to the utility of statistical probability models in understanding, or prescribing, the role of standards of proof in civil or

criminal litigation, but they are outside the scope of this paper. See Kaplan 1968; Tribe 1971, pp. 1378–93.

[3] In this case six characteristics identified by eye witnesses were used by the prosecutor to assert that under the product rule the possibility was only one in twelve million that the defendants would match by chance.

[4] A useful summary of some of the arguments may be found in Pancerz 1983.

[5] 42 U.S.C.A. §2000e et seq.

[6] 29 U.S.C.A. §621 et seq.

[7] See, e.g., *State v. Spann,* 617 A.2d 247 (N.J. 1993); *Imms v. Clarke,* 654 S.W.2d 281 (Mo.Ct.App. 1983).

[8] *Gregg v. Georgia,* 428 U.S. 153 (1976); *Bazemore v. Friday,* 478 U.S. 385 (1986); *McClesky v. Kemp,* 481 U.S. 279 (1987).

[9] *Ballew v. Georgia,* 435 U.S. 223 (1978).

[10] The report itself may be found in Fienberg 1989.

[11] The Supreme Court has recently revisited the whole subject of the use of scientific expert testimony in *Daubert v. Merrell Dow Pharmaceuticals, Inc.,* 113 S.Ct. 2786 (1993). The implications are explored at length in Cardozo Law Review 1994.

[13] See, e.g., Gastwirth 1988; Finkelstein and Levin 1990; Barnes 1983; Baldus and Cole 1980; and Finkelstein 1978.

# References

Baldus, D. C.., and J. W. Cole. 1980. *Statistical Proof of Discrimination.* New York: McGraw-Hill.

Barnes, D. W. 1983. *Statistics as Proof.* Boston: Little, Brown.

Cardozo Law Review 1994. "Scientific Evidence After the Death of Frye." *Cardozo Law Review* 15: 1745–2294.

Fienberg, S., ed. 1989. *The Evolving Role of Statistical Assessments as Evidence in the Courts.* New York: Springer-Verlag.

Fienberg, S., and M. Straf. 1991. "Statistical Evidence in the U.S. Courts: An Appraisal." *Journal of the Forensic Science Society* 31: 259–64.

Finkelstein, M. O., and W. Farley. 1970. "A Bayesian Approach to Identification Evidence." *Harvard Law Review* 83: 489–517.

Finkelstein, M. O. 1978. *Quantitative Methods in Law.* New York: The Free Press.

Finkelstein, M. O., and B. Levin. 1990. *Statistics for Lawyers.* New York: Springer-Verlag.

Gastwirth, J. 1988. *Statistical Reasoning in Law and Public Policy.* 2 vols. Boston: Academic Press.

Kaplan, J. 1968. "Decision theory and the fact-finding Process." *Stanford Law Review* 20: 1065–92.

Pancerz, C. 1983. "Statistics in the Law: Potential Problems in the Presentation of Statistical Evidence." *Washington and Lee Law Review* 40: 313–39.

Raiffa, Howard. 1968. *Decision Analysis.* Reading, Mass.: Addison-Wesley.

Thomson, J. 1986. "Liability and Individualized Evidence." *Law and Contemporary Problems* 49: 199–219.

Tribe, Laurence. 1971. "Trial by Mathematics: Precision and Ritual in the Legal Process." *Harvard Law Review* 84: 1329–93.

# Chapter 30

# Communication: Statistical Task and Statistical Tool

### Lincoln E. Moses

## 1. Introduction

I believe it was the statistician Churchill Eisenhart who said that the value of a statistical procedure should be assessed in terms of not only its type I and type II error rates, but also its type III error rate, where a type III error occurred when the procedure was not used at all because it was too complex or too difficult to apply. Analogously, a statistical report that goes unread, or that is misread is a failure. The practice of statistics consists largely of organizing information and presenting the results. Communication is thus a main activity in the practice of statistics and surely deserves systematic attention in statistical education. I shall organize my remarks around various kinds of communications that statisticians produce, namely, tables, graphs, writings, and talks.

# 2. Tables

Borrowed from a paper of John Bailar and Fred Mosteller (1988), Tables 30.1 and 30.2 are two presentations of the same data.[1] Nevertheless, they differ markedly in what can be learned from them for a moderate amount of effort. Indeed from Table 30.2 we can readily construct a verbal summary after a brief perusal. What is different about Table 30.2?

1. The individual entries have 2, not 4, significant figures.

2. Rows and columns have been interchanged. More interest attaches to comparing infant mortality rates between education groups than between regions. Since it is easier to compare numbers in the same column than in the same row, the row variable has been chosen to be education in Table 30.2.

3. Row and column averages, and an overall average have been added.

4. Finally, the columns (Regions) lacking a natural order, have been placed in order of increasing regional average.

The idea of reducing the number of digits in a table entry has wide applicability. Sometimes it helps to pose this question: At what fineness of digital reporting would I be able, for two entries differing in the last digit, to put down two distinguishable points in a graph? Surely, that is the maximum meaningful fineness; the example uses coarser digitization than that—and gains from doing so.

Another device sometimes useful in tables is to show in boldface type individual entries of special importance, like the row or column median or values that exceed a certain threshold. If boldface is hard to arrange, then underscoring such individual entries works well. I have never found it easy to read a correlation matrix—that is, until I took to reducing all correlations to one significant figure. This permits noting patterns of correlations at a glance.

## TABLE 30.1
### Infant Mortality Rates in the United States, All Races, 1964 to 1966, by Geographic Region and Level of Father's Education*

| Region | Education of Fathers (in Years of Schooling) | | | | |
|---|---|---|---|---|---|
| | ≤ 8 | 9–11 | 12 | 13–15 | ≥ 16 |
| Northeast | 25.32 | 25.29 | 18.26 | 18.29 | 16.34 |
| North Central | 32.09 | 29.04 | 18.78 | 24.32 | 19.02 |
| South | 38.81 | 31.02 | 19.33 | 15.66 | 16.79 |
| West | 25.37 | 21.09 | 20.29 | 23.97 | 17.52 |

SOURCE: U.S. Department of Health, Education, and Welfare
* Data given as number of deaths per 1000 live births


## TABLE 30.2
### Infant Mortality Rates in the United States, All Races, 1964 to 1966, by Geographic Region and Level of Father's Education*

| Education | Region | | | | |
|---|---|---|---|---|---|
| | Northeast | West | South | North | Average |
| ≤ 8 | 25 | 25 | 39 | 32 | 30 |
| 9–11 | 25 | 21 | 31 | 29 | 27 |
| 12 | 18 | 20 | 19 | 19 | 19 |
| 13–15 | 18 | 24 | 16 | 24 | 21 |
| ≥ 16 | 16 | 18 | 17 | 19 | 17 |
| Average | 20 | 22 | 24 | 25 | 23 |

SOURCE: U.S. Department of Health, Education, and Welfare
* Data given as number of deaths per 1000 live births

## 3. Graphs

From Ed Tufte (1983) we should now have heard his dictum "Less is more." It is a valuable and powerful thought. It means that noninformative lines, shadings and so on, are dysfunctional. But there is a little more to say. The amount of information that should be packed into one graph can depend strongly on the purpose of the chart. Suppose one presented graphically the function

$$f(t) = e^{\lambda t}$$

for a mesh of values, one curve for each value of $t$, like 1.01 (0.01) 1.10 over the range of $t$ from 1 to 100. A dense mesh of vertical and horizontal rulings would be needed if its purpose were to enable reading off values of $f(t)$ at any particular $t$. But such density of rulings would constitute interference if the purpose of the graph were merely to show the rapidity of exponential growth and its sensitivity to seemingly small changes in $\lambda$.

One of the finest examples of graphical presentation known to me is from W. S. Cleveland's book, *The Elements of Graphical Data* (1985, p. 203); see Figure 30.1. Here, presentation of the points on one graph using different symbols for different groups would produce chaos, but the presentation offered is beautifully clear. How does "Less is more" apply here? Surely there are more graphs, but each of them carries less ink than would the one superposed graph. The common-slope regression lines tie the chart together; they constitute an example of what I call *reference lines.*

I offer two more examples of reference lines. Table 30.3 (last column) shows fatal motorcycle accident rates (per 10,000 motorcycle registrations) in Colorado from 1964 to 1979. The black points in Figure 30.2 show those rates as a time series. Two kinds of reference lines have been added to the latter figure. The dashed vertical lines contain the years 1969 (in which a helmet law was enacted) and 1977 (when it was repealed). (Because 1969 and 1977 are partly with and partly without a helmet law, their data are not used in the analysis.) The horizontal lines are the (equally weighted) average rates over the three periods defined by the two pieces of legislation. Those lines strongly suggest a lower rate during the time of the law. Ranks (1=smallest) are also shown, and a Wilcoxon two-sample test ($2p = 0.02$) confirms the indication.

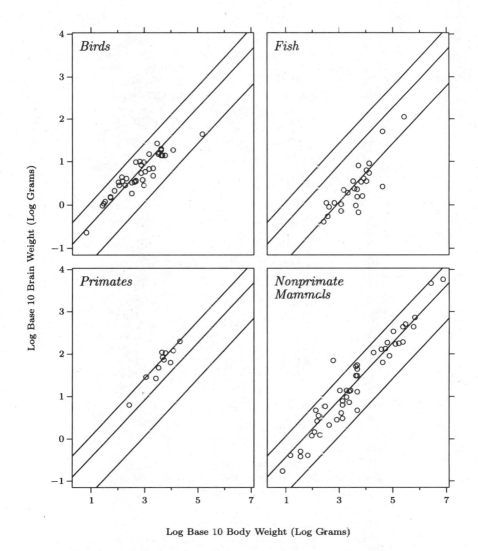

Figure 30.1. JUXTAPOSITION. Log brain weights are graphed against log body weights for four categories of species. The same three reference lines are drawn on the four panels. Each line has slope 2/3; the top line describes the primates, the middle line describes the birds and nonprimate mammals and the bottom line describes the fish. These strategically placed lines enhance our ability to compare data on different panels.

## TABLE 30.3
### Fatal Motorcycle Accidents in Colorado

| Year | Motorcycle Registrants | Fatal Accidents | Fatal Accident Rate[a] |
|------|-----------------------|-----------------|------------------------|
| 1964 | 16,645 | 10 | 6.02 |
| 1965 | 21,479 | 10 | 4.65 |
| 1966 | 24,811 | 14 | 5.65 |
| 1967 | 26,034 | 17 | 6.53 |
| 1968 | 28,594 | 23 | 8.04 |
| 1969[b] | 34,889 | 29 | 8.31 |
| 1970 | 44,851 | 27 | 6.01 |
| 1971 | 57,098 | 21 | 3.68 |
| 1972 | 68,908 | 28 | 5.51 |
| 1973 | 81,871 | 45 | 5.59 |
| 1974 | 92,833 | 39 | 4.20 |
| 1975 | 95,439 | 47 | 4.92 |
| 1976 | 98,051 | 31 | 3.16 |
| 1977[c] | 108,559 | 57 | 5.25 |
| 1978 | 110,000 | 63 | 5.73 |
| 1979 | 115,000 | 74 | 6.43 |

SOURCE: Krane 1981.

NOTE: During the Period 1970 Through 1976 a helmet law was in effect, but not in the periods before or after.

[a] Accidents per 10,000 registrants.

[b] Helmet law effective July 1, 1969.

[c] Helmet law repealed May 20, 1977.

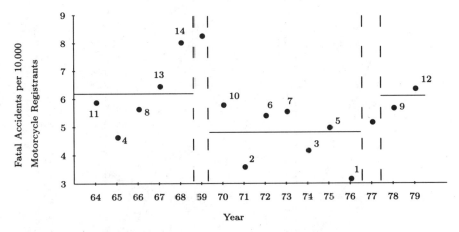

Figure 30.2. Fatal motorcycle accidents in Colorado with and without a helmet law. Numbers appearing near the data points are ranks; 1 is smallest; 14 is largest of the observations. Horizontal lines are simple averages of the rates for the period. The ranks justify the conclusion that the lower rate during the helmet law era is not likely to be a chance aberration.

SOURCE: *Annual Review of Public Health* 8 (1987): 325.

A second example is more reminiscent of Cleveland's graphical presentation. The data, from Jeanne Altmann (Moses, Gale, and Altmann 1992) concern weights of juvenile baboons in the wild over their first eight years (Figure 30.3). There are growth curves for four graphs: Male and Female from Troupe 1 and Troupe 2 (of whom the latter regularly fed at the garbage dump of the tourist hotel). Again the points would interfere with each other, but the four graphs allow one to see how well the Lowess-fitted curves fit their own points and how the four groups differ in growth pattern. Feeding on garbage is clearly more strongly related to rapid growth than is being male.

Depending on the context, an $(x, y)$ plot such as a scatter diagram may gain interpretability from adding a family of reference lines, such as the lines $x + y = c$ for several values of $c$, or lines where $y/x = k$ for several values of $k$.

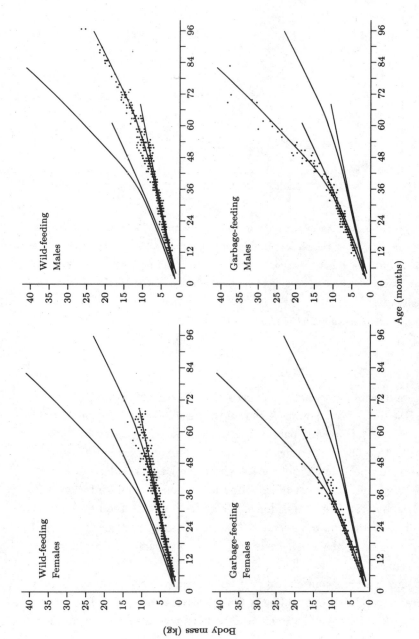

Figure 30.3 Body mass as a function of age for free-living baboons, plotted separately by sex and feeding condition. Each point represents the mean of measurements for an individual for that month. Individuals contributed from 1 to 23 points to the data set. Lines represent the LOWESS-smoothed curves for each of the subsets.

Another scatter plot graphical device that deserves careful planning is the choice of symbols to depict which group a point belongs to. If the groups have a natural order, then choose corresponding symbols having a natural order that is easily perceived, like disks that are hollow, hollow with one diameter, hollow with two crossed diameters, or solid. This helps the readers to keep the order in mind; a set of arbitrary symbols like triangles, squares, circles, and so on, do not help with this.

Another scatter plot problem is to suitably depict the statistical uncertainty of each point. Because the statistician tends to think of an ill-determined point as plausibly representing a larger area than it would if it was precisely determined, the first device entering his or her head can be to represent more uncertain points by larger disks. The eye gives more not less weight to these larger disks, so this plotting device is a mistake. Instead let all points have the same size disk, but let those with less uncertainty be shaded more darkly. The eye will correctly interpret these darker points as more important.

I cannot leave the subject of graphs without saying at least a little about scales; they are the key to the graphically encoded information. Figure 30.4 is a fair representation of two side-by-side graphs once considered for publication in the *Monthly Energy Review*. They suggest an approximate equality between petroleum exports and petroleum imports, with the latter more variable—until one finally locates the decimal points on the vertical scale for exports. This is an egregiously bad example of burying the information in the scale. The two series should appear in one figure, with one scale. The reader would then see that imports were very large compared to exports. Newspapers—and I think some software packages— often bury the information in the scale. Once one allows zero to be absent from the scale and the spacing on the vertical to be arbitrary, then any two positively sloping straight lines can be depicted identically. Or, at choice, either one can be represented as more steep than the other. Similar distortion is available for any pair of monotone functions. I regard it as unethical to bury the information in the scale. (Perhaps these abuses arise more from incompetence than from guile; they remain shameful.)

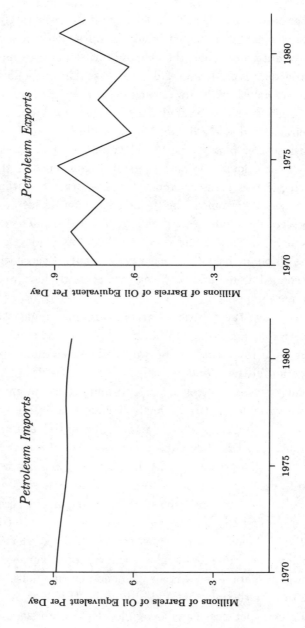

Figure 30.4. An example of burying the information in the scale.

It is often useful to graph data on a transformed scale like the logarithm. It can then sometimes be helpful to let the natural values identify the tick marks; additionally the transform can be shown on the corresponding scale on the opposite side of the figure.

# 4. Writings

Several aspects of written communication in the practice of statistics deserve systematic attention. First there is notation; we have come a long way. Greek letters are no longer assigned to random quantities (like $\chi^2$), at least without their wearing a circumflex, in the style $\hat{\chi}^2$. We have regular adherence to $\mathbf{X}, \mathbf{y}, c$ as representing respectively matrix, vector, and scalar. The importance of getting and using good notational conventions was impressed on me early when, as a graduate student, I was told by a strong mathematician about how he and a colleague struggled for a long time to read a paper and found it incomprehensible until they finally realized that the author was letting epsilon go to infinity!

Attention to mnemonics helps a lot with achieving transparent notation. Allow alphabetical order to help out. Thus, when we have two series of observations, $X$'s and $Y$'s, it helps to let the two sample sizes be $m$ and $n$, not vice versa. If we will transform $X$ and $Y$ into $U$ and $V$, let it be that way, rather than $V$ and $U$. If $U + V$ and $U - V$ are to be constructed, maybe the new variables should be named $S$ and $D$ for sum and difference. (Surely not $D$ and $S$!) A recently developed felicitous notational device states the $p$-value of a two-sided test in a form like $2p = 0.038$.

A second aspect of communication is words. Carefully using our own technical terms is important. We should avoid barbarisms like "We measured several parameters of behavior."

There are some interesting initiatives about words and statistics. Mosteller (1980) has been exploring the quantitative meanings of words and phrases dealing with uncertainty, like "probably," "possibly," "not likely" and so on. Names matter a lot; I remember when Brad Efron developed the main lines of thinking about what we call the bootstrap. He devoted considerable effort, time, and thought to choosing that name for it.

A third aspect of communication is writing style. Who is the intended audience? The lay public? Congressional staff? Archaeologists? The answer should inform the extent and form of introductory material, the mathematical level adopted, the choice of portions to be relegated to the appendices, and so on. Maybe there are multiple audiences of quite disparate technical background. This may argue very strongly for putting the technical material carefully into appendices.

What about the choice of language: Latin? Anglo Saxon? One must choose between "Increased quantities or intensities are conducive of augmented conviviality" and "The more the merrier." And what about motivation: the reader does the job of comprehending and storing your message; you cannot do it yourself. But you can try hard to recruit the reader's participation by making your writing clear and interesting, and by continually bearing in mind two questions: What are the reasons that the reader should care about this? and How can I help the reader to recognize these reasons?

Better and more interesting writing can be learned with the help of such books as Strunk and White 1959, entitled *The Elements of Style*, and Sir Ernest Gowers 1975, entitled *The Complete Plain Words* (for bureaucratic writing—of high quality).

## 5. Talks

I mention talks, for this survey would not be complete if we omitted them entirely and included only tables, graphs, and writings. For a general discussion of talks I refer you to Mosteller 1980.

## 6. Concluding Remarks

Clarity is the key consideration in communication in statistical practice. It surely helps the reader. It can help the writer. I once gave an idea to a postdoctoral fellow. He wrote a manuscript on it and asked me to look it over. It was not clear. I proposed that we introduce things with a clear, simple, special case, and I thereby found that the idea I had given him was actually wrong! Sweet are the uses of clarity.

Clarity is the touchstone by which to resolve certain tensions we have seen: (1) "Less is more" stands in tension with the values of redundancy as in the Cleveland graph and the baboon graph; (2) Greater generality is a form of additional information, but can be an obstacle to getting the main idea across; and (3) maximal precision of notation certainly favors the informativeness of the message sent, but it can work against absorption of the message.

Keep in mind the readers' level of skill and knowledge. Kendall (1970) set an interesting example; his book not only put a wealth of material in the appendices, but four times devoted an entire (skippable) chapter to proofs of the results in the preceding chapter.

Regard the preparation of a graph or a table (or a talk) as partly experimental. Do not settle for the first way you find for presenting certain information in graphical form. Think of another and maybe still another. Compare them; perhaps ask students or associates to compare them. Similarly, the circulation of early versions of a manuscript typically leads to improvements. But most of all, keep the readers in mind, and take it as a high good to communicate effectively with them.

# Note

[1] The discussion here also borrows from the paper of Bailar and Mosteller (1988).

# References

Bailar, John C., III, and Frederick Mosteller. 1988. "Guidelines for Statistical Reporting in Articles for Medical Journals." *Annals of Internal Medicine* 108: 266–73.

Cleveland, W. S. 1985. *The Elements of Graphing Data.* Monterey, Calif.: Wadsworth.

Gowers, Ernest. 1975. *The Complete Plain Words.* Revised by Bruce Fraser. London: Her Majesty's Stationery Office.

Kendall, M. G. 1970. *Rank Correlation Methods.* 5th ed. London: Griffin.

Krane, S. 1981. "Motorcycle Crashes, Helmet Use and Injury Severity: Before and After Helmet Law Repeal in Colorado." In *Symposium on Traffic Safety Effectiveness (Impact) Evaluation Projects, May 29–31, 1981, Chicago,* p. 330 (Table 1). (Conducted by National Safety Council under contract no. DTNH22-80-C-01564).

Moses, L. E., Lynn C. Gale, and Jeanne R. Altmann. 1992. "Methods for Analysis of Unbalanced, Longitudinal Growth Data." *American Journal of Primatology* 28: 49–59.

Mosteller, Frederick. 1980. "Classroom and Platform Performance." *The American Statistician* 34: 11–17.

Mosteller, Frederick, and Cleo Youtz. 1990. "Quantifying Probabilistic Expression." *Statistical Science* 5: 2–12.

Strunk, William, Jr., and E. B. White. 1959. *The Elements of Style*. New York: Macmillan.

Tufte, E. R. 1983. *The Visual Display of Quantitative Information*. Cheshire, Conn.: Graphics Press.

Library of Congress Cataloging-in-Publication Data

Education in a Research University / edited by Kenneth J. Arrow . . .
   [et al.].
       p.    cm.
     ISBN 0-8047-2595-0 (cloth : alk. paper)
       1. Universities and colleges—Research—United States—Management.
     2. Science—Study and teaching (Graduate)—United States.
     3. Research—Social aspects—United States.     4. Stanford University.
     I. Arrow, Kenneth Joseph.
     Q180.U5E38   1996
     378.1´55—dc20                                              96-10877
                                                                   CIP

⊚ This book is printed on acid-free, recycled paper.

Original Printing 1996
Last figure below indicates year of this printing:
05   04   03   02   01   00   99   98   97   96